TRATTORIA COOKING

Macmillan Publishing Company
New York

Maxwell Macmillan Canada
Toronto

Maxwell Macmillan International
New York Oxford Singapore Sydney

TRATTORIA
COOKING

Biba Caggiano

Macmillan Publishing Company   Maxwell Macmillan Canada, Inc.
866 Third Avenue   1200 Eglinton Avenue East Suite 200
New York, NY 10022   Don Mills, Ontario M3C 3N1

Macmillan Publishing Company is part of the Maxwell Communication Group of Companies.

Library of Congress Cataloging-in-Publication Data

Caggiano, Biba.
    Trattoria cooking / Biba Caggiano.
      p.   cm.
    Includes index.
    ISBN 0-02-520252-9
    1. Cookery, Italian.   I. Title.
TX723.C264   1992   92-27785   CIP
641.5945—dc20

Macmillan books are available at special discounts for bulk purchases for sales promotions, premiums, fund-raising, or educational use. For details, contact:

Special Sales Director
Macmillan Publishing Company
866 Third Avenue
New York, NY 10022

Book design by Maura Fadden Rosenthal

Illustrations by Charles Waller

10   9

Printed in the United States of America

CONTENTS

ACKNOWLEDGMENTS

In cooking we are only an extension of other people. One does not become a good cook in a vacuum, and certainly not overnight. It is a rather long process made up of years of exposure to good food and to talented cooks. Most of us have been molded by someone we admire. My mother was my first mentor. Her food was simple, wonderfully honest, tasty, and generous.

I want to thank
My husband, Vincent, for his constant encouragement, his love, and his honest criticism which made me try harder;

My daughters, Carla and Paola, for "just being there";

My friend Darrell Corti for always being there for me with his knowledge and advice, and for enriching my book with his "suggested wines";

My "kids" in the kitchen, Don Brown and Jim La Perriere, chef and sous chef of *BIBA* for all the help they gave me for this book and for their incredible energy which also rubbed off on me;

My agent, Maureen Lasher, for her patience and guidance while I was laboring on the book outline;

My editor, Pam Hoenig, for wanting this book as much as I did and for her support and kindness.

I want to thank also in one big sweep the many unsung cooks of the Italian *trattorie* who shared with me their generous cooking and their tradition.

Lastly, I want to thank Arcigola Slow Food Editore for having published a little gem of a book, *Osterie d'Italia,* which was invaluable to me during the research for this book.

INTRODUCTION

In 1945 the Second World War ended. Italy was half destroyed and my father, like most other Italians, was left without a job and with a young family to support. At that time I was nine years old, my brother was eleven, and my sister six. My mother, who was a homemaker and had not held a job outside the home since she was a young unmarried woman, found a part-time job to help put the bread on the table. She went to work in the kitchen of one of the oldest *trattorie* of Bologna, Trattoria Birreria Lamma. For several years she took care of all of us during the day and worked the evening shift at the trattoria. She started as a helper and shortly after she became one of Lamma's best cooks, cooking side by side with the owner and serving some of the best home-cooked meals in Bologna. My father eventually found a new job and my mother left Lamma to become a full-time mother again. I will never forget those years!

Today Lamma is still there and has not changed much. The same medieval dining room, very bare and pristine, with large, dark wooden tables and uncomfortable chairs. The same long counter where one could sip wine or beer and order a plate of pasta or Lamma's famous salad of white beans, sweet onions, and tuna fish. The reason for Lamma's success over the years was that they consistently served wonderful, down-to-earth home-cooked meals at very reasonable prices.

If you go to Italy and eat in a place that takes *no* credit cards, that gives you *no* menu, that places only *one* glass per person on the table for both wine and water and is family owned, you have found a gem—*an authentic Italian trattoria*!

A trattoria is a home away from home for many Italians. Eating in a trattoria is like eating with an Italian family. The mood can be relaxed or boisterous and most of the time very friendly. The food is basic, simple, and honest. The trattoria is a place patronized by young families, by older people on fixed incomes, by students, by singles, and by anybody who simply wants to recapture the aromas and taste of good home-cooked meals.

Trattoria cooking changes according to geographical location, climate, local traditions, and the inventiveness and mood of the cook. It also differs from other Italian cooking in the same way that home cooking does, with personal touches and personal interpretations.

Even though a trattoria can be rustic, homey, or upscale, it always has a personality of its own. It generally stays within a family for many years. The cooking is often done by the women of the family. These women don't wear fancy chef hats. They don't work out of large show kitchens and most of the time don't have gleaming copper pots hanging on their kitchen walls. Often their cooking space is cramped and their cooking utensils are limited, and yet they routinely produce wonderful food.

I have so many fond memories of great trattoria meals! When I was dating my husband, Vincent, while he was attending the Faculty of Medicine in Bologna, we used to go, whenever we could afford it, to a small neighborhood trattoria called Lo Sterlino. It was a very humble place, with the tables covered with paper instead of tablecloths and straw chairs. The bread was put on the table, and the house wine, which was not very good, was served in carafes. The dishes of the day were only a few, but we did not care, because the homemade pasta, the polenta, and the tortellini in broth were terrific. Today, thirty years later, Lo Sterlino is still there, all spruced up, serving the same wonderful traditional dishes.

I remember years ago while in Roma, my husband and I decided to cancel the reservation we had in a well-known fashionable restaurant and went instead to a small, tucked-away trattoria we had discovered earlier that day while walking through the city. It had an intimate, homey atmosphere, but what captivated us most was the friendliness of the owners and the tastiest *spaghetti alla carbonara* I had ever had in my life.

Another time, while I was filming a cooking segment in Southern Italy for station KCRA in Sacramento, we stopped for lunch in a pleasant-looking trattoria that had some outdoor tables under a rustic trellis. As we stepped out of the car, the aroma of grilled food hit us. A middle-aged woman was turning and basting sausages, chops, ribs, and vegetables on an open grill. We ordered a bottle of local wine and tasted everything, including some freshly made local mozzarella. It was pure heaven! Trends will come and go, but that is food that will *never* go out of style!

In Italy today, there is a new appreciation for the food of the trattoria. On weekends people from large cities drive to the country seeking out these small establishments. Unfortunately, true, authentic *trattorie* are beginning to disappear from the Italian landscape, especially in larger or very touristy cities, which have been invaded by snack bars and quick lunch counters. The modernization of Italy has created a more homogeneous gastronomic landscape, with many restaurants and *trattorie* catering to tourists. These establishments might have a "trattoria" sign on their door, but when the menu posted outside is written in four languages, and every credit card in the world is accepted, there is little hope for "ye who enter" to savor real trattoria food.

Because I have been seriously involved with food for many years, first as a cooking teacher, then as an author, and now as a restaurant chef-owner, I have spent many years traveling throughout my country getting to know the people and the food of other regions better. All this has enriched me with a considerable "memory bank" that transcends any written recipes, a memory bank which is made up of tangible flavors spoken with different dialects. When I began researching this book, I went through my file and began sorting through old menus, notes, and recipes. Even though I already had a lot of material at hand, I realized I needed to collect much more. So, like a hunting dog, I set out methodically to follow any lead that would take me to a real trattoria. I practically ate my way through Italy in search of real trattoria food, collecting on the way several unwanted pounds. Sometimes I would find a real gem, like Trattoria Vernizzi near Parma, where prosciutto, sausages, pasta, cheese, bread, and wine were made on the premises. On occasion I found some disappointments, but most often I found good, wholesome food and great passion and devotion for the *cucina casalinga*.

This book would not have happened without the help and assistance of all those great unsung Italian cooks, who, in spite of the culinary changes that Italy is going through today, have kept alive the tradition of good trattoria cooking.

USEFUL TIPS AND INFORMATION ABOUT ITALY, ITS FOOD AND ITS CUSTOMS

Italy has many types of eating establishments, the following being some of the most common:

Ristorante	Restaurant.
Trattoria	A family-owned restaurant, generally a small, unassuming establishment with a limited menu, serving homestyle food at reasonable prices.
Osteria	Generally a tavern or a wine shop where wine is served by the glass. It also serves a limited number of homey dishes or *spuntini* (savory treats such as *focacce*, cheese, sandwiches, crostini, and cold cuts).
Tavola Calda	An informal eatery that serves a limited number of hot and cold items quickly and at reasonable prices. Great for people on the run who can grab a plate of reasonably good pasta fairly inexpensively (almost the equivalent of an American fast-food restaurant).
Pizzeria	An informal establishment that serves pizza and often other dishes such as *calzoni*, savory pies, and composed salads.
Gelateria	An ice cream shop.
Pasticceria	A pastry shop, where products can be eaten there or taken away.
Bar	A "bar" in Italy is a place to stop for a quick espresso, cappuccino, tea, pastry, or an aperitif.
Caffè	A place to meet friends, sit at an outside table, munch on pastries, or sip espresso or tea and enjoy people watching.

In Italy, restaurant menus follow a classic structure and read as follows:

Antipasti	Appetizers
Primi piatti	First courses (pasta, risotto, gnocchi, and soup)
Secondi piatti	Entrees (meat, game, and fish)
Contorni	Vegetables
Insalata	Salad
Frutta	Fruit
Dolci	Desserts

Italian restaurant menus are generally *a la carte*; soup or salad are never offered with the entree.

On most menus, the vegetables, *contorni*, are listed and priced separately and don't come automatically with the entree.

In many restaurants the taxes and the service charge are already included on the bill. In that case it should appear as *servizio* at the bottom of the bill. Check with the server. If it is not included, a tip of ten to fifteen percent is expected.

At the bottom of many menus you will read *"coperto, Lire . . ."* That is an automatic charge per person for the bread, linen, and silverware. (It's the same as a "cover charge" in the United States.)

Restaurants and *trattorie* in Italy generally don't open for dinner until 7:30. Italians eat lunch generally from 1 to 2 P.M. and dinner from 8 to 11 or 12 A.M.

Trattorie often don't serve espresso because of the lack of a commercial espresso machine. (But Italians don't seem to mind, because they feel that the walk to a nearby bar is good for the digestion.)

Espresso can be served as

ristretto	(concentrated and strong)
macchiato	(with a touch of milk)
lungo	(thin and less concentrated)
corretto	(with grappa or brandy).

Cappuccino is consumed mostly in the morning and is almost never served after a meal. Espresso is.

Butter is generally never served in *trattorie*.

Italians smoke, and in the restaurants and *trattorie* of Italy there is generally no separation between smoking and nonsmoking (even though this is slowly changing).

The best Italian gelatos are found in *gelaterie* and caffè. Don't leave Italy without having tasted some. Sit at an outdoor caffè, have a *coppa di gelato*, and enjoy it leisurely, just like Italians do.

BASIC
INGREDIENTS

This is perhaps the most important little chapter in this book, because it tells you about Italian ingredients, and I firmly believe that the "secret" of Italian cooking lies in fidelity to its ingredients.

Years ago, many vital Italian ingredients were virtually unavailable, not only in the rural parts of this country, but also in large cities. I remember teaching classes in the late seventies and early eighties in Los Angeles and San Diego and finding an incredible lack of even the most basic ingredients. Fortunately, this is not the case anymore. Because of huge popularity of Italian cooking today, many indispensable ingredients are now widely available.

When Caroline Bates of *Gourmet* magazine reviewed my restaurant in the May 1989 issue, she wrote, "San Franciscans and Angelenos would consider themselves lucky to have an Italian restaurant as *authentically* Italian as Biba." Do you think that ingredients as wonderful as the parmigiano-reggiano, prosciutto di Parma, extra virgin olive oil from Toscana that I use on a daily basis at my restaurant have anything to do with the "authenticity" of my restaurant? You bet they do!

For this reason I urge you to go the extra mile to try to secure that particular cheese, or ham, or the olive oil and porcini mushrooms you need for your Italian dish, which will help you attain that particular Italian flavor. I could not have reproduced more than half the dishes in this book successfully if many of these "basic" ingredients had not been available, and neither can you.

CHEESES

Parmigiano-Reggiano

It is hard to imagine Italian cooking without parmigiano-reggiano. This noble cheese, produced under strict regulations in the provinces of Parma, Reggio, Modena, Mantua, and Bologna, is made with milk produced between the first of April and the eleventh of November. Twelve hundred cheese-making dairies produce this superlative cheese which is made by hand by artisan cheese makers, following a tradition that has remained unchanged for seven centuries.

A chunk of perfectly aged parmigiano can begin or end a meal. Its subtle flavor enriches pasta, soups, and risottos. It is a vital ingredient in many simple and complex preparations and often is a component of simple or composed salads.

Parmigiano-reggiano is a low-fat cheese, with a high protein content, produced simply from the best possible milk and rennet. (Parmigiano is completely free of additives.) The following figures from the Consortium of Parmigiano-Reggiano offer some interesting comparisons.

100 grams of parmigiano-reggiano contain approximately the same protein content as:

160 grams of ham   300 grams of trout
206 grams of beef   914 grams of milk
214 grams of pork   5 eggs.

When buying parmigiano, look for the words "Parmigiano-Reggiano" etched in tiny dots on the rind of the cheese. By law, parmigiano-reggiano is aged at least one year. Sometimes in this country we find a two-year-old parmigiano which is exceptionally good. Good parmigiano should have a straw yellow color with a crumbly but moist texture.

Parmigiano is an expensive cheese, but a little goes a long way. A nice chunk of parmigiano can be wrapped in plastic and kept in the refrigerator for two to three weeks without losing any of its freshness. If the cheese dries out a bit, wrap it in a damp cloth and leave it in the refrigerator for a few hours, then remove the cloth and wrap the cheese again in plastic. Grate the cheese as you need it.

Grated domestic "parmesan" has absolutely no relation to parmigiano-reggiano.

Grana Padana

Grana padana is an excellent cheese, similar to parmigiano-reggiano, but it is produced outside the restricted area that produces parmigiano. Grana padana is perhaps the only acceptable substitute for parmigiano.

Mozzarella

Mozzarella is a very popular cheese essential to many Southern Italian preparations.

The most prized mozzarella in Italy is made from the curd of water buffalo milk. Unfortunately, the number of domesticated water buffalo in Southern Italy is rapidly shrinking in number and it is getting harder to find real *mozzarella di buffala*. What we often find today is mozzarella prepared with a percentage of buffalo milk and a percentage of cow's milk. This is still an extremely delicious cheese, and can be found imported from Italy in Italian markets and specialty food stores across the country. If you are lucky enough to find some good mozzarella imported from Italy, buy more than you need and freeze what you don't use right away. (Freezing mozzarella is unanimously approved of by the cheese makers of Southern Italy.) Thaw the mozzarella overnight in the refrigerator.

Cow's milk mozzarella is also quite popular in Italy. In the United States good locally made cow's milk mozzarella, such as Polly-O's whole milk *Fior di Latte*, can be found in Italian neighborhoods and specialty stores. The factory-made mozzarella found on the supermarket shelves is tough and rubbery and has no relation to the real thing.

Smoked mozzarella is also available. Remember when seasoning that smoked mozzarella is quite salty.

Ricotta

Ricotta is a cheese by-product made from whey, the watery part of the cow's milk. This soft, delicious cheese is used in the filling for many pasta preparations and in the ricotta cakes and pastries of the South. Since ricotta is quite perishable, it is not often available imported from Italy. However, just like mozzarella, good fresh ricotta can often be found in Italian markets and specialty stores. The whole milk ricotta available in the supermarket is an acceptable substitute.

Gorgonzola

Gorgonzola is a soft, blue-veined table cheese made from cow's milk. This buttery cheese was originally produced in the small village of Gorgonzola, near Milano, and aged in rocky caves. Today, however, this delicious cheese is produced in specially designated areas of Piemonte and Lombardia.

While a mature gorgonzola, aged five to six months, has a pungent, direct taste, a two- to three-month-old gorgonzola is milder and sweeter. Even though gorgonzola is a delicious table cheese, often served with grapes, pears, and nuts, it shines when it becomes a component in a creamy, delicate pasta sauce.

Fontina

Fontina is another great table cheese. This tender, mild, cow's milk cheese produced in Val d'Aosta dates back to the Middle Ages. Because of its soft, melting quality, fontina cheese is frequently used for cooking.

Pecorino

Pecorino cheese is made from sheep's milk. There are many varieties of pecorino cheese and they vary greatly, depending on the area where they are made. The best-known pecorino in this country is pecorino romano, a sharp, strong, assertive hard cheese, mainly used as a grating cheese in Roman and Southern Italian preparations.

There are, however, other pecorino cheese which are milder and are generally used as table cheeses. My personal preferences are the pecorinos made in Toscana and Umbria, which are mild and tender, with just a bit of peppery bite to them.

Mascarpone

Mascarpone is a double cream cheese that originated in Lombardia. The heavy cream is coagulated by the addition of citric acid, which gives this cheese its characteristic slightly sour taste. Mascarpone cheese is high in butter fat and has a thick, heavy consistency that resembles that of sour cream. This delicious cheese is used primarily in delicate pasta dishes and desserts and is the essential ingredient in the famous Italian dessert *tiramisù*. (Cream cheese is not an acceptable substitute for mascarpone.)

MEAT PRODUCTS

Prosciutto

Prosciutto is unsmoked, salted, and cured ham. Perhaps the best and best-known prosciutto of Italy is produced in the hills of Langhirano just outside Parma. This prosciutto, just like parmigiano-reggiano, is produced under strict regulations by the Consortium of Producers of *Prosciutto di Parma*. Only the best-quality pigs are used for this prosciutto, and they are fed with a special high-protein diet. *Prosciutto di Parma* is now available for the first time in this country. It has a lovely dark pink color with just a bit of marbling of fat and it is deliciously sweet. This ham is widely used in Italian cooking. Sliced prosciutto, tightly wrapped in plastic, can be kept in the refrigerator for 1 to 2 days. After that it will dry out. Do not freeze prosciutto.

    Prosciutto di Parma is sold with or without its large central bone. American-made prosciuttos such as Volpi, Daniele, and Citterio are good substitutes.

Pancetta

Pancetta is bacon. But unlike bacon, pancetta is not smoked. It is cured in salt and spices, and aged a few months. Pancetta, which comes rolled up like a salami, is perhaps one of the most important Italian ingredients, since its flavor is essential to many dishes. Good pancetta should have approximately the same amount of lean and fat meat. Pancetta is still not imported from Italy. However, American-made pancetta can be extremely good and should be easily available in Italian markets and specialty stores. Because of its high fat content, sliced pancetta can be kept in the refrigerator several days longer than prosciutto—4 to 5 days would be safe.

Speck and Bresaola

Speck is smoked ham from the Alto Adige and bresaola (sometimes also called *carne seca*) is cured, dried beef. Both ingredients have become quite popular lately in this country and are often served in Italian restaurants as components of an *antipasto misto* or alone. Both ingredients are often available in Italian markets and specialty stores.

COOKING FATS

Butter

Italian butter is unsalted. This butter is sweet and delicious and also much more perishable than salted butter (salt is often used as a natural food preservative).

    Once you get hooked on unsalted butter, you will never cook with salted butter again. In this country unsalted butter is found in the freezer section of supermarkets.

Olive Oil

Olive oil is the ingredient that unites all Italian cooking. Even though butter is widely used in the North, olive oil has its own special place and its usage is increasing by leaps and bounds. The reason? Olive oil is very good and it is also very good for us.

Of course olive oil is *the* cooking fat of Central and Southern Italy because of the abundance of olive trees spread throughout the landscape.

The best, most popular, and most expensive oil is *extra virgin olive oil*. This oil is produced without chemical means, by stone crushing and cold pressing hand-picked olives. It also has the lowest acidity, under one percent.

Virgin olive oil is produced in the same manner, using riper olives which have fallen to the ground. This oil has a higher degree of acidity which can be up to, but not more than, four percent.

Pure olive oil is, in spite of its label, the most common oil. It is rectified (deodorized, deacidified, and decolorized by chemical means). Many brands available in supermarkets fall in the category of *pure olive oil*.

Italy has a wide range of extra virgin olive oils, from the deep green and strongly flavored oil of Sicilia to the light, golden oil of Liguria and the Veneto, and in between there are the great oils of Toscana, Umbria, and Puglia. Fortunately, today we can find Italian olive oils not only at our specialized markets but quite often also at our local supermarkets. Try several brands and settle on the one you prefer.

Extra virgin olive oil has a place of prominence in my home pantry and in my restaurant. Use extra virgin oil whenever you can obtain it or can afford it. A few drops of fragrant green extra virgin olive oil can go quite far and give your cooking that unmistakable Italian taste.

Storing olive oil. Olive oil can be kept quite well for many months, provided you store it in the coolest, darkest part of your pantry in a tightly closed bottle. (Do not store it in plastic.) Olive oil does not need to be refrigerated.

Oil for frying. Many Italians use a *pure olive oil* for frying. My preference, however, is a more neutrally flavored oil, such as corn or peanut oil.

WINES AND VINEGARS

Wine

In Italian home cooking, most sauces are produced from a reduction of pan juices added to some wine, broth, or cream. Therefore, the quality of the liquid we use to produce a sauce is important. Don't choose a ninety-cent bottle of wine for cooking. Choose a wine that you would enjoy drinking, then use a bit of that for your sauce. Of course, if a wine is expensive, you probably would rather drink it than cook with it. But if you think of wine as an important ingredient which will affect the quality of your dish, perhaps you won't mind using a cup of good wine for your sauce.

Marsala

A bit of good Marsala can transform an ordinary dish into a delicacy. This wonderful aromatic wine comes from Marsala in Sicilia. Most people know how delicious a few slices of veal are when they are tossed with a bit of Marsala, but this wine can be used for so many other preparations. A veal, pork, or turkey roast, for example, will become irresistible with the addition of some Marsala. A bit of Marsala will enrich the sauce of a stew and many desserts would not taste the same without it. Marsala comes sweet and dry. Use dry Marsala for cooking and sweet Marsala for desserts and pastries. Look for imported Marsala, such as Florio and Pellegrino, which is available in Italian markets and wine shops. Domestic Marsala is not an acceptable substitute.

Balsamic Vinegar

Balsamic vinegar is an aromatic, concentrated product made from the boiled-down must of white Trebbiano grapes, and it is a specialty of Modena, a lovely city in Emilia-Romagna. In the sixteenth century, this vinegar was considered so precious that it was often made part of a legacy in a will and given as a dowry. The production of *real* balsamic vinegar takes many decades. The boiled-down must of the grapes is aged for many years in a series of barrels, moving the contents of the barrel to another of diminishing size and wood after much of the vinegar has evaporated, all of which gives a different fragrance to the vinegar. This process is repeated approximately every ten years until the vinegar has acquired that special thick, velvety, highly aromatic quality that defines it.

In Modena seventy- or eighty-year-old vinegar can still be found among some families which have been making it for generations or, with luck, one can obtain it from some of the few remaining artisans who still make it for sale. (Years ago I had the good fortune to savor a thirty-year-old vinegar, and I thought I had died and gone to heaven!) Today most balsamic vinegar available is commercially produced and aged two, three, or five years. I suppose we should be grateful for little miracles, because even though this product is light-years away from the wonderful homemade product, it is still reasonably pleasant. Sometimes in this country, you can find a ten-, fifteen-, or twenty- year-old vinegar. If you can afford it, buy it and use it sparingly and wisely, keeping in mind that you will need only a few drops to enrich a dish. Balsamic vinegar should read *Aceto balsamico tradizionale di Modena* or *Reggio Emilio*.

Vinegar

In Italian home cooking, vinegar is used far beyond the regular salad. A few drops of good red wine vinegar can be added to a fish stew, to game, and to liver. Vinegar is also the essential element in many sweet-and-sour dishes. Choose a wine vinegar that has a deep red color and that is free of other seasonings, such as garlic or herbs. White wine vinegar is occasionally used.

HERBS

Herbs, just like garlic, should be used in moderation. Somehow we have this image of Italian food loaded with all kinds of herbs. A bit of fresh sage added to boiled potatoes will give a decisive delicious touch. Too much will be quite overpowering. A little chopped fresh rosemary added to stewed game will bring out the flavor of the meat. Too much will give the sauce a bitter taste. If fresh herbs are not available, we must use dried herbs, also with moderation, for some might be too assertive and others might lack their original aroma. Our good common sense should tell us to always start with a little, for we can always add more.

Parsley

Parsley, just like olive oil and parmigiano, is a basic Italian ingredient. The parsley used in Italy, however, is not the curly type most commonly available in supermarkets, but the flat, broad-leaved parsley, also called appropriately "Italian parsley." It has a sweet, fragrant flavor which enhances the taste of innumerable dishes. Today Italian parsley is quite often available in supermarkets.

Basil

Basil is one of the most popular herbs, with its sweet taste and pretty green leaves and the fact that it embodies the spirit of summer. We use it in the ever-popular pesto sauce, in salads, and over pasta. In Italy, even the most modest cook has a little pot with basil on her window. This is one of those herbs that I do not bother to use unless it is fresh.

Rosemary

A roast scented with fresh, leafy rosemary is simply irresistible. This wonderful aromatic herb is used extensively throughout Italy, especially in conjunction with grilled or roasted meat and fowl. Dried rosemary, if used in moderation, is quite acceptable.

Sage

Sage is more popular in the northern part of Italy than the south, where it is properly paired with game cooking. I also love sage in savory breads and roasted potatoes, as well as in marinades. Use dried sage leaves judiciously because they can be quite overpowering.

Oregano

Fresh oregano is mild and sweet and gently aromatic. It appears in many Southern Italian dishes, either fresh or dried, especially in the many appetizing tomato sauces. Again, use dried oregano in moderation.

Mint

Many Southern Italian dishes have the delicious added taste of mint. Mint is used in the stuffing of the famous carciofi alla Romana, in lamb, chicken, and fish cooking, and in many marinades. *Mentuccia*, the wild mint used in Italy, has a milder flavor than most mint found here. To achieve the approximate taste of Italian *mentuccia*, use a combination of fresh spearmint and fresh oregano. Or use whatever mint you have available in moderation.

MISCELLANEOUS BASIC INGREDIENTS

Arborio Rice

Not many people know that Italians are the greatest producers of rice in Europe. This short, thick-grained rice is consumed extensively especially in the North. Arborio is perhaps the best-known and most widely exported variety. This rice, which comes packaged in small cloth sacks or boxes, is fairly expensive, but it is indispensable for a truly authentic risotto, because of its farinaceous nature which, as it cooks, gives the risotto its creamy consistency.

Arborio rice is now widely available in Italian markets and specialty food stores. In a pinch, substitute a good brand of converted rice.

Funghi Porcini (Boletus edulis)

Perhaps the reason I prefer to go to Italy in the spring and fall is because it is porcini season. Porcini are wild Italian mushrooms which grow under chestnut trees. These succulent, woodsy mushrooms, with their unique fragrance and meaty texture, are one of the most important elements of Italian gastronomy. In the spring and fall even the most modest trattoria has a supply of fresh porcini available, which often are showcased in large baskets in full view of the patrons.

Fresh porcini can also be found in this country, but only by those who know how to hunt for them. (At my restaurant we can occasionally get fresh porcini which we grill or use in risottos, and they are quickly sold out.) What we can find here, however, are dried porcini imported from Italy. Dried porcini are quite delicious, with a highly concentrated flavor. These are the porcini which are extensively used by the Italian home cook, because they are less expensive than the fresh, and can be kept conveniently for several months in the pantry. As specific recipes will instruct you, these mushrooms must be soaked in water before using them. The soaking water, which becomes intensely flavored with the mushrooms, is also used in many preparations. Dried porcini are now widely available in Italian markets, specialty food stores, and some supermarkets.

Radicchio

An indigenous Italian chicory that has quickly captured the attention of many American cooks is radicchio. The most celebrated type of radicchio in Italy is *radicchio di Treviso*, as it is commonly called, with its elongated shape and purplish red leaves. The radicchio that most Americans are familiar with is the round red variety. Radicchio has a slightly bitter taste that lends itself to many dishes. For me, the best way to end a meal is with a refreshing radicchio salad.

A good head of radicchio should have crisp, compact, firm, bright leaves.

Tomatoes

Tomatoes were introduced to Italy from South America, and Italians have adopted them wholeheartedly, exploiting them to their fullest.

When ripe, meaty, fragrant, fresh tomatoes are not available, Italians rely on canned tomatoes. The best Italian canned tomatoes are the San Marzano variety, grown in Southern Italy, which are ripe, red, meaty, and flavorful.

In making tomato sauces, keep in mind that Italians use tomatoes with a light hand. Even in the South, where tomatoes appear in every other dish, the amount of tomato sauce used over a pasta is minimal. Also keep in mind that in order to retain their freshness, fresh or canned tomatoes should be cooked quickly and briefly. Let the many sauces in the pasta chapter guide you.

Peeling fresh tomatoes. Cut a cross at the root end of the tomatoes and drop them into a large pot of boiling water. Cook the tomatoes until the skin begins to split, about 1 minute. (The cooking time varies, depending on the ripeness of the tomatoes and the thickness of their skin.) Transfer the tomatoes to a bowl of cold water. Peel, seed, and dice the tomatoes as soon as you can handle them.

Sun-dried Tomatoes

Sun-dried tomatoes are the legacy of parsimonious Italian peasants, who put to good use the abundant summer tomato harvest by drying the fresh tomatoes in the sun; that is the reason for their intense fragrance. Sun-dried tomatoes imported from Italy are preserved in extra virgin olive oil.

There is no doubt that sun-dried tomatoes are more popular in this country than in Italy. In this country, they have become trendy and are used extensively in restaurants of every denomination. In Italy they are used, just like any other flavor enhancer, in moderation.

Garlic

A heavy hand with garlic doesn't make a dish "Italian." The basic principle that guides all Italian cooking applies also to the use of garlic—just enough to flavor a dish, but not too much to overpower it. Always use fresh garlic. *Never* use the dried-up garlic flakes or powder sold in supermarkets. The taste will kill a dish, not enhance it.

Capers

Capers are the green buds of nasturtiums, a plant that grows wild around the Mediterranean. Capers come in two sizes, the large "capote" caper and the small "nonpareil" caper. Both are deliciously appetizing and are used as a flavoring ingredient in many sauces, over pizza, salads, and appetizers. I generally use capers that are sold in jars and pickled in vinegar. Before using them, they should be rinsed to get rid of the vinegar taste.

Anchovies

In an Italian pantry, alongside the canned tomatoes, the olive oil, the garlic, the bag of Arborio rice, and the flour for polenta, you will find a few cans of anchovies packed in oil. With a few chopped anchovies, a bit of garlic, chile pepper, and extra virgin olive oil, you will have a quintessential Southern Italian sauce. A hint of anchovy on a pizza, on a salad, or in a sauce can give a special zest to the dish. Just keep in mind one word: "moderation." Also, make sure you rinse the anchovies of their brine before using them.

Peperoncino

Peperoncino (small hot red chile pepper) is a favorite ingredient in many Southern Italian regions. The cooking of Abruzzi and Lazio has an abundance of dishes that use this hot ingredient. Clusters of *peperoncini*, brightly tied together, are sold in the open food markets, and many Southern Italian kitchens have them hung on their walls.

Often, this red chile pepper can be found fresh in the vegetable section of the supermarket, or in the form of dried flakes in the spice section of the market.

Mostarda di Cremona

Mostarda di Cremona is a relatively new imported Italian ingredient. It is made with large pieces of plump, mixed fruit which are preserved in a sweet, mustardy syrup. This is a specialty of the city of Cremona, and it is used in fillings for traditional pasta dishes such as pumpkin ravioli. It is also traditionally served next to mixed boiled meats and as a component of some vegetable fillings.

Amaretti di Saronno

Amaretti di Saronno are imported almond macaroons that taste like no other. This delicious crisp cookie is used as a component in many desserts, as a stuffing for baked fruit, mixed with squash and mostarda di Cremona.

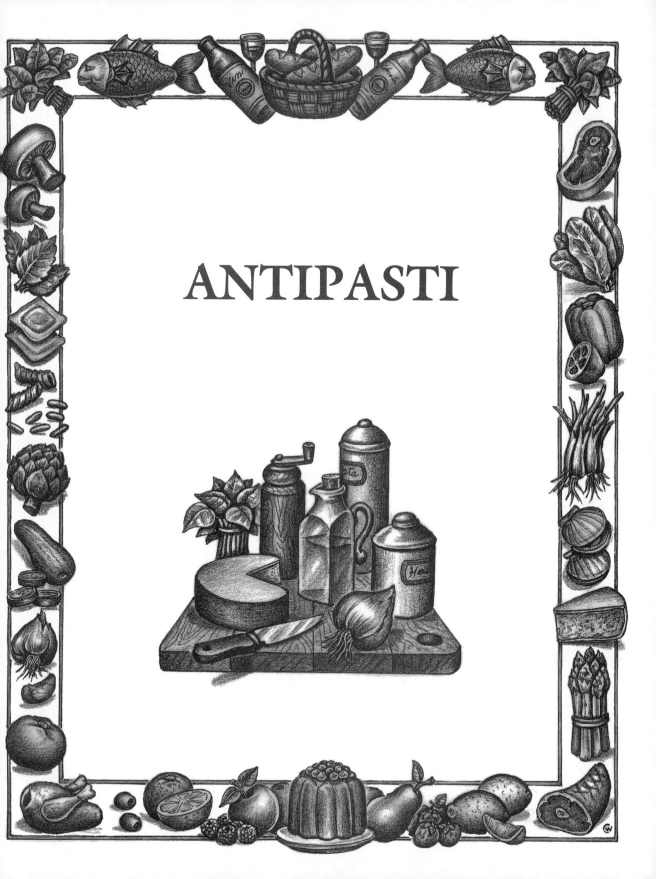

ANTIPASTI

Antipasto literally means "before the meal."

An antipasto is meant to tease the palate, stimulate the appetite, set the gastric juices in motion, and make you yearn for more.

But before that, an antipasto must catch your eye, since Italians believe that you eat first with your eyes, then with your palate. Every time I am in Italy, I am always mesmerized by the mouthwatering display of appetizers in restaurants and *trattorie*. Seafood salads, marinated and grilled vegetables, meat and fish carpaccio, marinated legumes, platters of prosciutto and sausages of every kind, pickled vegetables, figs, melon—suddenly your willpower fades and you want to reach out and try everything all at once.

Many *antipasti* can play a multiple role and be served at different stages of a meal, especially now that the traditional way of eating is less structured and more relaxed. (Often at my restaurant in Sacramento, I make a complete meal out of tastes of several *antipasti*.)

Although *antipasti* play a very important role in restaurants, they are almost shunned in an everyday family meal. However, when people entertain, the antipasto becomes the exciting prelude to a special meal.

An antipasto should fit into a meal and a setting. It is not an accident that in country *trattorie* the appetizers generally are made up of local salame, hams, pickled and fried vegetables, and crostini, while in elegant city restaurants they become more elegant and refined.

Because this book is about the food of the Italian *trattorie*, you will find the recipes for *antipasti* simple and hearty, like the Sicilian *panelle* (fritters made with chick-pea flour), which have centuries of tradition behind them, and the Tuscan *fettunta* (slices of bread that have been brushed with oil and grilled), which has been embellished by the addition of white beans and pancetta, and deep-fried zucchini blossoms and fried olives.

This is the food I get excited about. Real food that awakens my senses and speaks the unaffected language of the many good Italian cooks.

Carciofi alla Romana

Baked Artichokes Roman Style

Romans have a special way with artichokes. They fry them, stuff them, pickle them, and serve them raw in salads. One of the best-known artichoke preparations is this *carciofi alla Romana*. The artichokes are stuffed with a savory mixture of fresh mint, garlic, bread crumbs, and olive oil, then baked *upside down*, with their stalks upward, in a bit of water and oil. This most appetizing dish is generally served at room temperature as an appetizer, even though it will fit quite well almost anywhere in a menu.

The last time I had these lovely artichokes, I was eating *al fresco* in one of the most popular *trattorie* of Roma, La Carbonara, which delivers not only good food, but a colorful and exuberant ambiance.

    4 small artichokes
    ½ lemon
    3 fresh bread slices, crusts removed and finely chopped
    ⅓ cup chopped fresh parsley
    10 fresh mint leaves or 1 teaspoon dried, crumbled
    2 cloves garlic, minced
    ½ cup olive oil
    Salt and freshly ground black pepper to taste

Remove and discard the tougher outer leaves of the artichokes. Cut the remaining leaves halfway, with scissors, until you reach the central cone of leaves. At this point you will see that three-quarters of the leaves are white and the tip of the cone is pale green. Slice off the green top.

Gently open the artichokes with your hands and remove the fuzzy chokes with a spoon or a melon scooper. Rub the lemon over the cut edges of the artichokes to prevent discoloration.

With a small knife, trim off the outer green part of the artichokes' green bottoms. Trim the stalks, leaving about 2 inches intact. Trim away the greener outer part of the stalks, leaving the white part of the stalks intact. Rub the cut edges of the artichokes with more lemon.

In a small bowl, combine the bread, parsley, mint, garlic, and oil, and season. Push the stuffing between the artichoke leaves and into each artichoke cavity.

Place the artichokes, with their stalks pointing upward, in a small casserole. Add the remaining oil and just enough water to come halfway up the artichokes. (If you have any stuffing left, add it to the casserole.)

Brush a piece of parchment paper with olive oil and place over the artichokes. Cover the casserole with a tight lid and bake at 375°F until tender, 30 to 40 minutes. Cool to room temperature.

VARIATION

For a nontraditional but extremely appetizing variation, add 2 to 3 ounces of pancetta finely minced, to the stuffing.

SUGGESTED WINES

A white wine with a light, fruity body such as Frascati or a dry California chenin blanc such as Hacienda Winery. Remember, artichokes tend to change wine flavors.

Arrange the artichokes with their stems upward on a serving dish. If there is still quite a bit of watery juice in the casserole, cook it down over high heat until you have 4 to 5 tablespoons left. Pour the sauce over the artichokes, let cool, and serve.

Makes 4 servings

Carciofi alla Giudia

Deep-fried Artichokes, Jewish Style

NOTE OF INTEREST

Before becoming a trattoria, Gigetto was originally an osteria. Osterie *date back to Papal Rome and were originally wine shops or taverns, where the people of the neighborhood would gather to socialize, play cards, and drink wine. Often they would bring their own humble dinner along and would accompany it with wine sold by the* osteria.

The Ceccarellis, original owners of the Osteria da Gigetto, eventually began to serve food to their customers, and converted the osteria *into a trattoria.*

Today, the third generation of the Ceccarellis run this popular eating spot, but out of respect for their grandparents' humble beginning, they have maintained a corner of their trattoria for the fagottari, *as they are called, the old people who bring their own food along and enjoy it with the house wine.*

Roma is a living museum. A part of Roma that is perhaps older than Roma itself is the Jewish Ghetto. This is where the Jewish community settled over two thousand years ago. It is an area of synagogues, majestic old buildings, narrow cobblestoned streets, and ancient squares. Walking through the area is like walking back in time. Here there is also a great tradition of food. One of the most popular dishes of this area is *carciofi alla Giudia*, crisp, fried artichokes, Jewish style.

Gigetto, a popular family-owned trattoria that has been in the same location for over seventy years, prepares this dish with a sure hand and a delicate touch. The small Roman artichokes are trimmed of all hard leaves and fried in two stages with two separate batches of oil, until they are tender and crisp.

Eating a dish that has been prepared in the same manner for centuries, in a seventy-year-old trattoria in the heart of the oldest quarter of Roma, was a heartwarming, humbling experience.

4 small artichokes
½ lemon
Salt and freshly ground black pepper to taste
1 cup plain bread crumbs, spread over aluminum foil
Vegetable oil for frying

Cut off half of each artichoke stems. Remove and discard all outer green leaves until you reach the white central cone. At this point, you will see that three-quarters of the leaves are white and the tip of the cone is pale green. Slice off the green top.

With a small knife, trim off the outer green part of each artichoke's green bottom.

Gently open each artichoke with your hands and remove the fuzzy choke with a spoon or melon scooper. Rub the lemon over the cut edges of the artichokes and season them inside with salt and pepper. Gently open the artichoke leaves as far as they can go without breaking them off and, holding the artichokes by their stems, press the open leaves into the bread crumbs to coat lightly.

Heat two inches of oil in a medium-size saucepan over medium heat to 250° to 275°F. Lower the artichokes into the oil and cook about 10 minutes. Turn the artichokes a few times so they will fry evenly. Lower the heat if the artichokes turn golden too fast. With a thin knife, prick their bottoms to test for doneness. They are done when they can be easily pierced. Transfer the artichokes to paper towels to drain. (The artichokes can be prepared up to this point several hours ahead.)

Just before you are ready to serve them, pour two inches of oil in another medium-size saucepan over medium-high heat. When the oil is very hot, but not smoking, about 375°F, carefully add one artichoke. With two long wooden spoons, or a long tong, hold the artichoke open-face down, pressing the leaves gently against the bottom of the pan to open them further. Hold the artichoke in that position for about 30 seconds. Transfer the artichoke to paper towels to drain. Repeat with the other artichokes. The second frying should take no longer than 2 to 3 minutes. Sprinkle them lightly with salt and serve hot.

Makes 4 servings

Panelle

Chick-pea Flour Fritters

One of my Sicilian "discoveries" was a very appetizing local dish called *panelle*. In reality, *panelle* is not a dish per se. It is best categorized as a snack or a rustic appetizer. And appetizing it certainly is! It seems as if everyone in Palermo eats *panelle*. The child and the laborer who put a large piece of *panelle* between two slices of bread. The mother who buys a "sheet" of *panelle* from the *panillaru*, then fries them at home for her children. The shoppers who in the colorful A Vucciria open food market buy *panelle* from one of the many vendors who fry them while you wait. And in restaurants and *trattorie* a plate of hot, golden *panelle* appears on your table the moment you sit down.

Panelle are made with chick-pea (garbanzo) flour. First, the flour and water are combined to make a batter. Then the batter is cooked and mixed constantly. When the thickened mixture is ready, it is spread on a baking sheet and allowed to firm up for several hours or overnight, so it can be cut and fried.

This is basic, ancient street food. And in a world where everything seems to move faster every day, it is heartwarming to me to come across food that has been around for centuries.

> 3 cups cold water
> Salt to taste
> ½ cup chick-pea (garbanzo) flour (see note below)
> 2 tablespoons chopped fresh parsley
> ⅓ cup freshly grated parmigiano, optional
> Vegetable oil for frying

NOTE OF INTEREST
Garbanzo flour can be found in health or organic food stores.

In a medium-size bowl combine the water and salt. Add the flour slowly, mixing well with a wooden spoon or a wire whisk after each addition to prevent lumps. When all the flour has been added, you should have a smooth batter.

Pour the mixture into a medium-size saucepan and bring to a gentle boil over medium heat, stirring constantly. Cook and stir for 12 to 15 minutes. As it cooks, the mixture will thicken considerably. If it thickens too much, however, and sticks heavily to the spoon or the whisk, add a bit of cold water. Just before removing it from the heat, stir in the parsley and parmigiano and mix energetically to incorporate. The mixture should have the consistency of a medium-thick béchamel or a thick gravy.

Pour the mixture onto a medium-size baking sheet. Wet a spatula (keep a small bowl of cold water next to you to dip the spatula) and quickly spread the mixture evenly to a thickness of about ¼ inch. Refrigerate, uncovered, for several hours or overnight, until it is very firm. When you are ready to fry, cut it into 2-inch squares.

SUGGESTED WINES
A good, imported dry Marsala Vergine or Soleras, served chilled, would be perfect with the classic Sicilian flavor of this dish.

Heat one inch of oil in a heavy, medium-size skillet over medium heat. When the oil is hot, fry the *panelle* a few at a time until they are lightly golden on both sides, 3 to 4 minutes. Remove with a slotted spoon and drain on paper towels. Season lightly with salt and serve while hot.

Makes 30 *panelle*

Cavolfiore Fritto

Deep-fried Cauliflower

For centuries the Sicilian diet has relied heavily on pasta, fish, and vegetables. These are the elements that constitute the basis of what we today call the Mediterranean diet.

The pastas of Sicilia are vibrant and colorful. The fish preparations are simple and straightforward, needing nothing but the wonderful fresh local fish to be outstanding. The vegetables of Sicilia could fill up a whole cookbook because of the many ways in which they can be prepared.

At A Zammara in Taormina, I indulged in an appetizer of wonderfully crisp, fried cauliflower florets which had been dipped in a batter scented with a bit of anchovy. They were light and airy and not at all greasy. I found myself eating them like cherries, one after another, unable and unwilling to stop.

> 1 head cauliflower, about 1½ pounds, broken into florets
> 1 tablespoon salt
> 1 recipe flour-and-water batter (see page 35)
> 4 anchovy fillets, finely chopped, or to taste
> Vegetable oil for frying

Wash the florets under cold running water.

Bring a large pot of water to a boil over medium heat. Add the salt and the florets. Cook, uncovered, until tender, 3 to 5 minutes, depending on the size of the florets.

Drain and rinse the florets under cold running water to stop the cooking. Lay the florets on paper towels and pat dry. (The florets can be cooked several hours or a day ahead and kept tightly wrapped in the refrigerator.)

Prepare the batter and mix in the anchovies.

Heat two inches of oil in a medium-size saucepan over high heat. When the oil is hot, dip the florets in the batter, then slip a few at a time into the oil. When they are golden on one side, 1 to 2 minutes, turn them over to cook the other side. Remove from the oil with a slotted spoon and transfer to paper towels to drain. Sprinkle lightly with salt and serve while they are hot and crispy.

Makes 4 servings

SUGGESTED WINES
A crisp, light, somewhat fragrant white wine is called for here, such as a Pinot Bianco from the Alto Adige or a Verdicchio from the Marche region.

Melanzane Marinate

Marinated Eggplant

SUGGESTED WINES

A dry Marsala Vergine would stand up to the vinegary character of this dish, as would a very fruity red of medium alcohol and body such as a young Barolo.

Taormina is a resort town in Sicilia of incomparable beauty. It has a warm, sunny climate, the bluest, clearest sea in the Mediterranean and, as I discovered, wonderful food.

Sicilians can probably cook vegetables better than anybody in Italy, especially eggplant, which they love. At Trattoria La Botte, a fairly large, charming establishment in the heart of Taormina, I was captivated by the large table showcasing an array of mouthwatering vegetable *antipasti*. These marinated eggplant were one of the many *antipasti* I enjoyed that night, and they tasted like no other eggplant I had ever had. They were peeled and diced and boiled in water and vinegar. Then they were drained and tossed together with garlic, fabulously scented green extra virgin Sicilian olive oil, fresh oregano, and just a bit of strong white wine vinegar.

2 medium-size eggplant (about 2 pounds), trimmed, peeled, and cut into 1-inch dice
1 to 2 tablespoons salt
1 cup plus 2 tablespoons white wine vinegar
Salt and freshly ground black pepper to taste
½ cup extra virgin olive oil, preferably from Sicilia
2 cloves garlic, finely minced
¼ cup loosely packed fresh oregano leaves or
2 tablespoons chopped fresh parsley

Place the diced eggplant in a large colander and sprinkle with the salt. Let stand for about 1 hour. The salt will draw out the eggplant's bitter juices.

Bring a large pot of water to a boil and add 1 cup of the vinegar.

Rinse the eggplant quickly under cold running water and place them in the boiling water. Boil 1 to 2 minutes. (Do not boil them too long—test them after 1 minute—or they will become soggy.) Drain and rinse the eggplant under cold running water to stop the cooking. Shake the colander a few times to remove as much water as possible. Place the eggplant in a large bowl and refrigerate about 1 hour.

Just before serving, season the eggplant with salt and pepper and dress with the oil, garlic, the remaining vinegar, and the oregano. Serve alone as an appetizer or a salad, or as part of an *antipasto misto* (see sidebar on page 26).

Makes 6 servings

Melanzane al Forno alla Siciliana

Baked Eggplant Sicilian Style

In Italy there are many preparations called *alla parmigiana*. Many are made with vegetables and some with meat, especially veal. The best known, however, is *eggplant alla parmigiana*, which too often has been a very uninspired fixture in Italian-American restaurants in this country.

At Trattoria La Bussola in Mazzaro, a very small community just outside Taormina in Sicilia, they bread and fry the eggplant slices and combine them with a lightly cooked tomato sauce and fresh mozzarella, and bake the preparation just long enough for the cheese to melt. The result is a very satisfying yet fresh-tasting dish.

1 medium-size eggplant, trimmed, peeled, and cut lengthwise into twelve ¼-inch-thick slices

1 to 2 tablespoons salt

2 large eggs, lightly beaten in a medium-size bowl with a pinch of salt

2 cups plain bread crumbs, spread over a sheet of aluminum foil

Vegetable oil for frying

¼ cup olive oil

3 cloves garlic, finely minced

4 cups imported Italian tomatoes with their juices, put through a strainer or a food mill to remove the seeds

Salt and freshly ground black pepper to taste

2 tablespoons chopped fresh parsley

24 thin slices mozzarella (approximately 12 ounces)

Put the eggplant slices on a large platter or baking sheet, sprinkle with 1 to 2 tablespoons of salt, and let stand about 1 hour. The salt will draw out the eggplant's bitter juices. Pat the slices dry with paper towels.

Dip the slices into the beaten eggs, shake off the excess, and dredge completely in the bread crumbs.

Heat 1 inch of oil in a medium-size skillet over high heat. When the oil is very hot, slip a few slices into the oil. When they are golden on one side, less than 1 minute, turn to fry the other side. With a slotted spoon transfer to paper towels to drain. Repeat with the remaining eggplant. (This step can be done a few hours ahead. Keep the fried eggplant at room temperature.)

Preheat the oven to 350°F.

Heat the olive oil in a medium-size skillet over medium heat. Add the garlic and cook, stirring, until the garlic begins to color, less than 1 minute. Add the tomatoes and season with salt and pepper. Cook, uncovered, 7 to 8 minutes. Just before removing it from the stove, stir in the parsley.

Spread about ¾ cup of the sauce in the bottom of a baking dish. Cover the sauce with some eggplant slices and top each with two slices of mozzarella. Spread some more tomato sauce over them. Repeat until all the ingredients are used up. (If you are using a small baking dish, you might have two or three layers. If you are using a large one, you might have only one layer.)

Bake until the cheese is melted, 12 to 15 minutes. Serve warm or at room temperature.

Makes 6 servings as an appetizer or 4 as an entree

SUGGESTED WINE
Sicilia's famous Corvo Rosso, with its ruby red color and penetrating aroma, would accompany this dish perfectly.

Involtini di Melanzane

Baked Stuffed Eggplant Bundles

These delicious baked stuffed eggplant were part of a large display of appetizers at Trattoria La Botte in Taormina.

For lighter bundles, the eggplant slices can be grilled, instead of fried, then stuffed and baked as instructed here.

1 medium-size eggplant, peeled and cut lengthwise into twelve ¼-inch-thick slices

1 to 2 tablespoons salt

2 large eggs, lightly beaten in a medium-size bowl with a pinch of salt

2 cups plain bread crumbs, spread over a sheet of aluminum foil

Vegetable oil for frying

24 thin slices mozzarella (approximately 12 ounces)

12 anchovy fillets

Put the eggplant slices on a large platter or baking sheet, sprinkle with the salt, and let stand about 1 hour. The salt will draw out the eggplant's bitter juices. Pat the slices dry with paper towels.

Dip the slices into the beaten eggs, shaking off any excess, then dredge completely in the bread crumbs.

Heat one inch of oil in a medium-size skillet over high heat. When the oil is very hot, slip a few slices into the oil. When they are golden on one side, less than 1 minute, turn and fry the other side. With a slotted spoon transfer to paper towels to drain. Repeat with the remaining slices.

Preheat the oven to 375°F. Put two slices of mozzarella over each slice of eggplant and top with one anchovy fillet. Roll the eggplant up *loosely* into a soft bundle. Secure with a toothpick.

Brush a baking dish lightly with oil and add the bundles. Bake until the cheese is melted, 7 to 8 minutes. Serve hot.

Makes 6 servings

SUGGESTED WINES
The dry white wine of Rapitalà or Regaleali from Sicilia would be perfect, or try Gallo's French Colombard, which is similar in style and character.

Olive Fritte

Fried Green Olives

Cantina Do Mori in Venezia is a well-known bustling *osteria* where Venetians meet to drink wine and snack on some delicious morsels. It was there that I tasted these appetizing fried olives. When I asked Signor Biscontin, the owner, for the recipe, he smiled and said: "What recipe? Just roll the olives in flour, eggs, and bread crumbs and fry them." I wonder why I didn't think of that before. Now, I often have a bowl of fried olives on the bar of my restaurant, and my customers love them.

> 30 large Italian-style pitted green olives from jars
> 1 cup unbleached all-purpose flour, spread over a sheet of aluminum foil
> 2 large eggs, lightly beaten
> 1 cup plain bread crumbs mixed with ½ cup freshly grated parmigiano, spread over a sheet of aluminum foil
> Vegetable oil for frying

Roll the olives in the flour, dip them in the eggs, and coat with the bread crumb–parmigiano mixture.

Heat one inch of oil in a medium-size skillet over medium heat. When the oil is hot, fry a handful of olives at a time until they are lightly golden, less than 1 minute. Remove the olives with a slotted spoon and spread on paper towels to drain.

Serve the olives warm while your family or guests are enjoying a glass of wine.

Makes approximately 6 servings

SUGGESTED WINES
Try a dry Solera or Marsala Vergine from Pellegrino or Rallo served cool or a chilled glass of Fino sherry such as Tio Pepe.

Cipolle Ripiene di Magro

Baked Stuffed Onions

The deliciousness of a simple dish depends not only on the skill of the cook, but also on the quality of the ingredients. In this recipe we not only have onions and squash, but also Mostarda di Cremona, an imported candied fruit in heavy syrup, Amaretti di Saronno, imported almond cookies, and parmigiano-reggiano. There is no doubt that these ingredients make an otherwise humble dish outstanding. This is a traditional dish of Piemonte that used to be served on Christmas Eve. It was then a happy surprise for me to find it on the menu of the lovely Trattoria

Albero Fiorito in Dogliani, a small town about forty kilometers from Cuneo. It was served as an appetizer next to roasted red bell peppers with *bagna caôda* (pages 32–33). It was simply wonderful, because the onions with their sweet stuffing contrasted sharply but very pleasantly with the pungency of the peppers in their garlic, anchovy, and olive oil dressing.

1 pound butternut squash, cut in half lengthwise and seeded

3 ounces imported Mostarda di Cremona (see page 17), strained of the juices and finely chopped

5 pairs Amaretti di Saronno cookies (see page 17), finely crushed

½ cup freshly grated parmigiano

Salt to taste

⅓ cup plain bread crumbs, optional

5 medium-size onions, trimmed and peeled

Preheat the oven to 375°F.

Place the squash in a buttered baking pan and bake until tender, 1 to 1½ hours. Cool the squash. With a spoon, scoop out the pulp and place it in a medium-size bowl. Mash the pulp against the side of the bowl with the spoon. Do not puree it in a food processor or the squash will become too soupy. Add the mostarda, amaretti, and parmigiano, season with salt, and mix everything till well combined. At this point the mixture should have a medium-firm consistency. If too soft, add a bit more parmigiano or the bread crumbs. Cover the bowl and refrigerate until ready to use.

Bring a large saucepan of water to a boil and add the onions. Cook over medium heat, uncovered, until the onions are tender but still firm to the touch, 15 to 20 minutes. Drain, dry them on paper towels, and cool.

Cut the onions in half and with a knife or a spoon remove their centers. Season the inside of the onion with salt, then fill each onion with the squash mixture.

Butter a baking dish and put the stuffed onions in the dish. Bake until the onions are lightly golden and are easily pierced with a thin knife, 20 to 30 minutes. Serve hot or at room temperature.

Makes 10 servings

TIP

∽ *Boil the onions and prepare the squash filling up to one or two days ahead of time. Keep the onions well wrapped in the refrigerator. Fill the onions and bake them at the last minute.*

SUGGESTED WINES

With these unusual-tasting onions, try the uniquelly Italian Grignolino from one of the following producers: Mascarello, Scarpa, or Pio Cesare. Serve it cool.

Peperoni alla Bagna Caôda

Roasted Peppers with Bagna Caôda

In Piemonte, vegetables are often served raw with *bagna caôda*, a hot dip made with olive oil, butter, garlic, and anchovies. This is peasant food at its best, hearty, stout, and flavorful. Occasionally, vegetables for *bagna caôda* are treated differently, like the preparation of Trattoria Albero Fiorito of Dogliani, in Piemonte, where the peppers are roasted, peeled, and served with a generous topping of hot, fragrant *bagna caôda*.

4 large red bell peppers
½ cup olive oil
2 tablespoons unsalted butter
4 cloves garlic, finely minced
8 anchovy fillets, finely chopped
2 tablespoons chopped fresh parsley

Peppers can be roasted in several ways. They can be roasted over an open flame, a barbecue, a grill, or under a broiler.

To roast the peppers over a gas burner, raise the heat to high, to take advantage of a full flame, hold the pepper with a long thong, and place over the flame on its side. As soon as the skin over the fire is charred, 3 to 4 minutes, turn it to char the other sides.

To roast the peppers over a barbecue or grill or under the broiler, preheat the cooking unit well ahead of time. Place the peppers on their sides over the hot grill or under the broiler until they are charred all over (about 10 minutes for the grill and 10 to 12 minutes for the broiler).

Place the charred peppers in a plastic bag and secure tightly. Leave the peppers in the bag for 30 minutes to cool and soften.

Peel the peppers and discard the seeds (this step can be done quickly under cold running water). Pat the peppers dry with paper towels and cut them into two-inch strips. Place the strips on a large serving platter until you are ready to use them. (The peppers can be prepared several hours or a day ahead and kept tightly covered in the refrigerator. However, bring them back to room temperature before serving.)

TIPS

If you want to serve bagna caôda *in the classic Italian way as a hot dip for raw vegetables, prepare the dip as instructed above and keep it warm in a chafing dish. Place the dish in the center of the table and let everyone dip in their raw vegetables. Some of the vegetables to use for* bagna caôda *are mushrooms, peppers, cardoons, celery, radishes, carrots, and zucchini. Vegetables that are equally delicious, but not used traditionally are Belgian endives (my favorite), radicchio, asparagus, and sugar snap peas.*

When I have leftover bagna caôda, *I use it as a sauce for spaghetti, and what a dish it makes! In Piemonte, leftover* bagna caôda *is mixed into scrambled eggs.*

To prepare the *bagna caôda*, heat the oil and butter in a small skillet over medium-low heat. The moment the butter begins to foam, reduce the heat to low and add the garlic. Cook and stir for 1 to 2 minutes, making sure the garlic *does not color*. Add the anchovies and cook over very low heat, stirring, until the anchovies and garlic are cooked into a soft paste, about 10 minutes. Spoon the hot dip over the peppers, sprinkle with the parsley, and serve at once.

Makes 4 to 6 servings

SUGGESTED WINES
As with the Baked Stuffed Onions, try a Grignolino from Mascarello, Scarpa, or Pio Cesare, and serve it cool.

Pomodori Ripieni alla Salsa Verde

Plum Tomatoes Stuffed with Piquant Green Sauce

Salsa verde is a classic Northern Italian sauce that is the perfect accompaniment to *bollito misto* (mixed boiled meats). Each city in Northern Italy has a slightly different version of this sauce. In Piemonte, tuna, diced red bell peppers, and small gherkins are sometimes added to the sauce. This version, which comes from Trattoria Pertinace, near Alba in Piemonte, is used also as a stuffing for tomatoes or peppers, and served as an appetizer.

    1 slice white bread, crust removed
    2 tablespoons red wine vinegar
    2 cups loosely packed chopped fresh parsley
    3 cloves garlic
    2 anchovy fillets
    2 tablespoons capers, drained and rinsed
    3 ounces canned tuna packed in olive oil, drained
    6 small gherkins packed in vinegar, drained
    ½ cup olive oil
    Salt and freshly ground black pepper to taste
    4 large, firm but ripe tomatoes

Tear the bread into pieces and put in a food processor. Add the vinegar, parsley, garlic, anchovies, capers, tuna, gherkins, and olive oil and turn the machine on and off until everything is well chopped, but not completely smooth. Place the sauce in a

small bowl and season. Cover the bowl and refrigerate until ready to use.

Wash and dry the tomatoes. Slice them in half lengthwise and, with a small knife, remove the seeds and the inside of the tomato pulp. Place the tomatoes on paper towels facedown to let excess juices drain. Fill the tomatoes with the prepared sauce and serve at room temperature.

Makes 4 servings

Zucchine Fritte con la Pastella

Fried Zucchini Blossoms

There are some dishes that have no regional barrier. Deep-fried zucchini blossoms is such a dish. The last time I feasted on perfectly fried zucchini blossoms was at La Biscondola, an up-scale establishment in the Chianti area of Toscana.

This is a simple dish to prepare, provided you have on hand beautifully fresh (not wilted) zucchini blossoms and fry them properly.

The secret of good fried food lies in the temperature of the oil, which should be very hot, but not so hot that it will smoke and burn your food. Test the oil by adding a bit of what you are frying. If it turns golden brown almost immediately, the oil is ready.

Another important element of good frying is not to crowd the food in the pan. Keep in mind that each time you add something to the oil, you lower its temperature. Fry a few pieces, then as you remove those, fry a few more. This way the food will fry quickly, will absorb very little oil, and will be perfectly crisp.

> One recipe of batter (see page 35)
> 4 ounces fresh zucchini blossoms (approximately 12 blossoms)
> Vegetable oil for frying
> Salt to taste

Prepare the batter.

Cut the base from the blossoms and slice them in half length-wise. Remove the pistils. Wash the blossoms quickly under cold running water and thoroughly pat dry with paper towels.

Heat two inches of oil in a heavy, medium-size skillet over high heat. When the oil is very hot, dip the blossoms into the batter, and slip a few at a time into the oil. When they are lightly golden on one side, turn them over and cook till the other side is golden, about 1 minute. Remove with a slotted spoon and transfer to paper towels to drain. Sprinkle lightly with salt and serve piping hot.

Makes 4 servings

SUGGESTED WINE
A nice, dry Riesling such as Trefethen from California's Napa Valley would accompany this delicious dish very well.

Fiori di Zucchine Ripiene Fritte

Stuffed and Fried Zucchini Blossoms

One of the joys of summer is the abundance of its harvest. In Italy during the summer, the open markets are filled to capacity with a dazzling variety of fresh produce. Red and yellow peppers, sweet peas, tender asparagus, ripe juicy tomatoes, and clusters of orange-colored zucchini blossoms.

Zucchini blossoms are a delicacy. They are short-lived because they are very perishable. But if you can get your hands on them, by all means buy them and try this delicious dish which comes from Gigetto, one of the oldest *trattorie* in Roma.

In this country, zucchini blossoms can be found with a certain regularity in specialized markets.

For the batter
   1 cup water
   2 large eggs, lightly beaten
   1 cup unbleached all-purpose flour
   Salt to taste

To complete the dish
   4 ounces zucchini blossoms (approximately 12 blossoms)
   5 anchovy fillets, cut into small pieces
   1 ounce mozzarella, diced
   Vegetable oil for frying

Combine the water with the beaten eggs in a medium-size bowl. Gradually sift in the flour, beating well with a wire whisk after each addition. Season the batter lightly with salt. Set aside.

Remove the pistils gently from the zucchini blossoms. Wash the blossoms quickly under cold running water and thoroughly pat dry with paper towels. Place a very small piece of anchovy and a few pieces of diced mozzarella into the blossom cavity. Twist the long parts of the flower *very lightly* (it should look like the ends of a loosely wrapped candy) so that the filling will not escape during the frying. Repeat until all the blossoms have been stuffed.

Heat two inches of oil in a heavy, medium-size saucepan over high heat. When the oil is very hot, dip the stuffed blossoms in the batter and slip a few at a time into the oil. (Do not fry too many at one time or you will lower the temperature of the oil and the blossoms will not become crisp.) When the blossoms are lightly golden on one side, turn them over and cook till golden on the other side. Remove from the oil with a slotted spoon and transfer to paper towels to drain.

Season very lightly with salt (remember, the anchovies are already salty) and serve piping hot.

Makes 4 servings

SUGGESTED WINE

Try one of Italy's unique white wines, Prosecco from the Veneto region, in either its still or sparkling style, from producers such as Nino Franco and Foss Maral.

Frittata alle Zucchine e Pecorino

Frittata with Zucchini and Pecorino Cheese

NOTE OF INTEREST

My favorite way to eat a frittata is cold or at room temperature between two slices of bread.

I was told that at Lucia, an eight-table trattoria in the heart of Trastevere, you could eat true, homey Roman food. So, the last night I spent in Roma, I decided to give it a try. I got into a taxi, and when I gave the driver the address, he turned around and asked me whether I was sure I wanted to go there, alone. "Not a nice area for a woman alone," he said. But I had made up my mind and went anyway. The run-down trattoria located in a very narrow, very old street turned out to be just fine. The large woman who was screaming the food orders to the kitchen sat me at a little table near the kitchen, and hovered over me like a mother hen.

A carafe of Frascati wine and an *antipasto misto* instantly materialized on the table, even before I had time to say hello. I decided not to protest and just go with the flow. The antipasto turned out to be very satisfying—slices of local *salame*, prosciutto, pickled artichokes hearts, and thick wedges of zucchini frittata. There was enough on the plate to feed an army. Finally, I was allowed to choose my next dish, which was one of the two choices of the evening. Large *polpette* (meatballs) with small, sweet peas in a zesty tomato sauce (see pages 185–87). Perhaps that is why they say, "When in Rome, do as the Romans do."

⅓ cup olive oil
½ pound small zucchini, sliced into thin rounds
1 clove garlic, finely minced
3 tablespoons freshly grated pecorino romano or ⅓ cup
    freshly grated parmigiano
2 tablespoons chopped fresh parsley
6 large eggs, lightly beaten
Salt and freshly ground black pepper to taste

Heat the oil in an 8-inch nonstick skillet over medium heat. Add the zucchini and cook, stirring, until the zucchini are lightly golden, 4 to 5 minutes. Add the garlic and stir once or twice. Beat the pecorino cheese and the parsley into the eggs in a large bowl and season.

Remove the zucchini from the skillet with a slotted spoon and stir them into the beaten eggs. Return the egg mixture to the skillet and cook over medium heat until the bottom of the frittata is set and lightly browned, 5 to 6 minutes.

Put a large plate over the skillet and turn the frittata onto the plate. Slide it back into the skillet to cook the other side. Cook until the bottom is lightly browned, 3 to 4 minutes longer. Slide the frittata onto a serving dish, cut into wedges, and serve warm or at room temperature.

Makes 4 servings as an appetizer or 2 servings as an entree

SUGGESTED WINES
Try a medium-bodied white from Toscana, such as Frescobaldi's Pomino Bianco, or the fuller-bodied San Angelo Pinot Grigio of Villa Banfi.

Sopressata all'Aceto con Polenta Fritta

Sopressata with Vinegar and Fried Polenta

I always wonder why some of the dishes we long for and lust after are often the ones we should not eat because of their caloric or fat content!

It was in Venezia at Trattoria-Enoteca da Gigio that I succumbed to a stout appetizer of rich sopressata in a thick, glazy sauce of vinegar and sugar, accompanied by golden fried polenta. Not only did I eat the sopressata, setting aside the initial guilt, but I asked shamelessly for more fried polenta to scoop up a tiny bit of sauce left on my plate.

When I tested this dish at my restaurant in Sacramento, my pastry cook, Edna, licked her lips and said, "Wow, what a great breakfast this would make!"

> ½ recipe Basic Polenta (see page 176)
> Vegetable oil for frying
> 2 tablespoons unsalted butter
> ½ cup red wine vinegar
> ⅓ cup sugar
> 8 ounces sopressata (see note above), cut into 8 thick slices

Prepare the polenta several hours or a day ahead so it will become very firm. Pour the polenta onto a platter or a cookie sheet, and spread it uniformly to approximately ½ inch thick. When you are ready to fry the polenta, cut it into 8 slices.

Heat one inch of oil in a medium-size nonstick skillet over medium heat. When the oil is hot, fry the slices of polenta a few at a time until they are lightly golden on both sides, 3 to 4 minutes. Remove the polenta with a slotted spoon and drain on paper towels. Keep the polenta warm in a low oven while you are preparing the sopressata.

Heat the butter in a medium-size skillet over medium heat. When the butter foams, add the vinegar and sugar and cook,

NOTE OF INTEREST

Sopressata, or sopressa, is a large salame made from pork. This tasty sausage is eaten thinly sliced as an antipasto or in sandwiches. It is also delicious grilled. Sopressata is available in Italian specialty stores. Substitute with baked ham or prosciutto if not available.

TIP

This dish has to be served as soon as it is cooked, because the thick sauce will become firmer and thicker and hard to pour over the sopressata. If this happens, remove the sopressata from the skillet, add a bit of water to the sauce, and cook and stir over low heat until the sauce has reacquired the proper consistency.

stirring constantly, until the mixture has a medium-thick, glazy consistency, 3 to 4 minutes. Add the sopressata to the sauce and turn the slices in the hot mixture briefly to coat, 20 to 30 seconds. Place the sopressata on serving dishes, top with a bit of thick sauce, add the fried polenta, and serve at once.

Makes 4 servings

SUGGESTED WINES

Use a light, fruity, cooled red wine such as a Merlot from the Veneto or a Refosco from Friuli.

Bresaola con Olio, Limone e Parmigiano

Bresaola with Oil, Lemon, and Parmigiano

One of the appetizers often found in restaurants and *trattorie* of Northern Italy is bresaola. Bresaola is a fillet of beef that is cured in salt and dried. This delicious product is a specialty of the Valtellina, a beautiful sunny valley in the northern part of Lombardia.

At Cucina delle Langhe in Milano, the bresaola was cut very thin, topped by a bit of extra virgin olive oil, lemon juice, slivers of perfectly aged parmigiano, and black pepper.

After the bresaola is sliced, it should be kept tightly wrapped in plastic wrap, so that it won't dry out and change color. Try to use the bresaola as soon as possible, preferably within twenty-four hours, to fully appreciate its unique flavor.

    4 ounces bresaola (see page 11), very thinly sliced
    ¼ cup extra virgin olive oil
    Juice of 1 lemon
    Freshly ground black pepper to taste
    ¼ ounce parmigiano-reggiano, cut into slivers

Place the bresaola on individual dishes and sprinkle with the oil. Add a bit of the lemon juice and a few twists of pepper. Top with the parmigiano and serve.

Makes 4 servings

SUGGESTED WINES

A light red or a rosé with some character would work well served slightly chilled. Try Rivera Rosé from Puglia or Vin Ruspo of Capezzana in Toscana.

Insalata di Calamari

Calamari Salad

During my last trip to Sicilia, I ate fish wherever I went. The dishes I particularly enjoyed were the colorful, appetizing fish and shellfish salads.

At Trattoria Stella, located in a seventeenth-century palazzo in the oldest part of Palermo, I had a calamari salad that, in its simplicity, was sheer perfection.

The small calamari were very white and very tender and were dressed simply with aromatic green Sicilian olive oil, lemon juice (but then, the lemons of Sicilia are the best in the world), sweet garlic, and fresh basil.

For this salad, select the smallest calamari, which will need the briefest of boiling to be very tender.

2 pounds squid, the smallest you can find (approximately 18 ounces of cleaned squid)
Salt and freshly ground black pepper to taste
2 cloves garlic, finely minced
10 to 15 medium-size basil leaves, finely shredded
⅓ cup extra virgin olive oil
Juice of 1 large lemon

To clean the squid, hold it in one hand and gently pull away the tentacles. Cut the head off just below the eyes and discard it. Remove the little beak just inside the tentacles. Remove the squid bone from the body. (This is actually a piece of cartilage that resembles a piece of clear plastic.) Clean the inside of the squid body under cold running water, pulling out any matter still inside. Wash and peel away the grayish skin from the body and tentacles and discard.

Cut the squid body into one-inch-wide rings and the tentacles into one-inch pieces.

Bring a medium-size saucepan of water to a boil over medium heat and add the squid and tentacles. Cook less than one minute. I generally check the squid after 30 to 40 seconds, and if it is chalky white all the way through and tender, it is done.

Drain and rinse the squid under cold running water, pat dry with paper towels, and place in a large salad bowl. Cover the bowl with plastic wrap and refrigerate until ready to use. (The calamari can be prepared up to this point several hours ahead.)

Remove the squid from the refrigerator and leave at room temperature for half an hour. Season the squid with salt and several grinds of pepper and dress with the garlic, basil, oil, and lemon juice. Toss well and serve.

Makes 4 servings as an appetizer or 2 servings as an entree

SUGGESTED WINE

A delicate dish requires a delicate wine. Try a California Riesling such as Trefethen, Robert Mondavi, or Firestone.

Mozzarella Impanata

Fried Breaded Mozzarella

Neapolitans love fried food. They are fond of fried vegetables, fried pizzas, fried desserts, and fried cheese. Walking through the old, narrow, congested Neapolitan streets, you can smell fried food everywhere. It comes from the open windows, from the little *trattorie*, from the *friggitorie* (a "frying" store, where a variety of fried foods are sold), and from the vendors in the street who sell fried little *pizzette*.

So, naturally, once in Napoli, I had to have some fried food. At Salvatore alla Riviera, a colorful, well-known trattoria, I succumbed to a delicious *fritto misto* of fried, crunchy, yet voluptuous mozzarella, crisp, fried zucchini blossoms (pages 34–35), and deep-fried rice-and-cheese balls (pages 42–43).

> 10 ounces mozzarella (see page 9), cut into four ½-inch-thick slices
> 2 large eggs, lightly beaten with a pinch of salt
> 1 cup plain bread crumbs, spread over a sheet of aluminum foil
> Vegetable oil for frying
> 8 leaves fresh basil, finely shredded

Dip the mozzarella slices into the eggs, shake off the excess, and dredge completely in the bread crumbs, pressing the crumbs with the palms of your hands.

SUGGESTED WINES
The innovative Plinius from Mastroberardino or a Galestro from Frescobaldi or Antinori would diminish the oily character of this fried dish.

Heat one inch of oil in a medium-size skillet over high heat. When the oil is very hot, lower a few slices of mozzarella into the oil with a slotted spoon. When the slices are golden, less than one minute, turn and fry the other side. With a slotted spoon transfer to paper towels to drain. Serve piping hot with a bit of thinly shredded fresh basil over each serving.

Makes 4 servings

Supplì

Deep-fried Rice-and-Cheese Balls

Imagine strolling down Via Veneto in Roma on a beautiful, sunny afternoon. So you stop at an outdoor *caffè*, order an *aperitivo* and a *stuzzichino* (a very small appetizer). The waiter brings you a tray with miniature finger sandwiches and small, warm, golden, crisp, balls. You bite into one and find a divine filling of hot melted mozzarella. You have just discovered *supplì*. This Roman specialty is made with risotto. The risotto is left to cool, then it is shaped into small oval or round balls that are stuffed with mozzarella and sometimes with other ingredients.

Because I find it a bit time-consuming to cook a risotto in order to make this dish, I prepare a double amount of risotto with butter and parmigiano, eat the risotto one night, and make the *supplì* the day after with the leftover risotto.

For the risotto
6 cups chicken broth, preferably homemade (see pages 54–55)
5 tablespoons unsalted butter
1 small onion, finely minced
2 cups imported Italian Arborio rice
1 cup dry white wine
Salt to taste
½ cup freshly grated parmigiano

To complete the dish
4 medium-size eggs
¼ pound mozzarella, diced
¼ pound sliced prosciutto, diced

Salt to taste

2 cups plain bread crumbs, spread over a sheet of
  aluminum foil

Vegetable oil for frying

In a medium-size saucepan, heat the broth and keep it warm
over low heat. Melt 4 tablespoons of the butter in a large
saucepan over medium heat. When the butter foams, add the
onion and cook, stirring, until the onion is pale yellow and soft,
4 to 5 minutes. Stir in the rice and cook, stirring, until the rice
is well coated with the butter and onion. Add the wine and
cook, stirring constantly, until the wine has evaporated. Add
just enough broth to barely cover the rice. Cook, still over
medium heat, stirring, until the broth has been absorbed. Continue cooking and stirring the rice, adding the broth a bit at a
time until the rice is tender but still firm to the bite, 15 to 16
minutes. Season with salt, then add the remaining tablespoon
of butter and the parmigiano. Mix well and quickly to blend.
At this point the rice should have a moist, creamy consistency.

The risotto can be made up to this point several hours or a
day ahead of time. Keep it tightly wrapped in the refrigerator
until you are ready to make the *supplì*.

To prepare the *supplì*, beat 2 of the eggs in a small bowl and
add it to the cooled risotto. Mix well to incorporate. If the rice
is a bit too moist, mix in a little parmigiano.

Take a large tablespoon of rice, about the size of an egg, into
your hands, and roll it gently with the palms of your hands to
make a small, round ball. With one finger press gently into the
middle of the ball. Put a bit of mozzarella and prosciutto into
the cavity and close the cavity with a bit of extra rice.

Beat the remaining eggs in a small bowl and season with salt.
Dip the rice ball into the beaten eggs and roll it in the bread
crumbs. Repeat until you have used up all the ingredients.

Sprinkle a cookie sheet with some bread crumbs and set the
supplì on top. Refrigerate for 15 to 20 minutes to allow the
coating to dry and the rice balls to firm up.

Heat two inches of oil in a large pan over high heat. Using
a slotted spoon, lower the rice balls into the hot oil a few at a
time. When they are golden on all sides, about 2 minutes, remove from the oil with a slotted spoon and drain them on paper
towels. They should be served hot.

Makes approximately 25 balls

TIP

∽ *To test the frying oil for
the perfect frying temperature,
add a small piece of bread or a
few bread crumbs to the oil. If
the oil sizzles and the bread
turns golden almost immediately, you can begin to fry.*

SUGGESTED WINES
*Try one of Italy's dry Spumanti,
such as Castello Gancia of Gan-
cia, Berlucchi Brut, Cà del
Bosco, or a Maison Deutz from
California in the same style.*

Fettunta con Spinaci

Tuscan Garlic Bread with Spinach

In Toscana it is called *fettunta*, "oily slice." In Roma it is called *bruschetta*. In many places all over Italy it might not even have a definite name, but one thing is for sure, there is nothing better and more basic than a slice of good crusty bread rubbed lightly with garlic and dribbled with extra virgin olive oil. Today this simple preparation has been updated and the bread is topped by a variety of ingredients. Even though I am partial to the original preparation, I must admit that the following version was truly enjoyable. This dish is from Osteria del Cinghiale Bianco in Firenze.

> 8 slices crusty Italian bread, cut ½ inch thick
> 2 pounds fresh spinach, washed thoroughly, dried, and stems removed or one 10-ounce package frozen spinach, boiled until soft and squeezed of all water
> ¼ cup olive oil
> 2 cloves garlic, finely chopped
> 2 tablespoons finely chopped sun-dried tomatoes
> Salt and freshly ground black pepper to taste

Preheat the oven to 400°F. Brush the bread on both sides with olive oil, place it on a baking sheet, and bake until it is lightly golden on both sides, about 5 minutes.

If using fresh spinach, place in a large saucepan over medium heat with 1 cup of water and a pinch of salt. Cook until the spinach is soft, 2 to 3 minutes. Drain and squeeze well of all excess water.

Heat the olive oil in a large skillet over medium heat. Add the garlic and tomatoes and cook 1 to 2 minutes. Add the spinach, season with salt and several grinds of pepper, and cook, stirring, 2 to 3 minutes. Taste and adjust the seasonings. Let the spinach cool slightly, then spread over the toasted bread and serve.

Makes 4 servings

Fettunta con Cannellini e Pancetta

Fettunta with White Beans and Pancetta

Latini is a well-known trattoria in an old, narrow street in the center of Firenze. In fact, this trattoria is so well known that often you need to wait outside for a table. And when you are finally seated, you will find yourself sharing a large table, wine, and conversation with other customers.

During one of my frequent visits there, I had an appetizer of toasted bread topped with a savory mixture of cannellini beans, garlic, and pancetta. The beans kept falling off the bread, and I kept scooping them up and piling them back onto the bread, determined not to miss one single bit of that divine humble concoction.

> Eight ½-inch-thick slices crusty Italian bread
> 5 tablespoons olive oil, preferably extra virgin, plus extra
>   for brushing
> 4 ounces sliced pancetta, cut into small strips
> 3 cloves garlic, finely chopped
> 10 fresh sage leaves, shredded or 1 teaspoon dried
> 2 cups cooked cannellini beans (see page 69)
> Salt and freshly ground black pepper to taste

Preheat the oven to 400°F. Brush the bread on both sides with olive oil, place it on an ungreased baking sheet, and bake until it is lightly golden on both sides, about 5 minutes.

Heat 1 tablespoon of the olive oil in a small skillet over medium-high heat. Add the pancetta and cook, stirring, until the pancetta is golden in color and crisp. Remove with a slotted spoon and let drain on paper towels.

Heat the remaining oil in a large skillet over medium heat. Add the garlic and sage and cook, stirring, until the garlic begins to color, less than one minute. Add the beans and pancetta, season with salt and several grinds of pepper, and cook, stirring, 2 to 3 minutes. Cool the beans slightly, then place over the toasted bread and serve.

Makes 4 servings

NOTE OF INTEREST
When I make a white bean soup, I always cook more beans than I need for the soup. Later, I use the cooked beans in a salad or in the dish above.

SUGGESTED WINE
With this dish try a young Chianti served cool, such as Ricasoli or Frescobaldi.

Crostini Piccanti

Crostini with Spicy Topping

One of the most important elements of Tuscan cooking is bread—wonderful, unsalted, hard, crusty bread that appears on the dinner table in many disguised ways. The crostini that I enjoyed at the Trattoria Montagliari in the Chianti region of Toscana have a bread topping that can hardly be detected because it is so well mixed and camouflaged with other ingredients. However, without the bread, these crostini would not have their delicious, smooth, velvety consistency.

2 cups loosely packed shredded Italian bread, without
    its crust
¼ cup red wine vinegar
⅓ cup extra virgin olive oil
2 tablespoons tomato paste diluted in ½ cup water
½ cup finely minced fresh tomatoes
¼ cup finely minced red onion
2 tablespoons chopped fresh parsley
3 tablespoons capers, drained and rinsed
2 cloves garlic, finely chopped
Salt to taste
Pinch of dried red pepper flakes
20 small, thin slices toasted or grilled Italian bread

Place the shredded bread in a medium-size bowl with the vinegar and let soak for 10 minutes. Squeeze the bread with your hands to remove the excess vinegar. Wipe the bowl clean and return the bread to the bowl with the olive oil, tomato paste mixture, tomatoes, onion, parsley, capers, and garlic. Season with the salt and red pepper. Mix well with a wooden spoon to completely blend all the ingredients. Spread the topping over the toasted bread and serve.

Makes 20 crostini

SUGGESTED WINE
Try a Vernaccia di San Gimignano from Riccardo Falchini or Guicciardini-Strozzi.

Crostini alle Cipolle in Agrodolce

Crostini with Sweet-and-sour Onions

Crostini are Italian canapés. The bread is generally toasted or grilled and topped with a variety of ingredients. I enjoyed these appetizing sweet-and-sour crostini at Enoteca, a wine bar on the outskirts of Garlenda, a small town in Liguria, that also served some very appetizing food.

⅓ cup pine nuts
¼ cup olive oil
2 medium-size white onions, thinly sliced
Salt and freshly ground black pepper to taste
15 fresh sage leaves, cut into small pieces (see note)
¼ cup red wine vinegar
¼ cup sugar
15 small, thin slices toasted or grilled Italian bread

Preheat the oven to 350°F. Place the pine nuts on an ungreased cookie sheet and toast in the oven until they are lightly golden on both sides, about 6 minutes. Heat the oil in a large skillet over medium heat. Add the onions and cook, stirring, until the onions are lightly golden and soft, 10 to 12 minutes. Season, then add the sage, vinegar, and sugar. Cook, stirring, until the onions have a rich, golden color, 3 to 5 minutes. Stir in the pine nuts. Taste and adjust the seasoning. Cool the onions to room temperature, then spoon over the toasted bread when ready to serve.

Makes 15 crostini

NOTE OF INTEREST

The taste of fresh sage mixed in with the onions is delicate and appetizing. If fresh sage is not available, sprinkle the onions with chopped fresh parsley or shredded fresh basil. The onions are also excellent served as an accompaniment to a pork roast or grilled veal or pork chops.

SUGGESTED WINES

A medium-bodied white wine such as Orvieto or, when available, the white wines of the Italian Riviera, such as Pigato or Vermentino, would be a lovely accompaniment to these crostini.

Crostini alla Mozzarella

Crostini with Baked Mozzarella

In food, there are some dishes that are a "sure bet" because their appetizing, wholesome taste appeals to almost everyone.

When I tested these crostini one early morning at my restaurant and the aroma of the melted mozzarella and the sautéed garlic, anchovies, and sun-dried tomatoes spread throughout the kitchen, my cooks and dishwashers eagerly surrounded me, ready to try them.

This recipe comes from Pierino Jovene, the exuberant Neapolitan owner of the well-known Gambero Rosso of Cesenatico, which serves some of the best food on the Adriatic coast.

12 small, thin slices toasted or grilled Italian bread
10 ounces mozzarella, cut into 12 slices
2 tablespoons unsalted butter
1 tablespoon olive oil
2 cloves garlic, finely minced
4 anchovy fillets, finely chopped
1½ ounces sun-dried tomatoes

Preheat the oven to 375°F.

Top each slice of bread with one slice of mozzarella and place on a lightly oiled baking sheet. Bake 5 to 6 minutes, or until the cheese is soft and almost completely melted.

Meanwhile, heat the butter and oil in a small skillet over low heat. Add the garlic, anchovies, and tomatoes and cook, stirring constantly, for about 2 minutes. (The garlic will not burn if the heat is quite low and you stir constantly.)

Remove the crostini from the oven. Put some of the hot garlic mixture over each crostini and serve at once.

Makes 12 crostini

SUGGESTED WINE
A nice Verdicchio from the Marche region such as Fazi Battaglia or Umani Ronchi would be delicious.

Crostini di Polenta Fritta con Porcini

~~~~~~

Fried Polenta with Porcini Mushrooms

In spring and fall when fresh porcini are plentiful, they can be seen displayed in large clusters in restaurants and *trattorie* all over Italy. Their aroma is unsurpassed and their taste is simply wonderful. I am a porcini lover and I eat them anywhere I can find them.

At La Biscondola in the Chianti region of Toscana, the mushrooms were sliced and cooked quickly with a bit of garlic and olive oil, then they were piled over crisp, fried polenta. Because I loved the dish so much, I included it on my fall restaurant menu.

Since fresh porcini are hard to find in this country, I have revised the recipe using dried Italian porcini, chanterelles, and shiitake mushrooms, and the result is simply splendid.

½ recipe Basic Polenta (see page 176)
Vegetable oil for frying
2 ounces imported dried porcini mushrooms (see page 15), soaked in 2 cups lukewarm water for 20 minutes
3 tablespoons olive oil
1 tablespoon unsalted butter
¼ pound fresh shiitake mushrooms, wiped clean, stemmed, and sliced
¼ pound fresh chanterelle mushrooms, wiped clean, stemmed, and sliced
2 cloves garlic, finely minced
2 tablespoons chopped fresh parsley
Salt and freshly ground black pepper to taste

Prepare the polenta several hours or a day ahead so it will become very firm. Pour the polenta onto a platter or a cookie sheet and spread it uniformly to approximately ½ inch thick. When you are ready to fry the polenta, cut it into eight slices.

Heat one inch of oil in a medium-size nonstick skillet over medium heat. When the oil is hot, fry the slices of polenta a few at a time until they are lightly golden on both sides, 3 to 4 minutes. Remove the polenta with a slotted spoon and drain on paper towels. Keep the polenta warm in a low oven while you are preparing the mushrooms.

Strain the porcini and rinse well under cold running water several times to get rid of sandy deposits. (Reserve the soaking water for use in a mushroom soup or stew after straining it through a double thickness of paper towels.) Chop the porcini roughly.

Heat the olive oil and butter in a large skillet over medium heat. When the butter foams, raise the heat to high and add the mushrooms, making sure not to crowd the skillet or the mushrooms will not brown properly. Cook and stir until the mushrooms are lightly golden, 2 to 3 minutes. Add the garlic and parsley and cook briefly. Season with salt and several grinds of pepper.

Place the polenta on individual serving dishes, top with the mushrooms, and serve at once.

Makes 4 servings

SUGGESTED WINES

A light red wine that can follow into the next course would work well, such as an Oltrepo Pavese Bonarda, a Sangiovese di Romagna, or the unique Bianchi Lambrusco from California.

SOUPS

The popularity of pasta in this country has upstaged the great variety of Italian soups. Too bad, because soup, just like pasta, can be immensely satisfying.

When I was growing up in Bologna, the Sunday meal always began with a soup. But what a soup it was! I would wake up on Sunday morning with the aroma of rich broth gently simmering for hours on the stove. Later on my mother would add tiny homemade tortellini or light, golden tagliolini to the broth and that soup would turn into a small masterpiece.

A soup can tell you almost instantly where it originates. There are the rich, clear broth and pasta soups of the North and the water-based vegetable, bean, and chick-pea soups of the deep South. There are the rice soups of the Veneto and the thick bean and bread soups of Toscana. There are the hearty soups of the mountain areas and the fish soups of the seacoasts. And there are the incredible variety of *minestroni*, scented with garlic, herbs, and tomatoes in the South, or thickened with beans, pasta, or rice in the North.

A soup in Italy is called by many names. *Minestra in brodo* (a generic name for a variety of soups) often is clear soup with some type of pasta in it.

Minestrina, much like the above, is a light, delicate, clear broth soup with pastina—small pasta—added.

Minestrone is a thick or thin vegetable soup with or without the addition of pasta or rice.

Zuppa (which literally translates into "soup") is a thick, hearty soup, often made with simple elements, such as beans, lentils, or mushrooms.

Passato is a cream soup.

In an Italian meal, soup is always a first course and it is never served before, after, or next to another first course, such as pasta, risotto, or gnocchi.

While pasta is generally consumed at lunch, which in Italy is the most important meal of the day, soup is preferred at dinnertime.

Soup is perfect trattoria food because it is wholesome, nurturing, and generous. Tuscan *trattorie* strive and are glorified for their thick, wonderful soups, and so are the *trattorie* of other regions that still serve the traditional soups of the area, such as the celebrated Tortellini in Broth of Bologna (pages 55–56) and the Jota of Trieste (pages 62–63).

In this chapter you will find delicious soups made with a base of flavorful broth, and others, equally delicious, made with a base of . . . hot water! You will also find the recipes for Homemade Meat Broth (pages 53–54) and Homemade Chicken Broth (pages 54–55).

I love to make soup because I love the rich aroma that permeates the house the moment the soup begins to bubble. But what I love even more is the feeling of satisfaction I get when I ladle a hot, fragrant soup into the many waiting bowls.

Il Brodo di Carne

Homemade Meat Broth

Broth is a very important element of Italian cooking, and it is the basis for many wonderful soups, risottos, braised dishes, and sauces.

A good homemade broth is produced by assembling and cooking together a variety of bones, meat scraps, and vegetables. The best bones and meat scraps are from beef, veal, and chicken. (Lamb and pork are generally not used because of their strong flavors.) These ingredients are covered with cold water and allowed to simmer for 3 to 3½ hours in order to extract every bit of their flavor.

A good broth should be light and flavorful. The broth can develop a different identity depending on the kind and amount of bones and meat scraps used. For a richer, more intensely flavored broth, use more beef. For a lighter broth, use less beef and more chicken and veal.

When I prepare the broth I always try to make it one day ahead, so that I can refrigerate it overnight. The next day I remove all the fat that has solidified on the surface.

> 4 pounds bones and meat scraps from beef, chicken, and veal
> Few fresh parsley sprigs
> 2 carrots, cut into chunks
> 2 stalks celery, cut into chunks
> 1 small onion, quartered
> 2 ripe tomatoes, quartered
> Salt to taste

Put all the ingredients, except the salt, in a large stockpot and cover by two to three inches with cold water. Set the cover of the pot askew and bring to a gentle boil over medium heat. Reduce the heat to low and skim the scum that comes to the surface of the water with a slotted spoon or a skimmer.

Simmer 3 to 3½ hours. Season with salt during the last few minutes of cooking.

If you are planning to use the broth right away, strain it through a strainer into another pot. If you are planning to use it the next day or freeze it, strain the broth into a large bowl and allow to cool, then refrigerate it overnight. The next day remove the fat that has solidified on the surface. The broth is now fat-free, ready to use or to freeze. It will keep about 4 days in the refrigerator, about 1 month frozen.

Makes about 4 quarts

Brodo di Gallina

Homemade Chicken Broth

Many cooks make their chicken broth with chicken scraps, bones, and vegetables only. I like to make mine with the addition of a large, plump chicken, if I plan to eat the chicken as a second course, or with an old hen, if my intention is to use the hen only for the purpose of a very flavorful broth.

    3 pounds bones and meat scraps from chicken and veal
    One 3- to 3½-pound whole chicken
    Few fresh parsley sprigs
    2 carrots, cut into chunks
    2 stalks celery, cut into chunks
    1 small onion, quartered
    2 ripe tomatoes, quartered
    Salt to taste

Put all the ingredients, except the salt, in a large stockpot and cover by two to three inches with cold water. Set the cover on the pot askew and bring to a gentle boil over medium heat. Reduce the heat to low and skim the scum that comes to the surface of the water with a slotted spoon or a skimmer.

Simmer 1½ hours. Remove the chicken and set it aside. Simmer the broth 1 hour longer. Season with salt during the last few minutes of cooking.

If you are planning to use the broth right away, strain it into another pot. If you are planning to use it the next day or to freeze it, strain the broth into a large bowl and allow it to cool, then refrigerate it overnight. The next day remove all the fat that has solidified on the surface. The broth is now fat-free, ready to use or to freeze. It will keep about 4 days in the refrigerator, about 1 month frozen.

Makes about 6 quarts

I Veri Tortellini di Bologna

The Real Tortellini in Broth of Bologna

Alla Grada is a neighborhood trattoria in Bologna, a city well known throughout Italy for its food. This is one of those establishments that bursts with vitality and energy, with waiters who glide through the dining room and seem to be everywhere at once. The night my husband and I were there, the chef-owner, Pippi Bondi, whom I have known for years, treated us to some wonderful dishes, most especially the tortellini in broth. They were absolutely heavenly—tiny, almost transparent, and wrinkled, with the nutmeg flavor so characteristic of homemade Bolognese tortellini. I closed my eyes as I was eating them and, for a moment, I was a child again in Bologna, eating the same dish, lovingly prepared by my mother.

> NOTE OF INTEREST
> *Homemade tortellini are very dear to the heart of Bolognese people. In fact, tortellini in broth is one of the dishes most often requested in the* trattorie *and restaurants of Bologna. There is absolutely no relation between the real Bolognesi tortellini and the frozen or dry products sold in supermarkets.*

2 tablespoons unsalted butter
1 pound pork loin, cut into 1-inch pieces
1 cup dry white wine
¼ pound sliced mortadella
¼ pound sliced prosciutto
2 large eggs
½ teaspoon freshly grated nutmeg
Salt to taste
1½ cups freshly grated parmigiano
Basic Egg Pasta Dough (see pages 74–75), made with
    3 cups unbleached all-purpose flour and 4 large eggs
10 cups Homemade Meat Broth (see pages 53–54)

TIPS

✺ *Because it is so time-consuming, making tortellini is truly a labor of love. If you love to cook and decide to try this superlative dish, here are some ways you can lessen the work:*

✺ *Prepare the dish in steps. The broth can be prepared several days ahead of time and the filling and tortellini can be prepared and assembled the day before. However, cook the tortellini at the last moment.*

✺ *If you own a pastry bag, put the filling in it to facilitate stuffing the pasta.*

✺ *For a wonderful flavor and richer broth, add a plump four-pound capon or a roasting chicken to the ingredients when making the broth. The capon can be eaten as a second course after the tortellini.*

SUGGESTED WINE

A richly flavored broth and the time-consuming tortellini would marry well with a great, full-bodied, mature Chardonnay.

To prepare the tortellini, melt the butter in a medium-size skillet over medium heat. When it begins to foam, add the pork loin and cook until it is lightly golden all over. Stir in the wine, cover the skillet, and cook 5 to 6 minutes. Remove the lid, raise the heat to high, and cook until the wine is completely evaporated, 2 to 3 minutes. Put the pork and cooking juices in a food processor with the mortadella and prosciutto. Pulse the machine on and off until the meat is very finely ground. Add the eggs and nutmeg and season very lightly with salt. Turn the machine on briefly to mix. Remove the pork mixture to a large bowl and fold in 1 cup of the parmigiano. Taste and adjust the seasonings. At this point, the mixture should have a slightly moist consistency. If it is too dry, mix in another egg or a touch of broth or cream. Cover the bowl and refrigerate several hours or overnight.

Prepare the Basic Egg Pasta Dough and cut off a piece about the size of a large egg. Cover the remaining dough with a kitchen towel. Work the small piece of dough through the pasta machine until you have a thin sheet of pasta. Cut the sheet of pasta into 1½-inch squares and put a bit of filling in the center of each square. Fold one corner over the filling to form a triangle; press firmly to seal the edges. Bend each tortellini around your finger, pressing one pointed end slightly over the other. Repeat until the dough and filling have been used up, placing the tortellini on a tray lined with a kitchen towel. The tortellini can be cooked at once or can be kept in the refrigerator, covered with another kitchen towel, for several hours or overnight.

To cook the tortellini, bring the meat broth to a boil in a large saucepan over medium heat. Add the tortellini and cook gently until tender but still firm to the bite, 2 to 3 minutes. Ladle the soup into individual bowls, sprinkle with the remaining parmigiano, and sit back and enjoy. You have earned it!

Makes 4 to 6 servings

Lattughe Ripiene in Brodo

Stuffed Lettuce Bundles in Broth

Altare is a very small town in Liguria, next to the Piemonte region. Right on the main street of the town, there is Quintilio, a small, elegant family-run trattoria that serves great traditional Ligurian and Piemontese food.

The day my husband and I stopped at Quintilio, we were suddenly caught in an unusually heavy summer rainstorm and walked into the trattoria completely soaked. About fifteen minutes later, the wet clothes all forgotten, we were served one of the nicest of all Ligurian soups—small lettuce leaves stuffed with veal, vegetables, and parmigiano, floating in a divine, fragrant, clear broth.

Paolo Bazzano, the chef-owner of Quintilio, explained to me later that the only liberty he took with this classic dish was to steam the bundles, instead of boiling them, so that they would not break or open up during the cooking and could be prepared ahead of time, if needed. It's a great tip, which I have eagerly adopted.

For the lettuce

1 tablespoon salt
1 small head of butter lettuce
4 tablespoons unsalted butter
1 small onion, finely minced
1 small carrot, finely minced
1 small white stalk celery, finely minced
2 tablespoons chopped fresh parsley
½ pound veal shoulder, cut into ½-inch cubes
1 cup dry white wine
1 tablespoon flour
½ cup freshly grated parmigiano
Freshly ground black pepper to taste
6 to 8 cups meat broth, preferably homemade (see pages 53–54)

Bring a large pot of water to a boil and add the salt.

Cut off the root of the lettuce, remove the larger outside leaves, and save for a salad. Choose 10 of the nicest medium-size leaves and add them to the boiling water. Cook 15 to 20 seconds. Drain gently and place them on a large kitchen towel to dry.

Melt the butter in a medium-size skillet over medium heat. When the butter begins to foam, add the onion, carrot, celery, and parsley. Cook, stirring a few times, until the vegetables are lightly golden and soft, 7 to 8 minutes.

Add the veal and cook, stirring, until lightly golden, 2 to 3 minutes. Add ½ cup of the wine and the flour and raise the heat to high. Cook, stirring, until the wine is almost all reduced, 2 to 3 minutes. Put the mixture in a food processor with two of the cooked lettuce leaves.

Put the skillet back on the burner and turn the heat to high. When the skillet is very hot, add the remaining ½ cup of wine. Stir quickly with a wooden spoon to pick up the bits and pieces attached to the bottom of the skillet. When there are only 1 or 2 tablespoons of thick, juicy sauce left in the skillet, add it to the food processor. (This is the tastiest part of the sauce.)

Pulse the machine on and off until the mixture is finely ground but not completely pureed. Transfer it to a bowl and stir in the parmigiano. Taste and adjust the seasonings.

Put 1 tablespoon of the filling in the center of each leaf and wrap the leaf around the filling, forming a small bundle. Fold the ends of the leaf under the bundle so that the filling will not escape. When all the leaves have been stuffed, place them gently in the upper part of a steamer or in a large colander. Bring the broth to a boil in a large pot over medium heat and place the top part of the steamer or the colander over the simmering broth. Cover the colander with a lid or with a sheet of aluminum foil and steam the bundles 2 to 3 minutes, or until tender.

Gently transfer the bundles into individual soup bowls, ladle the hot broth over them, and serve.

Makes 4 servings

SUGGESTED WINE
Try a delicious unusual light red wine of Liguria, Rossese di Dolceacqua from Lupi. It will be perfect for this soup.

I Risi e Bisi della Ghiacceretta

Rice and Pea Soup

The soups of the Veneto very often have the addition of rice. Perhaps the best-known soup of the region is the classic *risi e bisi*, made with good homemade broth, fresh sweet peas, onion, pancetta, and rice. At All'Antica Ghiacceretta, a boisterous trattoria a short walk from the Trieste pier, patronized mostly by fishermen and laborers, I found a version of this soup that was stouter, thicker, and quite filling, but equally delicious. Dried split peas were cooked and pureed, then added to the classic version minutes before the soup was removed from the stove. This version was probably concocted because of the hearty appetites of the trattoria patrons. If you love thick soups, this is decidedly for you.

½ pound dried split peas, soaked overnight in cold water
    to cover generously
2 quarts chicken broth, preferably homemade (pages
    54–55)
3 tablespoons unsalted butter
1 small onion, finely minced
¼ pound thickly sliced pancetta, finely chopped
2 tablespoons chopped fresh parsley
2 cups imported Italian Arborio rice
1 cup shelled fresh peas (about 1 pound unshelled) or
    1 cup frozen peas, thawed
Salt and freshly ground black pepper to taste
½ cup freshly grated parmigiano

Discard any split peas that have come to the surface of the water. Drain and rinse the split peas under cold running water and put them in a medium-size saucepan. Cover the split peas completely with water and bring to a boil over medium heat. Reduce the heat to low and cook, uncovered, 25 to 30 minutes, stirring a few times during cooking.

Heat the broth in a medium-size saucepan and keep warm over very low heat.

Melt the butter in a large saucepan over medium heat. When the butter begins to foam, add the onion, pancetta, and parsley.

NOTE OF INTEREST

Because of the starchiness of the dried split peas, this soup will thicken up considerably if it is not served immediately. You can thin it down with some broth, and it is advisable to always have a bit extra at hand.

The fresh peas can also be cooked separately in a little broth and added to the soup during the last few minutes of cooking.

Cook, stirring a few times, until the mixture is lightly golden, 6 to 7 minutes. Add the rice and stir just enough to coat the rice thoroughly with the pancetta-onion mixture. Add the hot broth. Cook, stirring, 5 to 6 minutes. Add the fresh peas and continue cooking and stirring until the rice and the peas are tender, 6 to 7 minutes longer.

While the rice is cooking, strain the cooked split peas, and put them in a food processor with 1 cup of their cooking liquid. Process until smooth. Add the pureed peas to the soup during the last minutes of cooking. (If you are using thawed frozen peas instead of the fresh, add them to the soup at this point also.) Season with salt and several grinds of pepper, stir the soup once or twice, and serve hot, with a generous sprinkling of parmigiano.

Makes 6 servings

SUGGESTED WINES

This is a sweet-flavored dish that needs a moderately aromatic, dry white with flavor, such as a Riesling, Traminer Aromatico, Gewürztraminer, or Sauvignon Blanc.

Zuppa di Funghi

Mushroom Soup

The Ligurian region is also known as the Italian Riviera. This thin strip of land on the Mediterranean has probably the best climate in Italy and some of the finest and most beautiful seacoasts.

But Liguria is not all seacoast. Its *entroterra*, inland, is made up of mountainous, sparsely inhabited, lusciously green territory, which boasts a *cucina* of its own.

On a hot Sunday afternoon, my husband and I ventured inland to explore the small hamlets of this region. Along the way we stopped at Enoteca Il Gallo della Checca, near Ranzo, a small community in the province of Imperia, for a bit of local wine testing, and succumbed to the aroma coming from the kitchen. And so, in the middle of a hot Sunday afternoon, we happily snacked on a fragrant, thick, fresh porcini soup and on a tender, melt-in-your-mouth rabbit, loaded with fresh, ripe tomatoes and small, delicious local green olives (see page 226).

I wish I could have reproduced the soup exactly as I ate it, with the unrivalled taste of fresh, woodsy porcini. Unfortunately, fresh porcini are almost never available here, so I have used a combination of dried porcini, shiitakes, and white cultivated mushrooms and, even though a bit different, this soup is still a winner.

2 ounces dried porcini mushrooms (see page 15), soaked in 2 cups lukewarm water for 20 minutes
⅓ cup olive oil
1 small onion, finely minced
3 cloves garlic, finely minced
3 tablespoons chopped fresh parsley
1 pound shiitake mushrooms, thinly sliced
1 pound white cultivated mushrooms, thinly sliced
1 cup dry white wine
6 cups meat broth, preferably homemade (see pages 53–54)
Salt and freshly ground black pepper to taste
1 cup freshly grated parmigiano

Drain the porcini mushrooms and reserve their water. Rinse the mushrooms well under cold running water. Strain the soaking water through a few layers of paper towels over a small bowl to get rid of the sandy deposits and set aside.

Heat the oil in a large saucepan over medium heat. Add the onion, garlic, and parsley. Cook, stirring, until the onion begins to color, 4 to 5 minutes.

Add the fresh mushrooms and porcini. Raise the heat to high and cook 4 to 5 minutes, stirring a few times. (In this preparation, the mushrooms will not brown, they will stew in their own juices.) Add the wine. Cook and stir until the wine is almost all reduced, 4 to 5 minutes.

Add the reserved porcini soaking water and the broth, season with salt and pepper. Bring the liquid to a boil, then lower the heat and simmer over low heat, uncovered, 30 to 40 minutes. Taste and adjust the seasoning. Serve hot, with the parmigiano.

Makes 8 servings

VARIATION

For a heartier soup, place two small slices of toasted or grilled Italian bread in the soup bowls, ladle the soup over the bread, and sprinkle generously with parmigiano.

SUGGESTED WINES

For this dish try a simple, direct white wine from Liguria such as Vermentino, or a California French Colombard or dry Chenin Blanc, especially from the Clarksburg area.

La Jota Triestina

Bean and Sauerkraut Soup

One of the stoutest soups of Northern Italy is the *jota* of Trieste. This is a decidedly winter soup, loaded with beans, sauerkraut, salt pork, bacon, and potatoes, with a pronounced Slavic origin. Signor Pesaro, owner and chef of the small, cramped Acquario trattoria in Trieste, prepares this soup in four steps: *First*, he soaks the beans overnight, then cooks them with the potatoes. *Second*, he stews the sauerkraut with the bacon in a bit of the beans' cooking water. *Third*, he prepares the *pestata*, which is a delicious flavoring mixture of salt pork, onion, garlic, fresh sage, and parsley. And *finally*, he assembles all of the above and cooks it all together a bit longer.

> 2 cups dried red cranberry beans (about 12 ounces), picked over and soaked overnight in cold water to cover generously
> 4 quarts water
> 2 medium-size starchy potatoes, peeled and cut into medium-size pieces
> ¼ cup olive oil
> ¼ pound bacon, diced
> 1 pound sauerkraut, drained and rinsed

For the pestata
> 2 tablespoons olive oil
> ½ small onion, finely minced
> 6 medium-size fresh sage leaves, finely chopped or 3 dried, crumbled
> 2 tablespoons chopped fresh parsley
> 2 cloves garlic, finely minced
> ¼ pound salt pork, finely chopped

Discard any beans that have come to the surface of the water. Drain and rinse the beans under cold running water, and put them in a large pot. Cover the beans with the water, add the potatoes, and bring to a boil over medium heat. Cover and reduce the heat to low. Simmer gently, stirring several times, until the beans are tender, about 1 hour. (The potatoes will probably overcook and fall apart, but that's all right.)

Heat the oil in a medium-size saucepan over medium heat. Add the bacon and cook until it is lightly golden, 2 to 3 minutes. Add the sauerkraut, stir, and cook with the bacon 2 to 3 minutes longer. Add 1½ cups of the beans' cooking water, cover the pan, and stew the sauerkraut over low heat for about 30 minutes. Stir several times during cooking.

While the sauerkraut is cooking, prepare the *pestata*. Heat the oil in a small skillet over medium heat. Add the onion, sage, parsley, garlic, and salt pork. Cook, stirring a few times, until the mixture is lightly golden, 3 to 4 minutes.

Add the sauerkraut and the *pestata* to the beans and cook over medium heat 10 to 12 minutes longer. Season lightly with salt and pepper. (Remember that the salt pork and the bacon are already salty.) If the soup is too thick, add a bit more water. Serve piping hot.

Makes 8 to 10 servings

SUGGESTED WINES
The traditional grape varieties of Friuli, either red or white, would accompany this dish very well. Try Refosco or Schioppettino for reds or Ribolla Gialla and Tocai for the whites.

Acquacotta

Cooked Water Soup

Acquacotta is a water-based soup that literally means "cooked water." But what a delicious cooked water this is!

Fresh or dried porcini mushrooms are cooked together with tomatoes and water. The soup is then ladled over toasted bread which has been topped with a mixture of beaten eggs and parmigiano. Even though *acquacotta* is one of the classic soups of Toscana, it is not as well known as the famous *ribollita* or the *pappa al pomodoro*. It is, however, equally delicious.

Trattoria Toscana, in the small town of Capalbio, about forty miles from Grosseto, serves a wonderful *acquacotta*.

This is a variation of the classic *acquacotta* since, for a thicker soup, I have also added some white cultivated mushrooms to the dried porcini. Prepare it early in the day because, like most soups, even this one improves by sitting for a while.

1 ounce dried porcini mushrooms (see page 15), soaked in 2 cups lukewarm water for 20 minutes

⅓ cup olive oil

1 pound white cultivated mushrooms, thinly sliced

2 cloves garlic, finely minced

¼ cup chopped fresh parsley

2 cups imported canned Italian tomatoes with their juices, put through a strainer or a food mill to remove the seeds

4 cups water

Salt to taste

Pinch of dried red pepper flakes

3 large eggs

½ cup freshly grated parmigiano

8 small slices toasted or grilled Italian bread

Drain and rinse the porcini mushrooms well under cold running water to get rid of the sandy deposits. Chop the mushrooms roughly.

Heat the oil in a large skillet over high heat. When the oil is very hot, add the porcini and fresh mushrooms all at once. Cook, stirring a few times, until the mushrooms begin to color, 3 to 4 minutes. Add the garlic and 2 tablespoons of the parsley and stir once or twice. Transfer the contents of the skillet to a medium-size saucepan and put it over high heat. Add the tomatoes and water and season with the salt and hot pepper. Bring the liquid to a boil, then lower the heat to medium and simmer, uncovered, 25 to 30 minutes. Taste and adjust the seasonings. Set aside.

When you are ready to serve the soup, beat the eggs with the parmigiano and the remaining 2 tablespoons of parsley in a bowl. Put 2 slices of toasted bread into each soup bowl and cover with the beaten egg-parmigiano mixture. Ladle the hot soup over the eggs and the bread and serve at once.

Makes 6 servings

❖ ❖ ❖

V A R I A T I O N

For a nontraditional but very good result, strain the porcini soaking water through a few layers of paper towels and add to the tomatoes and water. Cook as instructed.

S U G G E S T E D   W I N E

A full-bodied Chardonnay would work very well with this dish.

Zuppa di Cipolle e Pane

Onion and Bread Soup

I sampled this delightful onion bread soup one hot summer day at Il Latini in Firenze and, for once, I was glad I had ordered a soup instead of a pasta. It was served at room temperature and I could fully taste the sweetness of the onions. The bread, which was cooked slowly with the onions, gave the soup a velvety texture that was immensely pleasing. I liked it so much that even though we had ordered a lot of food, I unashamedly asked for a second bowl.

- 5 tablespoons olive oil
- 8 large red onions (about 6 pounds), halved and thinly sliced
- 1 tablespoon sugar
- 6 cups chicken broth, preferably homemade (see pages 54–55)
- 6 cups dry white wine
- 1 cinnamon stick
- 6 slices several-day-old crusty Italian bread, broken into pieces
- Salt to taste
- ½ cup freshly grated parmigiano

Preheat the oven to 350°F.

Heat the oil in a large ovenproof saucepan or casserole over medium heat. Add the onions and cook, stirring, a few minutes, until the onions are pale yellow. Sprinkle with the sugar and mix. Add the broth and wine. Add the cinnamon stick and bring to a boil.

Cover the saucepan with a sheet of aluminum foil and place in the oven. Cook 1 hour, then remove the foil and add the bread, mixing well. Cook, uncovered, another 30 minutes.

Remove the soup from the oven and discard the cinnamon stick. With a wire whisk beat the soup lightly until the bread is completely broken up and the soup achieves a smooth, thick consistency. Season with the salt. Serve hot or at room temperature with a sprinkling of parmigiano.

Makes 4 to 6 servings

NOTE OF INTEREST
Broth and wine are used in equal proportions, giving the soup its distinctive flavor. You can reduce the amount of wine and increase the amount of broth if you wish. Like most soups, this is better the day after it is made. I suggest you double the recipe because you won't be able to put your spoon down.

SUGGESTED WINES
A fresh, not overly tannic, fruity red wine such as Chianti Colli Fiorentini or Classico is perfect for this dish. A young, light-bodied California Merlot would also fit.

La Pappa al Pomodoro del Cinghiale Bianco

~~~~~~

Tomato Bread Soup of the White Boar Osteria

NOTE OF INTEREST

In Florence this soup is served without cheese.

In the heart of Firenze, in a narrow, ancient street called Borgo San Jacopo, a few blocks from the famous Ponte Vecchio, there is Osteria del Cinghiale Bianco. It is here that we found perhaps the best *pappa al pomodoro* in Firenze. From the moment we were seated in the candlelit medieval dining room, we knew we were in for a treat. The soup arrived at our table thick and fragrant and dribbled with extra virgin olive oil. My husband and I savored each spoonful slowly and thoroughly, dreading seeing the soup slowly disappear.

Most cooks in Italy add their own special touches to the dishes they cook. Signor Maselli, the owner of the Cinghiale Bianco, prepares this soup without garlic and hot chile pepper. He uses fresh, ripe tomatoes in summertime and canned San Marzano tomatoes in winter and, of course, plenty of the wonderful Tuscan bread.

> ½ cup olive oil
> 1 large red onion, finely minced
> Four 28-ounce cans imported Italian pear tomatoes with
>   their juices, put through a strainer or a food mill
>   to remove the seeds
> 5 cups chicken broth, preferably homemade (see
>   pages 54–55)
> 10 slices 4- to 5-day-old crusty Italian bread, cut into
>   chunks
> 2 cups loosely packed fresh basil leaves, roughly chopped
> Salt and freshly ground black pepper to taste
> Extra virgin olive oil

Heat the oil in a large saucepan over medium heat. Add the onions and cook, stirring, until they are soft, about 5 minutes. Stir in the tomatoes and broth and bring to a gentle boil. Cook, uncovered, 15 to 20 minutes. Add the bread, mix well, and cook 20 to 25 minutes longer. Add the basil and season with salt and pepper.

Remove the saucepan from the heat and beat the soup with a wire whisk until the bread is completely broken into small pieces and becomes an integral component of the soup.

Serve the soup hot or at room temperature with a few drops of extra virgin olive oil dribbled over each serving.

Makes 8 servings

SUGGESTED WINES

Choose a full-bodied white with some structure or a light red wine like a Remole of Frescobaldi, or a dry California Zinfandel.

La Zuppa di Ceci del Corsi

Signor Corsi Chick-pea Soup

Signor Corsi, owner of Trattoria Corsi in Roma, loves food. His passion is evident in the way he explains the food to his customers, and his exuberance is contagious. This little trattoria is patronized by locals—bankers, government employees, and business people. Signor Corsi hops from table to table, balancing several dishes in his hands, advising his customers about the specials of the day, and pouring wine, while welcoming new customers. Because I enjoyed this trattoria so much, I had several meals there and each time Signor Corsi kept surprising me with his energy and hearty, mouthwatering dishes. This soup is quintessentially simple. The ingredients are basic and the execution of the dish is elementary. The taste, however, is outstanding.

NOTE OF INTEREST

This is a thick soup that becomes even thicker the day after it is made, since the starchiness of the chick-peas will soak up the liquid. As in all soups of this kind, they are even better the second day and it freezes well. Thin to taste with water or broth as desired.

- 2 cups dried chick-peas (garbanzo beans), picked over and soaked overnight in cold water to cover generously
- 2 quarts water
- ¼ cup olive oil
- 2 cloves garlic, finely chopped
- 2 tablespoons chopped fresh rosemary or 1 teaspoon dried
- 3 anchovy fillets, finely chopped
- 4 cups imported canned Italian plum tomatoes with their juices, put through a strainer or food mill to remove the seeds
- Salt to taste
- Small pinch of dried red pepper flakes
- 2 tablespoons chopped fresh parsley
- ½ cup freshly grated parmigiano

Discard any chick-peas that have come to the surface of the water. Drain and rinse the chick-peas well under cold running water and put in a large saucepan. Add the water and bring to a gentle boil over medium heat. Cover the pan and reduce the heat to low. Simmer until the chick-peas are tender, 45 minutes to 1 hour.

While the chick-peas are cooking, prepare the sauce. Heat the oil in a medium-size saucepan over medium heat. Add the garlic, rosemary, and anchovies and cook, stirring. As soon as the garlic begins to color, add the tomatoes. Season with the salt and red pepper. Cook the sauce, uncovered, 10 to 15 minutes.

Puree half of the chick-peas through a food mill or in a food processor and return to the saucepan. Stir in the tomato sauce and bring to a gentle boil. Simmer over low heat, uncovered, 4 to 6 minutes. Just before serving, stir in the parsley, and taste and adjust the seasonings. Ladle the soup into the soup dishes and serve hot with freshly grated parmigiano.

Makes 4 to 6 servings.

SUGGESTED WINES
With this soup, try a Barbera, a Dolcetto, or a Zinfandel. Either Californian or Italian.

Minestrone alla Toscana

Tuscan Minestrone

Even though minestrone changes according to the season and the mood of the cook, there are some basic rules to abide by if one wants a specific minestrone such as *alla Toscana, alla Milanese*, etc.

The most important ingredient for a *minestrone alla Toscana* is the white cannellini beans, also called Tuscan beans, which are extensively used in the cooking of the region.

The beans are cooked; then, in a separate saucepan, a *soffritto* is prepared with aromatic herbs, vegetables, and pancetta to which cabbage and tomatoes are added. This sauce is later combined and cooked briefly with the beans, turning it into a beautiful, thick minestrone. Sometimes pasta, rice, or grilled bread is added to the soup, depending on the preference of the cook.

This delicious heartwarming dish is regularly served at Locanda Marchetti in the small, medieval town of Castelnuovo di Garfagnana, about thirty-five miles north of Lucca. The great thing about this soup is that the day after, by simply adding a few slices of old bread, it can be turned into the delicious classic *ribollita*! (See the note right.)

½ pound dried cannellini beans or white kidney beans, picked over and soaked overnight in cold water to cover generously
3 quarts cold water
⅓ cup olive oil
¼ pound thickly sliced pancetta, finely chopped
3 cloves garlic, finely minced
1 small onion, finely minced
1 medium-size carrot, finely minced
1 medium-size white stalk celery, finely minced
¼ cup chopped fresh parsley
2 tablespoons chopped fresh rosemary or 1 teaspoon dried
1 pound Savoy cabbage, thinly sliced
4 cups imported canned Italian tomatoes with their juices, put through a strainer or a food mill to remove the seeds
Salt and freshly ground black pepper to taste
20 to 24 small slices Italian bread, toasted or grilled
Extra virgin olive oil

Discard any beans that have come to the surface of the water. Drain and rinse the beans under cold running water and put them in a large pot. Cover the beans with the water and bring to a gentle boil, uncovered, over medium heat. Cook 30 to 40 minutes, stirring a few times during cooking. At this point the beans should be tender but still a bit firm to the bite. Puree half of the beans through a food mill or a food processor and return to the pot.

While the beans are cooking, prepare the sauce. Heat the oil in a medium-size saucepan over medium heat. Add the pancetta, garlic, onion, carrot, celery, parsley, and rosemary. Cook, stirring, until the mixture begins to color, 6 to 7 minutes.

Add the cabbage and cook 2 to 3 minutes longer, stirring constantly. Add the tomatoes and season with salt and pepper. Cook 8 to 10 minutes, stirring a few times during cooking.

NOTE OF INTEREST

We know that many soups are even better the day after they are made, and there is no better proof of this than this Tuscan minestrone which, the day after, can be turned into the classic ribollita. Ribollita literally means "reboiled."

To make ribollita, simply bring any leftover Tuscan minestrone to a gentle boil over medium heat. Cut 4- to 5-day-old, hard-crusted Italian bread into pieces and add to the soup.

Reboil the soup gently for 15 to 20 minutes over medium-low heat, then let the soup rest for about 1 hour. The soup will become quite thick and utterly delicious.

Do not worry about the amount of bread you put in the soup. The thicker the better. Some trattorie in Firenze make a ribollita that is so thick it can be eaten with a fork!

Add the sauce to the beans and simmer gently 15 to 20 minutes longer. At this point the cabbage should be tender and the soup should have a medium-thick consistency.

When you are ready to serve, put two slices of toasted or grilled bread into each soup bowl, ladle the hot minestrone over them, and dribble with a few drops of extra virgin olive oil. Serve hot.

Makes 10 to 12 servings

SUGGESTED WINE
Try a light young Chianti Classico, from Antinori or Vignamaggio.

Zuppa d'Orzo

Barley Soup

There is a whole category of soups that is typical of the Italian high mountain range. They can be made with beans, lentils, sauerkraut, vegetables, potatoes, or barley, and they all have one thing in common. They are thick, gutsy, stick-to-the-ribs preparations, perfect for good appetites and cold winter nights.

This barley soup can be found, in one version or another, in the many homey *trattorie* of the Trentino Alto Adige and Friuli-Venezia Giulia regions.

½ pound pearl barley, soaked overnight in cold water to cover generously
⅓ cup olive oil
1 small onion, finely minced
2 cloves garlic, finely minced
2 tablespoons chopped fresh parsley
¼ pound sliced bacon or salt pork, finely chopped
4 quarts cold water
Salt and freshly ground black pepper to taste

VARIATIONS
A smoked ham shank can be added to the soup. At the end of the cooking, all the fat from the ham should be removed and the leaner meat should be diced and added back to the soup.

This soup can also be made with a base of broth, instead of water.

The bacon or the salt pork can be substituted with finely diced speck (smoked ham from the Alto Adige—see page 11).

Discard any grain that has come to the surface of the water. Drain and rinse the barley under cold running water.

Heat the oil in a large pot over medium heat. Add the onion, garlic, parsley, and bacon and cook, stirring, until the mixture begins to color, 4 to 5 minutes. Add the barley and stir a few times. Cover with the water and bring to a boil over medium heat. Cover the pot and reduce the heat to low. Simmer gently, stirring several times, until the barley is tender, about 1 to 1½ hours. Season with salt and several grinds of pepper. Add a bit more water if the soup becomes too thick. When done, allow the soup to sit for a few hours before serving. It will improve in flavor. If it's no longer warm enough, reheat over medium heat.

Makes 6 servings

Zuppa di Farro

Spelt Soup

Corsi in Roma is my favorite trattoria. The food is wholesome, honest, and unpretentious. One of the dishes I fell in love with was this stout, thick, energy-giving *zuppa di farro*, which I simply could not stop eating. What I liked so much about this soup, besides its flavor, was its chewy texture and the fact that after eating it, I felt full and completely satisfied.

When I decided to reproduce this soup back in Sacramento, I ran into trouble, because I could not find spelt (see the note right).

So I tried the next best thing, and made the soup with soft wheat berries, a similar, somewhat softer grain. This soup was very good, even though a bit different from the one I had in Roma. But then, there is only one Mona Lisa.

½ pound spelt or soft wheat berries, soaked overnight in cold water to cover generously
2½ quarts water
⅓ cup olive oil
½ medium-size onion, finely minced
1 small white stalk celery, finely minced
1 small carrot, finely minced
2 cloves garlic, finely minced
6 fresh sage leaves, finely chopped or 3 dried leaves, crumbled
¼ pound thickly sliced pancetta, finely chopped
½ pound ripe, juicy tomatoes, diced
Salt and freshly ground black pepper to taste

SUGGESTED WINES
For this dish, choose hearty red wines without a strong varietal character, like a Montepulciano d'Abruzzo, or even a stout, full-bodied beer.

NOTE OF INTEREST
Spelt is a small, hard, wheatlike grain that used to be the standard diet of the Roman legions because of its wholesome nutritional value. It was cooked in water or milk to a soft mush, much like a very soft polenta. Today spelt is grown mainly in Toscana, Umbria, Lazio, and Abruzzo.

For spelt substitute soft wheat berries or barley, which are the grains closest to spelt. These grains can be found in health food stores.

This soup can also be made with meat broth (pages 53–54) instead of water.

Discard any grain that has come to the surface of the water. Drain and rinse the grain under cold running water and put it in a large saucepan. Add the water and bring to a boil over medium heat. Reduce the heat to low and cook, uncovered, 1½ hours, stirring several times during cooking.

Heat the oil in a small saucepan over medium heat. Add the onion, celery, carrot, garlic, sage, and pancetta. Cook, stirring, until the mixture is lightly golden, 6 to 7 minutes. Add the tomatoes and cook 2 to 3 minutes. Add 1 cup of the grain cooking water and cook 10 to 15 minutes, stirring a few times.

Put the sauce in a food processor and process until smooth. Add the pureed sauce to the grain and season with salt and pepper. Cook 20 to 30 minutes longer, until the grain is tender. Add a bit more water if the soup thickens too much.

To improve the flavor, let the soup sit for a few hours, then reheat it over low heat and serve hot.

Makes 6 servings

SUGGESTED WINES
Fruity red wines and a good dry Lambrusco would complement this dish well, or a light California Zinfandel.

PASTA

Pasta! The mere word conjures up images of heaping, steaming bowls of multicolored, multishaped pasta preparations. To an Italian, there is nothing more appetizing or more tempting than a bowl of freshly cooked pasta, shining with green oil or luscious butter, topped with vegetables or fish or meat sauces, and sprinkled with incomparable cheeses.

Pasta is synonymous with Italy, colorful, ebullient, and gregarious in the South, and refined, restrained, and more complex in the North. Pasta is the food of peasants and kings alike, and it is, undoubtedly, one of Italy's greatest culinary assets.

The image of pasta in this country has changed considerably in the last few years. It is now fashionable and chic to make your own pasta and to order it in a restaurant. This ancient Italian staple, whose origins are still disputed, has become a favorite of American cooks.

Homemade or factory-made pasta begins by working flour and eggs, or flour and water, into a dough. This dough is then kneaded and rolled out for the homemade product, or it is put through the extruders of large commercial pasta machines to form various shapes for the factory made. (Since homemade and factory-made pastas are two entirely different products, I will discuss each separately.)

HOMEMADE PASTA

When I was growing up in Bologna, the only tools needed to make homemade pasta were a long rolling pin, a large wooden board, and your hands. A rolling pin and wooden board produce a pasta with a porous surface which absorbs the sauce. To make good pasta with a rolling pin, however, is not that easy. It is a craft that requires practice and patience, but just like everything else in life, it can be learned if you are willing to put in the time needed.

If making pasta entirely by hand makes you nervous and hesitant, then you should definitely try making it with a pasta machine. Making pasta with a pasta machine is not that difficult and can also be a lot of fun. There are several kinds of pasta machines on the market today that make the job easier. Pasta rolled out by a hand-cranked machine can be quite good. It will produce, however, a smoother, more slippery pasta because the rollers of the machine are made of steel.

A relatively new apparatus is an extruding machine for the home that makes instant pasta. Put the eggs and flour in and just push the button. The result is a pasta with a gummy, sticky texture that has absolutely nothing to do with the real thing.

The Ingredients

Flour. In Northern Italy, homemade pasta is made with a flour that is called *doppio zero* (double zero). This is a soft wheat flour which contains a moderate amount of gluten. (Gluten is the protein substance in wheat; it is the gluten that determines the consistency of the pasta. The lower the level of gluten, the softer and more delicate the dough is, and the easier it is to stretch it out by hand.) In this country the flour that is closest to *doppio zero* is unbleached all-purpose flour, perfect for making all kinds of fresh pasta.

In Southern Italy, homemade pasta is often prepared with a combination of unbleached all-purpose flour and durum wheat flour (semolina). Semolina flour has a high gluten content and will produce a firmer, more compact, and less stretchable dough. Most factory-made pasta is made with 100 percent semolina flour.

Eggs. All of my pasta dough recipes use large eggs. If smaller or extra large eggs are used, the amount of flour should be decreased or increased accordingly. Always keep in mind, however, that it is easier to add flour to a soft, sticky dough than it is to try to fix a dough to which too much flour has been added.

The proportions. Two large eggs and 1¼ cups of flour will make approximately seven ounces of string pasta and serve two people.

There are, however, many variables, like the level of humidity, the heat, and the altitude. All of these will have an effect on how much flour you will ultimately need. Don't worry too much about this. After you have made pasta a few times, you will be able to judge the proportions yourself.

Equipment Needed to Make Pasta by Hand

∾ A large wooden board is preferable. Formica or marble can also be used.

∾ A fork to mix the flour with the eggs.

∾ A long Italian rolling pin would be ideal. Check with your local gourmet cooking store. If all else fails, give it your best try with a regular rolling pin.

∾ A dough scraper which will clean the board of the sticky pieces of dough.

∾ A scalloped pastry wheel to cut the pasta into the desired shapes and lengths.

Making the Pasta by Hand

Heap the flour on a wooden board or other clean surface. With your fingers, make a round well in the center of the flour. Break the eggs into the well. Beat the eggs briefly with a fork, then begin to draw some of the flour from the edge of the well over the eggs. Add the flour a little at a time, always mixing with the fork. When you get to the point that a soft paste begins to form, switch to the dough scraper.

With the dough scraper push all the remaining flour to one side of the board while you scrape off the bits and pieces of dough attached to the board. Add some of the flour you have pushed aside to the paste and begin kneading it with your hands, gently at first. As you keep incorporating more flour into the dough, your kneading will become more energetic. Do not add the flour too hastily, because you might not need to use all of it. The moment you have a soft, manageable dough, clean the board again of the sticky pieces and wash your hands. Knead the dough more energetically now, pushing the dough away from you with the palms of your hands and folding half of the dough back over toward you. Keep turning the dough as you knead it. Push, fold over, and turn. Knead for about 8 minutes, adding a bit of flour if the dough sticks to the board and to your hands.

Push a finger in the center of the dough. If it comes out barely moist, the dough is ready to be rolled out. If the dough is sticky, knead it a little longer, adding a bit more flour. At the end of the kneading time, the dough should be compact, pliable, and smooth as a baby's bottom. Keep in mind that a well-kneaded dough is vital to good pasta. Don't skimp on it. Wrap the dough in plastic wrap and set aside to *rest* for about 30 minutes. After 30 minutes the gluten in the dough will be more *relaxed* and it will be easier to roll out by hand. If the dough should be too soft and somewhat limp when you remove the plastic wrap, give it a light kneading to regain a firmer consistency.

Rolling Out the Pasta Dough by Hand

After the dough has rested, dust a large wooden board or work surface very lightly with flour. Flatten the dough with your hands or with the rolling pin. Start rolling from the center of the dough forward, away from you, toward the edges. Rotate the dough slightly and roll out again from the center toward the edges. Keep rolling and turning the dough to produce a circular sheet of dough. If the dough sticks to the work surface, wrap it loosely around the rolling pin, lift the rolling pin, and dust the working surface lightly with more flour.

Once you have a nice, round circle of dough, about the size of an individual pizza, wrap the far edges of the pasta sheet around the rolling pin. Roll only half of the pasta sheet toward you. With the palm of one hand, hold the dough that is wrapped around the rolling pin. With the other hand, hold the part of the dough near you so that there will be some resistance once you start rolling the dough. Push the rolling pin back, away from you, stretching the dough. Repeat this motion a few times, then rotate the dough slightly. Wrap the far edges of the dough again around the rolling pin, while you are holding the dough near you with the other hand. Repeat a few more times, trying to keep a circular shape if possible, by rotating the dough. Make sure to dust your hands and the pasta sheet *very lightly*, so it won't stick to the board and the rolling pin. (Do not use too much flour, or the dough will dry out.)

When the sheet of dough has doubled in size, wrap the far edges of the pasta sheet around the rolling pin again, rolling only half of the pasta sheet lightly toward you. Now, the stretching of the pasta begins.

Put the palms of your hands in the center of the rolling pin, and gently roll the pin back and forth while stretching the dough forward. While you are doing this, your hands should never remain in the same position, but rather move from the center to the sides in a continuous motion, while stretching the dough sideways as well as forward. Your hands should move lightly and quickly over the dough. Too much pressure will make the dough stick to the rolling pin. Try to work as fast as you can, or the pasta will dry out and it will be impossible to stretch. Once you are experienced, it should not take longer than 10 minutes to roll out a small batch of dough.

To retain a circular shape, keep turning the dough, rolling and stretching, until the pasta is thin and almost transparent. At this point you should have a nice, large round circle of dough. Realistically, however, if you are a beginner, your dough might look more like a free-form creation. Don't worry about it. Remember, practice makes perfect.

If you are using the dough for stuffed pasta, it should be cut and stuffed immediately, while it is still moist, so that it can be sealed properly. (See the individual recipes for more detailed instructions.)

If you are using the dough for string pasta such as tagliatelle, angel hair, etc., the dough should be allowed to dry a little to prevent it from sticking together once cut. To do this, place the sheet of dough on a lightly floured tablecloth and let it dry for 8 to 10 minutes. Turn the sheet gently to dry on the other side. Keep in mind that the length of the drying time will depend greatly on the temperature of the room. On a hot day the pasta will dry much faster than on a rainy or humid day. What you are looking for here is pasta that is dry but still retains a touch of moisture. If pasta is too dry, it will crack and break. (If that should happen, do not discard it; after all, you have put in considerable effort producing it. Cut the pasta into odd-size pieces, place in a plastic bag, and save to add to bean or lentil soup.)

Cutting Pasta by Hand

When the pasta sheet is no longer sticky, fold it loosely into a flat roll not wider than three inches. With a large flat, sharp knife (a cleaver will work well), cut the pasta into the desired width by pressing down evenly with the knife. Unroll the noodles and place them in loose bundles on a wooden surface or tablecloth, uncovered. The noodles can be cooked immediately or allowed to dry and cooked later. (Pasta rolled out by hand can also be cut with a pasta machine, just as pasta rolled out by machine can be cut by hand.)

If you are planning to use the noodles a few days after you have made them, leave the bundles, uncovered, on the wooden board or tablecloth for 24 hours. After that the noodles will be *completely* dry. Place them in a large plastic container or plastic bags, tightly covered, until you are ready to use them. At this point you must handle them gently because they are dry and, therefore, very brittle. (Homemade string pasta, when dry does not require refrigeration or freezing. It keeps well for up to 1½ months in plastic bags in the cupboard.)

Equipment Needed to Make Pasta by Machine

ॐ A food processor or an electric mixer to mix the flour and eggs into a dough.

ॐ A pasta machine to roll out the pasta.

The most popular and inexpensive pasta machine is perhaps the little hand-cranked one. This machine has two cylindrical stainless steel rollers that roll out the dough. It comes with two attachments to cut the sheet of dough into fettuccine and tagliolini.

There is now on the market a little electric motor that can be attached to the hand-cranked machine which simplfies the task of manually operating the pasta machine. Both the machine and the motor can be found in most department stores.

Several years ago I had a small electric pasta machine made by Bialetti. This machine had plastic rollers instead of stainless steel rollers and it worked on the same principle as the hand-cranked one, with the advantage that the pasta it produced was less slippery and more porous. If you can still find it on the market, by all means invest in one.

Making Pasta Dough in a Food Processor

Break the eggs into a food processor fitted with the metal blade and process briefly to mix the eggs. Add the flour. Pulse the machine on and off until the dough is all gathered *loosely* around the blade. (It is important that you remove the dough *before* it turns into a ball, or it will become too tough.) At this point the dough should be moist and slightly sticky. If the dough is too dry, beat an extra egg in a small bowl and add half of it to the dough. If the dough is too wet, add a bit more flour.

Put the dough on a lightly floured wooden board or work surface. Dust your hands lightly with flour and knead the dough 2 to 3 minutes, adding a bit more flour if the dough is too sticky. Dough assembled in the food processor is not as delicate as dough kneaded by hand, because the assembling process happens too quickly and too violently; however, it should still be smooth, pliable, and quite satisfactory.

Push a finger in the center of the dough. If it comes out barely moist, the dough is ready to be rolled out. If the dough is sticky, knead it a little longer, adding a bit more flour. Dough assembled by food processor does not need to rest if it is going to be rolled out by machine. Let the dough rest for 30 minutes, though, if it is going to be rolled out by hand. Keep the kneaded dough wrapped in plastic wrap until you are ready to use it.

Making the Pasta Dough with an Electric Mixer

Break the eggs into the bowl of an electric mixer fitted with a dough hook and beat briefly at low speed. Add the flour a little at a time, beating well after each addition. When all the flour has been added, increase the speed and let the mixer knead the dough for 5 to 6 minutes. Check the consistency of the dough. If too moist, work in a bit more flour. If too dry, work in half of a beaten egg. Remove the dough from the bowl and knead it a few minutes by hand. Dough assembled with an electric mixer does not need to rest if it is going to be rolled out by machine. Let the dough rest for 30 minutes, wrapped in plastic wrap, if you are planning to roll it out by hand.

Rolling Out Pasta Dough by Machine

Set the rollers of the pasta machine at their widest opening. Cut off a small piece of dough, about the size of a large egg, and flatten it with the palm of your hand. Keep the rest of the dough wrapped in plastic wrap. Dust the flattened piece of dough lightly with flour, and run it once through the machine. Fold the dough in half, pressing it together with your fingertips. Run it through the machine again. Repeat this step four to five times, rotating the dough and rubbing it with flour until it is smooth and not sticky. During these steps the dough will acquire a firmer consistency, since the machine at this point is really doing the kneading for you. (Do not skimp on this step or, as you thin out the pasta, it will probably stick to the rollers.) Now that the dough is smooth and firm, it is ready to be stretched into a long, thin sheet of pasta.

Change the notch of the rollers to the next setting and run the dough through once without folding it anymore. Keep changing the setting and working the pasta sheet through the rollers *once* each time until it reaches the desired thinness. Gently pull the dough toward you as you run it through the machine.

If you are planning to make noodles, place the sheet of dough on a lightly floured tablecloth and let it dry for 8 to 10 minutes. Turn the sheet to dry on the other side. Roll out the remaining dough in the same manner.

If you are planning to make stuffed pasta, each sheet of dough should be stuffed immediately, before another sheet of dough is rolled out, so that it can be sealed properly. (See the individual recipes for detailed instructions.)

Cutting Pasta by Machine

When the sheet of dough is no longer sticky, put it through the cutting blades of the pasta machine, according to the width you wish to make. Arrange the noodles in soft bundles on a wooden board or a tablecloth. They can be cooked immediately or they can be allowed to dry and be cooked later on.

Colored Pasta

Colored pasta in Italy consists only of spinach pasta and sometimes beet pasta, compared to American chefs who make multicolored, multiflavored pasta. Perhaps we are dull. Or perhaps we understand that it is the neutrality of pasta that makes it the best vehicle for sauces. Because the pasta dishes in this book are traditional, the only colored pastas here are spinach and the short, chubby, brown-gray buckwheat noodles, called pizzoccheri (see pages 89–90).

Spinach Pasta

To make spinach pasta, add to the eggs 1 to 2 tablespoons of fresh or frozen spinach that has been cooked, chopped, and squeezed dry. Mix the spinach into the eggs, add the flour, and proceed to make the dough by hand or by machine.

A Short Glossary of Homemade Noodles

Tagliatelle are the classic noodles of Bologna, traditionally served with Bolognese meat sauce. The width of tagliatelle is 6 millimeters.

Fettuccine are the classic Roman noodles, generally associated with the butter-cream-parmigiano sauce, all'Alfredo. Their width is about ⅛ inch.

Pappardelle are the widest of the noodles, used in many regions with hearty meat or game sauces. Their width is about ⅝ inch.

Tagliolini are very thin noodles, traditionally served in clear broth soups. The width of tagliolini is about 1/16 inch.

Capelli d'angelo. Angel hair are even thinner than tagliolini. Traditionally they are served in clear broth soups.

Trenette is the classic noodle of Liguria, originally made with flour and water and traditionally served with pesto sauce. The width of trenette is approximately the same as for fettuccine.

Tips on Pasta Making

∽ The time element is very important in rolling out dough by hand. If it takes you longer than 8 to 10 minutes, the dough will dry out, lose its pliability, and will be impossible to thin out. Practice kneading with a small amount of dough before attempting the real thing.

∽ Unless you are skilled at pasta making, do not attempt to roll out pasta by hand on a hot day because the dough will dry out very quickly.

∽ Even if you are skilled at pasta making, when you roll it out by hand, you might have tears and breakage. Do not panic. Even the most experienced pasta maker sometimes has these problems. Simply patch the hole up and go over it gently with the rolling pin.

∽ Pasta dough made by hand, food processor, or electric mixer does not need to rest if it is rolled out by machine.

∽ If the pasta breaks when you put it through the cutters of the pasta machine, it means it was dried too long. If it sticks together when you put it through the cutters, it was not dried or kneaded long enough.

∽ I find that the last setting on most pasta machines produces a sheet of dough that is much too thin and breakable. Use the next to the last setting *twice* and you will have a perfect thin dough to use for stuffed pasta.

∽ For string pasta the dough should be rolled out a little thicker than for other types of pasta, otherwise it will have no character and stick together.

∽ When the pasta is dry enough to be cut into noodles, it will be slightly curled at the edges.

∽ The most important thing in pasta making, and for that matter in cooking in general, is to have fun and also to realize that if we mess it up, *it is only food*—we can try it again, until we get the hang of it.

SOME GOLDEN RULES FOR PERFECTLY COOKED AND PERFECTLY SAUCED PASTA

My mother used to say, "Pasta does not wait for anyone!" As a child, playing in the yard of our apartment building, I would hear my mother calling from the terrace, urging me to come up immediately because she was ready to drop the pasta in the water. Then I would join my father, brother, and sister around the kitchen table and watch the care with which my mother performed the daily rituals of the last-minute tasks. The tasting of the pasta for doneness. The quick draining of the pasta with several vigorous shakes of the colander. The gentle yet urgent mixing of the pasta with the sauce in a large, warm bowl. Then, at last, the enjoyment and the abandon of eating a perfectly cooked, perfectly sauced plate of pasta. Here are some tips for success.

∽ Always use a large pot with plenty of water. For one pound of pasta you will need approximately four to five quarts of water.

∽ When the water boils, add the salt and the pasta all at once. Cover the pot and bring the water back to a boil, then remove the lid. The salt will season the pasta thoroughly and lightly, highlighting its wholesome, unique character.

∽ Stir the pasta a few times as it cooks. If you have plenty of water in the pot and you give it an occasional stir, the pasta *will not* stick together. Adding oil to the water is unnecessary and not advisable, for it will make the pasta slippery.

∽ The cooking time of the pasta will depend on the size, the type, and the shape of the pasta. The fresher and thinner the pasta, the shorter the cooking time. Freshly made pasta will cook in no time at all. The longer it dries, the longer it needs to cook. Fresh homemade noodles will cook faster than fresh homemade stuffed pasta, since stuffed pasta has double the thickness.

∽ The cooking of factory-made pasta also depends on the shape, thickness, and brand of the pasta. To be safe, read the cooking instructions on the package, *but taste* the pasta for doneness often during cooking.

∽ Perfectly cooked pasta should be tender but still firm to the bite, *al dente*. To an Italian, there is no greater sin than overcooked pasta. Keep in mind that pasta keeps cooking even after it has been drained.

∾ Never precook your pasta *unless* you are making lasagne or cannelloni. These are the only instances when pasta is quickly precooked, rinsed to stop the cooking, and dried before it is stuffed and baked.

∾ *Never* rinse your pasta, *unless* you are making lasagne or cannelloni.

∾ Once pasta is cooked, drain it, then transfer it to a warm bowl and toss it immediately with the sauce. (This can be done in a large, warm bowl or in the skillet where the sauce is kept simmering.)

∾ *Never* add all the sauce at once—you might not need it or want it all. Start with half the amount and add more if you like. Keep in mind that pasta served the Italian way is *never* oversauced.

∾ If you are planning to add your pasta to the simmering sauce in the skillet, make sure to undercook your pasta a bit more than usual, so that it can be tossed together with the sauce over the heat briefly. By doing this, you will achieve two things. The pasta will be piping hot when it is served, and it will be thoroughly coated with the hot sauce. (This is an old restaurant trick.)

∾ Remember that pasta does not wait for anyone, so serve it at once, making sure that everyone is already sitting in anticipation at the table.

FACTORY-MADE PASTA

I was born and raised in Bologna and fed on a daily diet of homemade pasta at which my mother excelled. And yet today, when I crave pasta, I often reach for a box of imported penne, rigatoni, or orecchiette. Perhaps it is the immediacy of the product that is so appealing. No hassle, no fuss. Just reach for the box and drop the pasta into the water. Or, perhaps, I reach for factory-made pasta because it is very good.

Good factory-made pasta is made with durum wheat flour (100 percent semolina) and water. Nothing else. This pasta has the gold coloring of wheat and, when properly cooked, it swells in size while maintaining its toothsomeness. Nothing can appease hunger like a plate of large, firm *maccheroni*.

Factory-made pasta is, and has always been, more popular in the South. However, even in Northern Italy the consumption of factory-made pasta is increasing steadily every year, since experienced pasta makers are slowly disappearing.

There is today in this country a certain snobbism toward factory-made pasta and the assumption that *fresh is best*. Personally, I would rather buy good-quality factory-made pasta anytime over some of the mediocre-looking fresh pasta now available.

In choosing factory-made pasta, look for an Italian brand, preferably from Southern

Italy, such as Del Verde and DeCecco, which is made with 100 percent semolina flour. Read the tips for cooking pasta above before you cook your first batches. Be judicious with the amount of sauce you put on the pasta, and enjoy one of the best products that man has created.

THE PASTA AND ITS SAUCE

In all my years of cooking, I have never thought about matching the pasta with the sauce. I know that traditionally the tagliatelle of Bologna are served with Bolognese meat sauce (but not always) and the Roman fettuccine with a *ragù alla Romana* or with a butter and cheese sauce. I know that with pappardelle, the largest of all noodles, a nice assertive meat or game sauce is in order, and that linguine and spaghetti are the perfect vehicles for shellfish. I also know that with the colorful and zesty sauces of Southern Italy, a stubby cut of pasta such as rigatoni, bucatini, or fusilli is demanded. But matching the pasta with the sauce . . . really!

On second thought, how about the orecchiette with the broccoli of Puglia? And the *spaghetti alla chitarra* with the lamb sauce of Abruzzo? Now I am all confused, and probably so are you!

Yes, there are many sauces in Italy that traditionally belong to specific types of pasta shapes, and the explanation for all this would probably fill a small book. So, in order to simplify this topic, I will make a few simple suggestions:

∾ Spaghetti and linguine are the perfect vehicles for fish and shellfish sauces.

∾ Angel hair and taglioline, traditionally served in clear broth, can also be served with a light butter-cream sauce or with a fresh tomato sauce.

∾ Wide noodles and large *maccheroni* pair well with meat and game sauces.

∾ Factory-made pasta such as penne, ziti, bucatini, spaghetti, etc., are perfect for the bold oil-based sauces of Southern Italy.

∾ Orecchiette, penne, shells, and rotelle are great with vegetable sauces and tomato sauces.

∾ Fettuccine and tagliatelle are succulent with butter, cream, and cheese sauces, but also with meat sauces and with tomato-cream prosciutto or pancetta sauces.

If this is still too confusing to you, keep in mind the following:

- ∾ Use full-bodied pasta with full-bodied sauces.
- ∾ Use light, delicate pastas with delicate sauces.

But most of all, find the combination that works for you, and simply enjoy it!

Tagliatelle con Salsiccia, Funghi e Pomodoro

Tagliatelle with Sausage, Mushrooms, and Tomatoes

When I am in Bologna and I want to recapture the aroma and taste of the food that my mother used to cook, I go to Boni. This noisy, popular trattoria has been in the same location for over thirty years, and for thirty years the Boni family has consistently served some of the best home-cooked meals in Bologna. During my last visit to Bologna, I took my sister, my brother, their spouses, and their grown-up children to Boni. Signora Agnese, who is the soul of this cozy trattoria, came to greet us and, as usual, she fussed over us, just like a mother would do. Half an hour later the table was full of wonderful food: tortellini in capon broth, homemade tagliatelle with fresh porcini, tagliatelle with homemade sausage, *risotto alla Bolognese* (see pages 168–69). And we kept eating, and chatting, and laughing, and toasting each other with generous, bubbling, local Lambrusco. It was a wonderful family reunion, made possible by the terrific *cucina casalinga* (home cooking) of this great little trattoria.

For the tagliatelle
　　2 cups unbleached all-purpose flour
　　3 large eggs

For the sauce

> 1 ounce dried porcini mushrooms (see page 15), soaked in 2 cups lukewarm water for 20 minutes
> 3 tablespoons olive oil
> 2 tablespoons unsalted butter
> 6 ounces sweet Italian sausage, casings removed and finely chopped
> 4 cups canned imported Italian tomatoes with their juice, put through a strainer or food mill to remove the seeds
> Salt and freshly ground black pepper to taste
> ⅓ cup heavy cream
> 2 tablespoons chopped fresh parsley
> 1 cup freshly grated parmigiano

Prepare the dough for the tagliatelle using the proportions given here, according to the instructions on pages 75–77. Roll out the dough and cut it into tagliatelle (see page 80).

Strain the mushrooms and reserve the soaking water. Rinse the mushrooms well under cold running water and chop them roughly. Line a strainer with two layers of paper towels and strain the mushroom soaking water into a bowl to get rid of sandy deposits. Set aside.

In a large skillet, heat the oil and butter together over high heat. When the butter foams, add the sausage and cook, stirring, until the sausage loses its raw color, 3 to 4 minutes. Add the mushrooms and 1 cup of the reserved soaking liquid. Stir and cook until the liquid is reduced by half, about 2 minutes. Add the tomatoes and season with salt and several grinds of black pepper. Cook, uncovered, over medium heat for 8 to 10 minutes, stirring a few times. Stir in the cream and parsley.

While the sauce is cooking, bring a large pot of water to a boil. Add 1 tablespoon of salt and the tagliatelle. Cook, uncovered, over high heat until the pasta is tender but still firm to the bite, *al dente*, 3 to 4 minutes.

Drain the pasta and add it to the sauce in the skillet. Add ⅓ cup of the parmigiano. Mix over low heat until the pasta is well coated with the sauce. Serve immediately with the remaining parmigiano.

Makes 4 to 6 servings

SUGGESTED WINES
The woodsy, smokey character of the mushrooms and the rich flavor of the sausage call for a light yet assertive red wine, such as a young Cabernet Sauvignon or Merlot. If you can find it, a real *Lambrusco, dry and bubbly, would be perfect.*

Tagliatelle al Prosciutto e Piselli

Tagliatelle with Prosciutto and Peas

Emilia-Romagna is one of the wealthiest regions of Italy and has a great tradition of food. It is here that some of the best ingredients are produced: parmigiano-reggiano, prosciutto di Parma, mortadella, sausages, balsamic vinegar, and great home-made pasta. It is not unusual, then, to find all these elements incorporated into the cooking of Bologna. Tagliatelle with prosciutto is a staple in the homes, restaurants, and *trattorie* of Bologna, and with good reason. This dish, in its straightforward simplicity, is a small masterpiece. Lo Sterlino in Bologna adds a few fresh peas to this preparation.

For the tagliatelle
     2 cups unbleached all-purpose flour
     3 large eggs

For the sauce
     1 cup shelled fresh peas or frozen peas, thawed
     6 ounces prosciutto, cut into 4 thick slices
     5 tablespoons unsalted butter
     ½ medium-size onion, finely minced
     Salt and freshly ground black pepper to taste
     1 cup freshly grated parmigiano

Prepare the dough for the tagliatelle, using the proportions given here, according to the instructions on pages 75–77. Roll out the dough and cut it into tagliatelle (see page 80).

If you are using fresh peas, bring 2 cups of water to a boil in a small saucepan. Add the peas and cook until tender over medium heat, 4 to 6 minutes, depending on the size of the peas. Drain and set aside.

To prepare the sauce, remove the fatty part of the prosciutto and chop it up very fine. Cut the prosciutto into small cubes. Melt the butter in a large skillet over medium heat. When the butter foams, add the fat and onion and cook, stirring, until the onion is pale yellow and soft, 3 to 4 minutes. Add the prosciutto and peas and season lightly with salt and several grinds of pepper (keep in mind that the prosciutto is already salty). Cook 1 to 2 minutes longer, stirring a few times. Set aside.

Bring a large pot of water to a boil. Add one tablespoon of salt and the tagliatelle. Cook, uncovered, over high heat until the pasta is tender but still firm to the bite, *al dente*. Scoop out a bit of the pasta cooking water, then drain the tagliatelle and add it to the skillet with the sauce. Stir in ⅓ cup of the pasta cooking water and mix briefly over low heat to incorporate. (The water will be absorbed very quickly by the fresh pasta and will give the pasta additional moisture.) Serve at once with a generous sprinkling of freshly grated parmigiano.

Makes 4 to 6 servings

SUGGESTED WINES

The sweet character of the peas and onions calls for a rich ripe, white wine, such as a California Chardonnay or one of the new style Italian Chardonnays such as Antinori's Cervaro della Sala.

Fettuccine con i Porcini

Fettuccine with Porcini Mushrooms

Fettuccine, freshly made with a rolling pin by the expert hands of Signora Ida, the personable owner of Trattoria Paola in Roma, topped by the season's first fresh porcini mushrooms, was an absolute treat. The large slices of fresh porcini needed only to be tossed with some olive oil, a bit of garlic and parsley, and some white wine for their flavor to burst out.

Unfortunately, fresh porcini mushrooms are seldom available here, so we must compromise and make do with what we have. To try to recapture the flavor of this dish, I have used dried porcini, easily available in specialty stores, and chanterelles, which in Italy are called *galletti*. I have cooked this dish many times at my restaurant in Sacramento, and I have always been rewarded by enthusiastic praise.

For the fettuccine
> 2 cups unbleached all-purpose flour
> 3 large eggs

For the sauce
> 2 ounces dried porcini mushrooms (see page 15), soaked in 2 cups lukewarm water for 20 minutes
> ¼ cup olive oil, preferably extra virgin
> ½ pound chanterelles, wiped with a damp towel and thinly sliced
> 2 cloves garlic, finely chopped
> 1 cup dry white wine
> Salt and freshly ground pepper to taste
> 2 tablespoons chopped fresh parsley

Prepare the dough for the fettuccine, using the proportions given here, as instructed on pages 75–77. Roll out the dough and cut into fettuccine (see page 80).

Strain the mushrooms and reserve the soaking water. Rinse the mushrooms well under cold running water. Line a strainer with two paper towels and strain the mushroom soaking water into a bowl to get rid of sandy deposits. Set aside one cup of the soaking water to use in the sauce.

Heat the oil in a large skillet over high heat. Add the chanterelles and sauté until they are lightly golden. Add the garlic and porcini mushrooms and cook one minute longer, stirring, making sure not to burn the garlic. Stir in the wine and cook until it is almost all reduced. Stir in the reserved mushroom water and season with salt and pepper. Cook for a few minutes, until only a few tablespoons of liquid are left in the skillet.

Bring a large pot of water to a boil. Add one tablespoon of salt and the fettuccine. Cook, uncovered, over high heat, until the pasta is tender but still firm to the bite, *al dente*. Drain the pasta, add it to the skillet with the mushrooms, and add the parsley. Mix over low heat until the pasta is well coated and serve at once.

Makes 4 to 6 servings

SUGGESTED WINES

The woodsy, aromatic component of this dish calls for an aromatic, full-bodied, aged white wine with a bottle age of four to five years. It could be either Chardonnay- or Sauvignon Blanc–based.

Pizzoccheri

Buckwheat Noodles with Cabbage and Potatoes

Pizzoccheri are thick, short noodles made with a combination of buckwheat flour and white flour. They are cooked with potatoes and cabbage and tossed together with garlic-scented butter, soft cheese, and parmigiano until the cheese melts and coats the pizzoccheri. This hearty, no-nonsense dish comes from the Valtellina, a beautiful valley north of Milano, at the foot of the Alps.

When I began serving pizzoccheri at my restaurant in Sacramento, many of my customers were hesitant to order them. Then, as I began slowly to introduce the dish, tempting my customers with small portions of pizzoccheri, I developed a whole legion of pizzoccheri lovers. This substantial, filling dish is perfect for cold winter days.

For the pizzoccheri

¾ cup buckwheat flour thoroughly mixed with ¾ cup unbleached all-purpose flour
3 large eggs
1 to 2 tablespoons milk

To complete the dish

1 large boiling potato, peeled and cut into small cubes
¾ pound Savoy cabbage, cut into thin strips
4 tablespoons (½ stick) unsalted butter
1 tablespoon olive oil
3 large cloves garlic, minced
Salt and freshly ground black pepper to taste
6 ounces fontina cheese, cut into small pieces
½ cup freshly grated parmigiano

Prepare the Basic Pasta Dough (see pages 74–75) using the proportions given here. Roll out the dough by hand or by machine (see pages 76–77), approximately ⅛ inch thick and 6 to 7 inches long. (If you are using a pasta machine do not roll the sheet of dough past the number 3.) Let the sheet of dough dry for about 10 or 15 minutes, then cut it just as you would fettuccine.

TIP

↩ *Boil the potatoes and the cabbage ahead of time, making sure to leave them a bit under-cooked. Add the cooked vegetables to the boiling water with the pasta during the last minute of cooking, then proceed as instructed in the recipe.*

SUGGESTED WINES

Try a light red Valtellina Superiore or the vineyard wines of Sasella or Inferno of Nino Negri or Rainoldi.

Bring a large pot of water to a boil over medium-high heat. Add 1 tablespoon of salt and the potatoes. Cook 2 to 3 minutes, then add the cabbage and the pizzoccheri. Cook, uncovered, over high heat until the pizzoccheri are tender but still firm to the bite, 3 to 4 minutes. (Keep in mind that *very* fresh pasta will cook faster.)

While the pasta is cooking, heat the butter and olive oil in a large skillet over medium-low heat. Add the garlic, cook and stir until the garlic begins to color, about 1 minute.

Drain the pasta, potatoes, and cabbage and add them to the skillet. Season with salt and several grinds of pepper. Add the fontina and the parmigiano and mix well over the heat, until the cheese begins to melt, less than 1 minute. Add a few table-spoons of the pasta cooking water if the pasta seems a bit dry. Serve at once.

Makes 4 servings

Garganelli al Ragù Ricco

Homemade Maccheroni with Meat, Sausage, and Porcini Mushroom Sauce

NOTE OF INTEREST

Making garganelli is a bit time-consuming; however, if you know how to make pasta and have the time and patience, I urge you to try because this pasta is truly outstanding. Penne rigate (grooved penne) can be substitued for the homemade garga-nelli.

Both the pasta and sauce can be prepared well ahead of time.

Garganelli are small, handmade grooved maccheroni that are typical of the Emilia-Romagna region. There was a time when these lovely maccheroni would appear regularly on the menus of the restaurants and *trattorie* of the region. I remember many years ago when some restaurants in Bologna would have their *sfogline* (pasta makers) make pasta in front of the restaurant's large windows, in full view of passersby. It was fascinating to see these women, dressed all in white, their hair covered by a white net, prepare the garganelli and the tiniest tortellini at incredible speed. Today these *sfogline* have almost all disappeared and only a handful of establishments make their own pasta by hand.

I enjoyed this splendid dish at Rosteria Luciano in Bologna. This beautiful restaurant started out as a trattoria and for many,

many years the owner, Luciano, served wonderful regional food. Today, Luciano is gone, and the restaurant is owned and run by the two young men who were once the kitchen helper and busboy. The ambiance is now more upscale, but the name on the door and the wonderful food are still the same.

This pasta has an additional egg yolk, which will make the dough a little firmer than usual and will give the garganelli (see the note on page 90) a hardier consistency. The pasta will serve four, or it can be stretched to serve six. The sauce, however, makes much more than that, so there will be extra for you to freeze or to serve the day after over penne or fettuccine.

For the garganelli
    1¾ cups unbleached all-purpose flour
    3 large eggs
    1 large egg yolk

For the meat sauce
    2 ounces dried porcini mushrooms (see page 15), soaked
       in 2 cups lukewarm water for 20 minutes
    2 tablespoons unsalted butter
    3 tablespoons olive oil
    ½ small onion, finely chopped
    1 small carrot, finely chopped
    1 medium-size stalk celery, finely chopped
    ½ pound ground veal
    ½ pound mild Italian sausage, removed from its casing
       and finely chopped
    1 cup dry white wine
    3 cups canned imported Italian tomatoes with their juice,
       put through a strainer or food mill to remove the seeds
    1 cup chicken broth, preferably homemade (see pages
       54–55)
    Salt and freshly ground pepper to taste
    ⅓ cup milk
    1 cup freshly grated parmigiano

Prepare the dough for the garganelli, using the proportions given here, according to the instructions on pages 75–76.

Roll out the dough and cut into 1½-inch squares. Place a new, very clean comb with long, protruding teeth in front of you, with the teeth of the comb pointing away from you. Lay a pasta square over the comb, with one corner of the square pointing toward you. Place a pencil over the pasta square and wrap the corner closest to you around the pencil. Press gently away from you over the comb. The pasta square is now wrapped completely around the pencil, with ridges all around its surface made by the teeth of the comb. Gently slide the garganelli off the pencil and repeat with the remaining squares.

Line a tray or a cookie sheet with a kitchen towel and arrange the garganelli loosely over the towel. The garganelli are now ready to be cooked or they can be left to dry uncovered at room temperature and used several hours or a few days later.

To prepare the meat sauce, strain the mushrooms and reserve the soaking water. Rinse the mushrooms well under cold running water. Line a strainer with two paper towels and strain the mushroom water into a bowl to get rid of the sandy deposits. Set aside.

Heat the butter and oil in a large skillet over medium heat. Add the onion, carrot, and celery and cook, stirring, until the vegetables are lightly golden, about 5 minutes. Add the veal and sausage and cook, stirring to break up the meat with a large spoon, until the meat loses its raw color, 4 to 5 minutes. Add the wine and cook until it is almost all reduced, about 2 to 3 minutes. Add the porcini mushrooms and 1 cup of the reserved soaking water. Raise the heat to high and cook until the liquid is reduced by half, 1 to 2 minutes. Stir in the tomatoes and broth, and season with the salt and pepper. Cover the skillet and cook over low heat 1 to 1½ hours, stirring a few times. When done, the sauce should have a medium-thick consistency. If too dry, add a little more broth or a bit more of the soaking water. Add the milk and cook a few minutes longer.

Bring a large pot of water to a boil. Add 1 tablespoon of salt and the garganelli. Cook, uncovered, over high heat until the pasta is tender but still firm to the bite, *al dente.*

Drain the pasta and place it in a large warm serving bowl. Add half of the sauce and mix well to combine. Spoon the pasta into individual serving bowls and top each serving with a bit of additional sauce and a sprinkling of freshly grated parmigiano. Serve at once.

Makes 4 to 6 servings

SUGGESTED WINES
Since this dish is time-consuming to prepare and has a ragù-*type sauce, an elegant medium-bodied red wine with some acid and tannin would fit well. A Nebbiolo d'Alba from Piemonte, a Valpolicella-Valpantena from the Veneto, or even a five- to eight-year-old Chianti Classico Riserva would be delicious.*

Linguine alla Cannavota

Linguine with Shrimp, Tomatoes, Béchamel, and Hot Pepper

There are people who are always striving for originality in cooking. They mix and match unusual ingredients, borrowing ideas from the East and West, in the hope of creating something new.

I am afraid I am not one of them. The food that interests me is that which warms my soul, comforts and soothes me, and, at the same time, delivers all that good food should: Satisfaction!

At Cannavota in Roma, while I was twirling the linguine around my fork, picking up small chunks of shrimp perfectly coated with the creamy, pink sauce, I was incredibly and perfectly satisfied.

 3 tablespoons olive oil
 12 ounces medium-size shrimp, shelled, deveined, and
  cut into ½-inch pieces
 2 cloves garlic, finely minced
 ⅓ cup brandy
 4 cups canned imported Italian tomatoes with their juice,
  put through a strainer or food mill to remove the seeds
 Salt to taste
 Small pinch of dried red pepper flakes
 2 tablespoons heavy cream
 1 pound linguine or spaghetti
 2 tablespoons chopped fresh parsley

Heat the oil in a large skillet over medium heat. Add the shrimp and cook 1 minute. Add the garlic, and stir once or twice. As soon as the garlic begins to color, add the brandy. Stir and cook until the brandy is reduced by half, about 40 seconds. With a slotted spoon transfer the shrimp to a dish while you finish the sauce.

Add the tomatoes, salt, and dried red pepper. Cook, uncovered, over medium-high heat for 5 to 6 minutes. Stir in the cream. Lower the heat to medium and cook 1 minute longer. Add the shrimp and stir for a few seconds, then turn the heat off under the skillet.

TIPS

↬ *If you are not comfortable cooking with alcohol, and the flame that it can make as the alcohol evaporates scares you, this is what you should do:*

Remove the skillet from the heat and add the brandy. Lower the heat to medium and put the skillet back. Cook gently until the liquid in the pan is almost all reduced and the alcohol is evaporated.

↬ *Always use a skillet or saucepan large enough to cover the burners completely or you do run the risk of having some of the alcohol accidentally splash out of the pan and catch on fire, especially if you have a gas stove.*

SUGGESTED WINES
A simple dry white wine with some body such as Orvieto Secco or Vernaccia di San Gimignano will go well, as will a dry California Chenin Blanc.

While the sauce is cooking, bring a large pot of water to a boil. Add 1 tablespoon of salt and the linguine. Cook, uncovered, over high heat until the pasta is tender but still firm to the bite, *al dente*. Drain the pasta and add it to the skillet with the sauce. Turn the heat on again under the skillet to medium and add the parsley. Mix everything quickly until the pasta is well coated with the sauce. Serve at once.

Makes 4 to 6 servings

Spaghettini alla Carrettiera

Thin Spaghetti with Fried Bread Crumbs, Garlic, and Anchovies

This is an old classic dish of *la cucina provera* which shows the imagination and creativity of people who, in spite of meager means, could create sinfully appetizing dishes with just a few basic ingredients.

Extra virgin olive oil, garlic, anchovies, and some fried bread crumbs become the "sauce" for this pasta. The bread crumbs take the place of cheese which, at one time, was probably expensive.

There are today many variations of this dish, which is named after the men who used to haul carts full of produce. This version is from Il Barone, a very old trattoria in the center of Avellino, a city that is approximately forty miles southeast of Napoli.

The "sauce" is of the utmost simplicity. However, keep your eyes glued on the bread crumbs when they cook, because they will become golden almost immediately.

5 tablespoons extra virgin olive oil
2 tablespoons plain bread crumbs
3 cloves garlic, finely chopped
4 anchovy fillets, finely chopped
Salt and freshly ground black pepper to taste
1 pound thin spaghetti
2 tablespoons finely chopped fresh parsley

Heat the oil in a large skillet over medium heat. Add the bread crumbs and cook until the bread crumbs are lightly golden, 5 to 10 seconds. Remove the skillet from the heat and add the garlic and the anchovies. Stir vigorously and in less than 15 seconds even the garlic will be cooked. Season lightly with salt (remember, the anchovies are already quite salty) and several grinds of pepper. Set aside.

Bring a large pot of water to a boil. Add 1 tablespoon of salt and the spaghetti. Cook, uncovered, over high heat until the pasta is tender but still firm to the bite, *al dente*. Scoop out 1 cup of the pasta cooking water, and add it to the skillet. Drain the pasta and add it to the skillet. Add the parsley and mix everything together quickly over low heat until well coated. If the pasta is too dry, add a bit more olive oil. Taste and adjust the seasonings and serve at once.

Makes 4 to 6 servings

SUGGESTED WINES

This peasant dish from Campania calls for a light white wine from the same region, such as Mastroberardino's innovative Plinius or, for really showing off, a Fiano di Avellino would be perfect.

Spaghetti con le Vongole e il Diavolillo

Spaghetti with Clams and Hot Red Pepper

My family and I spent a glorious week years ago at a beautiful seaside resort in Southern Italy called Giulianova. The hotel we stayed in was practically on the beach and for a week we swam, laid in the sun, and ate. The meal I remember most was at Beccaceci, a family-owned establishment that, according to many, served the best fish on all the Adriatic coast.

The cooking of the Abruzzi region, just like the cooking of most of the South, is spirited, tasty, and very often quite spicy. One of the dishes I had that night was a sensational plate of spaghetti loaded with tiny clams and laced with fragrant extra virgin olive oil, garlic, and more hot chile peppers than I have ever had in my life. And, as if the spiciness of the dish was not enough, the waiter brought a jar of olive oil seasoned with bits of hot chile pepper to our table.

2 pounds clams, such as littleneck, the smallest you
  can get
1 cup water
5 tablespoons extra virgin olive oil
Salt to taste
1 pound spaghetti or linguine
2 cloves garlic, finely chopped
½ teaspoon dried red pepper flakes, or to taste
2 tablespoons finely chopped fresh parsley

Soak the clams in cold salted water for 20 to 30 minutes to
purge them. Wash and scrub them well under cold running
water. Discard any clams that are broken or already open. Put
the clams in a large skillet with the water and 1 tablespoon of
the oil. Cover the skillet and cook over high heat until the clams
open. Remove them with a slotted spoon to a bowl as they
open. Toss out any clams that do not open. Bring the cooking
liquid back to a boil and cook until it is reduced by half, 2 to
3 minutes. Line a strainer with two paper towels and strain the
liquid into a small bowl to remove any sandy deposits. Set aside.

Bring a large pot of water to a boil. Add 1 tablespoon of salt
and the spaghetti. Cook, uncovered, over high heat until the
spaghetti is tender but still firm to the bite, *al dente*.

While the pasta is cooking, heat the remaining oil over medium heat in the same large skillet you steamed the clams. Add
the garlic and red pepper flakes and cook, stirring, until the
garlic begins to color, less than 1 minute. Add the clams and
the reserved liquid, season with salt, and bring to a gentle boil.

Drain the pasta and add it to the skillet with the clams. Stir
in the parsley. Mix everything quickly over low heat to combine.
Taste and adjust the seasoning. Serve at once.

Makes 4 to 6 servings

SUGGESTED WINE
*A young, flavorful red wine of
light body and tannin, served
icy cold, would complement this
dish very well.*

Spaghetti con Peoci

Spaghetti with Mussels

Italians love mussels and clams and when the *frutti di mare* (fruit
of the sea), as they are called in Italy, are very fresh, the simpler
the preparation, the better the taste.

In Venezia at Trattoria Le Carampane, I dined on a divine plate of spaghetti with mussels; they were large and meaty, dressed only with their own juices, white wine, a bit of tomato, extra virgin olive oil, and garlic. The garlic, however, had been browned and discarded so that only the faintest hint of its aroma was left in the dish.

> 3 pounds fresh live mussels
> ⅓ cup extra virgin olive oil
> 2 cloves garlic, peeled
> 1 cup dry white wine
> 1 cup water
> 1 cup canned imported Italian tomatoes with their juice,
>   put through a strainer or food mill to remove the seeds
> Salt and freshly ground black pepper to taste
> 3 tablespoons finely chopped fresh parsley
> 1 pound spaghetti

Soak the mussels in cold salted water for 20 minutes to purge them. Remove the beard protruding from the shell and scrub the mussels under cold running water thoroughly. Discard any that are broken or already open.

Heat the oil over medium heat in a large skillet. Add the garlic and cook, stirring, until the cloves are golden on both sides, 1 to 2 minutes. Discard the garlic. Add the mussels, wine, and water, cover, and cook over high heat until the mussels open. Remove the mussels with a slotted spoon to a bowl as they open, and discard any that don't open during the cooking. Bring the cooking liquid back to a boil and cook until it is reduced to about 1 cup, about 4 minutes.

Line a strainer with two paper towels and strain the liquid into a bowl to remove any sandy deposits. Return the liquid to the skillet, add the tomatoes, and season with salt and pepper. Cook, uncovered, over high heat for 2 to 3 minutes. Add the mussels and parsley, stir a few times, and turn off the heat.

Bring a large pot of water to a boil. Add 1 tablespoon of salt and the spaghetti. Cook, uncovered, over high heat until the spaghetti is tender but still firm to the bite, *al dente*.

Drain the pasta and add it to the skillet. Mix everything quickly over low heat until well combined. Taste and adjust the seasoning and serve at once.

Makes 4 to 6 servings

SUGGESTED WINES
The creamy texture of mussels and the hint of cooked garlic are enhanced by a straightforward white especially from the Veneto. Try a Masi Soave or their single-vineyard Col Baraca.

Bucatini all'Amatriciana Bianca

Bucatini with Pancetta, Hot Red Pepper, and Pecorino

Bucatini all'Amatriciana Rossa (right) is a quintessential Roman dish in which thick, hollow bucatini are tossed together with a zesty sauce of tomatoes, pancetta, onions, and lots of hot red pepper. But there is another version of this popular dish, a version that the Romans who were born and raised in Roma claim as the most authentic. In this version, the sauce is made only with plenty of pancetta or *guanciale* (cured pork cheek), olive oil, and red chile pepper.

I had this "white" *amatriciana* sauce at Il Piedone in Roma, an eight-table trattoria frequented mostly by Roman laborers who speak the true Roman vernacular. I was fascinated by the intensity with which they ate their pasta. Their heads were bowed, only a few inches from the plate, to minimize the distance that the fork had to travel from the plate to the mouth.

As I began to eat the bucatini with the white *amatriciana* sauce, I understood why. This dish was so incredibly appetizing that one only wanted to pause long enough to wash the spicy pasta down with a large glass of Frascati wine.

> ¼ cup olive oil, preferably extra virgin
> 2 tablespoons unsalted butter
> ¼ pound thickly sliced pancetta, cut into small strips
> Pinch of dried red pepper flakes
> Salt to taste
> 1 pound bucatini or spaghetti
> 2 tablespoons chopped fresh parsley
> ¼ cup freshly grated pecorino romano cheese or ⅓ cup
>   freshly grated parmigiano

TIP

Ⓐ *When a sauce is comprised of only a few tablespoons of oil and/or butter, ham, pancetta, or vegetables, Italian housewives add a bit of starchy pasta water to the skillet, which, in cooking down, thickens the sauce and moistens the pasta.*

Heat the oil and butter together in a large skillet over medium heat. When the butter foams, add the pancetta and red pepper flakes. Cook gently, over medium heat, until the pancetta is lightly golden, 2 to 3 minutes.

Bring a large pot of water to a boil. Add 1 tablespoon of salt and the bucatini. Cook, uncovered, over high heat until the pasta is tender but still firm to the bite, *al dente*.

Scoop out ½ cup of the pasta cooking water and reserve. Drain the pasta and add it to the skillet. Stir in the reserved water, parsley, and cheese. Mix over low heat until the pasta is well coated. Taste and season with salt, if necessary. (The pancetta is already quite salty.) Serve piping hot with a bit more cheese, if desired.

Makes 4 to 6 servings

SUGGESTED WINES

With a Roman dish, a Roman wine, Frascati, such as Fontana Candida or Colli di Catone. A California French Colombard from Gallo would substitute well.

Bucatini all'Amatriciana Rossa

Bucatini with Pancetta, Tomatoes, and Hot Red Pepper

5 tablespoons olive oil
1 small onion, finely minced
1 clove garlic, finely chopped
¼ pound thickly sliced pancetta, cut into small strips
3 cups canned imported Italian tomatoes with their juice, put through a strainer or food mill to remove the seeds
Salt to taste
Pinch of dried red pepper flakes
1 pound bucatini, penne, or rigatoni
¼ cup freshly grated pecorino romano cheese or ⅓ cup freshly grated parmigiano

Heat the oil in a large skillet over medium heat. Add the onion and the garlic and cook, stirring, until the onion is pale yellow, 2 to 3 minutes. Add the pancetta and cook, stirring, until the pancetta begins to color, 1 to 2 minutes. Stir in the tomatoes and season with salt and red pepper. Cook, uncovered, over medium heat, stirring occasionally, for 7 to 8 minutes.

Bring a large pot of water to a boil. Add 1 tablespoon of salt and the pasta. Cook, uncovered, over high heat until the pasta is tender but still firm to the bite, *al dente*. Drain the pasta and add it to the skillet with the sauce. Stir in the pecorino cheese and mix over low heat until the pasta is well coated. Taste and adjust the seasoning. Serve at once.

Makes 4 to 6 servings

TIPS

∾ *For a preparation with less fat, sauté the pancetta in a separate skillet, scoop it out with a slotted spoon, drain it on paper towels, and then add it to the sauce.*

∾ *If you object to the sharp taste of the pecorino romano cheese, use 3 parts parmigiano and 1 part pecorino instead.*

SUGGESTED WINE

For this dish a young, hearty red wine would go very well, such as Gallo's Reserve Burgundy.

I Bucatini dell'Arancio d'Oro

Bucatini with Eggplant, Smoked Mozzarella, Olive Paste, and Tomatoes

So many pasta dishes, especially the ones of the South, are born out of simplicity and imagination. Humble ingredients are mixed together into perfect unions of taste. But what amazes me the most is that the people who create these small master-pieces are not "great chefs." They are simple, humble cooks who put their hearts and their passion into the food they cook.

I had this pasta dish in October 1990 at Arancio d'Oro (golden orange) trattoria in Roma, while on a television cooking assignment for station KCRA in Sacramento. We had filmed all day. We were tired and very hungry. The aroma of the pasta filled the tiny trattoria even before the plates arrived at the table. We sipped generous glasses of local wine, twirled the bucatini—a thick, hollow spaghetti—around our forks, and proceeded to devour this immensely satisfying pasta.

1 pound firm small eggplant, peeled and diced about the
    size of small grapes
Salt
4 to 5 tablespoons olive oil
2 cloves garlic, finely chopped
4 cups canned imported Italian tomatoes with their juice,
    put through a strainer or food mill to remove the seeds
1 tablespoon olive paste (see tip)
Small pinch of dried red pepper flakes
2 tablespoons chopped fresh parsley
1 pound bucatini or spaghetti
¼ pound smoked or regular mozzarella

Place the diced eggplant in a colander and season liberally with salt. Let stand for 30 minutes. The salt will draw out the bitter juices from the eggplant. Put the eggplant on a large kitchen towel and pat dry.

TIPS

↬ *Olive paste is available in specialty Italian markets or food stores. Several good brands are Ardoino, San Remo, and Min-assio.*

↬ *Eggplant absorbs oil quickly, so resist the temptation to add more oil or the eggplant will become too soggy. Grilled eggplant can also be used in this preparation. In that case peel and cut the eggplant into ¼-inch-thick slices, sprinkle them with salt, and let stand for 30 minutes. Pat dry with paper towels.*

Meanwhile, preheat the bar-becue, grill, or broiler. Cook until the slices are lightly golden on both sides. Dice them and proceed as instructed in the rec-ipe.

Heat the oil in a large skillet over high heat. Add the eggplant and cook, stirring, until it is golden in color, 2 to 3 minutes. Stir in the garlic and cook 1 minute longer. Add the tomatoes and olive paste, and season with salt and the red pepper. Reduce the heat to medium and cook, stirring a few times, until the sauce has a medium-thick consistency, 5 to 6 minutes. Stir in the parsley.

While the sauce is cooking, bring a large pot of water to a boil. Add 1 tablespoon of salt and the bucatini. Cook, uncovered, over high heat until the pasta is tender but still firm to the bite, *al dente*. Drain the pasta and place it in the skillet with the sauce. Add the smoked mozzarella. Mix well over low heat until the cheese begins to melt and the pasta is well coated with the sauce. Serve at once.

Makes 4 to 6 servings

SUGGESTED WINE
Choose a young, medium-bodied, flavorful red wine without tannin, such as Gianni Piccoli's Bardolino.

Tortiglioni con Melanzane, Pomodoro e Mozzarella Affumicata

Tortiglioni with Eggplant, Tomatoes, and Smoked Mozzarella

Il Verdi in Milano is a very unusual trattoria. It is a casual, comfortable place that has an old-fashioned feeling with dark wood paneling, massive tables, and an upscale yuppy Milanese clientele.

The Il Verdi menu is also unusual, handwritten and quite extensive, with dishes of many regions and an assortment of creative preparations.

Perhaps it was the chill and fog of Milano that night that prompted me to order a quintessential Southern Italian dish of pasta, loaded with a zesty tomato sauce, grilled eggplant, and smoked mozzarella. It was so good that it not only warmed my soul, but also brought color to my cheeks.

NOTE OF INTEREST
Tortiglioni are corkscrew-shaped macaroni. Penne or rigatoni can also be used.

1 firm medium-size eggplant, trimmed, peeled, and cut into ¼-inch-thick slices lengthwise
Salt
¼ cup olive oil
2 cloves garlic, finely chopped
Pinch of dried red pepper flakes
4 cups canned imported Italian tomatoes with their juice, put through a strainer or food mill to remove the seeds
2 tablespoons finely chopped fresh parsley
1 pound tortiglioni or penne
6 ounces smoked mozzarella (see page 9) or Gouda cheese, cut into small pieces about the size of an olive

Place the eggplant slices on a large dish or cookie sheet and sprinkle liberally with salt. (The salt will draw out the eggplant's bitter juices.) Let stand about 1 hour, then remove the salt and juices by patting the slices dry with paper towels.

Preheat the broiler. Place the slices on a broiling pan and brush lightly with oil. Broil until they are golden on both sides, about 2 minutes per side. Cool slightly, then cut the slices into ½-inch pieces. Set aside.

In a large skillet heat the oil over medium heat. Add the garlic and the pepper flakes and cook, stirring, until the garlic begins to color, less than a minute. Add the tomatoes and season with salt. Cook, stirring, over medium-high heat for 6 to 8 minutes. Add the eggplant and parsley and cook 1 to 2 minutes longer. Taste and adjust the seasoning. Leave the sauce a bit shy of salt because the smoked mozzarella is quite salty.

While the sauce is cooking, bring a large pot of water to a boil. Add 1 tablespoon of salt and the pasta. Cook, uncovered, over high heat until the pasta is tender but still firm to the bite, *al dente*.

Drain the pasta and add it to the skillet with the sauce. Stir in the mozzarella and mix everything over low heat until the mozzarella begins to melt and is completely blended with the pasta and the sauce, about 1 minute. Serve at once.

Makes 4 to 6 servings

SUGGESTED WINES
Some of the new Sicilian red wines such as Regaleali, Terre di Ginestra, or Donnafugata have the spicy, uncomplicated flavors complementary to this style of dish.

Conchiglie alla Pappagano

Shells with Calamari, Tomatoes, Anchovies, and Hot Red Pepper

The more I eat my way through Italy, the more I realize how wonderfully uncomplicated, tasty, satisfying, and varied the sauces for pasta are. A Roman friend told me about Cannavota, a trattoria run and operated by the whole Cannavota family, whose specialty is pasta dishes. Since there is nothing under the sun I would rather eat than pasta, I went, I ate, and I succumbed to some of the most appetizing pasta dishes I have ever had. The day after, in the Cannavota kitchen, I was given the recipes for three of my favorite dishes. This is one of them.

12 ounces uncleaned squid, or about 8 ounces cleaned
¼ cup olive oil
2 cloves garlic, finely chopped
4 anchovy fillets, finely chopped
4 cups canned imported Italian tomatoes with their juice,
    put through a strainer or food mill to remove the seeds
Salt to taste
Small pinch of dried red pepper flakes
1 tablespoon unsalted butter
2 tablespoons heavy cream
1 pound shells or penne

To clean the squid, hold it in one hand and gently pull away the tentacles. Cut the head off, just below the eyes, and discard it. Remove the tentacles. Remove the squid "bone" from inside the body (this is actually a piece of cartilage that resembles a piece of clear plastic). Clean the inside of the sac under cold running water, pulling out any matter still inside. Wash and peel any skin from the body and tentacles. (The skin will come away easily from the body, but not from the tentacles. If it does not bother you, leave it there because it is edible.)

Cut the squid body into 1-inch-wide rings. Set aside. (Reserve the tentacles for another use, such as a salad.)

Heat the oil in a large skillet over medium heat. Add the garlic and anchovies and cook, stirring, until the garlic begins to color, less than a minute. Add the tomatoes and season with

TIPS

The squid takes very little time to cook. For this reason I add the squid to the simmering sauce and, after a few seconds, turn the heat off. The squid will keep cooking in the hot sauce. Keep in mind that squid will become tough and rubbery if it is cooked longer than a few minutes.

Ideally, your pasta should be cooking at the same time your sauce is being prepared, since both will be cooked in less than 10 minutes.

When my daughters were young, I used to cook and keep this tomato sauce, without the squid, in the refrigerator for several days. After school, they would impress their friends by preparing their favorite "snack," a large plate of penne with a savory tomato sauce.

the salt and red pepper. Cook, uncovered, 7 to 8 minutes, stirring occasionally. Stir in the butter and cream and cook a few minutes longer. Add the squid, stir once or twice, then turn the heat off under the skillet.

While the sauce is cooking, bring a large pot of water to a boil. Add 1 tablespoon of salt and the pasta. Cook, uncovered, until the pasta is tender but still firm to the bite, *al dente*. Drain the pasta and add it to the skillet with the sauce. Turn the heat under the skillet to medium and mix everything until the pasta is well combined with the sauce. Serve at once.

Makes 4 to 6 servings

SUGGESTED WINES
A light, uncomplicated red wine is called for here, but a full-bodied, unoaked white could also be used. Try a Trebbiano d'Abruzzo.

Pasta con la Ricotta e Pecorino

Pasta with Ricotta and Pecorino Cheese

Some of the best ricotta in Italy comes from the South. The Roman ricotta, with its flavorful, granular consistency, is very often used as a topping for pasta or in the great *torte di ricotta*, ricotta cake.

At Gigetto, a very old, well-known Roman trattoria, I was served a large plate of steaming penne, coated abundantly with that marvelous Roman ricotta. This dish reflects the simplicity of old peasant cooking, when dishes were prepared simply with whatever ingredients one had at hand.

Since we don't have the lovely Roman ricotta, we must make do with what we have. Check your local Italian market or specialized food store for the best fresh product. If all else fails, buy the best possible brand.

    1 pound penne or shells
    8 ounces whole milk ricotta
    1 cup milk
    2 tablespoons freshly grated pecorino romano or parmigiano
    2 tablespoons chopped fresh parsley
    Salt to taste

Bring a large pot of water to a boil. Add 1 tablespoon of salt and the pasta. Cook, uncovered, over high heat until the pasta is tender but still firm to the bite, *al dente*.

While the pasta is cooking, combine the remaining ingredients in a bowl large enough to also accommodate the pasta. Mix the ingredients thoroughly with a large spoon until you have a soft, loose mixture. If your mixture is too thick, add a bit more milk.

Drain the pasta and add it to the bowl. Mix well and serve at once.

Makes 4 to 6 servings

SUGGESTED WINES

A light, uncomplicated red or white wine such as Bardolino is called for here. Serve the wine cool.

Maccheroni con il Ragù di Agnello

Pasta with Lamb Sauce

The cooking of the Abruzzi region is robust, rustic, and spiced with the ever-present hot red chile pepper. One of the best-known pasta dishes that should be eaten locally to fully appreciate its flavor and texture is *maccheroni alla chitarra*.

A square, homemade spaghettilike pasta made with eggs and hard wheat flour, it is cut by pressing the sheet of dough through the wires of a loom that is rectangular-shaped with wires running from end to end.

This *chitarra,* however, is seldom available outside Abruzzi. The sauces for this delicious pasta dish are many. One of the most popular is a lamb sauce that is cooked slowly with onions, garlic, rosemary, hot red pepper, and fragrant ripe tomatoes. This delicious version comes from the rustic trattoria Le Salette Aquilane in Coppito, a small country town outside the city of L'Aquila, famous for its saffron production. Since I don't have a *chitarra* at my restaurant, I serve this delicious lamb sauce over penne, rigatoni, or ziti.

NOTE OF INTEREST

Some pasta brands, such as La Rustichella, offer the thin, square-shaped pasta called chitarra.

5 tablespoons olive oil

1 small onion, finely diced

2 cloves garlic, finely chopped

1 tablespoon chopped fresh rosemary or 1½ teaspoons dried

Small pinch of crushed red pepper flakes

1 pound boneless leg of lamb, all fat removed and cut into small pieces, about the size of small white beans

1 cup dry red wine, such as Chianti

4 cups canned imported Italian tomatoes with their juice, put through a strainer or food mill to remove the seeds

Salt to taste

1 pound penne or rigatoni

2 tablespoons finely chopped fresh parsley

3 to 4 tablespoons freshly grated pecorino romano cheese or ½ cup freshly grated parmigiano

Heat the oil in a large skillet over medium-high heat. Add the onion, garlic, rosemary, and red pepper flakes and stir once or twice. Add the lamb and cook, stirring several times, until the meat is lightly colored, 4 to 6 minutes. Raise the heat to high and pour in the wine. Cook, stirring, until the wine is almost all reduced, about 2 minutes. Stir in the tomatoes, season with salt, and cover the skillet. Cook over low heat 45 minutes to 1 hour, stirring a few times. If the sauce thickens too much, add a bit of water.

Bring a large pot of water to a boil. Add 1 tablespoon of salt and the pasta. Cook, uncovered, over high heat until the pasta is tender but still firm to the bite, *al dente*. (The cooking time will depend on the kind of pasta used.) Drain the pasta and add it to the sauce. Stir in the parsley. Mix quickly over low heat until the pasta and the sauce are well combined. Taste and adjust the seasoning. Serve with a sprinkling of pecorino romano.

Makes 4 to 6 servings

SUGGESTED WINE
This classic pasta from Abruzzo cries for a wine of the same region. Try Montepulciano d'Abruzzo, Casal Thaulero.

Pasta con le Verdure

Pasta with Vegetables

The marriage of pasta and vegetables is a predominant characteristic of Southern Italian cooking. Some dishes are so well known that they are instantly associated with the sunny land where they originate. The orecchiette with mustard greens of Puglia and the pasta with cauliflower or with eggplant of Sicilia are just two. There are, however, lesser-known preparations that arise from people's imaginations and the products they have at hand. This dish comes from Trattoria Il Piedone in Roma, even though it can be found in slightly different versions in other parts of Southern Italy.

The basis for this appetizing dish is simple: extra virgin olive oil, garlic, anchovies, and red chile pepper. These standard ingredients are sautéed together with a variety of vegetables, then combined with the pasta. Nothing could be simpler, healthier, or more delicious.

> 1 teaspoon salt
> ¾ to 1 pound cauliflower (about ½ head), separated into florets
> 1 to 1½ pounds (about ½ head) broccoli, separated into florets
> ⅓ cup olive oil, preferably extra virgin
> 4 ounces thickly sliced pancetta, cut into small strips
> 4 ounces white cultivated mushrooms, thinly sliced
> 2 cloves garlic, finely chopped
> Pinch of dried red pepper flakes
> 1 pound penne, shells, or orecchiette

Bring a medium-size saucepan of water to a boil over medium heat. Add the salt and cauliflower florets. Cook, uncovered, 4 to 5 minutes, or until the florets are tender but still firm to the touch. Scoop out the florets with a large skimmer and set aside. Bring the water back to a boil, then add the broccoli florets, and cook until tender, 4 to 5 minutes. Drain and set aside.

Heat the oil in a large skillet over medium heat. Add the pancetta and sauté about 1 minute. As soon as the pancetta

NOTE OF INTEREST
Grated cheese is generally not added to garlic-oil-anchovy preparations.

Orecchiette are small, flat disks of pasta shaped like the lobe of an ear.

begins to color, add the mushrooms. Raise the heat to high and cook, stirring, until the mushrooms are golden, 4 to 5 minutes. Add the garlic and stir once or twice. Add the vegetables, season with the salt and red pepper, and stir less than 1 minute.

While you are sautéing the vegetables, bring a large pot of water to a boil. Add 1 tablespoon of salt and the pasta. Cook, uncovered, over high heat until the pasta is tender but still firm to the bite, *al dente*. Drain the pasta but leave it a bit "wet." Add it to the skillet with the vegetables. Mix briefly over low heat, taste, adjust the seasoning, and serve at once.

Makes 4 to 6 servings

SUGGESTED WINE
A light red wine such as Bardolino served cool would be perfect for this dish.

Penne al Radicchio e Pancetta

Penne with Radicchio and Pancetta

Many years ago, before Italy had super highways that allowed ingredients to be transported easily and safely from one end of Italy to the other, radicchio was known mostly to the people of Veneto, where it originated.

Today, radicchio is available all over Italy and in many parts of the world. One of the most popular dishes at Evangelista in Roma, besides its celebrated artichokes Roman style, is the penne with radicchio. The tartness of this delicious chicory becomes a bit milder as it cooks and blends perfectly with deliciously crisp pancetta.

> 1 pound radicchio (see page 16)
> ¼ cup extra virgin olive oil
> 6 ounces thickly sliced pancetta, cut into small strips
> 2 tablespoons unsalted butter
> Salt and freshly ground black pepper to taste
> 1 pound penne

Discard any bruised or wilted leaves from the radicchio. Detach the radicchio leaves and wash them under cold running water.

Pat dry with paper towels. Stack the leaves one over the other and cut them into thin strips.

Heat the oil in a large skillet over medium heat. Add the pancetta and sauté until the pancetta is lightly golden. Add the radicchio strips and sauté less than a minute. Add the butter and cover the skillet. Reduce the heat to low and cook 4 to 5 minutes, until the radicchio strips are soft and wilted. Season with salt and several grinds of pepper.

While the radicchio is cooking, bring a large pot of water to a boil. Add 1 tablespoon of salt and the penne. Cook, uncovered, over high heat until the pasta is tender but still firm to the bite, *al dente*. Drain the pasta and add it to the skillet with the radicchio. Mix well over low heat. Taste and adjust the seasoning. Serve at once.

Makes 4 to 6 servings

SUGGESTED WINES

Merlot from the Colli Euganei, a Bardolino, and Breganze Rosso are some of the natural choices for this dish. A Gamay Beaujolais from California would also work very well.

Penne con i Funghi, Tonno e Pomodoro

Penne with Mushrooms, Tuna, and Tomatoes

As a child I grew up with homemade pasta. Tagliatelle, which are the noodles of Bologna, were made fresh by my mother almost daily. Sometimes they were served with a Bolognese meat sauce, other times, with just a bit of tomato, cream, and butter. At that time regional Italian cooking was still well defined and only occasionally would my mother prepare a plate of maccheroni or spaghetti in the manner of Southern Italy.

Today, the regional differences have almost all disappeared, and on restaurant menus we can now find dishes from every part of Italy. I still maintain, however, that food, just like dialects, is best expressed and understood within its own borders. Nobody will ever prepare delicate, tasty tortellini like a Bolognese grandmother who has made them all her life, and a Northern Italian will not have that special magic touch in preparing the fabulous pastas of the South.

This dish comes from Trattoria Corsi in Roma. Perhaps there is nothing new or exciting in this dish, other than the fact that the pasta was cooked *perfectly* and that the sauce had just the right amount of garlic, hot pepper, tuna, mushrooms, and tomatoes. What was special, however, was the terrific feeling of satisfaction I felt while I was eating it. While in Roma, eat what the Romans eat!

⅓ cup olive oil
½ pound fresh white cultivated mushrooms, thinly sliced
3 cloves garlic, finely chopped
4 cups canned imported Italian tomatoes with their juice, put through a strainer or food mill to remove the seeds
One 7-ounce can white tuna packed in oil, drained, and broken into small pieces
8 to 10 fresh basil leaves, shredded
2 tablespoons chopped fresh parsley
Salt and freshly ground black pepper to taste
1 pound penne rigate

Heat the oil in a large skillet over high heat. Add half of the mushrooms, making sure not to crowd them, and cook, stirring, until they are lightly golden, about 4 minutes. Transfer the mushrooms with a slotted spoon to a bowl and finish cooking the remaining mushrooms. Return the mushrooms to the skillet, stir in the garlic, and cook until it begins to color, 20 to 30 seconds (the skillet is already very hot and the garlic will color almost immediately). Add the tomatoes, reduce the heat to medium, and cook 4 to 5 minutes. Add the tuna, basil, and parsley, season with salt and several grinds of pepper, and cook a few minutes longer. At this point the sauce should have a medium-thick consistency.

While the sauce is cooking, bring a large pot of water to a boil. Add 1 tablespoon of salt and the penne. Cook, uncovered, until the pasta is tender but still firm to the bite, *al dente*. Drain the pasta and place it in the skillet with the sauce. Mix, over low heat, until the pasta and sauce are well combined. Serve hot.

Makes 4 to 6 servings

TIP
~ *When fresh basil is not available, add 1 additional tablespoon of chopped fresh parsley.*

SUGGESTED WINE
In spite of the tuna in the sauce, a light- to medium-bodied red wine with low tannin is called for. Try a young Pinot Noir such as Saintsbury Garnet from California's Carneron region.

Pennette con le Zucchine Fritte, Piselli e Pomodori

Pennette with Fried Zucchini, Peas, and Tomatoes

Often the sauces for pasta are not "sauces" in the true sense of the word, but rather an assemblage of flavorful ingredients tossed together quickly with some oil or butter, so that one can savor the true identity of each ingredient used.

In this dish, the zucchini are quickly sautéed with some oil and combined with fresh tomatoes and fresh peas.

I had this dish at Trattoria Masuelli in Milano, on a hot, humid day, and it appealed to me because of its lightness. The zucchini were small and tender, the tomatoes ripe and fragrant, and the peas small and very sweet. Without these superlative, tasty ingredients, this dish would have been an ordinary one.

1 cup shelled fresh peas or frozen peas, thawed
¼ cup olive oil
2 medium-size zucchini, cut into ¼-inch-thick rounds
1½ pounds ripe, juicy tomatoes, peeled (see page 16), seeded, and cut into small strips
1 clove garlic, finely chopped
Salt and freshly ground black pepper to taste
1 tablespoon unsalted butter
1 pound pennette
1 cup freshly grated parmigiano

If you are using fresh peas, bring 2 cups of water to a boil in a medium-size saucepan. Add the peas and cook, uncovered, over medium heat until tender, 4 to 6 minutes, depending on the size of the peas. Strain the peas and set aside.

Heat the oil in a large skillet over medium-high heat. Add the zucchini and sauté until the zucchini are golden in color, 2 to 3 minutes. Add the tomatoes and the garlic, season with salt and pepper, and cook over high heat until the watery juice of the tomatoes is almost all reduced. Stir in the fresh or, if using frozen, thawed peas and butter. Cook just long enough to mix with the other ingredients, about 1 minute.

Meanwhile, bring a large pot of water to a boil. Add 1 tablespoon of salt and the pennette. Cook, uncovered, over high

---

NOTE OF INTEREST
Pennette are thin macaroni that are cut diagonally at the ends and can be smooth or ridged. If hard to find, substitute with penne rigate or shells.

SUGGESTED WINES
This light summer dish pairs well with a variety of wines, such as an Italian Rosato or a medium-bodied Sauvignon Blanc or a Chardonnay not overly oaked and fruity. A light Italian red such as Grignolino or Chiaretto del Garda is also perfect.

heat until the pasta is tender but still firm to the bite, *al dente*. Drain the pasta and add it to the skillet with the sauce. Add ⅓ cup of the parmigiano and mix briefly over low heat to combine. Serve at once with the remaining parmigiano.

Makes 4 to 6 servings

Pennette con Fiori di Zucchine

Pennette with Zucchini Blossoms

My first encounter with zucchini blossoms was on my honeymoon, when my husband and I took a trip to Salerno in Southern Italy, where we visited my husband's aunt, who prepared a Lucullan dinner for us. One of the most delicious dishes she prepared was stuffed deep-fried zucchini blossoms. The blossoms were fresh from her garden, stuffed, dipped into a light batter, and fried to a perfect crispness. Years later I had these delicious stuffed zucchini at Gigetto in Rome (see pages 35–36). They were marvelous. Since then, every time I come upon zucchini blossoms, either at the market or at restaurants and *trattorie*, I feast upon them shamelessly.

This lovely dish is from La Biscondola in the Chianti region of Toscana. The day we were there, there were large baskets of tiny zucchini with their blossoms wide open displayed on a large table.

The sauce for this dish can be made in minutes. The pancetta is sautéed quickly with some oil and butter. The zucchini blossoms are added and tossed with the pancetta briefly, and the sauce is completed when the wine, broth, and cream are reduced and the mixture smooth and creamy. The result is a wonderful, light dish that is as pretty to look at as it is good to eat.

Zucchini blossoms are seasonal, and are available starting midspring and throughout the summer. They are very delicate and perishable. Check with your specialty market and, by all means, go the extra mile to try to locate them. You will be richly rewarded.

12 small zucchini with the blossoms still attached, about
   1 pound
¼ cup olive oil
1 tablespoon unsalted butter
¼ pound sliced pancetta, cut into small strips
2 cloves garlic, finely chopped
1 cup dry white wine
½ cup chicken broth, preferably homemade (see
   pages 54–55)
1 cup heavy cream
Salt and freshly ground black pepper to taste
1 pound pennette, penne rigate, or shells
½ cup freshly grated parmigiano

Detach the zucchini blossom from the zucchini. Remove the
stems and pistils from the blossoms; wash gently under cold
water and drain on paper towels. Slice the blossoms lengthwise
into four pieces. Wash and dry the zucchini and cut them into
thin rounds.

Heat the oil and butter in a large skillet over medium heat.
Add the pancetta and cook until the pancetta is lightly golden,
1 to 2 minutes. Add the zucchini blossoms and garlic to the
skillet and toss briefly. Stir in the wine and cook until it is almost
all reduced, 2 to 3 minutes. Stir in the broth and cream, season
with salt and pepper, and cook until the sauce has a medium-
thick consistency, about 4 minutes.

While the sauce is cooking, bring a large pot of water to a
boil. Add 1 tablespoon of salt and the pasta. Cook until the
pasta is tender but still firm to the bite, *al dente*.

Drain the pasta and add it to the skillet. Mix well over medium
heat until the sauce thickens and is well combined with the pasta.
Serve with a generous sprinkling of freshly grated parmigiano.

Makes 4 to 6 servings

SUGGESTED WINES
*A good dry Tuscan white such
as Galestro or San Gimignano
would complement this dish very
well.*

Pennette con Sugo di Pesce Ligure

Pennette with Ligurian Fish Sauce

NOTE OF INTEREST
This delicious sauce is typical of the Ligurian seacoast. The type of fish used changes according to the season and the availability. Fresh herbs are very important to this dish; if they are not available, use dry herbs sparingly.

Even though pennette is suggested for this dish, spaghetti or linguine can also be used.

When I am in Italy, I can never really relax because I am always tuned in to the sights and smells of the food around me. This particular day I told my husband that I needed a day off from eating and researching. I wanted to lounge on the beach, read a book, and swim. My good intentions did not last long. Around noon the bathers and sun worshippers began to disappear and soon the odor of food was everywhere. Not far from where I was sitting, there was a very small *caffè*, the sort of establishment that offers pizza, sandwiches, and occasionally a few pasta dishes. This *caffè* had a few tables that were practically on the beach where people sat in their bathing suits eating. After a heavenly plate of penne with fish sauce and a glass of local white wine, I decided that while in Italy I would fast only on the eighth day of the week.

¼ cup olive oil
½ cup finely minced onion
2 cloves garlic, finely chopped
2 tablespoons finely chopped fresh parsley
3 tablespoons finely chopped fresh basil
1 tablespoon finely chopped fresh rosemary
1 tablespoon finely chopped fresh sage
10 ounces mixed fish fillets and seafood, such as orange roughy, sole, sea bass, halibut, shrimp, and scallops, finely diced
1 cup dry white wine
2 cups canned imported Italian tomatoes with their juice, put through a strainer or food mill to remove the seeds
2 tablespoons tomato paste diluted in 1 cup water
1 cup finely diced, peeled (see page 16), and seeded fresh tomatoes
Salt to taste
Pinch of dried red pepper flakes
1 pound pennette, penne rigate, or shells

Heat the oil in a large skillet over medium heat. Add the onion and garlic and cook, stirring, until the onion is lightly colored, 4 to 5 minutes. Add the parsley, basil, rosemary, and sage and cook about 1 minute. Add the diced fish and cook, stirring, 1 to 2 minutes. Raise the heat to high, stir in the wine, and cook until it is almost all reduced. Add the strained tomatoes, diluted tomato paste, and diced tomatoes, and cook, uncovered, 5 to 6 minutes over medium heat, until the sauce has a medium-thick consistency. Season with the salt and red pepper.

While the sauce is cooking, bring a large pot of water to a boil. Add 1 tablespoon salt and the pasta. Cook, uncovered, until the pasta is tender but still firm to the bite, *al dente*. Drain the pasta and place it in the skillet with the sauce. Mix well and serve at once.

Makes 4 to 6 servings

SUGGESTED WINES
Typical Ligurian wines such as Vermentino and Cinqueterre would be good white wine choices, or a light red such as the lovely Dolcetto d'Asti would also work well.

Ziti con Uova e Pecorino

Ziti with Eggs and Pecorino Cheese

Years ago, long before this book was ever conceived, my husband and I were traveling south, from Roma to Salerno, on the *autostrada*, and we were starving. We took the next exit and after a few minutes we stumbled upon the sort of place one finds not too far from the freeways, patronized mostly by truck drivers and hungry travelers. This little place, whose name I don't even remember, had a few outside tables under a trellis. As we approached, the aroma of food hit us. A large, middle-aged woman was turning and basting sausages, chops, ribs, and vegetables over an open rudimentary grill. It was a hot day and the mood of the patrons was mellow and slow. We ordered the local house wine and a plate of fragrant tomatoes and locally made mozzarella. Afterward, I tried an intriguing pasta dish, ziti with eggs and pecorino cheese. Once again, I discovered that the cooking born of poverty is rich with ingenuity, imagination, and taste.

5 very fresh large eggs
2 tablespoons freshly grated pecorino romano cheese
¼ cup freshly grated parmigiano
3 tablespoons finely chopped fresh parsley
Salt to taste
1 pound ziti or rigatoni
4 tablespoons (½ stick) unsalted butter

Beat the eggs together in a medium-size bowl. Add the pecorino, parmigiano, and parsley and season with salt. Mix well to combine. Set aside.

Bring a large pot of water to a boil. Add 1 tablespoon of salt and the ziti. Cook, uncovered, over high heat until the pasta is tender but still firm to the bite, *al dente*.

Melt the butter in a large skillet over medium heat. Drain the pasta, add it to the skillet, and toss briefly to coat it with the butter. Add the egg mixture and mix quickly over low heat, for less than a minute, until the eggs become creamy and thick, and coat the pasta evenly. Do not cook too long, or the eggs will scramble. Taste and adjust the seasoning and serve at once.

Makes 4 to 6 servings

SUGGESTED WINES
Choose a young, simple dry wine, either red or white, with a fruity flavor such as J. Lohr Monterey Gamay from California or Bonny Doon Il Pescatore.

Rigatoni Strascicati

Rigatoni with Vegetables, Tomato, and Cream Sauce

When I was growing up in Bologna, we used to patronize on occasion a little neighborhood trattoria. I remember vividly the sign they had in the window that listed the specials—"Monday, Tripe, Tuesday, Pasta e Fagioli, Wednesday, Tortellini in Brodo . . ." That sign was meant to attract customers and to reassure them that they were serving homey fare.

Today *trattorie* are generally packed with customers and those signs have disappeared. So, when at Trattoria Antico Fattore, in Firenze, the waiter began to describe the dishes, "and of course, today that is Wednesday, we have our wonderful Rigatoni Strascicati," the memories came back.

This is a wonderful, uncomplicated sauce to prepare, and is equally good served over rigatoni, fettuccine, shells, or penne. *Strascicare* means "to drag," which is exactly what we do once we have the pasta and the sauce in the skillet. We cook and "drag" the pasta and the sauce together with a large spoon until they are blended together.

6 tablespoons olive oil
1 medium-size onion, diced
1 large carrot, diced
1 stalk celery, diced
1 medium-size red bell pepper, diced
3 cloves garlic, finely chopped
4 to 5 fresh sage leaves, chopped
1 small sprig fresh rosemary, chopped
4 cups canned imported Italian tomatoes with their juice,
    put through a strainer or food mill to remove the seeds
1 tablespoon unsalted butter
¼ cup heavy cream
Salt and freshly ground black pepper to taste
1 pound rigatoni
10 to 12 fresh basil leaves, finely shredded
1 cup freshly grated parmigiano

Heat the oil in a large skillet over medium heat. Add the diced vegetables, garlic, sage, and rosemary and cook, stirring, 4 to 5 minutes, until the vegetables are lightly golden. Add the tomatoes and cook, uncovered, over low heat for 12 to 15 minutes, stirring a few times. Transfer the sauce to a food processor or a blender and blend until smooth.

Melt the butter over medium heat in the skillet used to cook the sauce. Return the tomato mixture to the skillet. Add the cream, season with salt and pepper, and simmer gently over medium-low heat 1 to 2 minutes. If the sauce is too thick, add a bit of chicken broth or water.

While the sauce is cooking, bring a large pot of water to a boil. Add 1 tablespoon of salt and the rigatoni. Cook, uncovered, over high heat until the pasta is tender but still firm to the bite, *al dente*. Drain the rigatoni and place it in the skillet with the sauce. Stir in the basil and ⅓ cup of the parmigiano. Mix over low heat until the pasta is completely coated with the sauce, less than 1 minute. Serve with the remaining grated parmigiano.

Makes 4 to 6 servings

SUGGESTED WINE
The sweet, light flavor of these vegetables is enhanced by a slightly tart, medium-bodied Chianti Classico or other such style wine. A bit of zippy acidity gives a lift to the flavor of the sauce.

Rigatoni alla Fornaia

Rigatoni with Tomatoes, Pesto, and Ricotta

If there is one thing that unites Italians everywhere, it is pasta. Italians are in love with pasta. They talk about it. They argue about it, and they cannot let a day go by without their pasta fix. Signor Cappelli, the cheerful and colorful owner of the trattoria that bears his name in the heart of the Chianti region, prepared this pasta with his own hands. "It is not fancy, but it is very good," he said. And he was right. Of course, the fact that the ricotta had been made on the premises and the tomatoes and the basil were picked that morning from his vegetable garden, certainly did not hurt.

For the pesto sauce
    3 cups loosely packed fresh basil leaves
    ½ cup olive oil
    ¼ cup pine nuts
    2 cloves garlic, peeled
    Salt to taste
    ⅓ cup freshly grated parmigiano
    2 tablespoons freshly grated pecorino romano cheese, or
        2 additional tablespoons parmigiano

To complete the dish
    ¼ cup olive oil
    ½ large red onion, finely diced
    1 clove garlic, finely chopped
    1 cup dry white wine
    4 cups canned imported Italian tomatoes with their juice,
        put through a strainer or food mill to remove the seeds
    2 tablespoons pesto
    Salt and freshly ground black pepper to taste
    3 tablespoons whole milk ricotta
    1 pound rigatoni
    ½ cup freshly grated parmigiano

Prepare the pesto sauce. Put all the ingredients, except the cheese, in a food processor and process until smooth. Pour the sauce into a small bowl and stir in the parmigiano and pecorino cheese. Taste and adjust the seasoning. Use whatever pesto you need, then cover the bowl with plastic wrap and freeze or refrigerate it (it can be kept in the refrigerator quite well for several days).

Heat the oil in a large skillet over medium heat. Add the onion and garlic and cook, stirring, until the onion is soft, 4 to 5 minutes. Add the wine and cook until the wine is almost all reduced. Stir in the tomatoes and cook, uncovered, 8 to 10 minutes. Add the pesto and mix well. Season with salt and pepper, then add the ricotta and mix well with a wooden spoon or a small wire whisk until it is completely incorporated into the sauce.

While the sauce is cooking, bring a large pot of water to a boil. Add 1 tablespoon of salt and the rigatoni. Cook, uncovered, over high heat until the pasta is tender but still firm to the bite, *al dente*.

Drain the rigatoni and add it to the sauce. Mix well to combine.

Serve immediately, accompanied by a sprinkling of freshly grated parmigiano.

Makes 4 to 6 servings

SUGGESTED WINES
If you can find it, serve Chianti Classico Montagliari or Vignamaggio or Castello dei Rampolla, and choose the youngest vintage available.

Rigatoni con Prosciutto, Pomodoro, Panna e Peperoncino

Rigatoni with Prosciutto, Tomato, Cream, and Hot Chile Pepper

There are some places in this world where one feels instantly at home. Pippo lo Sgobbone, a trattoria on the outskirts of Roma, patronized mostly by Romans, is such a place. Our waiter, who had an abundance of personality, greeted us like long-lost friends and proceeded to tell us in no uncertain terms what we should eat. He brought us large plates of wonderful, spicy rigatoni, followed by the most succulent small lamb chops I have ever

TIPS

Putting the pasta in the skillet with the sauce instead of in a bowl is an old restaurant trick. In doing so, the pasta and the sauce will cook together briefly. The sauce will thicken and coat the pasta perfectly. It will also get to the table piping hot.

When a sauce is cooked in a large skillet over high heat, instead of in a saucepan, the liquid will evaporate faster and the sauce will cook and reduce much faster.

You might want to double the amount of this sauce and keep half in the refrigerator. I can assure you that after a day, you will be yearning again for this delicious pasta dish, and the sauce will be waiting for you in the refrigerator.

SUGGESTED WINES

For a traditional matching, serve Frascati wine. For a non-traditional, but equally good matching, choose a dry Riesling from the Alto Adige, Alsace, or Washington State.

had in my life. We drank local Frascati wine and struck a lively conversation with the people sitting at the next table. Toward the end of the meal, we were exchanging tastes of food and phone numbers and were showing photographs of our kids to each other! And because of all of this, the food tasted better and the evening was a memorable one.

4 tablespoons (½ stick) unsalted butter
4 ounces sliced prosciutto, cut into small, thin strips
4 cups canned imported Italian tomatoes with their juice, put through a strainer or food mill to remove the seeds
⅓ cup heavy cream
Salt to taste
Small pinch of dried red pepper flakes
1 pound rigatoni
½ cup freshly grated parmigiano

Melt the butter in a large skillet over medium-high heat. When it begins to foam, add the prosciutto and cook 30 to 40 seconds only. Add the tomatoes and cream, season with the salt and red pepper, and cook, uncovered, until the sauce has a medium-thick consistency, 7 to 8 minutes. Set aside.

While the sauce is cooking, bring a large pot of water to a boil. Add 1 tablespoon of salt and the rigatoni. Cook, uncovered, over high heat until the pasta is tender but still firm to the bite, *al dente*. Drain the pasta and add it to the sauce in the skillet. Mix it, over low heat, until the pasta is completely coated with the sauce. Serve at once, with a sprinkling of freshly grated parmigiano.

Makes 4 to 6 servings

Rigatoni alla Carbonara

Rigatoni with Prosciutto, Eggs, and Pecorino Cheese

Romans love their pastas with distinct, direct flavors. Some of these pasta dishes are so good, they have become famous not only in Italy, but also abroad. *Spaghetti alla carbonara* is such a dish. Here, the spaghetti is cooked and tossed together with pancetta that has been sautéed in oil and butter, then they are mixed quickly with raw eggs, parmigiano, and pecorino cheese and lots of black pepper.

At Angelino ai Fori in Roma, a trattoria facing the spectacular Roman Forum, I enjoyed a variation of this dish. Large rigatoni took the place of the spaghetti, and prosciutto was used instead of pancetta. Everything was tossed together with the cheese, eggs, and plenty of hot red chile pepper.

> 3 very fresh large eggs
> 2 tablespoons olive oil
> 2 tablespoons unsalted butter
> 2 cloves garlic, peeled
> 6 ounces prosciutto, cut into 4 thick slices and diced
> 1 pound rigatoni or penne
> Salt to taste
> Generous pinch of dried red pepper flakes
> ¼ cup freshly grated pecorino romano cheese
> ⅓ cup freshly grated parmigiano

Beat the eggs in a large, shallow serving dish that can later accommodate the pasta.

Heat the oil and the butter in a large skillet over medium heat. Add the garlic and cook, stirring, until the garlic begins to color. Discard the garlic. Add the prosciutto and stir for 10 to 15 seconds. Turn the heat off under the skillet.

Bring a large pot of water to a boil. Add 1 tablespoon of salt and the rigatoni. Cook, uncovered, over high heat until the pasta is tender but still firm to the bite, *al dente*. Drain the rigatoni and add it to the skillet. Season with the salt and red pepper flakes. Mix over low heat until the pasta is well coated with the sauce.

Put the rigatoni and its sauce in the bowl with the eggs. Add the pecorino and the parmigiano and mix quickly and thoroughly. Serve immediately with additional parmigiano if desired.

Makes 4 to 6 servings

SUGGESTED WINE
Again, this is a typical Roman dish that should be complemented by a typical Roman wine. Serve Frascati.

I Ravioli con lo Stracotto

Braised Beef Ravioli with Butter and Sage

A traditional dish of Northern Italy that is cooked in homes, restaurants, and *trattorie* alike is *stracotto* (beef braised in wine). The beef is lightly floured and browned in butter and oil. A mixture of diced vegetables is added and browned with the beef, then the wine is poured in and the beef is left to cook very slowly, three to four hours. At that point the meat is so tender that it can be cut with a fork. Any leftover meat becomes a delicious filling for pasta.

In Milano, at the well-known Antica Trattoria al Matarel, I had a plate of ravioli that were stuffed with the braised beef and topped only with sweet butter, fresh sage, and parmigiano. It was sheer perfection! Since then, I have made these ravioli regularly at my restaurant in Sacramento, and they are one of my best-selling pasta dishes.

For the filling
>   1 pound cooked Beef Braised in Wine (see pages 181–82) and ½ cup of the sauce
>   2 large eggs
>   1 cup freshly grated parmigiano
>   Salt and freshly ground black pepper to taste

For the ravioli
>   2 cups unbleached all-purpose flour
>   3 large eggs

To complete the dish
>   1 tablespoon salt
>   6 tablespoons (¾ stick) unsalted butter
>   ⅓ cup loosely packed shredded fresh sage leaves or 3 tablespoons chopped fresh parsley
>   1 cup freshly grated parmigiano

To prepare the filling, cut the beef into small pieces, then put it into a food processor and pulse the machine on and off until it is coarsely chopped. Add the sauce, eggs, and parmigiano and season with the salt and a bit of pepper. Pulse the machine on and off again to chop the meat a bit more and to mix it with the other ingredients. Do not process the meat too long; it should still retain a bit of coarse consistency. (The meat can also be chopped by hand using a large knife.) At this point the mixture should be firm but moist. Place it in a bowl and set aside until you are ready to use it.

Prepare the dough for the ravioli, using the proportions given here, as instructed on pages 75–76. Roll out the dough and trim so it has straight edges and is 6 inches wide. Starting at the top of the sheet, center large tablespoons of the filling on the pasta sheet, spacing the mounds 3 inches apart from each other, until you reach the middle of the sheet. Fold the sheet in half over the filling. (If the sheet of pasta is quite long, you might want to cut its length into two to three parts for easier folding.) Press the edges together firmly to seal. Cut between the fillings in a straight line with a scalloped pastry wheel and press the cut edges of ravioli firmly to seal.

Cover a large tray or a cookie sheet with a kitchen towel. Sprinkle the towel with some flour and place the ravioli in a single layer over it. Use another cookie sheet or tray if you run out of room.

Bring a large pot of water to a boil. Add the salt and ravioli. Cook, uncovered, over high heat, until the pasta is tender but still firm to the bite, *al dente*, about 2 or 3 minutes.

While the pasta is cooking, melt the butter in a large skillet over medium heat. When the butter foams, add the sage and stir for 15 to 20 seconds. Drain the pasta and put it in the skillet. Add ⅓ cup of the parmigiano and season lightly with salt. Coat the ravioli with the mixture quickly over low heat and serve at once, with the remaining parmigiano.

Makes 6 to 8 servings

TIPS

༚ *The ravioli will keep well in the refrigerator for about 24 hours. Never cover the ravioli with plastic wrap. It will make the pasta sticky. It is not necessary to cover the ravioli with a towel.*

༚ *Even though ravioli and most other stuffed pasta can be frozen, I never freeze mine, because it changes the consistency and therefore, the quality of the pasta.*

༚ *If the ravioli look a bit dry when tossed in the butter, add a few tablespoons of the pasta cooking water and mix quickly over low heat.*

SUGGESTED WINES
A rich, buttery, and moderately old California Chardonnay would go well with the dish and, if available, a Ligurian red such as Lupi Rossese di Dolceacqua would be very traditional.

Ravioli con Sugo di Carne

Ravioli with Meat Sauce

There must be hundreds of variations for filling and topping ravioli. These small "pillows" of freshly made pasta can be stuffed with cheese, meat, vegetables, fish, and, often, with a combination of all of the above.

The dish comes from The Pantheon, an upscale trattoria that faces the majestic Pantheon in Roma. It is a filling dish, since the ravioli are stuffed with a wonderful meat mixture and topped with a sauce of vegetables, sausage, veal, porcini mushrooms, and tomatoes. Fortunato, the owner of the trattoria, allowed me in the kitchen when the chef was preparing these ravioli. It was almost lunchtime and the chef was rolling out pasta with fast determination in a few square feet of crowded countertop, filling, folding, and cutting the dough into chubby large ravioli.

For the filling
¼ cup olive oil
½ medium-size onion, finely diced
½ small carrot, finely diced
½ stalk celery, finely diced
1 pound chicken breast, boned, skinned, and ground
1½ cups dry white wine
Salt and freshly ground black pepper to taste
2 small eggs
2 tablespoons chopped fresh parsley
½ cup freshly grated parmigiano

For the sauce
1 ounce dried porcini mushrooms (see page 15), soaked in 2 cups lukewarm water for 20 minutes
2 tablespoons unsalted butter
2 tablespoons olive oil
½ medium-size onion, finely diced
1 small carrot, finely diced
½ pound ground veal

½ pound mild Italian sausage, casings removed and finely
   chopped
1 cup dry red wine
3 cups canned imported Italian plum tomatoes with their
   juice, put through a strainer or food mill to remove
   the seeds
Salt and freshly ground black pepper to taste
1 cup freshly grated parmigiano

For the ravioli
2 cups unbleached all-purpose flour
3 large eggs

TIP

∽ *To simplify this time-consuming dish, divide it into two
stages:*
*1. Prepare the filling and sauce
for the ravioli a day or two
ahead and keep it tightly
wrapped in the refrigerator.*
*2. Prepare and stuff the pasta
the day you are going to serve it
and keep it refrigerated until
you are ready to cook it.*

To prepare the filling, heat the oil in a large skillet over medium heat. Add the onion, carrot, and celery and cook, stirring, until they are lightly golden and soft, 4 to 5 minutes. Add the chicken, raise the heat to high, and cook, stirring, until the meat is lightly colored. Add the wine and season with salt and pepper. Cook until the wine is completely evaporated, 2 to 3 minutes. Put the mixture in a bowl and let cool to room temperature.

Put the cooled mixture in a food processor and add the eggs, parsley, and parmigiano. Pulse the machine on and off a few times to chop the meat a bit more and to mix it with the eggs and cheese. Do not process the meat too long; it should still retain a bit of a coarse consistency. Put the mixture back into the bowl, cover it tightly, and refrigerate until ready to use.

To prepare the sauce, strain the mushrooms and reserve the soaking water. Rinse the mushrooms well under cold running water. Line a strainer with two paper towels and strain the mushroom soaking water into a bowl to get rid of the sandy deposits. Set aside.

Heat the butter and oil together in a large skillet over medium heat. When the butter foams, add the onion and carrot and cook, stirring, until the vegetables are lightly golden and soft, 4 to 5 minutes. Add the veal and sausage and cook, stirring, until the meat is lightly colored. Add the mushrooms and wine, raise the heat to high, and cook until the wine is almost all evaporated, about 2 minutes. Stir in the tomatoes and 1 cup of the reserved porcini soaking water. Season with salt and pepper. Cover the skillet, reduce the heat to medium-low, and let simmer for 45 minutes to 1 hour, until the sauce has a medium-thick consistency. If the sauce is too thick, add a little more of the porcini soaking water. Set aside until ready to use.

Prepare the dough for the ravioli, using the proportions given here, according to the instructions on pages 75–76. Roll out the dough and trim so it has straight edges and is 6 inches wide. Starting at the top of the sheet, center large tablespoons of the filling on the pasta sheet, spacing the mounds 3 inches apart from each other until you reach the middle of the sheet. Fold the sheet in half over the filling. (If the sheet of pasta is quite long, you might want to cut its length into two to three parts for easier folding.) Press the edges together firmly to seal. Cut between the fillings in a straight line with a scalloped pastry wheel and press the cut edges of the ravioli firmly to seal.

Cover a large tray or a cookie sheet with a kitchen towel. Sprinkle the towel with some flour and place the ravioli in a single layer over it. Use another tray or cookie sheet if you run out of room.

Bring a large pot of water to a boil. Add 1 tablespoon of salt and the ravioli. Cook, uncovered, over high heat until the pasta is tender but still firm to the bite, *al dente*, about 2 to 3 minutes. Meanwhile, reheat the sauce over medium heat. Drain the pasta and put it in a large, warm bowl. Add half of the sauce and ½ cup of the parmigiano and mix gently to combine. Spoon the ravioli onto serving dishes, top with the remaining sauce and parmigiano, and serve at once.

Makes 6 to 8 servings

SUGGESTED WINES
This relatively rustic dish calls for a fresh, young, tasty red wine such as a California Zinfandel or Gamay, or an Italian wine such as a Merlot from the Veneto or a Dolcetto or Barbera d'Asti from Piemonte.

Pasta al Forno con la Besciamella

~~~~~~

Pasta Baked with Béchamel and Parmigiano

My mother was a very traditional regional cook. One of the dishes she used to make in wintertime was a hearty baked preparation. She would roll out a large sheet of spinach pasta, cut it into tagliatelle, and bake them with a velvety nutmeg-scented béchamel, parmigiano, and butter. It was terrific. Years ago I found a version of this dish at a little trattoria in Modena that was run by two not very friendly sisters. Trattoria Cervetta made this dish with large, chewy rigatoni that were golden and crunchy when they came out of the oven, oozing béchamel, butter, and melted parmigiano.

This is a simple, inexpensive dish to prepare. It can feed a few or a crowd and can be prepared completely ahead of time and baked at the last moment.

For the béchamel sauce
   3 cups milk
   6 tablespoons (¾ stick) unsalted butter
   5 tablespoons unbleached all-purpose flour
   Salt to taste

To complete the dish
   1 pound rigatoni
   ¼ teaspoon freshly grated nutmeg, optional
   ¾ cup freshly grated parmigiano
   3 tablespoons unsalted butter, cut into small pieces

To prepare the béchamel sauce, heat the milk in a small saucepan over low heat. Melt the butter in a medium-size saucepan over medium heat. When the butter foams, add the flour. Lower the heat to medium-low and stir the mixture with a wooden spoon. Cook and stir about 2 minutes, without letting the flour brown.

Remove the saucepan from the heat and add the milk all at once. Mix energetically to prevent lumps. Put the saucepan back over low heat, season with salt, and cook gently, mixing constantly, until the sauce has a medium-thick consistency, 3 to 5 minutes. If the sauce is too thick, stir in a bit more milk. If the sauce is too thin, cook it a little longer. Cover the pan and set aside until ready to use.

Preheat the oven to 375°F. Butter a baking pan generously. Bring a large pot of water to a boil. Add 1 tablespoon of salt and the rigatoni. Cook, uncovered, over high heat for 7 to 8 minutes. (The rigatoni should still be quite firm because they will finish cooking in the oven.)

Drain the pasta and place it in the baking dish. Season the béchamel with the nutmeg and mix to combine. Add the béchamel to the pasta and mix well. Sprinkle the pasta with the parmigiano and dot with the butter. Bake until the cheese is melted and the pasta has a nice golden color, 12 to 15 minutes. Serve hot.

Makes 4 to 6 servings

SUGGESTED WINES
This dish would be a good foil for a great red wine such as old Barolo or Barbaresco, especially if nothing else follows the pasta. As a pasta course with meat following, serve a young Barolo or Barbaresco.

Cannelloni di Ricotta e Spinaci al Forno

Baked Cannelloni with Spinach and Ricotta

Evangelista is an upscale trattoria in Roma that, in spite of its beautiful interior, serves traditional Roman food with a few dishes from the neighboring regions. The night I was there I was served a splendid cannelloni dish, stuffed with that superlative Roman ricotta and fresh spinach. The pasta for the cannelloni was tender and delicate and the tomato topping light and fresh.

In spite of the several steps needed to produce this dish, cannelloni is perhaps one of the easiest stuffed pasta dishes to prepare, with the added bonus that it can be prepared completely in advance.

Prepare the tomato sauce and the filling a day ahead. Make the pasta and assemble the dish early in the day you plan to serve the cannelloni—then the only thing left to do at dinnertime is the baking.

For the filling

    1 pound fresh spinach, thoroughly washed and stems removed, or one 10-ounce package frozen spinach, thawed

    2 cups water

    Pinch of salt

    1 tablespoon unsalted butter

    ¼ cup heavy cream

    1 cup freshly grated parmigiano

    1 pound whole milk ricotta

    ½ teaspoon freshly grated nutmeg

For the cannelloni

    1¼ cups unbleached all-purpose flour

    2 large eggs

To complete the dish

    3 tablespoons olive oil

    2 cloves garlic, peeled

    3 cups canned imported Italian tomatoes with their juice, put through a strainer or food mill to remove the seeds

    Salt to taste

    12 thin slices mozzarella (about 10 ounces)

To prepare the filling, place the spinach in a large saucepan with the water and salt. Cook, uncovered, over medium heat until tender, 2 to 3 minutes, or according to package instructions if you are using frozen spinach. Drain the spinach well, squeeze all the water out, and chop it fine. If you are using a food processor, make sure not to puree the spinach.

Heat the butter in a medium-size skillet. Add the cream, spinach, and ½ cup of the parmigiano. Cook over medium heat, stirring, until the spinach is completely coated with the cream and parmigiano, 1 to 2 minutes.

In a large bowl or in the bowl of an electric mixer, combine the buttered spinach with the ricotta, nutmeg, and remaining parmigiano. Season with salt and mix until well combined. Cover the bowl and set aside until ready to use.

Prepare the pasta dough according to the instructions on pages 75–76. Cut off a small piece of dough about the size of an egg and work it through the pasta machine until you have a thin sheet of pasta. Cut the sheet of pasta into 3- by 4-inch rectangles. Roll out the remaining dough.

Bring a large pot of water to a boil and add 1 tablespoon of salt. Drop 6 or 7 pieces of pasta into the water and cook about 20 to 25 seconds, stirring. Scoop out the pasta with a large strainer and place in a large bowl of very cold water to stop the cooking. Remove the pasta immediately and spread it on kitchen towels. Pat dry with another towel. Cook all the pasta pieces in this manner.

Lay the dried pasta on a work surface and place 2 heaping tablespoons of the filling down the center of each rectangle. Fold the two opposite edges of the pasta over the filling, loosely, to make a tube.

Butter a large baking dish generously, and put in the cannelloni. Cover with plastic wrap and set aside or refrigerate until you prepare the tomato sauce.

Heat the oil in a medium-size saucepan over medium heat. Add the garlic and cook, stirring occasionally, until they are golden brown. With a wooden spoon, remove and discard the garlic. Add the tomatoes and season with salt. Cook, uncovered, 8 to 10 minutes, stirring a few times.

Preheat the oven to 400°F. Spread a bit of tomato sauce over the cannelloni and top each *cannellone* with two slices of mozzarella. Bake until the mozzarella is melted and the cannelloni are lightly golden, 10 to 15 minutes. Serve hot.

Makes 6 servings

SUGGESTED WINES

The acidity of the tomatoes and the "milky" taste of the cheese with the slightly metallic taste of the spinach require a light, aromatic red wine. A young Chianti or a California Zinfandel would be a good choice.

GNOCCHI, RISOTTO, AND POLENTA

We all know that the cooking of Italy is instantly identified with its first courses. While pasta is universally known and loved, and risotto begins to be appreciated and understood by Americans, gnocchi have yet to make a culinary statement in this country. And yet, almost every region of Italy has a dumpling of its own.

Gnocchi come in different shapes, sizes, and flavors. They are made with potatoes, ricotta, spinach and ricotta, semolina, bread, squash, and prunes, just to mention a few. They can be served with sauces or in broth. They can be round, flat, or oblong. They might have ridges or might be smooth, and they can be dressed with an incredible variety of sauces. Many regions claim to be the "inventor" of the gnocchi, but regardless of where they were invented, gnocchi are an important part of the culinary tradition of Italy.

I grew up with gnocchi, made mostly with potatoes or sometimes with ricotta. During the Second World War, they were "fillers." A few potatoes and a bit of flour was all that was needed to make a filling, delicious meal. Today gnocchi is one of those dishes that you need to seek out because, like most traditional handmade dishes, it is beginning to disappear.

In Italy, old potatoes are used for potato gnocchi because their drier, floury content makes for lighter, not gummy, gnocchi. Idahoes or russets are best. Do not use "new" potatoes for this dish.

Most recipes for potato gnocchi call for boiling the potatoes. Several years ago, I picked up a wonderful trick from a Florentine friend of mine who bakes the potatoes instead of boiling them. The result is lighter gnocchi, because the potatoes do not absorb unnecessary water and, therefore need less flour. (You will also have one less pot to clean!)

If you have never made gnocchi before, try a small batch first. "Play" with the dough. Knead, roll, and shape the gnocchi until you get the hang of it.

I have compiled a short list of tips that should help you through your first batch of homemade gnocchi.

Tips

The flour. When you add the flour to the other ingredients, always start with a bit less than the recipe suggests. You can always add more, but you can't take it out once it is incorporated into the dough.

The dough. For any kind of gnocchi, the dough should not be kneaded too long (see the individual recipes); the longer the dough is kneaded, the more flour it will absorb. The result will be heavier gnocchi.

The eggs. There is no doubt that eggless gnocchi are lighter. They are, however, considerably trickier to keep together. After you have made gnocchi several times and feel comfortable, then you might want to try the eggless version (this applies only to potato gnocchi).

Testing the gnocchi. Before you prepare a whole batch of gnocchi, cook one to determine its consistency. If it is too soft or it falls apart in the water, you must knead in a bit more flour. If the dumpling is heavy and chewy, you have probably added too much flour.

To boil the gnocchi. Use a large pot with plenty of water (5 to 6 quarts for 4 servings) so that they won't stick together.

Freezing. Even though frozen gnocchi are available on the market, I *NEVER* freeze mine. Frozen gnocchi, when cooked, are mushy and quite unappetizing.

And finally, let me assure you that homemade gnocchi are much easier to prepare than homemade pasta, and once you get the hang of it, you will breeze through it and have a lot of fun.

Gnocchi di Patate

Basic Potato Dumplings

> 4 medium-size Idaho or russet potatoes (about 2 pounds)
> 1 tablespoon salt
> 1 large egg yolk, lightly beaten
> 1½ to 2 cups unbleached all-purpose flour

Preheat the oven to 375°F. Wash and dry the potatoes. With a knife, make a long incision in the potatoes lengthwise, about ½ inch deep. Put the potatoes in the oven and bake until they are tender, 45 to 55 minutes. When cool enough to handle, peel the potatoes and puree them through a food mill or a potato ricer directly into a large bowl. Add the salt, egg yolk, and 1½ cups of the flour. Mix it all together with your hands until the dough begins to stick together.

Transfer the mixture to a wooden board and knead lightly, gradually adding the remaining flour if the dough sticks heavily to the board and to your hands. (The making of the dough should take no longer than 4 to 5 minutes.) The dough is ready when it is soft, pliable, and just a bit sticky.

Cut the dough into pieces the size of an orange. Flour your hands lightly. Using both your hands, roll out each piece of dough with a light back-and-forth motion into a roll about the thickness of your thumb. Cut each roll into 1-inch pieces.

Hold a fork with its tines against a work board, the curved part of the fork facing away from you. Starting from the outside bottom of the curve, press each piece of dough with your index finger firmly upward along the length of the tines. Let the gnoc-

❈ ❈ ❈

VARIATION

For eggless gnocchi, simply omit the egg yolk, and follow the recipe as instructed above.

chi fall back onto the surface. Roll out the remaining pieces of dough. Place the gnocchi on a lightly floured platter or baking sheet; they can be cooked immediately or be kept in the refrigerator uncovered for several hours or overnight, until ready to cook.

Makes 4 servings

Gnocchi di Patate con la Fontina

Potato Gnocchi with Fontina Cheese

Fontina is a delicious Italian cheese, produced in the Val d'Aosta, an autonomous region bordering the Piemonte region. Besides being a table cheese, this whole cow's milk cheese is used quite often in cooking. One of the best-known dishes often found in the *trattorie* of the region is *gnocchi alla bava* (gnocchi with fontina). Sweet mountain butter is heated with chunks of fontina which, upon melting, are mixed with homemade potato dumplings. The result is a robust, yet delicate dish.

> 1 recipe Gnocchi di Patate (see above)
> 1 tablespoon salt
> 4 tablespoons (½ stick) unsalted butter
> ¼ pound Italian fontina cheese, diced
> 2 tablespoons chopped fresh parsley

Prepare the gnocchi and set aside. Bring a large pot of water to a boil. Add the gnocchi and salt. Cook, uncovered, over high heat until the gnocchi rise to the surface of the water, about 1 to 2 minutes.

While the gnocchi are cooking, melt the butter in a large skillet over medium heat. Remove the gnocchi with a slotted spoon or a skimmer and place the gnocchi in the skillet, season lightly with salt, then add the diced fontina and parsley. Mix gently over low heat for a few seconds, until the cheese begins to melt and the gnocchi are well coated. Stir in a few tablespoons of the gnocchi cooking water if the sauce seems too dry. Serve immediately.

Makes 4 servings

SUGGESTED WINES

Fontina is an aromatic yet flavorful cheese. Use light, aromatic red wines such as Spanna or, when you can find it, the incomparable Luigi Ferrando Carema.

I Gnocchi di Patate con la Salsa di Leonida

Potato Gnocchi with Leonida's Sauce

At Leonida in Bologna, I had this tasty sauce served over spinach tagliatelle. It was so good and so simple to prepare that I serve it also over other types of pasta and on gnocchi.

> 1 recipe Gnocchi di Patate (see pages 133–34)
> 4 tablespoons (½ stick) unsalted butter
> 1 small onion, finely minced
> 1 clove garlic, finely minced
> ¼ pound pancetta, cut into 4 thick slices, diced
> 1 cup dry white wine
> 3 tablespoons tomato paste mixed with 2 cups chicken broth, homemade (see pages 54–55) or canned
> Salt and freshly ground black pepper to taste
> 2 tablespoons heavy cream
> ½ teaspoon freshly grated nutmeg
> 1 cup freshly grated parmigiano

Prepare the gnocchi and set aside. Heat the butter in a large skillet over medium heat. Add the onion and cook 3 to 4 minutes, stirring a few times. Add the garlic and pancetta and cook, stirring, until the pancetta is lightly golden, 2 to 3 minutes. Stir in the wine and cook until the wine is reduced by half, about 1 minute. Add the tomato paste and broth and season with the salt and a pinch of pepper. Cook, uncovered, 7 to 8 minutes, stirring a few times. During the last minute or so of cooking, add the cream and nutmeg and stir once or twice.

While the sauce is cooking, bring a large pot of water to a boil. Add 1 tablespoon of salt and the gnocchi. Cook uncovered, over high heat, until the gnocchi rise to the surface of the water, 1 to 2 minutes. Remove the gnocchi with a slotted spoon or a skimmer, draining off the excess water against the side of the pot. Place the gnocchi in the skillet with the sauce and mix briefly over low heat. Serve at once with a generous sprinkling of freshly grated parmigiano.

Makes 4 servings

SUGGESTED WINE
Try this dish with a light red wine such as Valpolicella.

Gnocchi di Patate alla Sorrentina

Potato Gnocchi with Fresh Tomatoes and Mozzarella

When I returned home from my last trip to Italy to research this book, I had with me a carry-on bag full of notes and recipes that I had collected, names and addresses of *trattorie*, and people I had met. Some places and dishes stuck out in my mind with great clarity. As I was munching on some kind of airline lasagne, I thought nostalgically about one of the most appetizing dishes I had enjoyed in Italy.

It was at Salvatore alla Riviera in Napoli that I was served *gnocchi alla Sorrentina*, named after the picturesque town of Sorrento, halfway between Napoli and Salerno. The dish looked like a still-life painting, with the colors of the Italian flag. The plump white gnocchi had been tossed together with very fragrant fresh tomato fillets, cubes of delicate buffalo mozzarella, and aromatic fresh oregano. The mozzarella was soft and half melted and laced the gnocchi voluptuously. It was pure, simple Italian food at its best.

1 recipe Gnocchi di Patate (see pages 133–34)
¼ cup olive oil
3 cloves garlic, finely chopped
2 pounds juicy, ripe Roma or pear tomatoes, peeled (see page 16), seeded, and diced
Salt and freshly ground black pepper to taste
4 ounces whole milk mozzarella, diced (see page 9)
¼ cup loosely packed fresh oregano leaves or basil leaves, finely shredded

Prepare the gnocchi and set aside.

Heat the oil in a large skillet over medium heat. Add the garlic and cook, stirring, until the garlic begins to color, less than a minute. Add the diced tomatoes and season with salt and several grinds of pepper. Raise the heat under the skillet to high and cook the tomatoes, stirring, until the tomatoes lose their excessive watery juices, 3 to 4 minutes.

While the sauce is cooking, bring a large pot of water to a boil. Add 1 tablespoon of salt and the gnocchi. Cook, uncovered,

NOTE OF INTEREST
The wider the surface of the skillet, the faster the moisture from the tomatoes will evaporate.

over high heat until the gnocchi rise to the surface of the water, 1 to 2 minutes. Remove the gnocchi with a slotted spoon or a skimmer, draining off the excess water against the side of the pot. Place the gnocchi in the skillet with the sauce. Add the mozzarella and mix gently over medium heat until the mozzarella begins to melt, about 1 minute. Add the fresh oregano, stir once or twice, and serve at once.

Makes 4 servings

SUGGESTED WINES

Nothing accompanies this better than a light Rosé such as Ravello Rosé of Caruso, or a dry Vin Gris–style Pinot Noir from California.

Gnocchi di Ricotta e Spinaci al Burro e Parmigiano

Ricotta and Spinach Gnocchi with Butter and Parmigiano

My mother's cooking was the simple, delicious fare of Bologna. She was a master at pasta making, which she would roll out effortlessly with a long rolling pin. She was also the best gnocchi maker I have ever come across in my life. Her hands would slide back and forth on a long, thin roll of dough and, in no time at all, there were enough gnocchi on the board to feed an army.

I was blessed with these culinary head starts, even though at a young age I didn't want or care to cook. So when I come across a plate of good homemade pasta or gnocchi, I know it instantly.

I tasted these little spinach-ricotta dumplings at Dei Corrieri Trattoria in Parma, the charming city which supplies Italy and the world with the great parmigiano-reggiano and prosciutto di Parma. At Dei Corrieri, the gnocchi were made without the "ridges" so typical of most gnocchi. They were served only with sweet butter and, of course, a generous sprinkling of parmigiano.

When I prepare them at my restaurant, I sometimes add strips of prosciutto or pancetta, which I quickly toss in hot butter or I stir into the butter a bit of fresh sage. Nothing gastronomically earth-shattering, but this dish is so deliciously addictive that you will want to prepare it on a regular basis.

For the gnocchi

> ½ pound whole milk ricotta
> 1¼ cups unbleached all-purpose flour
> 2 small eggs, thoroughly beaten in a small bowl and mixed with 2 tablespoons very finely chopped cooked fresh or frozen spinach
> ½ cup freshly grated parmigiano
> ½ teaspoon finely ground nutmeg
> 2 tablespoons salt

For the sauce

> 4 to 5 tablespoons unsalted butter
> Salt to taste
> 1 cup freshly grated parmigiano

In a large bowl, combine all the gnocchi ingredients, except ¼ cup of the flour and 1 tablespoon of the salt. Mix with your hands until everything sticks together in a sort of dough.

Put the mixture on a wooden board and knead lightly for 2 to 3 minutes, gradually adding the remaining flour if the dough sticks heavily to the board and to your hands. When the dough is soft, pliable, and just a bit sticky, divide it into pieces the size of an orange.

Using both your hands, roll out each piece of dough with a light back-and-forth motion into a roll about the thickness of your little finger. Cut each roll into ½-inch pieces and place the gnocchi on a lightly floured platter or baking sheet. The gnocchi can be cooked immediately or be held in the refrigerator, uncovered, for several hours or overnight. (Ricotta gnocchi can be held a longer in the refrigerator than potato gnocchi without losing any of their wonderful texture.)

Bring a large pot of water to a boil. Add the remaining tablespoon of salt and the gnocchi. Cook, uncovered, over high heat until the gnocchi rise to the surface of the water, about 1 to 2 minutes.

While the gnocchi are cooking, melt the butter over medium heat. Remove the gnocchi with a slotted spoon or a skimmer, draining off the excess water against the side of the pot. Place the gnocchi in the skillet with the butter, season with salt, and add ⅓ cup of the parmigiano. Stir gently over medium heat until the gnocchi are well coated with the butter and parmigiano, less than a minute. Serve at once with the rest of parmigiano.

Makes 6 servings

SUGGESTED WINES
Try a nice Albana di Romagna, or a new California label, Bonny Doon's Cà del Solo Malvasia from California.

Gnocchi di Patate al Pesto e Pinoli Tostati

Potato Gnocchi with Pesto and Toasted Pine Nuts

They say that the Ligurian basil is the best in the world, and perhaps that is true because I cannot explain why a sauce that I have made a thousand times tasted so much better in Liguria. Perhaps it was the basil, or the light Ligurian olive oil, or the experienced cooks who make the pesto on a daily basis, mixing the various ingredients into a perfect balance of flavors.

Pasta or gnocchi with pesto is quintessentially Ligurian. This version comes from Bruxiaboschi, a country trattoria in the small town of San Desiderio, not too far from Genova.

    1 recipe Gnocchi di Patate (see pages 133–34)
    ⅓ cup pine nuts
    1 tablespoon salt
    ½ cup Pesto Sauce (see pages 118–19)
    ½ cup freshly grated parmigiano

Prepare the gnocchi and set aside.

Preheat the oven to 375°F. Place the pine nuts on an ungreased cookie sheet and toast in the oven until lightly golden, 1 to 2 minutes. Set aside.

Bring a large pot of water to a boil. Add the salt and gnocchi. Cook, uncovered, over high heat until the gnocchi rise to the surface of the water, about 1 to 2 minutes.

While the gnocchi are cooking, combine in a large bowl the pesto and ⅓ cup of the gnocchi cooking water.

Remove the gnocchi with a slotted spoon or a skimmer, draining off the excess water against the side of the pot. Place the gnocchi in the bowl with the pesto, the toasted pine nuts, and the grated parmigiano. Mix well and serve at once.

Makes 4 servings

SUGGESTED WINES
A Vermentino or Cinqueterre from Italy or a light-bodied Chardonnay from California such as Parducci are perfect with this dish.

Gnocchi di Patate con Sugo di Pesce Veloce

Potato Gnocchi with Quick Fish Sauce

Antico Pizzo is a small trattoria hidden behind the popular Rialto fish market in Venezia. I fell in love with this little place the moment I walked in. It was not the decor, or lack of it, that won me over. It was the delicious aroma that came from the kitchen and the chatters of the animated patrons who spoke real Venetian. And, in a city bursting at the seams with tourists from all over the world, this was truly a find. Then the food arrived. Small, featherlike gnocchi topped with a divine fish sauce. Then an entree of deep-fried shellfish that too quickly disappeared from my sight, and lastly, delicious Venetian biscotti with a double espresso. I sat there, trying to take notes of all I had eaten, blissfully satisfied, with a smile on my face. Today Antico Pizzo is only a memory . . . until I visit it again on my next trip to Venezia.

1 recipe Gnocchi di Patate (see pages 133–34)
¼ cup olive oil
2 cloves garlic, finely minced
2 tablespoons chopped fresh parsley
10 to 12 fresh sage leaves, chopped (see note)
½ pound mixed fish fillets, such as orange roughy, sea bass, tuna, and halibut, finely diced (about the size of a large pea)
¼ cup brandy
2 cups imported canned Italian tomatoes with their juice, put through a strainer or food mill to remove the seeds
2 tablespoons heavy cream
Freshly ground black pepper to taste
1 tablespoon salt

Prepare the gnocchi and set aside.

Heat the oil in a large skillet over medium heat. Add the garlic, parsley, and sage and cook, stirring, less than a minute. Before the garlic turns golden, add the cut-up fish. Cook, stirring, less than 1 minute. Add the brandy and cook 30 to 40

NOTE OF INTEREST

The taste and aroma of fresh sage is so deliciously distinctive that, if unavailable, I prefer to omit it rather than add dried sage. In that case, use a little more parsley or, if you prefer, a bit of fresh basil.

seconds, until it is almost all reduced. Stir in the tomatoes and cream and season. Cook, stirring, 4 to 5 minutes.

While the sauce is cooking, bring a large pot of water to a boil. Add the salt and gnocchi. Cook, uncovered, over high heat until the gnocchi rise to the surface of the water, about 1 to 2 minutes. Remove the gnocchi with a slotted spoon or a skimmer, draining off the excess water against the side of the pot. Place the gnocchi in the skillet with the sauce and mix gently and quickly over low heat until the gnocchi are well coated with the sauce. Serve at once.

Makes 4 servings

SUGGESTED WINES
A typical accompaniment to this dish would be an uncomplicated dry white wine such as Soave, Lugana, or Bianco Di Custoza.

Gnocchi di Patate allo Storione Affumicato e Rucola

Potato Gnocchi with Smoked Sturgeon and Arugula

Years ago as a cooking teacher, I used to tell my students that it would take them longer to prepare a frozen dinner than to cook a great plate of pasta from scratch. Once you have the ingredients you need at hand, most Italian sauces for pasta and gnocchi can be done in the time it takes for the water to boil, as the dishes in this chapter prove.

This is a somewhat refined and tasty preparation which combines red onion, cream, smoked sturgeon, arugula, and delicious Gewürztraminer wine in an unusual matching of tastes. It is the creation of the fancy Osteria Trattoria Laguna, located in the small town of Cavallino near Venezia.

NOTE OF INTEREST
This dish does not call for cheese so that the flavor of the smoked sturgeon can be fully savored.

1 recipe Gnocchi di Patate (see pages 133–34)
4 tablespoons (½ stick) unsalted butter
1 small red onion, very finely minced
1 cup Gewürztraminer or any good, dry, aromatic white wine
¼ cup heavy cream
Ground white pepper to taste
4 ounces smoked sturgeon, cut into thin strips
1 ounce arugula leaves, cut into thin strips
1 tablespoon salt

Prepare the gnocchi and set aside.

Melt the butter in a large skillet over medium heat. Add the onion and cook, stirring, until it is pale yellow and completely wilted, 6 to 7 minutes. Add the wine and cream, and season with a bit of white pepper. (Do not use salt, since the sturgeon is already quite salty.) Cook, stirring, until the sauce begins to thicken, 2 to 3 minutes. Add the sturgeon and the arugula and mix once or twice.

While the sauce is cooking, bring a large pot of water to a boil. Add the salt and the gnocchi. Cook, uncovered, over high heat until the gnocchi rise to the surface of the water, about 1 to 2 minutes. Remove the gnocchi with a slotted spoon or a skimmer, draining off the excess water against the side of the pot. Place the gnocchi in the skillet with the sauce and stir briefly over medium heat, until the gnocchi are well coated with the sauce. Serve at once.

Makes 4 servings

SUGGESTED WINES
Try a Traminer Aromatico (Gewürztraminer) from a good producer in the Alto Adige or Collio area of Friuli. From California a dry Riesling such as Trefethen or Renaissance would work splendidly.

Gnocchi di Patate con Ragù alla Romagnola

Potato Gnocchi with Meat Sauce

NOTE OF INTEREST
Freeze any meat sauce that is left—it will last two or three months. It can be tossed later with noodles, penne, or rice.

There are eateries where we feel more at ease with ourselves and more comfortable with everything around us. Boni, an old-fashioned trattoria in the center of Bologna that serves the traditional food of the area, makes me feel that way. Perhaps it is because the aromas from the kitchen are the ones dear to me, or because this little trattoria has a sense of place and a warm soul.

The last time I was there I ate a plate of homemade gnocchi, light and fluffy, topped by a delicious traditional meat sauce that was so good, it could have been prepared by my mother.

1 recipe Gnocchi di Patate (see pages 133–34)

4 tablespoons (½ stick) unsalted butter

1 small onion, finely minced

1 small carrot, finely minced

2 tablespoons chopped fresh parsley

10 ounces ground veal

¼ pound sliced prosciutto, finely diced

½ cup dry Marsala wine, preferably imported such as Florio

3 cups canned imported tomatoes with their juice, put through a strainer or food mill to remove the seeds

1 cup chicken broth, homemade (see pages 54–55) or canned

¼ teaspoon freshly grated nutmeg

Freshly ground black pepper to taste

2 tablespoons heavy cream

1 tablespoon salt

1 cup freshly grated parmigiano

Prepare the gnocchi and set aside.

Melt the butter in a medium-size saucepan over medium heat. Add the onion, carrot, and parsley and cook, stirring a few times, until the onion is pale yellow and soft, 4 to 5 minutes. Add the veal and prosciutto. Cook, stirring, until the meat is no longer pink, 2 to 3 minutes. Add the Marsala and cook until it is almost all reduced, 2 to 3 minutes. Stir in the tomatoes, broth, and nutmeg, and season. Cook, uncovered, over low heat 40 to 45 minutes, until the sauce has a medium-thick consistency. During the last few minutes of cooking, add the cream and stir once or twice.

While the sauce is cooking, bring a large pot of water to a boil. Add the salt and gnocchi. Cook, uncovered, over high heat until the gnocchi rise to the surface of the water, about 1 to 2 minutes. Remove the gnocchi with a slotted spoon or a skimmer, draining off the excess water against the side of the pot. Place the gnocchi in a warm serving bowl and add about half of the sauce and ½ cup of the parmigiano. Mix well and quickly. Serve at once topped by additional sauce or parmigiano if desired.

Makes 4 servings

SUGGESTED WINE

A light-bodied red wine such as a Chianti Classico would work very well with this dish.

Gnocchi di Pane

Bread, Parmigiano, and Smoked Ham Gnocchi

Bread gnocchi is a specialty of Trentino-Alto Adige where they are called *canederli*. This dish, of Austro-Hungarian derivation, can also be found in one form or another in the neighboring Friuli-Venezia Giulia region. Gabriella Gregori, a one-hundred-year-old trattoria in the town of Padriciano outside Trieste, makes them with milk-soaked bread, smoked prosciutto (speck), parsley, and parmigiano. This is a humble, filling dish, which has a unique texture and a wholesome, delicious flavor. The gnocchi can be topped with a meat sauce or some of the sauce left over from making ossobuco (see pages 203–204).

My favorite way of preparing these gnocchi, however, is to dress them simply with butter, fresh sage, and parmigiano, so that the wonderful taste of the gnocchi will not be altered.

For the gnocchi
1 large loaf Italian bread, about 1 pound, 1 to 2 days old
2 to 3 cups milk (see note)
1 large egg
2 tablespoons finely chopped fresh parsley
4 ounces speck (see page 11) or prosciutto, cut into 4 to 5 thick slices and very finely diced
1 cup freshly grated parmigiano
1 cup unbleached all-purpose flour, spread evenly over a sheet of aluminum foil
1 tablespoon salt

For the sauce
4 to 5 tablespoons unsalted butter
8 to 10 fresh sage leaves, finely shredded, or 2 tablespoons chopped fresh parsley
About ½ cup freshly grated parmigiano

NOTE OF INTEREST
If necessary, low-fat milk can be substituted for whole milk.

Cut the bread into 4 to 5 thick slices and remove the crust. Break the bread into pieces, place in a medium-size bowl, and cover completely with the milk. Let it soak for 15 minutes.

Strain the milk and squeeze the bread dry with your hands, trying to remove as much milk as possible. Put the bread in a large bowl. Add the egg, salt to taste, speck, and parmigiano. Mix with your hands until all the ingredients are well combined.

Take a heaping tablespoon of the bread mixture and shape it into a small ball, about the size of a cherry tomato. Roll the dumpling in the flour, coating it lightly, and place on a lightly floured platter or cookie sheet. Repeat until all the mixture is used up. Refrigerate, uncovered, until ready to cook, up to overnight.

Bring a large pot of water to a boil. Add the salt and dumplings. Cook, uncovered, over high heat 4 to 5 minutes, until the gnocchi rise to the surface of the water.

While the dumplings are cooking, melt the butter in a large skillet over medium heat. Add the sage and stir once or twice.

Remove the dumplings with a slotted spoon or a skimmer, draining off the excess water against the side of the pot. Place them in the skillet. Season lightly with salt. Stir in ¼ cup of the parmigiano, and mix quickly over low heat. Serve at once with the additional parmigiano.

Makes 4 to 5 servings

SUGGESTED WINES
The delicate, flavorful red wines of the Alto Adige area are perfect for this dish. Try Santa Maddalena or Lago di Caldaro. Sometimes the labels on these wines will also be in German, the other language spoken in this area.

Gnocchi di Zucca con Mozzarella Affumicata

Butternut Squash Gnocchi with Smoked Mozzarella

Trattoria da Toni in the town of Gradiscutta di Varmo near Udine is an upscale, beautiful establishment that serves great traditional food. Among the many delicious dishes on their menu, the butternut squash gnocchi with smoked ricotta stands out. Because it is very hard to find smoked ricotta in this country, at my restaurant in Sacramento I top the gnocchi with smoked mozzarella. This is one of those dishes that captures your attention at first sight.

Squash gnocchi are a bit tricky to prepare because squash contains a lot of water, read the recipe and the tips carefully, and you'll be able to prepare wonderful gnocchi.

For the gnocchi

1 butternut squash (about 2 pounds), cut in half lengthwise
1 large egg, lightly beaten
1½ to 1¾ cups unbleached all-purpose flour
½ cup freshly grated parmigiano
2 cups unbleached all-purpose flour, spread evenly over a sheet of aluminum foil
1 tablespoon salt

For the sauce

4 to 5 tablespoons unsalted butter
Salt to taste
4 ounces smoked mozzarella (see page 9), diced
2 tablespoons chopped fresh parsley

Preheat the oven to 350°F. Place the squash halves on an ungreased baking sheet, cut side up, and bake until tender, 40 to 50 minutes.

Cool slightly, then remove the pulp with a spoon and discard the seeds. Put the pulp in a large kitchen towel and squeeze out approximately ½ cup of the squash juices. (Do not squeeze out too much or the gnocchi will be dry.)

Put the squash in a large bowl and season with salt. Add the egg, 1½ cups of the flour, and the parmigiano. Mix well with a spoon or your hands until it is thoroughly combined. Place the mixture in a lightly floured bowl, cover with a clean kitchen towel, and freeze it for about 1 hour. The mixture will firm up and be much easier to shape into dumplings.

Remove the dough from the freezer. Take a teaspoon of the mixture and shape it into a small ball about the size of a cherry tomato. Roll the dumpling in the flour until lightly coated and place on a lightly floured platter or cookie sheet. Repeat until all of the mixture is used up. Refrigerate the dumplings, uncovered, until ready to use, up to several hours.

Bring a large pot of water to a boil. Add the salt and gnocchi. Cook, uncovered, over high heat until the gnocchi rise to the surface of the water, about 1 to 2 minutes.

While the gnocchi are cooking, melt the butter in a large skillet over medium heat. Remove the gnocchi with a slotted spoon or a skimmer, draining off the excess water against the side of the pot. Place in the skillet. (The smoked mozzarella is already salty, so there is no need to add salt.) Add the mozzarella and the parsley and mix gently over low heat for a few seconds, until the cheese begins to melt and the gnocchi are well coated. Stir in a few tablespoons of the gnocchi cooking water if the sauce seems too dry. Taste and adjust seasonings. Serve hot.

Makes 6 servings

Ravioli Nudi alla Fiorentina

Naked Ravioli Florentine

One of the lightest gnocchi of all is the Florentine variation called *ravioli nudi* (naked ravioli) which is made with ricotta, parmigiano, egg yolks, and only a few tablespoons of flour to keep them together. At Il Chinghiale Bianco in Firenze, these little round dumplings were served simply with butter, fresh sage, and parmigiano. I asked for another half of a portion, but this time they came topped with a light tomato sauce.

The day after when I met with the owner, Massimo, I was given the recipe for the dish and also a few helpful tips on how to prepare and cook the dumplings successfully. First, because the dumplings are held together only by the egg yolks and the few tablespoons of flour, they should be handled gently. After the ricotta mixture has been put together, it will be somewhat soft and sticky. Do not add more flour. Instead, freeze the mixture for about 1 hour to firm it up. It will then be much easier to shape the dumplings. Once the dumplings have been shaped, refrigerate them for a few hours. They will firm up a little more.

For the ravioli

- 1½ pounds fresh spinach or two 10-ounce packages frozen spinach
- 1 teaspoon salt
- 1 pound ricotta
- 4 large egg yolks, lightly beaten
- 1 cup freshly grated parmigiano
- 3 to 4 tablespoons unbleached all-purpose flour
- 2 cups unbleached all-purpose flour, spread evenly over a sheet of aluminum foil

For the tomato sauce

3 tablespoons unsalted butter
4 cups canned imported Italian tomatoes with their juice,
  put through a strainer or food mill to remove the seeds
Salt and freshly ground black pepper to taste

To complete the dish

1 tablespoon salt
½ cup freshly grated parmigiano

If you are using fresh spinach, remove the stems and wash them well under cold running water. Bring a large pot of water to a boil. Add the salt and spinach. Cook, uncovered, until the spinach is tender, about 3 to 4 minutes. If you are using frozen spinach, cook it according to the package directions. Drain the spinach and cool under cold running water. Squeeze the spinach dry. (A good way to do this is to put the spinach in a large kitchen towel and squeeze out as much water as possible.) Chop the spinach very fine and place in a large bowl. Add the ricotta, egg yolks, parmigiano, and the 3 to 4 tablespoons of flour. Season with salt. Mix well with your hands or a wooden spoon until the mixture is thoroughly combined. Place it in a lightly floured bowl and freeze it for about 1 hour.

While the dough is in the freezer, prepare the tomato sauce. Melt the butter in a wide-bottomed saucepan. Add the tomatoes and cook, uncovered, over medium heat for 8 to 10 minutes. Season with salt and pepper. Set aside.

Remove the ricotta dough from the freezer. Take a teaspoon of the mixture and shape it into a small ball about the size of a cherry tomato. Roll the dumpling in the flour until lightly coated and place on a lightly floured platter or a cookie sheet. Repeat until all of the mixture is used up. Refrigerate, uncovered, until ready to cook, up to several hours.

Bring a large pot of water to a boil and add the salt and one-third of the dumplings. Cook, uncovered, over high heat until they rise to the surface of the water, about 1 to 2 minutes.

Reheat the tomato sauce and put it in a large serving dish. Remove the dumplings with a slotted spoon or a skimmer, draining off the excess water against the side of the pot. Place them in the serving dish. Keep the dish warm in a low oven while you cook the remaining dumplings. When cooked, mix them lightly with the sauce. Serve with the parmigiano.

Makes 6 to 8 servings

SUGGESTED WINES
For a classic Tuscan dish, a classic Tuscan wine. Try a young, fresh Chianti or Chianti Classico such as Isole e Olena, Ricasoli, or Ruffino's Aziano.

Pisarei e Fasò

Flour and Bread Dumplings with Tomato and Bean Sauce

Between Parma and Piacenza, in the flat, prosperous region of Emilia-Romagna, there is a very small town, Frascarolo di Busseto, that doesn't even appear on the map. Here, in the middle of fertile farm land near a cluster of pretty homes and a lonely gas station, is Trattoria Vernizzi.

The food at Vernizzi is real food. Bold, well defined, and, most of all, true to its peasant background. Everything is made there according to the old traditions. Prosciutto, *salame*, sausages, bread, pasta, and even wine. And the pride shows.

Pisarei e fasò was my favorite dish. Small flour-and-bread dumplings that looked like little shells, in a rich, thick, satisfying sauce of tomatoes, beans, and pancetta. A wonderful, hearty, classic dish of the Emilia-Romagna region that today is almost all forgotten.

For the dumplings
  2 cups unbleached all-purpose flour
  ½ cup plain bread crumbs, preferably homemade (see tip on page 269), mixed with ¾ cup warm water
  1 tablespoon salt

For the bean sauce
  ⅓ cup dried red kidney beans or 1 cup canned
  2 tablespoons olive oil
  2 tablespoons unsalted butter
  ½ medium-size onion, finely diced
  2 cloves garlic, finely chopped
  2 tablespoons finely chopped fresh parsley
  One 2-ounce slice pancetta, finely chopped
  3 cups canned imported Italian tomatoes with their juice, put through a strainer or food mill to remove the seeds
  10 to 12 large fresh basil leaves, shredded
  Salt and freshly ground black pepper to taste
  1 cup freshly grated parmigiano

If you are using the dried beans, put them in a large bowl, cover abundantly with cold water, and let soak overnight. Drain and rinse the beans thoroughly. Place the beans in a medium-size saucepan and cover them again abundantly with cold water.

NOTE OF INTEREST
These dumplings have a firmer, more compact consistency than regular potato or ricotta dumplings and require a longer cooking time.

Cover the pot and bring the water to a boil. Cook the beans over low heat until tender, 40 to 50 minutes. Stir a few times during cooking.

Reserve 2 cups of the cooking water. Drain the beans and set aside in a bowl until needed.

To prepare the dumplings, combine the flour and wetted bread crumbs in a large bowl. Mix them together well with your hands, until the mixture sticks together easily and can be combined into a ball. If the dough is too dry, add a bit more water.

Lightly flour your work surface, then knead the dough for 3 to 4 minutes. At this point the dough should be soft and pliable. If the dough is too sticky, knead in a bit more flour. If it is too dry, wrap it in plastic wrap and let it rest for 5 to 10 minutes. (The dough will become softer.)

Cut off a small piece of dough about the size of an egg, and keep the larger piece wrapped in plastic. Shape the small piece of dough into a long roll, about the size of your little finger. Cut the roll into ½-inch pieces. With your index finger, press into each small piece of dough, pulling it toward you on the board. The pressure made by your finger will give the pieces the shape of little shells. Arrange the finished dumplings on a lightly floured tray. Repeat until all dough has been used up. Refrigerate the dumplings, uncovered, until ready to cook. (They can be prepared up to this point several hours or a day ahead.)

To prepare the sauce, heat the oil and butter together in a medium-size saucepan. Add the onion, garlic, parsley, and pancetta and cook, stirring, over medium heat 2 to 3 minutes. Add the tomatoes and 1 cup of the reserved cooking water. Cook, uncovered, 5 to 6 minutes. Add the beans and basil, and cook 4 to 5 minutes longer, or until the sauce has a medium-thick consistency. If the sauce should thicken too much (and it might happen because the beans are starchy and absorb a lot of liquid), add more of the reserved cooking water. Taste and adjust the seasonings.

While the sauce is cooking, bring a large pot of water to a boil. Add the salt and dumplings. Cook, uncovered, over high heat until the dumplings rise to the surface of the water and are tender but still firm to the bite, 8 to 10 minutes.

Drain the dumplings and transfer to a warm dish. Add the sauce and ½ cup of the parmigiano. Mix well to combine. Serve immediately sprinkled with the remaining parmigiano.

Makes 4 to 6 servings

SUGGESTED WINES
A robustly flavored, medium-bodied, young red wine is what is called for here, such as a Barbera from Italy or a dry Burgundy from California.

RISOTTO

Risotto, yellow with saffron, black with cuttlefish, purple with Barolo wine, green with spinach, white with parmigiano, or colored with a kaleidoscope of tiny vegetables, can be considered one of the glories of Italian gastronomy. Risotto is a cuisine all by itself. It can be made with one or a multitude of ingredients. It can be elegant, refined, delicate, hearty, or aggressive. It is one of those dishes that, once discovered, hooks you for life. Risotto is the quintessential comfort food. Eating it brings perfect satisfaction.

Risotto is a specialty of Northern Italy, because it is in Northern Italy that rice is extensively cultivated and consumed. In regions such as Piemonte, Lombardia, and Veneto, risotto is a staple of life and is much more popular than pasta. And yet, until a few years ago, many people in America had never heard of, let alone tasted, a risotto.

Risotto is made using a cooking technique that is uniquely Northern Italian. This dish begins by stirring the rice briefly with onion that has been sautéed in butter, or sometimes olive oil. The rice is then cooked with small additions of hot broth and stirred constantly. Other ingredients—shellfish, cheese, herbs, vegetables, sausage, game, etc.—are added to the rice at different stages, giving the risotto a particular identity.

During the last minute or two of cooking, butter and—except in the case of a seafood risotto—parmigiano are stirred into the rice energetically. This important final step is called *mantecare* (meaning to beat together) and will give the risotto its ultimate velvety, creamy consistency.

In Italy, risotto is always served as a first course, with the exception of the classic, time-honored combination of *risotto alla Milanese* and ossobuco.

To make a perfect risotto, you need the perfect rice. There are today on the market several varieties of medium-grain rice imported from Italy that are used exclusively for risotto. The best and best known is Arborio. This chubby rice is a favorite of Italian cooks because of its starchy quality which gives the risotto its unique texture and consistency. Other excellent varieties are Carnaroli, Vialone Nano, and Maratelli. Because the success of a risotto is unavoidably related to the kind of rice used, do not try to prepare a risotto with a normal long-grain rice; you will probably find yourself with a sticky mess.

Another important ingredient in risotto is the broth. A flavorful, homemade meat or chicken broth will give the risotto a richness of taste that canned broth won't ever achieve. Many Italian cooks make a "quick" broth with bouillon cubes when they have no time to prepare the homemade product. If you are going to use canned broth or bouillon cubes, keep in mind that they can be quite salty and should be diluted with some water.

Fish risotto is often prepared with a light fish broth, and vegetable risottos are sometimes cooked with the blanching water of the vegetables.

Risotto should take approximately eighteen minutes to cook. During this time you need to watch it like a newborn baby. Don't be intimidated by this, however, because after you have cooked several risottos you will have developed a sense of timing and an understanding of the dish. Then you will begin to relax, to improvise, and to take great joy and pride in your accomplishment.

The following is a short list of tips that will help you avoid the mistakes that many first-timers make.

A Few Tips for Cooking Perfect Risotto

Risotto, like pasta, cannot be prepared ahead of time or the rice will become overcooked and sticky when reheated. Once you start the risotto cooking, be prepared to give it your undivided attention.

For a perfectly cooked risotto, use a heavy-bottomed pan or skillet that can accommodate all the rice comfortably.

Prepare all your ingredients in advance and line them up on a tray. Start cooking the risotto fifteen minutes before you want your guests or family to sit down for dinner.

Practice cooking a risotto for your family before you make it for company.

Risotto is always cooked uncovered over medium heat.

Stir the risotto as you cook it so it cooks evenly and won't stick to the bottom of the pan.

It is almost impossible to give the exact amount of broth needed to cook a risotto because there are too many variables. To be safe, have an additional amount of broth at hand—you can always freeze whatever broth you have left.

The difficult stage in cooking a risotto is in the last few minutes of cooking. At that point add very little broth. It is easier to add broth if needed than to have a rice with a soupy consistency.

Keep in mind that rice keeps cooking even after it is removed from the heat and tends to dry out fast. So make sure your rice is still gently firm to the bite and moist and creamy when you serve it.

And finally, after you have read the recipe and followed it through completely, you must taste everything you do several times during the cooking of the dish, because only you will be able to determine if the dish needs extra seasoning and the rice is perfectly *al dente*. It is only through trial and error that we become accomplished cooks.

Risotto al Barolo

Risotto with Barolo

When in Roma do as the Romans, and when in Milano—you must eat a risotto! In Milano you will find risotto everywhere, in restaurants, *trattorie*, and family dining tables, and it will be served in innumerable preparations.

At Alla Cucina delle Langhe, an upscale trattoria, I had wonderful risotto with Barolo. It had the dark, rich color and aroma of a good Barolo wine. It was moist and creamy, with each grain of rice perfectly separated and properly cooked, and it was incredibly good.

The owner told me later that the risotto had been cooked completely with Barolo wine. At my restaurant in Sacramento, I have also cooked this risotto with wine only and found that most people objected to the strong wine taste (what a pity!). As a result, I have changed the recipe slightly, and I cook it with almost equal parts of wine and broth.

> 3½ cups chicken broth, preferably homemade (see
>   pages 54–55)
> 5 tablespoons unsalted butter
> 1 small onion, finely minced
> 2 cups imported Italian Arborio rice
> 2½ cups Barolo wine, or another nice full-bodied
>   red wine
> Salt to taste
> 1 cup freshly grated parmigiano

Heat the broth in a medium-size saucepan and keep it warm over low heat.

Melt 4 tablespoons of the butter in a large saucepan over medium heat. When the butter foams, add the onion and cook, stirring until the onion is pale yellow and soft, 3 to 4 minutes. Add the rice and cook until it is well coated with the butter and onion, about 1 minute. Add 1 cup of the wine. Cook, stirring constantly, until the wine is almost all reduced. Add the remaining cup of wine and cook until it has been absorbed. Add just enough hot broth to barely cover the rice. Cook, still over

❈ ❈ ❈

VARIATION

To make a risotto with Barolo and sausage, remove 4 ounces of mild Italian sausage from its casing, chop it up very fine, and cook it together with the onion, then proceed as instructed above.

SUGGESTED WINES

Although the recipe calls for Barolo, a slightly lighter Italian red such as Dolcetto or Barbera should be served. A California Zinfandel, Barbera, or even Gamay would fit as well. Barolo gives flavor and color to the dish but is too heavy for it.

medium heat, until the broth has been absorbed almost completely. Continue cooking and stirring the rice in this manner, adding the broth a bit at a time until the rice is tender but still firm to the bite, about 15 to 16 minutes. Season lightly with salt. Stir in the remaining tablespoon of butter and ⅓ cup of the parmigiano. Mix well and quickly to combine. At this point the rice should have a moist, creamy, and slightly loose consistency. Serve at once with a sprinkling of additional parmigiano.

Makes 4 to 6 servings

Risotto con Verdurine e Zafferano

NOTE OF INTEREST

I didn't want to confine this dish to specific vegetables. Use the best the season has to offer—asparagus, peas, tomatoes, and small zucchini with their blossoms still attached in spring and summer; carrots, broccoli, cauliflower, and mushrooms in winter. Or use a combination of all of the above

Dice up all the vegetables and boil or steam them separately until they are tender but still firm to the bite. You can prepare all this ahead of time and use it when needed.

If you have any leftover vegetables, just toss them with olive oil, vinegar, salt, and pepper to make a lovely salad.

Risotto with Spring Vegetables and Saffron

Traditional cooks don't strive to be innovators. They are happy to make the classic dishes they love daily. Occasionally they add a touch of this and that, more to experience a momentary emotion than believing they are creating anything new.

At Trattoria dei Cacciatori on the outskirts of Milano, the owner, Signor Temporali, added a handful of fresh, tender summer vegetables to his golden risotto. As I tasted it, I was once again hooked on the wonders of a perfectly made risotto.

    6 cups chicken broth, preferably homemade (see
      pages 54–55)
    5 tablespoons unsalted butter
    1 small onion, finely minced
    2 cups imported Italian Arborio rice
    1 cup dry white wine
    ¼ teaspoon powdered saffron
    2 cups cooked, mixed, diced fresh vegetables (see
      note below)
    1 cup freshly grated parmigiano

Heat the broth in a medium-size saucepan and keep warm over low heat.

Melt 4 tablespoons of the butter in a large saucepan over medium heat. When the butter foams, add the onion and cook, stirring, until the onion is pale yellow and soft, 2 to 3 minutes. Add the rice and cook until it is well coated with the butter and the onion, about 1 minute. Add the wine and cook, stirring, until the wine is almost all reduced. Add just enough broth to barely cover the rice. Cook, still over medium heat, stirring constantly, until the broth has been absorbed almost completely. Continue cooking and stirring the rice in this manner, adding broth a bit at a time, until the rice is tender but still firm to the bite, about 15 minutes.

Dilute the saffron in ½ cup of the broth and add it to the rice. Add all the vegetables and cook a couple of minutes. Taste and adjust the seasoning, then add the remaining tablespoon of butter and ⅓ cup of the parmigiano. Mix well and quickly to combine. At this point the rice should have a moist, creamy, and slightly loose consistency. Serve at once with a sprinkling of the remaining parmigiano.

Makes 4 to 6 servings

SUGGESTED WINES
This dish, with its saffron character and sweet taste from the vegetables, needs a light, fragrant red wine, like Valpolicella, a young Chianti, or a full-bodied, creamy white such as Pinot Grigio.

Risotto alla Parmigiana con Asparagi

Risotto with Parmigiano and Asparagus Tips

Risotto with butter and parmigiano is a specialty of Parma, and rightly so, because it is in Parma that the glorious parmigiano-reggiano cheese is produced. At Alla Grada in Bologna, this classic preparation was given a bonus with the addition of fresh, tender asparagus tips.

Risotto is not a difficult dish to prepare. It takes, however, a little bit of attention and tender loving care to produce a perfect risotto. At Alla Grada, the risotto came to the table still in its cooking pot, with the waiter vigorously stirring the rice, giving it the last, ultimate swirl before spooning it into the dishes. It was steaming hot, moist, and immensely appetizing.

> 6 cups chicken broth, preferably homemade (see pages 54–55)
> 5 tablespoons unsalted butter
> 1 small onion, finely minced
> 2 cups imported Italian Arborio rice
> 1 cup dry white wine
> 1½ pounds fresh, thin asparagus, cleaned, tips cut off, and stalks reserved for another use
> Salt to taste
> 1 cup freshly grated parmigiano

Heat the broth in a medium-size saucepan and keep it warm over low heat.

Melt 4 tablespoons of the butter in a large saucepan over medium heat. When the butter foams, add the onion and cook, stirring, for 3 to 4 minutes, until the onion is pale yellow and soft. Add the rice and cook until it is well coated with the butter and onion. Add the wine and cook, stirring constantly, until the wine is almost all reduced. Add just enough hot broth to barely cover the rice. Cook, still over medium heat, stirring constantly, until the broth has been absorbed almost completely. Add more broth as the liquid is absorbed, continually stirring. After 6 to 7 minutes of cooking, add the asparagus tips. Continue cooking and stirring the rice, adding the broth a bit at a time, until the rice is tender but still firm to the bite, another 7 to 8 minutes. Season with salt. Stir in the remaining tablespoon of butter and ⅓ cup of the parmigiano. Mix well and quickly to blend. At this point the rice should have a moist, creamy, and somewhat loose consistency. Serve at once with a sprinkling of additional parmigiano.

Makes 4 to 6 servings

SUGGESTED WINES

The fresh taste of asparagus will be enhanced by the sprightly fresh taste of Sauvignon Blanc. From Italy try Ruffino Libaio or Antinori Borro della Sala. From California try a medium-bodied, not overly varietal style such as the Mondavi Fumé Blanc.

Risotto con Fagioli, Pomodoro e Rosmarino

Risotto with White Beans, Tomatoes, and Rosemary

Tuscans are nicknamed *mangia fagioli* ("bean eaters") because of their fondness for beans. Some preparations, such as *Fagioli all'Uccelletto* (pages 264–65) and the thick, rich *pasta e fagioli*, cooked with the fabulous Tuscan olive oil, are almost legendary. The beans widely used in Toscana are cannellini, small white beans that are also known as Tuscan beans.

To simplify this dish, prepare the bean sauce several hours, or even a day, ahead. When you are ready to cook the risotto, reheat the sauce gently. Make sure to stir the risotto, especially after you add the bean sauce because the starchiness of the beans and the rice will absorb the liquid in the risotto very quickly.

For the bean sauce

    3 tablespoons olive oil
    2 cloves garlic, finely chopped
    1 small sprig fresh rosemary, finely chopped (about 2 tablespoons)
    1½ cups cooked cannellini or white kidney beans (see page 69)
    3 tablespoons tomato paste diluted in 2 cups chicken broth, preferably homemade (see pages 54–55)
    Salt to taste

For the risotto

    5 cups chicken broth, preferably homemade (see pages 54–55)
    4 tablespoons (½ stick) unsalted butter
    1 small onion, finely minced
    2 cups imported Italian Arborio rice
    1 cup dry white wine
    1 cup freshly grated parmigiano
    2 tablespoons chopped fresh parsley

TIP

↪ *This bean sauce is also terrific tossed over homemade or factory-made pasta.*

To prepare the bean sauce, heat the oil in a medium-size saucepan over medium heat. Add the garlic and rosemary and cook, stirring, until the garlic begins to color, less than 1 minute. Add the beans and stir once or twice. Add the diluted tomato paste and season lightly with salt. Cook, uncovered, over medium heat for 10 to 12 minutes, stirring a few times, until the sauce has a medium-thick consistency. At this point the sauce should be reduced to about 2 cups. Set aside.

Heat the broth in a medium-size saucepan and keep warm over low heat. Melt 3 tablespoons of the butter in a large saucepan over medium heat. When the butter foams, add the onion and cook, stirring, until the onion is pale yellow and soft, 3 to 4 minutes. Add the rice, and cook until it is well coated with the butter and the onion, about 1 minute. Add the wine and cook, stirring, until the wine is almost all reduced. Add just enough hot broth to barely cover the rice. Cook, still over medium heat, until the broth has been absorbed almost completely. Continue cooking and stirring the rice in this manner, adding the broth a bit at a time, for 10 to 12 minutes.

Add the bean sauce and continue cooking and stirring the rice 4 to 5 minutes longer.

At this point the bean sauce should be absorbed almost completely and the rice should be tender but still firm to the bite. Add a bit more broth if the rice looks too dry. Stir in the remaining tablespoon of butter, ⅓ cup of the parmigiano, and the parsley. Mix well and quickly to combine. At this point the rice should have a moist, creamy, and slightly loose consistency. Taste and adjust the seasoning, then serve at once, with a sprinkling of the remaining parmigiano.

Makes 4 to 6 servings

SUGGESTED WINES

A light, fragrant Rosé such as Brolio Tramonto or Capezzana Vin Ruspo would be perfect.

Risotto alla Boscaiola

Risotto with Porcini Mushrooms and Smoked Prosciutto

There is no better place in Italy to eat a risotto, with the exception perhaps of Venezia, than in Milano. Risotto in Milano is taken very seriously and risotto is to a Milanese what good homemade pasta is to a Bolognese. Every eating establishment in that city has risotto on its menu. There is even a place in Milano where one can eat twenty-five different kinds of risotto, and if you want one that is not on their menu, they will gladly cook it for you. Casa Fontana is truly the paradise of the risotto. This risotto with porcini mushrooms and smoked prosciutto is one of several I enjoyed at Casa Fontana. The risotto was made with large, meaty fresh porcini and with speck, smoked Italian prosciutto which is a specialty of the Alto Adige. If you can't locate it, substitute prosciutto. Since fresh porcini are very seldom available in markets across the country, I have substituted dried imported Italian porcini. If you have specialty markets in your area, look for fresh chanterelles, which will be terrific as a substitute or addition to the porcini mushrooms.

> 6 cups meat broth, preferably homemade (see pages 53–54)
> 1 ounce dried porcini mushrooms (see page 15), soaked in 2 cups lukewarm water for 20 minutes
> 5 tablespoons unsalted butter
> 1 small onion, finely minced
> 2 cups imported Italian Arborio rice
> 3 ounces speck (see page 11), cut into 4 or 5 thick slices and diced
> 1 cup dry full-bodied red wine, like a Barbera or California Zinfandel
> Salt to taste
> 2 tablespoons finely chopped fresh parsley
> 1 cup freshly grated parmigiano

Heat the broth in a medium-size saucepan and keep it warm over low heat. Strain the mushrooms and reserve the soaking water. Rinse the mushrooms well under cold running water. Line a strainer with two layers of paper towels and strain the mushroom soaking water into a bowl to get rid of the sandy deposits. Set aside.

Melt 4 tablespoons of the butter in a large saucepan over medium heat. When the butter foams, add the onion and cook, stirring, until the onion is pale yellow and soft, 3 to 4 minutes. Add the rice and cook until it is well coated with the butter and onion, about 1 minute. Add the speck and mushrooms and stir once or twice. Add the wine and cook, stirring constantly, until the wine has evaporated. Add 1 cup of the reserved mushroom water and cook until it is almost all reduced. Add just enough hot broth to barely cover the rice. Cook, still over medium heat, stirring constantly, until the broth has been absorbed almost completely. Continue cooking the rice in this manner, adding the broth a bit at a time and stirring, until the rice is tender but still firm to the bite, about 15 to 16 minutes. Season lightly with salt. Stir in the remaining tablespoon of butter, the parsley, and ⅓ cup of the parmigiano. Mix well and quickly. At this point the rice should have a moist, creamy, and somewhat loose consistency. Serve at once with a sprinkling of the remaining parmigiano.

Makes 4 to 6 servings

Risotto con e Biete

Risotto with Swiss Chard

NOTE OF INTEREST

In Italy, the white stalks of the Swiss chard are generally boiled until tender, then baked with butter and parmigiano.

Swiss chard when cooked is silky and sweet. It is great in salads or sautéed with a bit of oil and garlic. And now, I have discovered, it is also delicious in risotto. Pippo lo Sgobbone in Roma served a risotto that was loaded with Swiss chard, moist, buttery, and incredibly pleasing.

> 12 ounces Swiss chard
> 1 tablespoon salt
> 6 cups chicken broth, preferably homemade (see pages 54–55)
> 5 tablespoons unsalted butter
> 1 small onion, finely minced
> 2 cups imported Italian Arborio rice
> 1 cup dry white wine
> 1 cup freshly grated parmigiano
> Salt to taste

Remove the Swiss chard leaves from the stems and reserve the stems for another use (see note below). Wash the leaves well under cold running water.

Bring a medium-size saucepan of water to a boil. Add the salt and Swiss chard and cook, uncovered, over medium heat for 3 to 4 minutes. Drain and rinse the Swiss chard under cold running water. Press the leaves lightly with a large spoon to remove excess water. Put the Swiss chard on a cutting board and mince it very finely. Set aside.

Heat the broth in a medium-size saucepan and keep warm over low heat.

Melt 4 tablespoons of the butter in a large saucepan over medium heat. When the butter foams, add the onion and cook, stirring, until the onion is pale yellow and soft, 3 to 4 minutes. Add the rice and cook until it is well coated with the butter and the onion, about 1 minute. Add the wine and cook, stirring constantly, until the wine is almost all reduced. Add just enough hot broth to barely cover the rice and cook, still over medium heat, stirring constantly, until the broth has been absorbed almost completely. Continue cooking and stirring the rice in this manner, adding the broth a bit at a time, until the rice is tender but still firm to the bite, about 15 minutes. During the last 2 to 3 minutes of cooking, add the Swiss chard, the remaining tablespoon of butter, and ⅓ cup of the parmigiano. Mix everything together well and quickly. Season lightly with salt. At this point the rice should have a moist, creamy, and slightly loose consistency. Serve immediately with a sprinkling of the remaining parmigiano.

Makes 4 to 6 servings

SUGGESTED WINES
A light, fruity red wine, Sangiovese di Romagna or a young Chianti, or a youthful California Pinot Noir without a lot of tannin, such as Saintsbury Garnet, complements the chard taste.

Risotto con i Funghi Misti

Risotto with Mixed Fresh Mushrooms

One of the reasons I love to go to Italy in the spring and fall is that those are the fresh porcini seasons. These large, meaty, wild Italian mushrooms have a taste and a succulence all their own. Every season the restaurants and *trattorie* of Italy proudly display large baskets of these expensive mushrooms in their windows or on tables at the entrances of their restaurants.

There have been times when I have eaten nothing but fresh porcini—grilled as appetizers, sautéed over pasta, cooked in a risotto, baked as an entree, and raw in a salad. Of all of those wonderful preparations, perhaps the loveliest is risotto with fresh porcini.

During the last ten years fresh porcini, just like radicchio, balsamic vinegar, and sun-dried tomatoes, have become more available at American markets. Sometimes they are imported from Italy, other times they are found locally. Often, however, fresh porcini are simply not available. With that in mind, I prepare this risotto with a mixture of assorted fresh mushrooms, such as chanterelles, shiitake, and oyster mushrooms, realizing the necessity to compromise. And a good compromise it must be, because every time I feature this dish at my restaurant in Sacramento, it outsells everything else!

For the mushrooms

¼ cup olive oil

½ pound mixed mushrooms, such as cultivated white mushrooms, chanterelles, shiitake, and oyster mushrooms, finely sliced

2 cloves garlic, finely minced

½ cup dry white wine

Salt and freshly ground black pepper to taste

For the risotto

6 cups chicken broth, preferably homemade (see pages 54–55)

4 tablespoons (½ stick) unsalted butter

1 small onion, finely minced

2 cups imported Italian Arborio rice

1 cup dry white wine

2 tablespoons chopped fresh parsley

TIP

~ *The mushrooms should be cooked quickly over very high heat. Let the oil in the skillet become very hot before you add the mushrooms, and they will turn golden in almost no time at all.*

Heat the oil in a large skillet over high heat. When the oil begins to smoke, add the mushrooms and cook, stirring, until the mushrooms are lightly golden, 1 to 2 minutes. Add the garlic and stir quickly once or twice. Add the wine and season lightly with salt and just a bit of pepper. Cook and stir until the wine is almost all reduced. Turn the heat off under the skillet while you prepare the risotto.

Heat the broth in a medium-size saucepan and keep it warm over low heat.

Melt 3 tablespoons of the butter in a large saucepan over medium heat. When the butter foams, add the onion and cook, stirring, until the onion begins to color, 3 to 4 minutes. Add the rice and cook until it is well coated with the butter and the onion, about 1 minute. Add the wine and cook, stirring, until the wine is almost all reduced, less than 1 minute. Add just enough broth to barely cover the rice. Cook, still over medium heat, until the broth has been absorbed almost completely. Continue cooking and stirring the rice in this manner, adding the broth a bit at a time, for about 15 minutes.

Add the mushrooms and all of the mushrooms' juices. Cook and stir 1 to 2 minutes longer. Stir in the parsley and the remaining tablespoon of butter. At this point the rice should have a moist and slightly loose consistency. Taste and adjust the seasoning and serve at once.

Makes 4 to 6 servings

SUGGESTED WINES
The earthy flavor of mushrooms can take a rich, buttery-tasting, and creamy-textured Chardonnay, three to four years old, such as Sonoma-Cutrer and Saintsbury in California or Gaja or Maurizio Zanella from Italy.

Risotto Verde

Spinach and Fresh Basil Risotto

My husband and I were driving through the beautiful landscape of the Chianti area in Toscana, toward a trattoria we had heard about, when I spotted the sign of La Biscondola. That was the same trattoria where years back I had done a television story for KCRA-TV of Sacramento. I had chosen that place because it was in such a gorgeous setting and because Florentine friends had told me that the food was exceptionally good. I convinced my husband to change our destination and to eat instead at La Biscondola. And what a meal we had! The setting was about the same as I had remembered, rustic and warm. We feasted on an appetizer of fried polenta topped with sautéed fresh porcini, on deep-fried zucchini flowers, light and crunchy, and a spinach and basil risotto so aromatic and so perfectly cooked that we almost ordered another portion. We ended with the taste of several desserts. All of this while we were sipping different vintages of exquisite Chianti wine. This is the recipe for the great risotto we enjoyed at La Biscondola and, throughout the book, you will find the recipes for the other dishes mentioned above.

1 pound fresh spinach or 4 ounces frozen chopped
    spinach, thawed
6 cups chicken broth, preferably homemade (see pages
    54–55)
5 tablespoons unsalted butter
1 small onion, finely minced
¼ pound sliced pancetta, finely diced
2 cups imported Italian arborio rice
1 cup dry white wine
10 to 15 fresh basil leaves, finely chopped
Salt to taste
1 cup freshly grated parmigiano

If using fresh spinach, remove the stems and wash it well under cold running water. Put the wet spinach in a large saucepan with a pinch of salt and 1 cup of water and cook over medium heat until the spinach is tender, 3 to 4 minutes. If using frozen spinach, cook according to the package instructions. Drain the spinach well of all water and chop very fine by hand or with a food processor. If using a food processor, make sure not to puree the spinach. Set aside.

Heat the broth in a medium-size saucepan and keep it warm over low heat.

Melt 4 tablespoons of the butter in a large saucepan over medium heat. When the butter foams, add the onion and cook, stirring, for 3 to 4 minutes, until soft. Add the pancetta and cook until the pancetta is lightly golden, about 2 minutes. Add the rice and cook until it is well coated with the butter, onion, and pancetta, about 1 minute. Add the wine and cook, stirring constantly, until the wine is almost all reduced. Add just enough broth to barely cover the rice and cook, still over medium heat, until the broth has been absorbed. Continue cooking the rice in this manner, adding the broth a bit at a time, until the rice is tender but still firm to the bite, about 15 to 16 minutes. Stir in the spinach and basil and mix well to combine. Season lightly with salt, then stir in the remaining tablespoon of butter and ⅓ cup of the parmigiano. Mix well and quickly. At this point the rice should have a moist, creamy consistency. Serve at once with additional parmigiano if you wish.

Makes 4 to 6 servings

SUGGESTED WINES
Villa Antinori Chianti Classico Riserva or Santa Cristina would be a wonderful accompaniment. Reds from California, such as a Cabernet/Merlot blend, without too much tannin would also do.

Risotto con Radicchio e Pancetta

Risotto with Radicchio and Pancetta

Radicchio might be trendy in America, but it is commonplace in many parts of Northern Italy, especially in the Veneto region where it originates. I simply adore the slightly bitter taste of radicchio and look for and try out any dish made with it. At Antica Trattoria al Matarel in Milano, I tasted a risotto while researching this book that basically had the same ingredients as Penne with Radicchio and Pancetta (pages 108–109). However, since the same ingredients were given a completely different treatment, they produced two deliciously unrelated dishes.

In the risotto, the radicchio and pancetta are cooked together with the rice for the entire time it takes to cook the risotto. The brilliant red color of the radicchio changes during cooking to a darker hue, giving the risotto a most appealing, appetizing color. As it cooks the radicchio strips become meltingly soft, forming a perfect union with the creamy risotto. This is a dish not to be missed!

> 6 cups chicken broth, preferably homemade (see
>   pages 54–55)
> 5 tablespoons unsalted butter
> 1 small onion, finely minced
> 6 ounces sliced pancetta, diced
> 2 cups imported Italian Arborio rice
> 1 small head radicchio, about 10 to 12 ounces, sliced into
>   very thin strips
> 1 cup dry white wine
> Salt to taste
> 1 cup freshly grated parmigiano

TIP
◦ *What kind of wine to use for cooking? Any wine that is good enough to drink is good enough to cook!*

Heat the broth in a medium-size saucepan and keep warm over low heat.

Melt 4 tablespoons of the butter in a large saucepan over medium heat. When the butter foams, add the onion and cook, stirring, until the onion begins to color, 3 to 4 minutes. Add the pancetta and cook until the pancetta begins to color, 1 to 2 minutes. Add the rice, and cook until it is well coated with the butter, onion, and pancetta, about 1 minute. Add the radicchio and stir once or twice, then add the wine. Cook, stirring, until the wine is almost all reduced. Add just enough broth to barely cover the rice. Cook, still over medium heat, until the broth has been absorbed almost completely. Continue cooking and stirring the rice in this manner, adding the broth a bit at a time until the rice is tender but firm to the bite, about 15 minutes. Season lightly with salt, taste, and adjust the seasonings. Stir in the remaining tablespoon of butter and ⅓ cup of the parmigiano. Mix well and quickly to combine. At this point the rice should have a moist, creamy, and slightly loose consistency. Serve at once with a sprinkling of additional parmigiano.

Makes 4 to 6 servings

SUGGESTED WINES
The slightly bitter component of radicchio is accompanied well by a good Verdicchio from Umani Ronchi or Fazi-Battaglia.

Il Risotto di Pierino

Pierino's Sausage and Spinach Risotto

The Romagna part of the Emilia-Romagna region has perhaps some of the most beautiful and popular resort towns of the Adriatic coast. Rimini, Riccione, Milano Marittima, and Cesenatico are well known to Italians and foreigners not only for their large, sandy white beaches, but also for their great tradition of food. My friend Pierino Jovene, owner of the Gambero Rosso of Cesenatico, is a gregarious, exuberant man. He is also a very talented cook whose preference is simple, tasty fish preparations. The day I was there, I was served a risotto that was prepared not with fish, as would have been expected on a seacoast, but with sausage and spinach.

The risotto came to the table steaming hot, moist, and bright green, with specks of sausage scattered throughout the rice. It was deliciously appetizing. Then, faithful to the old saying "When on the coast, you must eat fish," I followed the rice with a wonderfully fresh, perfectly grilled swordfish with mint sauce and all of this, while I was sipping wine and looking out at the ocean. I felt very, very blessed!

6 cups chicken broth, preferably homemade (see
   pages 54–55)
½ pound fresh spinach or ½ of a 10-ounce package frozen
   spinach
1 teaspoon salt
5 tablespoons unsalted butter
1 small onion, finely minced
2 cloves garlic, finely minced
½ pound mild Italian sausage, casings removed and finely
   chopped
2 cups imported Italian Arborio rice
1 cup dry white wine
1 cup freshly grated parmigiano

Heat the broth in a medium-size saucepan and keep warm over low heat.

If you are using fresh spinach, remove the stems and wash well under cold water. Bring a medium-size pot of water to a boil. Add the salt and spinach and cook, uncovered, over medium heat until the spinach is tender, 3 to 4 minutes. If you are using frozen spinach, cook it according to the package directions. In either case, drain the spinach and cool under cold running water. Squeeze the spinach dry, then chop it very fine and set aside until ready to use.

Melt 4 tablespoons of the butter in a large saucepan over medium heat. When the butter foams, add the onion and garlic and cook, stirring, for 3 to 4 minutes, until the onion begins to color. Add the sausage and cook, breaking it apart with a large spoon until it begins to lose its raw color.

Add the rice and stir it with the sausage for about 1 minute, then add the spinach and wine. Cook, stirring, until the wine is almost all reduced. Add just enough chicken broth to barely cover the rice. Cook, still over medium heat, until the broth has been absorbed almost completely. Continue cooking and stirring the rice in this manner, adding the broth a bit at a time, for 16 to 18 minutes. Taste and adjust the seasoning. Stir in the remaining tablespoon of butter and ⅓ cup of the parmigiano. Mix well and quickly to combine. At this point the rice should have a moist, creamy, and slightly loose consistency. Serve at once with a sprinkling of additional parmigiano.

Makes 4 to 6 servings

SUGGESTED WINE
One of Italy's little-known red wines, Rosso Cònero from the Marche region, is perfect for this dish.

Risotto alla Bolognese

Risotto with Bolognese Meat Sauce

Many years ago, when my husband and I were dating while he was attending the University of Bologna, we used to eat occasionally at Trattoria Lo Sterlino. This was a very humble neighborhood trattoria which catered to students and older people on fixed incomes. There was no menu to speak of, only the few dishes that the owner's wife had cooked that day. The food was, however, very good, and perhaps because we were young and in love, we thought the place was also very romantic. Thirty years later, Lo Sterlino is still there.

For the Bolognese meat sauce
2 tablespoons unsalted butter
2 tablespoons olive oil
½ medium-size onion, finely minced
1 small carrot, finely minced
1 small stalk celery, finely minced
2 ounces pancetta, finely chopped
1 pound ground veal
1 cup dry white wine
3 cups canned imported Italian tomatoes with their juice, put through a strainer or a food mill to remove the seeds
1 cup chicken broth, preferably homemade (see pages 54–55)
2 tablespoons milk
Salt and freshly ground black pepper to taste

For the risotto
6 cups chicken broth, preferably homemade (see pages 54–55)
5 tablespoons unsalted butter
1 small onion, finely minced
2 cups imported Italian Arborio rice
1 cup dry white wine
Salt to taste
1 cup freshly grated parmigiano

To prepare the Bolognese sauce, heat the butter and oil in a medium-size skillet or saucepan over medium heat. Add the onion, carrot, and celery and cook, stirring, until the vegetables are lightly golden, about 5 minutes. Add the pancetta and veal and cook, stirring to break up the meat with a large spoon, until the meat loses its raw color, 4 to 5 minutes. Add the wine and cook until it is almost all reduced, 2 to 3 minutes. Add the tomatoes, broth, and milk, and season with salt and pepper. Cover the skillet and cook over low heat about 1 hour, stirring a few times. When done the sauce should have a medium-thick consistency. If too dry, add a bit more broth. Keep warm.

Heat the broth and keep warm over low heat. Melt 4 tablespoons of the butter in a large saucepan over medium heat. When the butter foams, add the onion and cook, stirring, 3 to 4 minutes, until the onion is pale yellow and soft. Add the rice and cook 1 to 2 minutes or just long enough to coat the rice with the butter and the onion. Add the wine and cook, stirring constantly, until the wine is almost all reduced. Add just enough hot broth to barely cover the rice. Cook, still over medium heat, stirring constantly, until the broth has been absorbed. Continue cooking and stirring the rice in this manner, adding the broth a bit at a time, for 12 to 15 minutes.

At this point the rice should still be firm to the bite. Add 1 to 1½ cups of the meat sauce and cook 3 to 5 minutes longer. Season lightly with salt. Add the remaining tablespoon of butter and ⅓ cup of the parmigiano. Mix well and quickly. Now the rice should be tender but still firm to the bite, and should have a moist, creamy, and somewhat loose consistency. Serve at once with a sprinkling of additional parmigiano.

Makes 4 to 6 servings

NOTE OF INTEREST
The Bolognese meat sauce yields about 2½ to 3 cups of sauce. You might want to double or triple the recipe and freeze what you don't use right away. It can be later used over any kind of pasta.

SUGGESTED WINES
This is a rich dish that requires a fairly high acid red wine, such as a Bardolino or a good, dry Lambrusco. From California, try a young, light style Zinfandel such as Santa Barbara Winery's Beaujour.

Risotto con Mozzarella Affumicata

Risotto with Smoked Mozzarella

Good food should provoke our senses. First, we should be able to smell it. Second, we should feast on its presentation with our eyes, and finally, we should be able to enjoy it wholeheartedly.

The first time I prepared this risotto, the aroma of the melted smoked mozzarella was all over the kitchen. The risotto was shining with melted cheese and butter and was incredibly appetizing. This is a hearty, filling dish, best suited for cold winter nights. It is also a very addictive dish, and you might scoop out a second helping without even realizing it. In that case, just follow it with a nice mixed green salad, or with a nice mixed cooked vegetable salad (see pages 260–61)

> 6 cups chicken broth, preferably homemade (see pages 54–55)
> 5 tablespoons unsalted butter
> 1 small onion, finely minced
> 2 cups imported Italian Arborio rice
> 1 cup dry white wine
> 3 ounces smoked mozzarella (see page 9) or smoked Gouda cheese, cut into small pieces
> ⅓ cup freshly grated parmigiano
> 2 tablespoons chopped fresh parsley
> Salt to taste

Heat the broth in a medium-size saucepan and keep warm over low heat.

Melt 4 tablespoons of the butter in a large saucepan over medium heat. When the butter foams, add the onion and cook, stirring, until the onion is pale yellow and soft, 3 to 4 minutes. Add the rice and cook until it is well coated with the butter and onion, about 1 minute. Add the wine and cook, stirring constantly, until the wine is almost all reduced. Add just enough broth to barely cover the rice. Cook, still over medium heat, stirring constantly, until the broth has been absorbed almost completely. Continue cooking and stirring the rice in this manner, adding the broth a bit at a time, until the rice is tender but firm to the bite, about 16 minutes. Add a last, small bit of broth, the mozzarella, the remaining tablespoon of butter, and the parmigiano. Mix well and quickly for less than a minute. At this point the mozzarella should be melted and the rice should have a moist, creamy, and slightly loose consistency. Stir in the parsley, season lightly with salt, and serve at once.

Makes 4 to 6 servings

TIP

◌ꙨꙨ *This risotto needs to be served immediately or it will dry out faster than the other risottos because of the cheese content. For this reason, make sure to leave the risotto a bit moister than usual during the last few minutes of cooking.*

SUGGESTED WINES

A recent vintage white Frascati from Fontana Candida or Plinius from Mastroberardino would lend the special "local touch" to this dish.

Risotto con Crema di Scampi

Risotto with Cream of Shrimp

Italian food would not be what it is without the glories of its pastas, gnocchi, and risottos, and, just like pasta, risotto can be prepared in innumerable ways. Risotto can be as straightforward and simple as a risotto with butter and parmigiano, or as rich and complex as a risotto with sausage, beans, salami, and red wine.

This version comes from Cannavota in Roma, a place well known to the Romans for their great first courses. Severino, the headwaiter who is practically as well known as the great pastas he serves, since he has been on the premises for thirty years, brought me a sample. The risotto was moist and creamy, with an appealing pink color, a delicious shrimp and basil aroma, and a very delicate taste.

For the cream of shrimp
    2 tablespoons olive oil
    6 ounces medium-size shrimp, shelled and deveined
    1 cup canned imported Italian plum tomatoes with their juice, put through a strainer or food mill to remove the seeds
    ¼ cup heavy cream

For the risotto
    6 cups chicken broth, preferably homemade (see pages 54–55)
    5 tablespoons unsalted butter
    1 small onion, finely minced
    2 cups imported Italian Arborio rice
    1 cup dry white wine
    Salt to taste
    10 to 12 leaves fresh basil, shredded, or 2 tablespoons chopped fresh parsley
    ¼ cup freshly grated parmigiano

Heat the oil in a large skillet over medium heat. Add the shrimp and cook until the shrimp are lightly golden on both sides, about

TIPS

∾ *You can turn this dish into a "one-dish meal" by doubling the amount of shrimp. After the shrimp are sautéed, reserve half. A few minutes before the risotto is done, cut the reserved shrimp into ½-inch pieces and stir them into the risotto briefly.*

∾ *Generally, parmigiano is omitted in risottos made with fish. At Cannavota, this risotto was given the ultimate swirl with a bit of parmigiano and was simply delicious.*

2 minutes. With a slotted spoon transfer the shrimp to a food processor. Add the tomatoes and cream and process until smooth. Set aside.

Heat the broth in a medium-size saucepan and keep it warm over low heat.

Discard the oil in the skillet and melt 4 tablespoons of the butter over medium heat. When the butter foams, add the onion and cook, stirring, for 3 to 4 minutes, until the onion is pale yellow and soft. Add the rice and cook until it is well coated with the butter and onion, about 1 minute. Add the wine and cook, stirring constantly, until the wine is almost all reduced. Add just enough hot broth to barely cover the rice. Cook, still over medium heat, stirring constantly, until the broth has been absorbed almost completely. Continue cooking and stirring the rice in this manner, adding the broth a bit at a time, for about 12 minutes.

Stir in the cream of shrimp and cook, stirring, 3 to 4 minutes longer. Add the remaining tablespoon of butter, the basil, and the parmigiano. Mix well and quickly. At this point the rice should be tender but still firm to the bite, and should have a moist, creamy consistency. Serve at once.

Makes 4 to 6 servings

SUGGESTED WINES
The slightly smokey character of Mastroberardino Lachryma Christi or the round flavor of Lungarotti Torgiano Bianco Torre di Giano would marry with this dish very well.

Risotto con Gamberi e Cape Sante

Risotto with Shrimp and Scallops

NOTE OF INTEREST
"Fish frames" are a mixture of fish heads, bones, and fish scraps available in fish markets and sold for the purpose of making fish broth. You can assemble your own fish frames by freezing any odd pieces of fish.

When my husband and I married in 1960, we spent our honeymoon in Rimini, a nice resort town on the Adriatic coast, about sixty miles from Bologna. We were young students, with little money, in love, and had great appetites. Ittico was a small trattoria near the pier patronized more by locals than by tourists. The food at Ittico was homey and delicious and of course they served a great deal of fish. My husband and I could not afford to eat several courses, so we limited ourselves to either pasta with fish or risotto with fish. I still have memories of those pastas and risottos, laced with all kinds of fish that still carried the aroma of the sea.

I don't know if Ittico is still there, but I still prepare one of the risottos I fell in love with. I don't know if I do this out of nostalgia or because it is simply wonderful.

For the fish broth

3 pounds fish frames (see note on page 172)
1 large onion, coarsely chopped
2 stalks celery, cut into pieces
2 carrots, cut into pieces
3 sprigs fresh parsley
2 cups dry white wine
3 quarts cold water
Salt to taste

For the shellfish

3 tablespoons olive oil
4 ounces shrimp, peeled, deveined, and cut into pieces
4 ounces bay scallops, cut into pieces
2 cloves garlic, minced
½ cup dry white wine
Salt to taste

For the risotto

4 tablespoons (½ stick) unsalted butter
1 small onion, finely minced
2 cups Italian Arborio rice
1 cup dry white wine
6 cups fish broth
2 tablespoons chopped fresh parsley

Prepare the fish broth. Rinse the fish frames under cold running water. Combine all the ingredients in a large saucepan and bring to a gentle simmer. With a skimmer or slotted spoon, remove the scum that comes to the surface of the water. Simmer the broth uncovered for 1 hour. Strain the broth into another saucepan if you are going to use it right away, and keep it warm over very low heat. Strain the broth into a bowl and cool it to room temperature if you are planning to refrigerate it for a few days or freeze it.

Heat the oil in a large skillet over high heat. Add the shrimp and scallops and cook, stirring, until they begin to color, 1 to 2 minutes. Add the garlic and stir quickly once or twice. Add the wine and cook, stirring, until only a few tablespoons are left in the skillet. Season lightly with salt and turn the heat off under the skillet.

SUGGESTED WINES

With this dish, try a Soave from Bolla or Bertani, or from a small estate like Anselmi or, from California, the dry Riesling of Trefethen or Firestone, which will complement this dish beautifully.

Melt 3 tablespoons of the butter in a large saucepan over medium heat. When the butter foams, add the onion and cook, stirring, until the onion begins to color, 3 to 4 minutes. Add the rice. Cook until it is well coated with the butter and onion, about 1 minute. Add the wine and cook, stirring, until the wine is almost all reduced. Add just enough broth to barely cover the rice. Cook, still over medium heat, until the broth has been absorbed almost completely. Continue cooking and stirring the rice in this manner for about 15 minutes, adding the broth a bit at a time.

Add the shellfish and every bit of their juices. Cook, stirring, 1 to 2 minutes longer. Stir in the parsley and the remaining tablespoon of butter. Taste and adjust the seasoning and serve at once.

Makes 4 to 6 servings

Risotto al Salto

Crisp Risotto Cake

NOTE OF INTEREST

The perfect risotto for these delicious crisp cakes is risotto alla Milanese, *or risotto with parmigiano. (See Risotto with Parmigiano and Asparagus Tips, pages 155–56, and prepare the risotto without the asparagus. When it is completely cool, prepare the* risotto al salto.)

In Milano, leftover risotto is turned into a delicious rice cake. The first time I tasted this dish, many years ago, was at Alfredo Gran San Bernardo, an old classic restaurant which is a bastion of traditional Milanese cooking. The rice cake came to the table piping hot, golden, and crisp, and sprinkled with parmigiano.

Since then, every time I make a risotto, I always cook a bit more, and the day after I turn the leftovers into rice cakes.

    6 cups loosely packed leftover risotto (see note)
    1 large egg, lightly beaten
    2 tablespoons olive oil
    ½ cup freshly grated parmigiano

In a large bowl combine the leftover risotto and egg. Heat ½ tablespoon of the oil in an 8-inch nonstick skillet over medium heat. Take 1½ cups of the rice mixture and spread it over the bottom of the skillet with a spatula, pressing the rice down evenly to form a round pancake. Cook until the bottom of the rice is lightly browned, 7 to 8 minutes.

Brush a large flat plate lightly with oil. Put the plate over the skillet and turn the rice cake onto the plate. Slide it back into the skillet to cook on the other side another 4 to 5 minutes. Place the cake on a serving dish and keep it warm in a low oven while you prepare the remaining cakes. Serve hot with a sprinkling of freshly grated parmigiano.

Makes 4 rice cakes

SUGGESTED WINES
Either a young red, light and fragrant, or an aromatic, not overly structured white. For reds try Valpolicella or Spanna, for whites, Gavi or Pinot Grigio.

POLENTA

I have a clear, vivid image of my mother stirring the polenta in the *paiolo* (the large copper pot used exclusively for polenta) with a long wooden spoon. My mother was not very tall, so she had to strain to reach the bottom of the *paiolo*. She would stir and stir; then, with surprising strength for a woman of her size, she would pick up the *paiolo* and turn it upside down, letting the thick, golden polenta fall slowly onto the *tagliere*. The steaming polenta was left to cool and firm up briefly on the wooden board; then my mother would slice it with a long string, and serve it with whatever sauce she had prepared.

But what is polenta exactly? Polenta is produced by cooking water (or sometimes broth or milk) and cornmeal together. As the cornmeal cooks, it absorbs the cooking water and swells and thickens into a soft, golden mass. The polenta is stirred constantly during cooking, so it won't stick to the pot and won't produce lumps. The cooked, soft polenta can then be served immediately with butter and cheese or other sauces, or with stews or braised meats and game, or poured onto a large wooden board and allowed to cool and firm up. When it is quite firm it can be baked, fried, or grilled and served alongside an infinite number of dishes.

At my restaurant in Sacramento, we serve polenta soft with stewed rabbit and ossobuco. We serve it grilled, topped with sautéed mushrooms or creamy gorgonzola. We bake it with Bolognese meat sauce, and fry it and serve it alongside a roasted meat or fowl.

The texture of polenta depends on the flour used. Cornmeal is available in Italian specialty stores *coarse grained* and *fine grained*. The recipes in this book use a combination of the two which produces a lovely medium-textured polenta.

Polenta is an extremely versatile food. It can be an appetizer, a first course, an entree, or a side dish. The recipes for polenta will be scattered throughout this book, in their proper places, and they will refer back to page 176 for the basic method.

When I started teaching Italian cooking in California twelve years ago, not many people knew about polenta. Today polenta can be found in many Italian and non-Italian restaurants in this country. Often, however, what they call polenta is nothing but a sad imitation of the real thing because too many shortcuts or changes in the cooking method have been taken to produce it. While I realize that ingenious cooks have devised nontraditional ways of cooking polenta, I still maintain that certain things in life need the time, the effort, the attention, and the traditions in order to be outstanding.

Polenta—Basic Method

To make polenta the old-fashioned way, you need only one thing—elbow grease. If you are not willing to put in twenty minutes of effort which will give you perfect polenta, you might just as well buy "instant" polenta in a store.

9 cups cold water
2 tablespoons salt
2 cups coarsely ground cornmeal mixed with 1 cup finely ground cornmeal

Bring the water to a boil in a large, heavy saucepan over medium heat. Add the salt and reduce the heat to medium-low. As soon as the water develops a gentle simmer, start pouring in the cornmeal by the handful, in a thin stream, very slowly, and stir constantly with a long wooden spoon to avoid lumps. When all the cornmeal has been added, you can relax a bit. Keep the water at a steady low simmer and stir frequently. (It is not necessary to stir constantly if the polenta is cooked gently.) Cook the polenta 20 to 25 minutes. As it cooks, the polenta will thicken considerably and it will bubble and spit back to you. Keep stirring, and crush any lumps that might form against the side of the pan. The polenta is done when it comes away effortlessly from the sides of the pan.

If you are planning to serve the polenta soft, spoon directly out of the pot into the serving dishes.

If you want to firm it up a bit (or a lot), pour the polenta onto a large wooden board, shaping it with a large, wet spatula into a 2-inch-thick round, or spread the polenta onto a baking sheet. Let the polenta "settle" for a few minutes, then cut into slices and serve it with your favorite sauce.

Makes 8 servings

TIPS

∾ *For additional taste, stir into the polenta 3 to 4 tablespoons of unsalted butter and 1 cup of freshly grated parmigiano a few minutes before you remove it from the stove.*

∾ *If you want to prepare the polenta a few hours ahead and still serve it* soft, *keep it in a large bowl over a large pot of simmering water. When you are ready to serve it, stir the polenta energetically with a large wooden spoon. If it is still a bit too firm for your taste, stir in a bit of chicken broth or milk and mix energetically to blend.*

MEAT, POULTRY, AND GAME

In 1960 when I first arrived from Italy, I attended my first barbecue party at a neighbor's house. Grilling on the barbecue were the largest steaks I had ever seen in my life. When one of these giant steaks was put on my plate, completely covering it, I began to cut it into large pieces and passed the pieces around to the other guests. My neighbor explained to me that the steak was *all mine*, and he put the pieces back on my plate. I was completely stunned! In Italy a steak of that size would have fed easily a family of four.

Meat in Italy is generally not eaten in large amounts, because in an Italian meal, the meat course is generally preceded by a *primo* (pasta, rice, or soup). The Italian diet, as many have already discovered, is one of the healthiest in the world because of its sequence of small diversified courses.

Because pasta is so strongly identified with the food of Italy, many of its wonderful second courses are still relatively unknown. Italy has a whole glorious category of *secondi*. The ones that are closest to my heart are the simple, traditional dishes of the home. These are exuberant dishes, prepared with basic, often inexpensive, cuts of meat, and they come to life and shine because of the sense of place and tradition and the fertile imagination of the cook.

When I compiled a list of the dishes I wanted to include in this chapter, I became very excited. There, printed on a few pages, were dishes I had enjoyed all over Italy. The ossobuco with porcini of Bologna, the rabbit with balsamic vinegar of Modena, the many versions of *polpette* (meatballs) I had eaten in Roma, where it seemed that every single trattoria had its own version. The beef goulash of Trieste and the chicken with fried eggplant and zucchini of Palermo. All those dishes were simply prepared and simply presented, and were wholesome, unpretentious, and delicious.

For this chapter I tried to choose dishes that are truly representative of the food of the trattoria, and stayed away from the ones that, even though wonderful, had ingredients that would have been hard to find in this country. (How often can we find a suckling pig or a two-month-old lamb in our markets?)

As you can see from the selection of recipes in this chapter, many of the dishes are stewed and cooked slowly with delicious sauces. (These are my favorite dishes because they can be prepared ahead, can be reheated or frozen, and can also feed a crowd.) Others are grilled, broiled, or barbecued, and others again are quickly pan-fried and will cook in practically no time at all, giving you that instant feeling of accomplishment and satisfaction, and will make you doubt the convenience of your microwave oven.

Bistecca alla Pizzaiola

Pan-fried Steaks with Garlic, Anchovies, Tomatoes, and Oregano

There are various *pizzaiola* preparations in Italy that can be made with beef, veal, or pork. However, the best and most authentic is the Neapolitan *bistecca* or *manzo alla pizzaiola*. In this dish, the beef is browned quickly over high heat and cooked briefly with a savory sauce of garlic, anchovies, tomatoes, and fresh oregano or other fresh herbs.

This dish comes from Antica Pizzeria Port'Alba, which, besides wonderful *pizze*, also serves some delicious local Neapolitan dishes.

> ⅓ cup olive oil
>
> Four ½-inch-thick sirloin steaks, about 6 ounces each
>
> 2 cloves garlic, finely minced
>
> 4 anchovy fillets, finely chopped
>
> 1 cup dry white wine
>
> 2 cups canned imported Italian tomatoes with their juice, put through a strainer or food mill to remove the seeds
>
> Salt and freshly ground black pepper to taste
>
> ⅓ cup loosely packed fresh oregano leaves or 2 tablespoons chopped fresh parsley

Heat the oil in a large skillet over high heat. Add the meat and cook until it is lightly golden on both sides, about 2 minutes. Transfer the meat to a dish.

Add the garlic and anchovies to the skillet and stir quickly once or twice. (The garlic will turn brown almost immediately because the skillet is now very hot.) Add the wine and cook, stirring, until the wine is reduced by half, 3 to 4 minutes. Add the tomatoes and season with salt and several grinds of pepper. Reduce the heat to medium and cook, stirring, 2 to 3 minutes. Stir in the fresh oregano, then return the meat and the meat juices in the dish to the skillet. Cook 1 to 2 minutes, stirring and basting the meat.

Taste and adjust the seasoning and serve at once.

Makes 4 servings

NOTE OF INTEREST

Pizzaiola means "pizza-maker's wife's style." Perhaps the creator of this dish was the wife of a pizzaiolo, a pizza maker.

With the exception of bistecca alla Fiorentina, *Italians generally don't eat steaks that are too thick. A quarter-inch or half-inch steak can be pan-fried very quickly and served with or without a sauce.*

A great deal of the cooking of Italy is made up of dishes that can be prepared in less time that it takes for a large pot of water to come to a boil!

SUGGESTED WINES

A tomato-based sauce calls for a young but not too light red wine such as Lachryma Christi Rosso from Mastroberardino or Rivera Castel del Monte. One of the new California Rhône-style reds would also work well.

Bistecca di Manzo alla Boscaiola

Steak with Porcini Mushroom and Tomatoes

Italians are not great red meat lovers and, with the exception of the famous and delicious *bistecca alla Fiorentina*, most beef preparations are either boiled (as in *bollito misto*) or are prepared with sauces.

In Italian homes, *bistecca di manzo* is often a very thin steak quickly sautéed in a bit of oil with some garlic and rosemary. Sometimes the same steak has the addition of a sauce. *Bistecca alla boscaiola* is a dish often found in *trattorie* because it is tasty, homey, and because it makes a small amount of beef go a long way. This preparation, which has a delicious sauce of onions, porcini mushrooms, Marsala wine, and tomatoes, comes from Coco Lezzone, one of the best-known *trattorie* in Firenze.

It is a dish that can be prepared in a short amount of time, provided that you have the basic ingredients at hand. In this recipe the steak is only ½ inch thick. You can use a thicker steak if you prefer. Make sure to have at hand a large loaf of Italian bread to dip into the sauce and a good bottle of Chianti Classico to sip with it.

> 1 ounce dried porcini mushrooms (see page 15), soaked in 2 cups lukewarm water for 20 minutes
> ¼ cup olive oil
> 4 ½-inch-thick steaks, such as New York or rib eye steaks, about 8 ounces each
> 1 small onion, finely minced
> 1 cup dry Marsala
> 2 cups canned imported Italian tomatoes with their juice, put through a strainer or food mill to remove the seeds
> Salt and freshly ground black pepper to taste
> 2 tablespoons finely chopped fresh parsley

Drain the mushrooms and reserve the soaking water. Line a strainer with two paper towels and strain the mushroom water into a bowl to get rid of the sandy deposits. Set aside. Wash the mushrooms well under cold running water and chop them into rough pieces.

Heat the oil in a large skillet over high heat. Add the steaks and cook until the meat is lightly golden on both sides, 2 to 3 minutes. Transfer the meat to a platter. (If the oil becomes too dark during cooking, discard it and add a bit of fresh oil to the skillet.)

Reduce the heat to medium, add the onion, and cook, stirring, until they are lightly golden, 2 to 3 minutes. Add the mushrooms and Marsala. Cook and stir until the Marsala is almost all reduced, 3 to 4 minutes. Add 1 cup of the reserved porcini soaking water and stir once or twice. Add the tomatoes, season with salt and pepper, and cook 4 to 5 minutes.

Return the steaks to the skillet and cook 2 to 3 minutes longer. Place the steaks on individual serving dishes. Add the parsley to the sauce and stir quickly a few times. Taste and adjust the seasoning. Spoon the sauce over the steaks and serve at once.

Makes 4 servings

SUGGESTED WINES

A good Italian Chianti Classico from Antinori, Ruffino, or Brolio would be perfect, especially a Chianti Classico Riserva, five to eight years old.

Stracotto di Manzo alla Piemontese

Beef Braised in Wine

Beef braised in wine is a classic dish of many Northern Italian regions. The best version is perhaps the one from Piemonte, because of the high quality of Piemontese wine and beef.

In this preparation the beef is browned over high heat to seal in the juices. A mixture of vegetables is added and browned with the beef. Then the wine is added and sometimes even some broth or a bit of tomato sauce. The meat is then cooked very slowly for 3 to 4 hours. The result is a juicy, tasty dish with a melt-in-the-mouth quality.

Trattoria Della Posta on the outskirts of Torino serves this classic dish regularly and cooks it in the great Barolo wine of the region. In winter, they serve it with a soft, delicious polenta.

1 tablespoon unsalted butter
3 tablespoons olive oil
3 pounds beef bottom round
½ cup unbleached all-purpose flour
1 medium-size onion, finely minced
1 medium-size carrot, finely minced
1 medium-size stalk celery, finely minced
2 cloves garlic, finely minced
3 cups medium-bodied red wine, such as a Chianti
    Classico or a light Pinot Noir
1 cup canned imported Italian tomatoes with their juice,
    put through a strainer or food mill to remove the seeds
Salt and freshly ground black pepper to taste

TIPS

ᔜ *This is one of those dishes that tastes even better the day after it is made. Prepare it in the morning and let the meat steep in its own sauce for several hours or overnight.*

ᔜ *Use any leftovers to make the delicious Braised Beef Ravioli (see pages 122–23).*

SUGGESTED WINES

This dish requires an important red wine, such as a Barolo or Barbaresco Riserva from one of the many great producers of Piemonte, such as Conterno, Ceretto, or Bruno Giacosa.

Heat the butter and oil in a large, heavy casserole over high heat. When the butter foams, sprinkle the meat with the flour and add it to the casserole. Cook until it is golden brown on all sides, 6 to 7 minutes. Transfer the meat to a platter, reduce the heat to medium, and add the onion, carrot, and celery to the casserole. Cook until they are lightly golden, 4 to 5 minutes. Add the garlic and cook less than 1 minute.

Return the meat to the casserole. Raise the heat to high and add the wine and tomatoes. Season with salt and pepper. Cook and stir until the liquid comes to a boil, then cover the casserole, leaving the lid slightly askew, and reduce the heat to medium-low. Simmer 3 to 3½ hours, stirring a few times and making sure that there is plenty of liquid in the pan. Add a bit more wine or tomatoes if the wine reduces too much. (At the end of the cooking time there should be about half of the original amount of wine and tomatoes still left in the casserole.) The meat will have shrunk to about three-quarters of its original weight and should have a nice darkish color.

Place the meat on a cutting board and let it settle for about 5 minutes. Check the consistency of your sauce. If too thin, cook it down over high heat until it has a medium-thick consistency. If too thick, add a bit more tomato or a bit of broth. Taste and adjust the seasonings, then slice the meat and serve topped by a bit of this delicious sauce.

Makes 6 servings

Involtini di Manzo al Pomodoro

Stuffed Beef Bundles with Tomato Sauce

My mother-in-law was a very good Southern Italian cook. One of the dishes she prepared often was *braciola alla Napoletana*, a large slice of beef that was stuffed with garlic, herbs, cheese, and whatever else she decided to add. It was rolled up into a large, fat bundle, browned in oil, and cooked slowly with tomatoes for about two hours. The sauce of the *braciola* was served over fusilli or rigatoni, and the meat was sliced and served as a second course after the pasta. It was wholesome and delicious.

During one of my visits to Roma, I came across a similar dish. This one, however, used small, thin slices of beef instead of a large one, that were cooked very quickly over high heat. This version from Vecchia Roma trattoria is a welcome one, since it can be prepared from beginning to end in about fifteen minutes.

1½ pounds top sirloin of beef, cut into 12 small, thin slices, pounded very thin (see tip below)
2 cloves garlic, finely minced
2 tablespoons chopped fresh rosemary or 1 tablespoon dried, crumbled
6 thin slices prosciutto (about ¼ pound), cut in half
⅓ cup olive oil
1 cup dry red wine
2 cups canned imported Italian tomatoes with their juice, put through a strainer or food mill to remove the seeds
Salt and freshly ground black pepper to taste
2 tablespoons chopped fresh parsley

Put the slices of beef on a work surface, and with a spoon, spread a bit of the minced garlic and rosemary over each slice. Place a half slice of prosciutto over each piece of meat and roll up into a small bundle. Secure each bundle with a toothpick.

Heat the oil in a large skillet over medium-high heat. Add the bundles and brown on all sides, 3 to 4 minutes. Transfer the bundles to a plate and discard half of the cooking fat.

Put the skillet back on the heat and add the wine. Cook and

TIPS

ↄ◞ *Since the beef slices are very thin, make sure not to overcook them or they will become tough.*

ↄ◞ *Whenever you sauté, make sure not to crowd the skillet so that the meat will brown evenly and quickly.*

SUGGESTED WINES
Try one of California's new Italian varietals such as Il Podere dell'Olivos Nebbiolo or Robert Pepi or Atlas Peak Sangiovese or Montevina's Montanaro.

stir to pick up the bits and pieces attached to the bottom of the skillet. When the wine is reduced by half, 1 to 2 minutes, add the tomatoes. Season with salt and pepper and cook, stirring a few times, until the sauce has a medium-thick consistency, 4 to 5 minutes. Stir in the parsley.

Remove the toothpicks from the bundles and put them back into the skillet. Cook about one minute, until the bundles are heated through and well coated with the sauce. Serve at once.

Makes 6 servings

Goulash alla Triestina

Beef Stew Trieste Style

There are so many dishes that are instantly identified with a city—the tortellini of Bologna, the black risotto of Venezia, the fettuccine all'Alfredo of Roma, and the goulash of Trieste, just to mention a few.

The goulash I enjoyed at Re di Coppe in Trieste was a melt-in-the-mouth preparation with a a dense wine-tomato sauce made sweet by the addition of onions, which came accompanied by slices of fried polenta.

The secret of a good stew lies in the long, slow cooking. After the initial browning of the meat and the addition of the required liquid, the stew will cook all by itself, needing only an occasional stir.

¼ cup olive oil
2 pounds beef chuck, cut into 2-inch pieces
2 large onions, thinly sliced
Salt and freshly ground black pepper to taste
½ teaspoon paprika
3 to 4 bay leaves, crumbled
¼ cup red wine vinegar
2 cups dry full-bodied red wine
2 cups canned imported Italian tomatoes with their juice, put through a strainer or food mill to remove the seeds
1½ cups meat broth, preferably homemade (see pages 53–54)

Heat the oil in a large skillet over high heat. Add the meat and cook, stirring, until it is lightly golden on all sides, 4 to 5 minutes. Transfer the meat to a plate, reduce the heat to medium, and add the onions. Cook and stir until the onions are lightly golden, 4 to 5 minutes.

Return the meat to the skillet and season with salt and pepper. Add the paprika, bay leaves, and vinegar, and stir once or twice. Add the wine and cook, stirring, until it is reduced by half, 6 to 7 minutes.

Add the tomatoes and 1 cup of the meat broth and mix well with the other ingredients. Cover the skillet, leaving it slightly askew, and reduce the heat to low. Simmer 1 to 1½ hours, stirring a few times. If the sauce dries out too much during cooking, add some more meat broth. (At the end of the cooking time, the meat should be so tender that it can be cut with a fork.)

Makes 4 to 6 servings

SUGGESTED WINES
Tasty, not too tannic reds will work well. Try an Italian Merlot from the Collio or from the Colli Orientali in Friuli, or a lighter vintage Merlot from a good California producer.

Polpettine di Manzo in Umido con Piselli

Beef Meatballs with Tomatoes and Peas

With a bit of ingenuity and imagination, basic ground beef or ground veal can be turned into many delicious preparations.

Polpette, polpettoni, and *ragù* can be produced with these economical meats and they are fixtures of the *buona cucina casalinga*.

This simple, satisfying dish comes from Lucia, a supermodest trattoria in the old Trastevere quarter of Roma. The look and taste of this dish reminded me of the one my mother used to make. She would prepare a large batch of *polpette* (meatballs). She would fry some and stew the others. The fried *polpette* became our school lunch or after-school snack, and at night, we would eat the stewed *polpette*, dipping the bread into that simple, satisfying sauce.

For the polpette

2 slices Italian bread without the crust, broken into pieces and soaked in 1 cup milk for 5 minutes

1 pound ground beef

1 clove garlic, finely minced

6 to 8 sage leaves, minced or a few dried, very finely crushed

2 tablespoons chopped fresh parsley

¼ cup freshly grated pecorino romano cheese or ½ cup parmigiano

3 large eggs, 2 of them lightly beaten

Salt and freshly ground black pepper to taste

1 cup fine plain bread crumbs, spread evenly over a sheet of aluminum foil

Oil for frying

For the sauce

2 cups shelled fresh peas or frozen peas, thawed

¼ cup olive oil

1 small carrot, finely minced

½ medium-size onion, finely minced

2 ounces sliced pancetta, finely chopped

2 cups chicken broth, preferably homemade (see pages 54–55)

2 cups canned imported Italian tomatoes with their juice, put through a strainer or food mill to remove the seeds

Salt and freshly ground black pepper to taste

NOTE OF INTEREST

When I tested this dish at my restaurant in Sacramento and received the unanimous approval of my kitchen staff, I took home the polpette *that were left over, so that the next day, Sunday, I did not have to cook. My husband, who that weekend had been on call for his medical group, came home late at night and ate the* polpette *cold, straight out of the container, proclaiming that "they were even better cold."*

If you are using fresh peas, bring a small saucepan of water to a boil over medium heat. Add the peas and cook until tender but still a bit firm to the bite, 4 to 6 minutes, depending on the size (they will finish cooking in the sauce). Drain the peas and set aside in a bowl until ready to use.

Drain the bread and squeeze it out with your hands into a soft pulp.

In a medium-size bowl, combine the bread, beef, garlic, sage, parsley, pecorino romano, and 1 egg and season with salt and pepper. Mix well with your hands or with a large spoon until the ingredients are well blended.

Take one heaping tablespoon of the beef mixture between the palms of your hands and roll it into a ball about the size of a small egg, then flatten it a bit. Repeat this with the remaining mixture. When all the *polpette* have been shaped, dip them into the beaten eggs and coat them with the bread crumbs.

Heat one inch of oil in a heavy medium-size skillet over medium heat until it begins to sizzle and smoke. Lower a few *polpette* at a time into it with a slotted spoon. Cook until they are lightly golden on both sides, 2 to 3 minutes. Remove them with a slotted spoon and transfer to paper towels to drain.

To prepare the sauce, heat the oil in a large skillet over medium heat. Add the carrot and onion and cook, stirring, until they begin to color, 2 to 3 minutes. Add the pancetta and cook, stirring, until it turns lightly golden, 2 to 3 minutes. Add the broth and tomatoes and season with salt and pepper. Bring the sauce to a gentle boil, then add the *polpette* and reduce the heat to medium-low. Cover the skillet, leaving it slightly askew, and cook until the sauce has a medium-thick consistency, 7 to 8 minutes. Add the peas and cook a few minutes longer. Taste and adjust the seasoning and serve immediately.

Makes 4 servings

SUGGESTED WINES
Use some of the red wines suggested for the previous recipe or, for white wine lovers, try a Pinot Grigio from Jermann or Schiopetto in Friuli.

Polpettone al Forno

Baked Meat Loaf with Spicy Tomato Sauce

Because trattoria food is synonymous with the classic, homey food of the immediate area, often there is very little difference in the variety of dishes offered in *trattorie*. In Roma, for example, a trattoria worthy of its name always serves *bucatini all'Amatriciana* (pages 98–99) or some kind of fetuccine and *abbacchio* (milk-fed lamb) That is precisely the reason why these dishes are so outstanding, because they have been prepared in the same classic manner a thousand times before. Then, of course, there are dishes where the cook puts in his own personal touch, adding or subtracting an ingredient or two to fit his own mood.

This delicious *polpettone* comes from Trattoria Zarazà in the colorful area of Frascati just outside Roma. The meat loaf was moist and juicy and was topped by a spicy tomato sauce, which gave me a good reason to drink a few glasses of very pleasant local Frascati wine.

For the polpettone

> 4 slices Italian bread without the crust, broken into rough pieces and soaked in 1 cup milk
>
> 2 pounds ground beef
>
> ¼ pound sliced prosciutto, finely chopped
>
> 2 large eggs, lightly beaten
>
> ¼ cup loosely packed chopped fresh parsley
>
> 1 cup freshly grated parmigiano
>
> Salt and freshly ground black pepper to taste
>
> 1 cup fine plain bread crumbs, evenly spread over a sheet of aluminum foil
>
> 3 tablespoons olive oil

For the tomato sauce

> 2 tablespoons olive oil
>
> 2 cloves garlic, finely minced
>
> 4 cups canned imported Italian tomatoes with their juice, put through a strainer or food mill to remove the seeds
>
> Salt to taste
>
> ¼ teaspoon dried red pepper flakes
>
> 2 tablespoons chopped fresh parsley

Preheat the oven to 375°F.

Drain the bread and squeeze it with your hands into a soft pulp. In a large bowl combine the bread, beef, prosciutto, eggs, parsley, and parmigiano, and season with salt and just a bit of black pepper. Mix well with your hands or with a large spoon until the ingredients are thoroughly combined. Shape the mixture into a large, rectangular loaf and coat with the crumbs.

Pour the oil in a large baking dish and place the *polpettone* in it. Brush some oil over the top of the *polpettone* and bake until it is golden brown, 30 to 40 minutes.

While the *polpettone* is in the oven, heat the oil for the sauce in a medium-size saucepan over medium heat. Add the garlic and stir until it begins to color, less than 1 minute. Add the tomatoes and season with salt and the red pepper. Cook 7 to 8 minutes, stirring a few times. Add the parsley and stir.

Carefully tilt the baking dish and discard about three-quarters of the fat and watery juices that have accumulated. Pour the tomato sauce over the *polpettone* and cook 15 minutes longer.

Cool the *polpettone* 5 minutes before slicing it. Serve topped with a few tablespoons of tomato sauce.

Makes 6 to 8 servings

SUGGESTED WINES

Try a Frascati Conte Zandotti or Orvieto from producers such as Antinori or Barberani.

Cotechino Bollito

Boiled Pork Sausage from Emilia-Romagna

Emilia-Romagna is famous throughout Italy for its superlative handmade pasta and pork products. One of the many wonderful pork specialties is cotechino, a large fresh sausage which is boiled and served as a component of the classic *bollito misto*, or simply by itself.

Cotechino, just like any other sausage, is down-to-earth food. One of my favorite way of eating cotechino is with fluffy mashed potatoes, enriched by plenty of butter and parmigiano (pages 275–76), or with stewed beans (pages 263–64), or stewed lentils (pages 265–66). This is an item that is quite often found in the *trattorie* of the region, especially country *trattorie* where sausages are often made on the premises.

Even though the cotechino of Emilia-Romagna is in a class by itself, it is possible to find an acceptable substitute here. Twenty years ago, when I first moved to Sacramento, I used to drive 160 miles round trip to San Francisco to buy cotechino and other special Italian ingredients. Check with your local Italian market or specialty food store.

1 cotechino sausage (generally 1 to 1½ pounds)

Bring a medium-size saucepan of water to a boil over medium heat. With a fork, puncture the cotechino skin in several places and add to the boiling water. Cover the saucepan and lower the heat to medium-low. Simmer the cotechino 45 minutes to 1 hour, depending on its weight. (If the skin of the cotechino breaks, that's okay; keep cooking it gently for the required time.)

Keep the cotechino in its own warm broth until you are ready to use it, then slice it into rounds and serve with one of the above-mentioned dishes.

Makes 4 servings

SUGGESTED WINES
A young, slightly acidic wine is needed. Try a young Amador County Zinfandel/Barbera blend such as Montanaro from Monteviña or a young Chianti from Ricasoli.

Involtini di Maiale alle Verze Piccanti

Grilled Pork Bundles Stuffed with Spicy Cabbage

In trattoria cooking there are many *involtini* dishes. They can be prepared with a variety of meats, fish, and vegetables and can be stuffed with savory ingredients. *Involtini* can be sautéed and cooked with sauces or they can be grilled. They are delicious, easy to prepare, and economical because a few thin slices of beef, veal, or pork can go a long way.

At Evangelista, an upscale trattoria in Roma, I had these delicious grilled *involtini*. They were prepared with veal and stuffed with a spicy mixture of cabbage. Interestingly, Evangelista refused to tell me how the dish was prepared. However, since it was quite simple, with recognizable ingredients, once I got back to my restaurant in Sacramento, I managed to reproduce them quite successfully. But, instead of veal, I used pork, because the idea of pork and cabbage appealed to me more.

> ⅓ cup olive oil
> ¼ pound sliced pancetta, chopped
> ½ pound Savoy cabbage, finely chopped
> ¼ cup red wine vinegar
> 1 cup water
> Salt to taste
> ¼ teaspoon dried red pepper flakes
> 1 large egg, lightly beaten with ⅓ cup freshly grated parmigiano
> 1½ pounds center-cut pork loin, cut into 12 slices, pounded thin into scaloppine
> 2 tablespoons olive oil mixed in a small bowl with 2 tablespoons red wine vinegar

Heat the oil in a large skillet over medium heat. Add the pancetta and cook, stirring, until it begins to color, about 1 minute. Add the cabbage and stir briefly. Add the vinegar and water, and season with the salt and red pepper. Cover the skillet and reduce the heat to medium-low. Cook 12 to 15 minutes, stirring a few times, until the cabbage is soft and tender and the liquid in the skillet is all reduced. If the juices are not reduced completely, remove the lid, raise the heat, and cook, stirring, until no more moisture is left in the skillet. With a slotted spoon, transfer the cabbage to a bowl and let cool.

Add the egg and parmigiano to the cabbage and mix to incorporate. Taste and adjust the seasonings.

Place the pork scaloppine on a work surface and place a heaping tablespoon of cabbage mixture in the center of each one. Fold the two lateral sides of the scaloppine so they are just barely over the filling, then roll up the meat around the filling to make a bundle. Secure each bundle with a toothpick and place on a plate until you are ready to cook them. (This can be done several hours ahead of time.)

Preheat the grill or the barbecue. When your heat source is very hot, brush the bundles with a bit of the oil-vinegar mixture and place on the grill. Cook until the bundles are golden on all sides, 8 to 10 minutes. (When you turn the bundles, do so gently or they may open and spill out their filling.)

Serve them hot with nice, fluffy mashed potatoes (see pages 275–76).

Makes 4 servings

SUGGESTED WINES
Try a spicy, aromatic dry white such as Château Ste. Michelle dry Riesling from Washington State or Felluga Terre Alte from Italy.

Involtini di Maiale al Pomodoro

Stuffed Pork Bundles with Tomato-wine Sauce

This dish is a delicious variation of the grilled pork bundles stuffed with spicy cabbage in the preceding page, and it came about because of a surplus of bundles I had prepared.

This dish can be prepared completely several hours ahead. When ready to serve, reheat it gently over low heat, making sure not to overcook it.

1 recipe Pork Bundles Stuffed with Spicy Cabbage (see
    pages 190–91)
¼ cup olive oil
2 cloves garlic, finely minced
1 cup dry white wine
3 cups canned imported Italian tomatoes with their juice,
    put through a strainer or food mill to remove the seeds
Salt to taste
2 tablespoons chopped fresh parsley

Prepare the bundles as instructed, but don't grill them.

Heat the oil in a large skillet over medium heat. Add the pork bundles, making sure not to crowd the skillet. Cook until they are lightly golden on all sides, 2 to 3 minutes. Transfer the bundles to a plate.

Add the garlic to the skillet and stir quickly once or twice. Add the wine and cook, stirring, until it is almost all reduced, 5 to 6 minutes, then add the tomatoes and season with salt. Reduce the heat to medium and cook, stirring, 3 to 4 minutes.

Return the bundles to the skillet, reduce the heat to medium-low, and cover the skillet, leaving the lid slightly askew. Cook 4 to 5 minutes longer. Stir in the parsley, taste, and adjust the seasoning. Serve hot.

Makes 4 servings

SUGGESTED WINES

Light red wines, low in tannin but with some acid, go well with the tomato-pork flavors. Try a Rosso Cònero from the Marche region, a Dolcetto d'Asti from Piemonte, or a light Zinfandel from California.

Cassoela

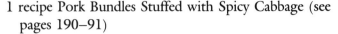

Milanese Short Ribs, Sausage, and Cabbage Stew

I first tasted *cassoela* many years ago at the venerable Antica Trattoria della Pesa in Milano. I had been told that for authentic, classic Milanese food, nobody could beat the food of this trattoria. I remember that I was somewhat disappointed by the modest, unadorned look of the old trattoria and by the cold, almost bored attitude of the waiter. All of this, however, became completely irrelevant when the food I had ordered came to the table.

A large plate of stewed pork ribs, sausage, salt pork, onions, and cabbage was put in front of me, next to a generous amount of soft, steaming polenta. I remember thinking that there was no way I could eat all that food, but somehow, a bit later, my plate had been wiped clean!

Today this hearty, robust, and filling dish is almost forgotten, because it is considered "too heavy" for today's dietary standards.

While I agree that this is, in fact, a rich, filling dish, I still maintain that sometimes there are reasons to prepare it. If you should hear a forecast for heavy snow in your area, run out immediately and buy all the ingredients for *cassoela*, because this is the perfect, quintessential winter dish.

    6 tablespoons olive oil
    2 tablespoons unsalted butter
    2 medium-size onions, thinly sliced
    1 stalk celery, sliced
    2 small carrots, sliced
    1 pound Savoy cabbage, coarsely shredded
    2 cups meat broth, preferably homemade (see pages 53–54)
    1 pound mild Italian sausage, cut into 2- to 3-inch pieces
    1 pound pork short ribs, cut into 8 single rib pieces
    4 ounces thickly sliced pancetta, cut into wide strips
    1 cup dry white wine
    Salt and freshly ground black pepper to taste

Heat 3 tablespoons of the oil and the butter in a large, heavy casserole over medium heat. Add the onions and cook, stirring, until they begin to color, 2 to 3 minutes. Add the celery, carrots, and cabbage, stir for about 1 minute, then add 1½ cups of broth. Cover the casserole, reduce the heat to medium-low, and cook 25 to 30 minutes, stirring a few times.

Heat the remaining oil in a medium-size skillet over high heat. Add the sausage and short ribs and cook until everything has a nice, golden color on all sides, 5 to 6 minutes. Transfer them to a plate as they brown.

Add the pancetta to the skillet and cook, stirring, until it begins to color, about 1 minute. (Remember that the skillet is already very hot and the pancetta will brown in no time at all.) With a slotted spoon transfer the pancetta to the plate with the sausage.

Discard the fat in the skillet. Raise the heat to high and add the wine. Cook, stirring to pick up the bits and pieces attached to the bottom of the skillet. When the wine is almost all reduced,

4 to 5 minutes, return the sausage, ribs, and pancetta to the skillet and mix briefly until everything is well coated with the thickened wine and pan juices.

Add everything to the casserole with the cabbage and mix well. Add the remaining broth, cover the casserole, and simmer gently until the meat is tender and the cabbage mixture is very soft, 40 to 50 minutes. Taste and, if necessary, season lightly with a bit of salt and pepper. (Keep in mind that both the sausage and pancetta are already quite salty.)

Serve hot with soft, grilled, or fried polenta.

Makes 4 servings

Costine di Maiale in Padella con Fagioli Piccanti

Pork Spareribs with Spicy Beans

Many trattoria dishes have an unmistakable peasant feeling that is reflected in the humble ingredients used and the simple, basic execution of the dish. At Trattoria "Max" on the outskirts of Trieste, I had a succulent dish of pork ribs which were browned in oil and cooked slowly with wine, vinegar, white beans, and plenty of *peperoncino* (crushed hot red pepper). The sauce consisted only of a few tablespoons of reduced pan juices and oil which gave the ribs and the beans a shiny coating.

½ cup dried white cannellini beans, picked over and soaked overnight in plenty of cold water in a medium-size bowl

⅓ cup olive oil

8 pork spareribs, cut into single ribs (about 2½ to 3 pounds)

1 medium-size onion, finely minced

2 cups dry white wine

¼ cup red wine vinegar

Salt to taste

½ teaspoon dried red pepper flakes

Discard any beans that come to the surface of the water. Drain and rinse the beans under cold running water and put them in a medium-size saucepan. Cover the beans with cold water and bring to a boil over medium heat. Reduce the heat to medium-low and cook the beans a little more than halfway, 35 to 40 minutes. (The beans should be tender but still quite firm, because they will continue cooking with the spareribs.) Drain the beans and place in a bowl until ready to use.

Heat the oil in a large skillet over medium-high heat. Add as many ribs as can comfortably fit into the skillet without crowding. Cook until the ribs are golden brown on both sides, 7 to 8 minutes, then transfer them to a plate and brown the remaining ones. Discard half of the fat.

Add the onion to the skillet, and cook, stirring a few times, until it is lightly golden, 2 to 3 minutes. Add the wine and vinegar and season with the salt and hot pepper. Bring the liquid to a fast boil, then reduce the heat to medium-low. Return the ribs to the skillet, add the beans, and mix well. Cover the skillet and cook until the meat is tender and begins to fall away from the bone, 45 minutes to 1 hour. Stir a few times during cooking and add a bit of broth or water if the liquid in the pan reduces too quickly. At the end of the cooking time there should be about ½ cup of pan juices left in the skillet. Serve hot.

Makes 4 servings

SUGGESTED WINES
Try an Italian Merlot from Felluga or Volpe Pasini or a California Zinfandel from Santa Barbara Winery.

Le Costicine di Maiale in Umido con la Polenta

Stewed Spareribs with Tomatoes and Soft Polenta

As a teenager growing up in Bologna, I remember the fun of a Sunday excursion in the country with friends which were made for the sole purpose of eating large quantities of country food. We would dash to the hills outside Bologna in search of farmhouses and *trattorie* that could feed a crowd for very little money. Those meals were made up of home-cured salamis, prosciutto, and sausages, fried polenta, and tasty spareribs.

At Vernizzi, a country trattoria smack in the middle of the flat, fertile farmland of Emilia-Romagna, between Modena and Parma, I was taken back in time with this dish of deliciously succulent spareribs which were served with a soft polenta!

⅓ cup olive oil
8 pork spareribs, cut into single ribs (about 2½ to 3 pounds)
2 cloves garlic, finely minced
8 to 10 fresh sage leaves, finely minced or 3 to 4 dried, crumbled
1 tablespoon minced fresh rosemary
¼ pound sliced pancetta, finely chopped
1 cup dry, medium-bodied red wine, such as Sangiovese di Romagna
4 cups canned imported Italian tomatoes with their juice, put through a strainer or food mill to remove the seeds
Salt and freshly ground black pepper to taste
½ recipe Basic Polenta (see page 176)

Heat the oil in a large skillet over medium heat. Add as many ribs as can comfortably fit in the skillet without crowding. Cook until the ribs are golden brown on both sides, 7 to 8 minutes. As they brown, remove them from the skillet to a plate and brown the ones that are left.

Discard half the cooking fat and add the garlic, sage, rosemary, and pancetta. Cook, stirring, until the mixture is lightly golden, about 2 minutes. Add the wine and cook, stirring, until it is reduced by half, 2 to 3 minutes. Add the tomatoes and season with salt and several grinds of pepper.

Return the ribs to the skillet (at this point it does not matter if they fit tightly together). Reduce the heat to medium-low, cover the skillet, and cook until the meat is tender and begins to fall off the bone, about 1 hour. Stir and turn the ribs a few times during the cooking.

While the spareribs are cooking, prepare the polenta and when done, keep it warm over *very* low heat, stirring occasionally.

Taste the sauce and adjust the seasoning. (If the sauce has thickened up too much during cooking, thin it down with a bit of water, meat broth, or additional tomato sauce.) Serve the ribs with a generous amount of sauce and polenta.

Makes 4 servings

SUGGESTED WINES
For the budget-minded, choose a red California jug wine from a serious producer such as Pedroncelli or Mondavi. From Italy, try a Frescobaldi Chianti or Riunite Lambrusco Rosso, served chilled.

Spiedini di Agnello e Salsiccia

Lamb and Sausage Skewers

There are people who assume that the right kitchen equipment will make them better cooks. I wish I could have taken these people to Italy with me when I was researching this book to show them the small, cramped kitchens of the *trattorie* I visited, where space and equipment were down to the bare essentials. One of my favorite little places in Roma was Trattoria Paola. Signora Ida, the owner, was the undisputed queen of the tiniest kitchen I have ever seen in my life. The day I had these delicious grilled *spiedini* for lunch, I went into her kitchen to tell her how much I had enjoyed them and asked her where her grill was. "Here," she said, and showed me a large cast-iron pan lined with elevated ridges. "It is not the equipment that makes this dish so delicious," she confided, "it is the ingredients. The lamb is very young, and we make our own sausage."

Romans love lamb and they eat it as often as they can. Lamb in Roma generally means *abbacchio*, which is milk-fed baby lamb that is just one month old. Since *abbacchio* is not available in this country, we must content ourselves with the youngest lamb available, which is generally six months to one year old.

> 1 pound spicy Italian sausage, cut into 1½-inch pieces
> 1 pound boneless leg of lamb, fat removed and cut into 1½-inch pieces
> 10 to 15 small fresh sage leaves
> 2 large red onions, quartered
> ⅓ cup olive oil
> 2 tablespoons red wine vinegar
> Salt and freshly ground black pepper to taste

Bring a small saucepan to a boil over medium heat. Puncture the sausage in a few places with a fork and place in the boiling water. Cook about 2 minutes. Drain the sausage and dry it on paper towels. Thread the lamb, sausage, sage leaves, and onions onto the skewers alternately.

In a small bowl combine the oil and vinegar. Brush the meat with this mixture and season with salt and several grinds of pepper.

TIPS

~ *In this preparation the sausage is given a quick boiling so that it will cook evenly with the meat. (Keep in mind that the sausage should cook all the way through, while the lamb should still be pink inside.)*

~ Spiedini *can be cooked on a grill, a barbecue, a "grill pan," or under a broiler. Whatever you use, make sure to have your heat source very hot so that the meat will "sear" immediately and when cooked will be lightly charred on the outside and pink and juicy on the inside.*

~ *If fresh sage is not available, crumble some dried sage, mix it with the oil and vinegar, and brush it over the lamb.*

~ Spiedini *can be prepared in the morning and cooked at the last moment.*

SUGGESTED WINES

Choose a straightforward, uncomplicated wine for this dish, such as a Gallo Hearty Burgundy from California or a Folonari Valpolicella from Italy, served slightly chilled.

Preheat the grill or broiler well ahead of time so it will be nice and hot when you are ready to use it. Cook the *spiedini* until the meat is well seared and golden in color, 3 to 4 minutes on each side. Brush the meat again with the oil and vinegar just before serving.

Makes 4 to 6 servings

Agnello a Scottadito

Grilled Marinated Lamb Chops

There is no better place to eat lamb than in Roma. There, young, tender lamb is cooked in many different ways. At Pippo lo Sgobbone in Roma, a fun, boisterous trattoria, I dined on small, succulent lamb chops that had been brushed with melted lard and cooked quickly on a very hot grill. They were simply outstanding! Because lard is not very popular in this country, the chops can be marinated first in olive oil, salt, and a bit of hot chile pepper flakes. Since I don't have a grill in my home, I use a heavy cast-iron pan with elevated ridges (also known as a "grill pan") or a nice, hot barbecue. A great accompaniment to these chops would be Baked Tomatoes with Mint (page 279) or Potato Cake with Garlic and Parmigiano (pages 276–77).

12 single lamb chops, cut from the rib, each ½ inch thick
    (about 2 pounds)
½ cup olive oil
Salt to taste
A pinch of dried red pepper flakes
Juice of 1 lemon

Place the chops in a shallow dish. Add the oil and season with the salt and crushed red pepper. Leave the chops in the oil for 30 to 40 minutes, turning them a few times.

Preheat the grill, barbecue, or grill pan. When your heat source is very hot, add the chops and cook about 2 minutes on each side. Arrange the lamb on a warm serving dish, season lightly with salt, add the lemon juice, and serve at once.

Makes 4 servings

Agnello alla Cacciatora con Polenta Fritta

Lamb Stew with Fried Polenta

Lamb is used extensively in the cooking of Roma and the Lazio region. It can be grilled, roasted, braised, or stewed, and since the lamb used is generally very young and often milk-fed, these preparations become thoroughly succulent.

This dish comes from Taverna Romana in the old quarter of Trastevere, and the owners, Lucia and Tonino, pride themselves on their old-fashioned *cucina casareccia*—home cooking.

For this preparation, choose the youngest lamb possible and after the initial browning of the meat, cook it very gently. The slow cooking and occasional basting will produce a tender, melt-in-your-mouth lamb.

NOTE OF INTEREST
The beautiful thing about stews is that they are even better the next day, so don't be afraid to double the recipe. The stew can be kept in the refrigerator, tightly sealed, for two to three days.

½ recipe Basic Polenta (see page 176)
⅓ cup red wine vinegar
3 cloves garlic, finely minced
3 anchovy fillets, finely chopped
2 tablespoons finely chopped fresh rosemary or 1 table-spoon chopped dried
3 pounds boneless lamb shoulder, all fat removed and cut into 2-inch cubes
1 cup unbleached all-purpose flour
⅓ cup olive oil
2 cups canned imported Italian tomatoes with their juice, put through a strainer or food mill to remove the seeds
1 cup meat broth, preferably homemade (see pages 53–54)
Salt and freshly ground black pepper to taste
2 tablespoons chopped fresh parsley
Oil for frying

Prepare the polenta several hours or a day ahead of time so it will become very firm. Pour the polenta onto a platter or cookie sheet and spread it evenly to approximately a ½-inch thickness. Cut the polenta into slices and set it aside until you are ready to use it.

In a medium-size bowl combine the vinegar, garlic, anchovies, and rosemary.

Place the lamb in a large strainer and put the strainer over a large bowl. Sprinkle the meat liberally with the flour, then shake off the excess.

Heat the oil in a large casserole over medium-high heat. Add the lamb and brown on all sides, about 6 to 7 minutes, stirring a few times. Raise the heat and add the vinegar mixture. Stir and cook until the vinegar is almost reduced, about 1 minute. Add the tomatoes and broth and season with the salt and several grinds of pepper. Bring the liquid to a boil, then reduce the heat to low and cover the skillet, leaving the lid slightly askew. Simmer until the lamb is tender and the sauce has a medium-thick consistency, 40 to 45 minutes. Stir occasionally during cooking. (If the sauce becomes too thick, add a bit more broth or water.) Add the parsley and stir once or twice. Taste and adjust the seasonings. Keep the stew warm over low heat while you fry the polenta.

Heat one inch of oil in a medium-size nonstick skillet over medium heat until it begins to smoke. Fry the polenta slices a few at a time until they are lightly golden on both sides, 3 to 4 minutes. Remove the polenta with a slotted spoon and drain on paper towels.

Spoon the stew onto individual serving dishes and serve with a few slices of polenta.

Makes 6 servings

SUGGESTED WINES

Try a young, light California Cabernet Sauvignon such as Fetzer or Parducci, or Castello dei Rampolla Chianti Classico from Italy.

Scaloppine di Vitello all'Aceto Balsamico

Veal Scaloppine with Balsamic Vinegar

Modena is the small, lovely town north of Bologna that produces the incomparable balsamic vinegar. It is only natural then that in Modena, more than anywhere else in Italy, one can find dishes employing this delicious condiment. La Francescana is an old trattoria in the center of Modena that has been modernized and updated, not only in its interior, but also in the food they serve. Two of the dishes I enjoyed thoroughly were a delicious aromatic Onion Frittata with Balsamic Vinegar (see pages 303–304) and these delicious scaloppine with balsamic vinegar. The balsamic vinegar was well aged, with an intense, rich, fragrant taste that complemented the milk-fed veal perfectly.

3 tablespoons unsalted butter
3 tablespoons olive oil
1½ pounds veal scaloppine from the top round, thinly
    sliced and pounded
Salt to taste
1 cup dry white wine
¼ cup balsamic vinegar (see page 13)

Heat 2 tablespoons of the butter and the oil in a large, heavy skillet over high heat. When the butter foams, add the scaloppine, making sure not to crowd the skillet. If you need to, cook the veal in two batches. Season with salt. Cook until the veal is lightly golden on both sides, about 2 minutes. Transfer the veal to a plate.

Add the wine, balsamic vinegar, and the remaining butter to the skillet. Cook over high heat and stir quickly to dissolve the meat deposits attached to the bottom of the skillet. When the wine is reduced by half, 3 to 4 minutes, return the veal to the skillet. Reduce the heat to medium and mix briefly until the veal is well coated with the sauce, 30 to 40 seconds. Serve at once with a bit of sauce over each serving.

Makes 4 servings

TIPS

෨ *It is important that you do not crowd the skillet when cooking scaloppine, or the veal will not brown properly. Cook the scaloppine in a few batches, then put them on a plate until you are ready to put them back in the skillet with the sauce.*

෨ *Always cook the scaloppine over high heat. The meat should be golden outside and pink and juicy inside.*

෨ *Scaloppine are fairly easy to cook; however, this is a dish that is not fit for a crowd. Have all your ingredients ready on a tray, cook the veal quickly, and zip to the table to enjoy them while they are still hot.*

SUGGESTED WINES
The unique Villa Bianchi Lambrusco from California would be nice, or one of the Emilia-Romagna reds, such as Fattoria Paradiso Sangiovese or Vallania Cabernet Sauvignon, would complement this dish quite well.

Scaloppine di Vitello ai Funghi

Veal Scaloppine with Mushrooms

The simplicity of trattoria cooking, just like the cooking of the home, can be improvised on the spur of the moment, depending on the ingredients at hand. One night, at Trattoria Il Cinghiale

Bianco in Firenze, there was a large, wonderful display of fresh porcini mushrooms which were served grilled as an appetizer. Since I adore fresh porcini, I asked the waitress if she could cook whatever veal they had at hand with some fresh porcini. Shortly after, I was presented with a plate of milk-fed veal scaloppine, topped by large slices of sautéed fresh porcini which had been tossed with a bit of garlic and just a touch of dry Marsala wine. The veal had been cooked without the usual coating of flour and had a lighter, cleaner taste and consistency.

In Italy, porcini mushrooms are a delicacy that can be found only in spring and fall. In this country they are seldom available in food markets. For this reason, I have made this dish with white cultivated mushrooms which, while lacking the intense flavor of the porcini, still give a delicious flavor to the dish.

⅓ cup olive oil
6 ounces cultivated white mushrooms, thinly sliced
2 tablespoons unsalted butter
1½ pounds veal scaloppine from the top round, thinly sliced and pounded
Salt to taste
1 cup dry Marsala, preferably imported Florio
¼ cup heavy cream

Heat the oil in a large, heavy skillet over high heat. Add the mushrooms and cook, stirring, until they are lightly golden. With a slotted spoon transfer the mushrooms to a bowl.

Add the butter and a bit of additional oil if necessary to the skillet. When the butter foams, add the scaloppine, making sure not to crowd the skillet. Cook them in two batches if necessary. Season lightly with salt and cook over high heat until the veal is lightly golden on both sides, about 2 minutes. Transfer the veal to a plate.

Add the wine and cream to the skillet. Cook over high heat and stir quickly to dissolve the meat deposits attached to the bottom of the skillet. When the liquid is reduced by half, 3 to 4 minutes, return the veal and mushrooms to the skillet and reduce the heat to medium. Mix briefly until the veal and the mushrooms are well coated with the sauce, 30 to 40 seconds. Serve at once, spooning a bit of sauce and mushrooms over each serving.

Makes 4 servings

SUGGESTED WINE
A great white Italian wine such as Jermann Vintage Tunina, or a full-bodied California Chardonnay such as Au Bon Climat would be perfect.

Ossobuco con Porcini

Veal Shanks with Porcini Mushrooms

In Italy veal shanks are used in various preparations, the best known is perhaps the classic *ossobuco alla Milanese*. Even though veal shanks can be cooked in many different ways, they really shine when they are stewed very slowly with other flavorful ingredients.

This delicious version comes from the great little trattoria Boni in Bologna. The veal is browned with vegetables, deglazed with good, dry Marsala wine, and cooked slowly with porcini mushrooms, homemade meat broth, and tomatoes. At the end of the cooking, the veal is soft and tender, and falls away from the bone.

1 ounce imported dried porcini mushrooms (see page 15), soaked in 2 cups lukewarm water for 20 minutes

8 medium-size veal shanks (3½ to 4 pounds), cut about 2 inches thick

2 cups unbleached all-purpose flour, evenly spread over a sheet of aluminum foil

2 tablespoons unsalted butter

3 tablespoons olive oil

1 large carrot, diced

2 stalks celery, diced

1 cup dry Marsala, preferably imported Florio Marsala

1 cup meat broth, preferably homemade (see pages 53–54)

1 cup canned imported Italian tomatoes with their juice, put through a strainer or food mill to remove the seeds

Salt and freshly ground black pepper to taste

2 tablespoons finely chopped fresh parsley

Strain the porcini and reserve the water. Rinse the porcini well under cold running water and chop them roughly. Line a strainer with two paper towels and strain the porcini water to get rid of sandy deposits. Reserve one cup of the soaking liquid.

Dredge the veal shanks in the flour and shake off any excess. Heat the butter and oil in a large, heavy skillet over medium

NOTE OF INTEREST

Twenty years ago when I first came to Sacramento, Corti Brothers, a specialized Italian market, was practically the only store in town that carried veal shanks. Today they are easily available fresh or frozen in many markets and specialized meat stores.

In Italy, the shanks for ossobuco are generally obtained from milk-fed veal or from very young veal. In this country, the veal is somewhat older. When buying ossobuco, ask for the hind shank, which is the meatier part of the shank. In Italy the marrow of the bone is considered a delicacy.

heat. When the butter foams, add the veal and cook until golden on both sides, 6 to 7 minutes. Transfer the meat to a dish and add the carrots and celery to the skillet. Cook, stirring, until they are lightly golden, 5 to 6 minutes. Add the porcini and stir a few times. Return the meat to the skillet, raise the heat to high, and add the Marsala wine. Cook until the wine is almost all reduced, 5 to 6 minutes. Add the broth, tomatoes, and the reserved soaking water, and bring to a boil. Season with salt and pepper. Reduce the heat to low, cover the skillet, leaving it slightly askew, and cook until the meat begins to fall away from the bone, 1 to 1½ hours. Stir in the parsley. Taste and adjust the seasonings and serve piping hot with soft polenta (page 176), if you wish.

Makes 4 servings

SUGGESTED WINES
Try one of Italy's Valtellina red wines such as Inferno or Sassella. A full-bodied Chardonnay or a delicate red such as a Pinot Noir from California will also complement the delicate taste of veal.

Costolette alla Milanese

Breaded Veal Chops Milanese Style

With only five ingredients and ten minutes of cooking time, a great, classic dish is put together. *Costolette alla Milanese*, as the name implies, it is a specialty of Milano.

During my last trip to Milano, while filming a week of food segments for KCRA-TV of Sacramento, the producer, Bob Murphy, and I dined at Alla Cucina delle Langhe, a stylish, popular trattoria. When Bob saw the breaded veal chop on the menu, he ordered it without hesitation. It came to the table in all its glory, redolent with sweet butter, golden and crisp outside and slightly pink and juicy inside.

Four ¾-inch-thick veal loin chops
2 large eggs, lightly beaten in a bowl with ½ teaspoon salt
2 cups fine plain bread crumbs, evenly spread over a sheet of aluminum foil.
3 tablespoons unsalted butter
2 tablespoons olive oil

Put the meat part of the veal chops between two sheets of plastic wrap or waxed paper and pound them until they are about half their original thickness.

Dip the veal chops into the beaten eggs, letting the excess egg fall off the veal. Coat the chops with the bread crumbs, lightly pressing the crumbs onto the meat with the palms of your hands.

In a large, heavy skillet heat the butter and oil over medium heat. As soon as the butter foams, slide the veal chops into the skillet. Cook for about 3 minutes on each side, or until the chops are golden brown in color. Serve at once.

Makes 4 servings

SUGGESTED WINES
Choose a good, young, fruity red wine such as a Bardolino from the Veneto or a Dolcetto d'Astia from the Piemonte.

Cotolette ai Pomodori Freschi

Veal Cutlets with Diced Fresh Tomatoes

Cutlets are very popular throughout Italy. A cutlet is a slice of meat or vegetable that is dipped into egg, then breaded and fried. The most popular and best-known cutlet is made with veal. This is a simple dish to put together, and it is often the dinner choice of hurried housewives, because it is fast to prepare.

This variation of the classic theme comes from a Roman trattoria, Pippo lo Sgobbone. I was intrigued and a bit skeptical about the unusual pairing of the cold tomato condiment served over the cutlet. But I was proven wrong, because the lively fresh taste of the tomatoes, celery, onions, and basil deliciously contrasted with the warm cutlet. A great dish for a summer day.

For the cutlets
   1 pound veal cutlets, sliced ¼ inch thick
   2 large eggs lightly beaten with a pinch of salt in a small bowl
   1½ cups plain bread crumbs combined with ½ cup freshly grated parmigiano
   3 tablespoons unsalted butter
   ¼ cup olive oil

TIPS

∽ *A perfectly cooked cutlet is golden brown outside and pink and juicy inside. In order to achieve this you should:*

∽ *Make sure to use a large, heavy skillet or a nonstick skillet to cook the veal and to have your cooking fat very hot so that the cutlet will cook fast and won't stick to the pan.*

∽ *The perfect thickness for the veal slices is ½ inch. If the slices of veal are too thin, they will overcook.*

∽ *Leftover veal cutlets are terrific in a sandwich, with slices of tomatoes, lettuce, and sweet onions.*

SUGGESTED WINES

Simple, straightforward light red wines such as a Regaleali Rosso from Sicilia or a Lohr Monterey Gamay from California would be perfect.

For the condiment

> 4 medium-size tomatoes, diced about the size of large peas
> 1 medium-size white stalk celery, finely sliced
> 4 scallions, white and green parts, finely sliced
> 8 to 10 large fresh basil leaves, finely shredded or
>   1 tablespoon finely chopped fresh parsley
> ¼ cup olive oil
> 1 tablespoon red wine vinegar
> Salt and freshly ground black pepper to taste

Dip the veal slices into the eggs and coat well with the bread crumb–parmigiano mixture. Lightly press the crumbs onto the meat with the palms of your hands. Place the cutlets on a large plate and refrigerate for 30 minutes, so that the coating will settle and dry and will remain attached to the meat during cooking.

In a large, heavy skillet, heat the butter and oil over medium-high heat. When the butter foams, add the cutlets without crowding the skillet. Cook in two batches if necessary. Cook until they are golden brown, about 2 minutes on each side. Put the cutlets on paper towels and pat dry to remove excess fat.

In a medium-size bowl, combine all the ingredients for the tomato condiment and mix well. Taste and adjust the seasoning. Place the cutlets on individual serving dishes, top with a few tablespoons of the tomato mixture, and serve.

Makes 4 servings

Involtini di Vitello alla Genovese

Stuffed Veal Rolls Genoa Style

Meat is not the predominant element of the Ligurian table—fish, herbs, and vegetables are. Yet, on occasion, one encounters a meat dish that is so utterly simple and restrained and yet so very appetizing. At Trattoria Piccolo Mondo in San Remo, I enjoyed these veal bundles, stuffed with a delicious mixture of poached chicken, porcini mushrooms, pine nuts, and herbs. The bundles are cooked quickly over high heat, then they are added to a flavorful sauce of tomatoes, wine, mushrooms, and fresh basil. It was so good that I scooped up every bit of sauce with the bread.

For the filling

2 ounces dried porcini mushrooms (see page 15), soaked in 2 cups lukewarm water for 20 minutes

One 6-ounce chicken breast, boned, skinned, and halved

4 slices Italian bread without the crust, broken into rough pieces and soaked in 1 cup chicken broth, homemade (see pages 54–55) or canned

3 tablespoons pine nuts

1 clove garlic, chopped

4 to 5 fresh basil leaves, finely shredded or 1 tablespoon chopped fresh parsley

1 large egg, lightly beaten in a small bowl with ⅓ cup freshly grated parmigiano

Salt and freshly ground black pepper to taste

16 slices veal scaloppine from the top round, approximately 1¼ pounds, pounded thin

2 tablespoons unsalted butter

3 tablespoons olive oil

For the sauce

1 cup dry white wine

1 cup canned imported Italian tomatoes with their juice, put through a strainer or food mill to remove the seeds

Salt and freshly ground black pepper to taste

8 to 10 fresh basil leaves, finely shredded

For the filling, drain the mushrooms and reserve the soaking water. Rinse the mushrooms well under cold running water. Line a strainer with two paper towels and strain the mushroom soaking water to get rid of the sandy deposits. Reserve 1 cup of the water for the sauce. (The remaining liquid can be used in a stew or mushroom soup.)

Bring a small saucepan of water to a boil. Add the chicken breast and cook over medium heat until the chicken is no longer pink, about 10 minutes. Transfer the chicken to a plate and cool.

Drain the bread, squeeze it with your hands into a soft pulp, and place in a medium-size bowl.

Combine the pine nuts, garlic, basil, half of the mushrooms, and the chicken on a board or in a food processor, and chop very fine. Place in the bowl with the bread. Add the egg and parmigiano mixture and season with salt and pepper. The mixture should be fairly soft. If too firm, add an additional egg. If too soft, add more parmigiano.

Place the scaloppine on a working surface and spread 1 tablespoon of filling over each scaloppine. Roll up the veal loosely in a bundle. Secure each bundle with a wooden pick and set aside. (The veal bundles can be prepared up to this point several hours ahead.)

Heat the butter and oil in a large skillet over medium heat. When the butter foams, add as many bundles as can comfortably fit in the skillet without crowding. Cook until the veal is golden on all sides, about 2 to 3 minutes. As they brown, transfer them from the skillet to a plate, and brown the ones that are left.

To prepare the sauce, raise the heat to high and add the wine. Stir to pick up the bits and pieces attached to the bottom of the skillet. When the wine is almost all reduced, 5 to 6 minutes, add the remaining mushrooms, the reserved soaking water, and the tomatoes. Season with salt and pepper. Cook, stirring, until the sauce has a medium-thick consistency, 3 to 4 minutes.

Return the veal bundles to the skillet, add the basil, and stir once or twice until the veal is well coated with the sauce.

Remove the wooden picks and serve the veal topped by a bit of its sauce.

Makes 4 servings

TIP

If you assemble the bundles ahead of time, it will take no longer than 10 minutes to complete this dish.

SUGGESTED WINES

Try a little-known Ligurian wine such as Rossese di Dolceacqua of Lupi, or a delicate, light red such as Saintsbury Garnet and Phelps Grenache Rosé.

Polpettine con Zucchine Fritte e Zafferano

Small Meatballs with Fried Zucchini and Saffron Sauce

There must be hundreds of ways in Italy to prepare *polpettine*, since each cook uses the ingredients at hand and his imagination. Settimio all'Arancio, a very popular Roman trattoria, serves this delicious version. The interesting thing here is that the small meatballs are not coated with bread crumbs and fried, but rather are baked, then combined briefly with a quick savory sauce of sautéed onions, broth, saffron, and fried zucchini. These *polpettine* are so tender that they almost dissolve in the mouth, and the sauce is simply mouthwatering. Bravo Settimio!

For the polpettine

2 large eggs
½ cup freshly grated parmigiano
3 tablespoons chopped fresh parsley
1 pound ground veal
Salt and freshly ground black pepper to taste
1½ cups unbleached all-purpose flour, evenly spread over a sheet of aluminum foil
3 tablespoons olive oil

For the saffron sauce

Vegetable oil for frying
1 pound small zucchini, cut into thin rounds
3 tablespoons olive oil
½ medium-size onion, finely chopped
A pinch of powdered saffron
2 cups meat broth, preferably homemade (see pages 53–54)
Salt and freshly ground black pepper to taste
2 tablespoons finely chopped fresh parsley

Preheat the oven to 350°F.

In a large bowl, beat the eggs with the parmigiano and parsley. Add the veal and season with salt and pepper. Mix everything together well with a large tablespoon or your hands until the ingredients are thoroughly combined. If the mixture is too soft, add a little more parmigiano.

Take a scant tablespoon of the meat mixture between the palms of your hands, and roll it into a small ball. When all the *polpettine* have been shaped, coat them lightly with the flour.

Coat the bottom of a baking dish with the olive oil, and add the *polpettine*. Bake until the meat balls are lightly golden, 10 to 12 minutes.

While the *polpettine* are in the oven, prepare the sauce. Pour ¼ inch of vegetable oil into a large, heavy skillet. When the oil is hot, add the zucchini, making sure not to crowd the skillet. When the zucchini are golden brown on both sides, remove from the oil with a slotted spoon and drain on paper towels.

TIPS

෧ *The meatballs can be shaped ahead of time, but should be baked and combined with the sauce at the last moment, because in reheating they will become dry.*

෧ *The zucchini can be fried ahead of time—don't refrigerate them—and added to the sauce.*

SUGGESTED WINES

The exotic, pungent taste of saffron calls for a wine that will stand up to it. Try a well-aged Semillon from California's Livermore Valley or a Vernaccia di San Gimignano Riserva from Toscana.

In another large skillet, heat the olive oil over medium heat. Add the onion and cook, stirring, until the onion is pale yellow. Dissolve the saffron in the broth and add to the skillet. Season with salt and just a bit of pepper. Cook over high heat until the sauce is reduced by half, 5 to 6 minutes. Stir in the parsley, *polpettine*, and fried zucchini. Cook 1 minute longer, until all ingredients are well combined. Serve hot.

Makes 4 servings

Polpette Fritte

Fried Meatballs

Re di Coppe in Trieste is a very pleasant wine shop–trattoria, where one can stop by for a glass of wine, a snack, or a light lunch or dinner. The food of the trattoria is cooked in plain view of the customers by an able middle-aged woman who commands attention because of her dexterity with pots and pans and because of the delicious aroma of her food. The few dishes that she prepares daily are basic and homey, typical of the area, such as the popular beef stew (pages 184–85) and these *polpette*, which are served either fried or with a tomato-based sauce.

For the polpette
> 4 slices Italian bread without the crust, broken into rough pieces and soaked in 1 cup milk for 5 minutes
> 2 pounds ground veal
> 2 cloves garlic, finely minced
> ¼ cup loosely packed chopped fresh parsley
> 1 cup freshly grated parmigiano
> 2 large eggs, lightly beaten
> Salt and freshly ground black pepper to taste

To complete the dish
> 2 large eggs, lightly beaten
> 2 cups fine plain bread crumbs
> Oil for frying

Drain the bread and squeeze it out with your hands into a soft pulp. In a large bowl combine the veal, squeezed bread, garlic, parsley, parmigiano, and eggs and season with salt and pepper. Mix well with your hands or with a large spoon until the ingredients are thoroughly blended.

Take one heaping tablespoon of the meat mixture between the palms of your hands and roll it into a ball, about the size of a small egg. When all the *polpette* have been shaped, dip them into the eggs and coat them with the bread crumbs.

Heat one inch of oil in a heavy medium-size skillet over medium heat. When the oil is very hot, lower a few *polpette* at a time into the oil with a slotted spoon. Cook until they are lightly golden, about 2 minutes, then turn them gently and cook the other side until golden. Remove with a slotted spoon to paper towels to drain. Serve piping hot.

Makes approximately 30 *polpette*

SUGGESTED WINES
Try a Friulan Tocai or Ribolla Gialla. For a New World treat, Oregon Pinot Gris or Washington State Semillon.

Pollo alla Cacciatora

Chicken Hunter Style

Stiore is a tiny community on the outskirts of Bologna that has been progressively overtaken and incorporated by the growing city. Years ago, to go to Stiore was to go to the country. It meant getting away from the city to breathe fresh air and to enjoy the simple, authentic country food.

On the main street of Stiore there was La Perla, a trattoria that had only a few tables and a large bar where the locals met ritually to sip a glass of wine or an espresso, to play cards or shoot pool, and talk about politics, women, and sport. Or they would simply sit at the outside tables and watch the world go by. If they were hungry, the small kitchen of La Perla would provide local cheeses, *salame*, prosciutto, pickled vegetables, and bread for a delicious *spuntino*—snack—or one could order one of the few dishes that were served daily.

I still have memories of La Perla's *pollo alla cacciatora* in a fragrant *battuto* of onion, pancetta, rosemary, and garlic, splashed with Marsala wine and simmered slowly in tomatoes. It was a most appetizing dish.

> One 4-pound chicken or rabbit, cut into 8 serving pieces, washed, and dried on paper towels
> 2 cups unbleached all-purpose flour, evenly spread over a sheet of aluminum foil
> ¼ cup olive oil
> 1 medium-size onion, finely minced
> 3 ounces sliced pancetta, chopped
> 3 cloves garlic, finely minced
> 2 tablespoons finely chopped fresh rosemary or 1 tablespoon dried, crumbled
> 1 cup dry Marsala, preferably imported Florio Marsala
> 3 cups canned imported Italian tomatoes with their juice, put through a strainer or food mill to remove the seeds
> Salt and freshly ground black pepper to taste

Coat the chicken liberally with the flour and shake off the excess.

Heat the oil in a large skillet over high heat. Add the chicken, making sure not to crowd the skillet. (The chicken can be browned in two batches.) Cook until it is golden on all sides, 6 to 7 minutes. Transfer the chicken to a platter. (If the oil becomes too dark during the browning of the chicken, discard it and add a bit more oil.) Reduce the heat to medium, then add the onion, pancetta, garlic, and rosemary and cook, stirring, until the mixture begins to color, 4 to 5 minutes.

Return the chicken to the skillet, raise the heat to high, and add the Marsala. Cook and stir until the Marsala is almost all reduced, 5 to 6 minutes. Add the tomatoes and season with salt and pepper. Bring the tomatoes to a boil, then reduce the heat to medium-low and cover the skillet, leaving it slightly askew. Cook until the chicken is tender, 40 to 50 minutes. Stir and turn the chicken a few times during cooking. Taste and adjust the seasoning and serve hot with good Italian bread or with soft (page 176) or grilled (page 49) polenta.

Makes 4 servings

SUGGESTED WINES
A California Chardonnay without a lot of oak character would work quite well. Try one from Sterling Vineyards or Louis Martini. Or try a Chianti from Antinori or Vignamaggio.

Pollo in Padella con Melanzane e Zucchine

Pan-roasted Chicken with Eggplant and Zucchini

Eggplants and tomatoes are perhaps Sicilia's most-loved vegetables, and under the hot, intense Sicilian sun, those vegetables taste like nowhere else in the world. At Trattoria A Cuccagna, in Palermo, I dined on a deliciously appetizing chicken dish that had all the colors of this beautiful sunny island. The chicken had been browned with the addition of pancetta and garlic and cooked with ripe, fragrant tomatoes; then during the last few minutes of cooking, it was tossed together with fried eggplant and zucchini.

1 small, firm eggplant (12 to 14 ounces), trimmed and
    cut lengthwise into ½-inch slices
¼ cup olive oil
One 4-pound chicken, cut into 8 serving pieces, washed,
    and dried on paper towels
3 ounces sliced pancetta, finely chopped
2 cloves garlic, finely minced
1 cup dry white wine
3 medium-size, ripe tomatoes, seeded and cut into small
    pieces
Salt and freshly ground black pepper to taste
2 small zucchini, cut into thin rounds

Place the eggplant slices on a large platter and sprinkle with salt. Let stand for 30 minutes to allow the salt to draw out the bitter juices. Pat the eggplant dry with paper towels, cut into medium-size cubes, and set aside until ready to use.

Heat half of the oil in a large skillet over high heat. Add the chicken, without crowding it, and cook until golden on all sides, 6 to 7 minutes. You can brown the chicken in two batches. Transfer the chicken to a dish.

Add the pancetta to the skillet and cook, stirring, until it begins to color, 1 to 2 minutes.

Return the chicken to the skillet and stir briefly with the pancetta. Add the wine and cook, stirring, until the wine is reduced by half, 3 to 4 minutes.

Add the tomatoes and season with salt and pepper. Reduce the heat to medium-low and cover the skillet, leaving it slightly askew. Cook 30 to 40 minutes, stirring a few times. (If the sauce dries out too much during cooking, add a bit of water or broth.)

While the chicken is cooking, heat the remaining oil in a medium-size skillet over high heat. Add the zucchini and cook, stirring, until it begins to color, about 2 minutes. With a slotted spoon, remove them to a plate.

Add the eggplant to the same skillet and cook until it begins to color, 1 to 2 minutes. Stir the eggplant as it cooks and resist the urge to add more oil because the spongy quality will absorb it very quickly and it will become too soggy.

With a slotted spoon, remove the eggplant and transfer to the plate with the zucchini. (The eggplant and zucchini can be fried a few hours ahead of time.)

Add the eggplant and the zucchini to the chicken and stir to combine. Cook 1 to 2 minutes, then serve immediately.

Makes 4 servings

SUGGESTED WINES

Try to serve this Sicilian dish with a Sicilian wine such as the red Corvo Rosso, or Regaleali Rosso, or Rapitalà.

Pollo al Lambrusco

Chicken Stewed in Lambrusco Wine

There are many *trattorie* in Emilia-Romagna, especially country *trattorie*, that cook rabbit, pheasant, or chicken in the delicious, locally made Lambrusco wine. This is a frothy wine, purple in color, light and flowery, that has no ambition of greatness, but is nevertheless the perfect accompaniment to many dishes of the area.

At Osteria di Rubbiara in Modena, I once had a lovely rabbit cooked in Lambrusco. And at Boni, my favorite little trattoria in Bologna, I had a wonderful chicken stewed in Lambrusco. This is a great winter dish that should be served with grilled, soft, or fried polenta to scoop up every bit of its tasty sauce.

⅓ cup olive oil

1 large onion, thinly sliced

1 cup unbleached all-purpose flour, evenly spread over a
sheet of aluminum foil

One 4-pound chicken, cut into 8 serving pieces, washed,
and dried on paper towels

2 cups Lambrusco

1 cup meat broth, preferably homemade (see pages
53–54)

Salt and freshly ground black pepper to taste

Heat the oil in a large skillet over medium heat. Add the onion
and cook, stirring, until the onion begins to color, 3 to 4 minutes. With a slotted spoon transfer the onion to a dish, draining
the excess oil against the side of the skillet.

Flour the chicken pieces lightly, shaking off any excess, and
add to the skillet without crowding them. If necessary, you can
cook the chicken in two batches. Cook until the pieces are lightly
golden on both sides, 6 to 7 minutes. Return the onion to the
skillet and add the wine and broth. Season with salt and pepper.
Cover the skillet and reduce the heat to medium-low. Cook until
the chicken is tender, 40 to 50 minutes. Stir a few times during
cooking. At the end of the cooking, there should be about 1 to
1½ cups of nice thick sauce left in the skillet. Serve hot with
some crusty Italian bread or some grilled polenta (page 176).

Makes 4 servings

SUGGESTED WINES
*Try the unique Bianchi Lam-
brusco from California or the
largest seller from Italy, Riunite
Rosso.*

La Gallina Bollita con Salsa Verde

Boiled Chicken with Piquant Green Sauce

For a while I was not sure whether to include this dish in the
book or not. After all, who could be tempted by a dish of
"boiled chicken"? Two things made me change my mind. First,
gallina bollita is quite often a standard traditional dish in many
Northern Italian *trattorie*, especially in Emilia-Romagna and
Lombardia. Second, I simply adore boiled chicken.

TIPS

෴ *When I prepare this sauce
at my restaurant, I also add
about ½ cup of finely diced red
or yellow bell peppers for color
and texture.*

෴ *When I use this classic
sauce for fish, I substitute the
juice of 1 lemon for the vinegar.*

With a nice, plump chicken, a few bones, and some vegetables, you can prepare a delicious broth, which in turn will give you a wonderful soup. The chicken can be eaten straight out of its hot broth and served with several condiments or vegetables. My favorite way of eating a boiled chicken is with a *peperonata*, a medley of cooked peppers, onion, and tomatoes (pages 272–73).

At trattoria Da Ornella in Bergamo, the chicken was served with tender asparagus topped by butter and parmigiano and by this delicious *salsa verde*.

Leftover chicken can be used cold in a salad (with potatoes, grilled red bell peppers, and peas) or turned into a wonderful light sandwich with the addition of some sweet-and-sour onions (pages 231–32), or it can be diced and turned into a frittata.

For this dish choose a large plump chicken, capon, or stewing hen.

> One 5- to 6-pound chicken, cooked as instructed in Homemade Chicken Broth (see pages 54–55)

For the green sauce
>   1 slice white bread without the crust, broken into pieces
>   ½ cup olive oil
>   2 tablespoons red wine vinegar
>   2 tablespoons capers, drained and rinsed
>   2 cloves garlic
>   2 cups loosely packed parsley sprigs, preferably Italian (flatleaf) parsley
>   4 anchovy fillets
>   1 teaspoon Dijon mustard

Put the bread in a small bowl and add the oil and vinegar. Soak for about 5 minutes.

Put the bread and all the oil and vinegar in a food processor. Add the capers, garlic, parsley, anchovies, and mustard and pulse the machine on and off until everything is chopped very fine, but not completely smooth. Place the sauce in a bowl and taste the seasoning. Adjust with a bit of salt if necessary. The sauce should have a somewhat loose consistency, resembling a soft pesto sauce. Add a bit more oil if needed.

Remove the chicken from the broth and let it settle for a few minutes, then cut it into serving pieces and serve it with 1 or 2 tablespoons of *salsa verde* (remember that it is a condiment and you need just a little) and any of the vegetables mentioned above.

Makes 4 to 6 servings

SUGGESTED WINE

*Try a young Dolcetto from the
Piemonte from such well-
respected producers as Renato
Ratti, Aldo Conterno, or
Mauro Mascarello.*

Scaloppe di Tacchino al Forno con Funghi e Mozzarella

Baked Turkey Breast with Mushrooms and Mozzarella

Italians are not enthusiastic meat lovers, and when they do eat meat, the preference is generally toward veal and poultry. Turkey is a favorite, especially turkey breast.

Because turkey is delicious and economical, it is often found on the menu of *trattorie*. At Cannavota in Roma, I found a new variation. There, the thick slices of turkey are quickly browned in butter and oil, topped with golden, glazy, and moist mushrooms, topped again with slices of mozzarella, and baked just long enough for the cheese to melt.

    3 tablespoons olive oil
    2 tablespoons unsalted butter
    1½ pounds turkey breast, cut into eight ¼-inch-thick
       slices
    6 ounces white cultivated mushrooms, sliced
    ⅓ cup dry Marsala
    2 tablespoons heavy cream
    Salt to taste
    ¼ pound mozzarella, sliced

Preheat the oven to 400°F.

Heat the oil and butter in a large skillet over medium-high heat. When the butter foams, add the turkey and cook until the slices are lightly golden on both sides, about 2 to 3 minutes. Transfer the meat to a baking dish.

Raise the heat to high and, if necessary, add a bit more olive oil to the skillet. When the oil is hot, add the mushrooms and cook, stirring, until they are lightly golden, 2 to 3 minutes. Stir in the Marsala and cream and season lightly with salt. Cook until the liquid is reduced and the mushrooms are moist and glazy, 1 to 2 minutes longer.

Spoon the mushrooms over each turkey slice, and top with one or two slices of mozzarella. Bake until the cheese is melted, 1 to 2 minutes. Serve at once.

Makes 4 servings

SUGGESTED WINES

Lighter red wines go well with turkey, especially Pinot Noir. Try a Pinot Nero from the Alto Adige or a California Pinot from the Carneros region or Santa Maria Valley.

Cotolette di Tacchino con Piselli

Sautéed Turkey Breast with Wine and Peas

Even the world's most talented choreographer could not have come up with a better setting for La Carbonara. This well-known trattoria is housed in a medieval building in one of the most colorful old squares of Roma. The outside tables are only a few feet away from the vendors in the noisy open market, and as with everything else in Roma, sitting in one of La Carbonara's tables is pure theater.

Andreina Solomone, the owner and inspiration of La Carbonara, serves no-nonsense Roman fare. The day I was there, I resisted the urge for more pasta, and opted instead for a "lighter" dish, a large turkey cutlet with fresh peas in a wine sauce. The thick turkey slice was so tender that it practically melted in the mouth. The sauce consisted only of a few table-spoons of pan juices, cooked and reduced with a bit of wine and a touch of cream and tossed together with very fresh, very small, and very tender Roman peas.

> 1 cup shelled fresh peas or 1 cup frozen peas, thawed
> 1½ pounds turkey breast, cut into ¼-inch-thick slices
> 1 cup unbleached all-purpose flour, evenly spread over a
>   sheet of aluminum foil
> Salt to taste
> 3 tablespoons unsalted butter
> 2 tablespoons olive oil
> 1 cup dry white wine
> ½ cup chicken broth, preferably homemade (see
>   pages 54–55)
> 2 tablespoons heavy cream

If you are using fresh peas, bring a small saucepan of water to a boil over medium heat. Add the peas and cook until tender, 5 to 7 minutes, depending on their size. Drain the peas and set aside.

Dredge the turkey slices lightly in the flour, shaking off any excess, and season with salt.

Heat 2 tablespoons of the butter and the oil in a large skillet over medium-high heat. When the butter foams, add the turkey and cook until the slices are lightly golden on both sides, 2 to 3 minutes. Transfer the meat to a plate and keep it warm in a very low oven.

Discard the fat in the skillet, which at this point might be a bit burned, and add the wine, broth, cream, and the remaining butter. Cook over high heat, stirring to pick up the bits and pieces attached to the bottom of the skillet. When the sauce is reduced by half, 5 to 6 minutes, and has a medium-thick consistency, add the peas and stir a few times. Taste and adjust the seasoning, then place the turkey on serving dishes and top with the sauce. Serve at once.

Makes 4 servings

SUGGESTED WINES

Fontana Candida Frascati from Italy or a fruity, not austere, Sauvignon Blanc from Sonoma County, such as Preston or Viansa, will complement this dish.

Arrosto di Tacchino Farcito

Roasted Stuffed Turkey Breast

The most beautiful and best-known food store in Bologna is Tamburini. This venerable store has become widely known because of the richness, abundance, and succulence of the food it sells. For the *Bolognesi*, Tamburini is more than a food shop, it is an institution. You are first lured inside the shop by the breathtaking array of hams, sausages, cheeses, and fresh pastas. Once inside you marvel at the long counter filled to capacity with cooked and marinated foods of all sorts, and at the tantalizing aroma that comes from the spit, where many kinds of roasts are slowly cooking. People from all walks of life go to Tamburini to buy a little or a lot, depending on their pocketbook. One of the dishes that I particularly love at Tamburini, besides their fried cream, baked apples, marinated red and yellow peppers, and roast pig, is this wonderful roasted stuffed turkey breast.

One 3½- to 4-pound boneless breast of turkey
2 cloves garlic, finely minced
2 tablespoons chopped fresh rosemary or 1 tablespoon
    dried, crumbled
Salt and freshly ground black pepper to taste
¼ pound sliced pancetta
2 tablespoons unsalted butter
3 tablespoons olive oil
1 cup dry white wine

Preheat the oven to 375°F.

Ask your butcher to open the turkey breast and flatten it out. It should look like a large veal cutlet. Rub the garlic and rosemary on the inner side of the turkey and season with salt and pepper. Cover the meat with the slices of pancetta. Roll up the turkey breast tightly and tie securely with string.

Heat the butter and oil in a large, heavy casserole over medium-high heat. When the butter foams, add the turkey and cook until it is golden on all sides, 6 to 7 minutes. Add the wine and cook, stirring, until the wine is almost all reduced.

Place the casserole in the oven and bake for 45 minutes to 1 hour. Baste the roast with its pan juices several times during cooking. Check the roast for doneness by piercing it with a thin knife. If the juices that come out are clear or barely pink, the roast is done. If the juices are visibly pink, cook it a bit longer.

Transfer the roast to a cutting board and let it "settle" a few minutes. Remove the string and slice the meat. Arrange the slices on serving dishes, and serve at once.

Makes 6 to 8 servings

VARIATION

When I cook this dish for my family, after I brown the roast and reduce the wine, I add large pieces of carrots, onions, potatoes, bell peppers, and several cloves of garlic to the pot. The vegetables, cooked together with the roast and the roast juices, acquire a delicious taste that complements the roast perfectly.

SUGGESTED WINES

Try a well-matured Tignanello from Antinori in Toscana or a six- to eight-year-old, not too tannic Cabernet from a good California producer.

Fagiano Arrosto con Patate

Roasted Pheasant with Roasted Potatoes

The cooking of Toscana favors simple grilled and roasted dishes. One of the dishes I thoroughly enjoyed at Trattoria Montagliari in the Chianti area of Toscana was a splendid roasted pheasant that had been smothered with chopped fresh rosemary and sage, garlic, and oil and cooked in a very hot oven until the skin was golden and crisp. Chunks of potatoes were added to the baking dish and also tossed with some of the herb mixture.

1 tablespoon chopped fresh rosemary or 1 teaspoon dried
6 to 8 fresh sage leaves, finely chopped
3 cloves garlic, finely minced
⅓ cup olive oil
One 2½- to 3-pound domestic pheasant, washed and dried thoroughly
2 large potatoes, peeled and cut into medium-size pieces
Salt and freshly ground black pepper to taste

Preheat the oven to 400°F.

In a small bowl, combine the rosemary, sage, garlic, and 3 tablespoons of the olive oil. Rub the pheasant inside and out with half of this mixture and place in a baking dish with the potatoes. Add the remaining oil and herb mixture to the pan and toss well to coat the potatoes. Season everything with salt and several grinds of pepper.

Bake until the pheasant and the potatoes are golden, 30 to 40 minutes. Baste a few times during cooking with the oil in the baking dish. The pheasant is done if the juices run clear when the thickest part of the leg is pierced with a thin knife.

Put the pheasant on a cutting board and let it cool a minute or two, then cut it into pieces and serve with the potatoes, topped by a few tablespoons of pan juices.

Makes 4 servings

SUGGESTED WINES
Choose a mature red from Italy, such as a six- or seven-year-old Barbaresco of Ceretto or Gaja. From California a ten-year-old Napa Valley Cabernet from Sterling or Beringer would be perfect.

Coniglio Arrosto

Roasted Rabbit with Rosemary and Vinegar

A favorite way of cooking rabbit in Emilia-Romagna is to marinate it with fresh herbs, olive oil, garlic, and vinegar, and to roast it with part of its marinade. The result is a delicious, aromatic rabbit with meat that is so tender it falls away from the bone.

This version comes from Osteria di Rubbiara in the small hamlet of Rubbiara outside Modena, where the cooking relys heavily on the local peasant heritage.

> 10 fresh sage leaves, finely chopped or 3 to 4 dried, finely crumbled
> 3 tablespoons chopped fresh rosemary or 1 tablespoon dried, finely chopped
> 4 cloves garlic, finely minced
> Salt and freshly ground black pepper to taste
> ½ cup olive oil
> ½ cup red wine vinegar
> One 4-pound rabbit, cut into serving pieces, washed, and dried with paper towels
> 3 large potatoes, peeled and cut into large pieces

In a small bowl, combine the sage, rosemary, garlic, salt, pepper, olive oil, and vinegar. Place the rabbit in a deep dish or large bowl and pour the marinade over it. Cover the bowl and marinate, unrefrigerated, 2 to 3 hours, basting the rabbit a few times.

Preheat the oven to 375°F. Put the rabbit and the potatoes in a baking dish and spoon over about a fourth of its marinade. Place in the oven and bake about 1 hour. Baste a few times during cooking. At this point the rabbit and the potatoes should have a nice golden color and the marinade should be almost all reduced and have a thick, shiny consistency. Serve hot.

Makes 4 servings

SUGGESTED WINE
Try a full-bodied Chardonnay with oakiness and richness, such as Sanford or Simi Riserve.

Coniglio all'Aceto Balsamico

Rabbit with Balsamic Vinegar

Savignano sul Panaro is a small, hilly town that, like thousands of others in Italy, does not even appear on the map and is known only by the people of the area. Here there is an *osteria* that offers, besides good, local wine, some wonderful food.

Gianni Negrini, the owner, is a man of passion. He realizes that the food he serves shines because of the ingredients he uses. Gianni raises pigs so that he can make his own prosciutto and *salame*. He hunts for truffles and porcini mushrooms in the woods of the area and uses them abundantly in his cooking.

The food of Gianni's trattoria, Osteria Novecento, is the traditional, straightforward cooking of the area. Plenty of good homemade pasta and great roasted meats, especially lamb, chicken, and rabbit, and also *alla cacciatora* preparations. Occasionally there are wonderful specials, like this rabbit with balsamic vinegar, which takes advantage of another superlative ingredient of the area, the balsamic vinegar of Modena.

When I cook this at my restaurant in Sacramento, I serve it with soft or grilled polenta.

> One 4-pound rabbit, cut into serving pieces
> 3 cups of dry white wine
> ½ cup red wine vinegar
> 7 tablespoons olive oil
> 1 small onion, finely minced
> 1 medium-size celery stalk, finely minced
> 2 cloves garlic, finely minced
> 2 cups canned imported Italian tomatoes with their juice, put through a strainer or food mill to remove the seeds
> 1 to 2 cups meat broth, preferably homemade (see pages 53–54)
> 2 tablespoons chopped fresh rosemary or 1 tablespoon dried, crumbled
> Salt and freshly ground black pepper to taste
> ¼ cup balsamic vinegar (see page 13)

Wash the rabbit, place it in a large bowl, and cover it with the wine and vinegar. Cover the bowl and marinate 4 to 5 hours in the refrigerator.

Heat 4 tablespoons of the oil in a medium-size skillet over medium heat. Add the onion and celery and cook, stirring, until they are lightly golden, 4 to 5 minutes. Stir in the garlic and cook about 1 minute.

Add the tomatoes and 1 cup of the broth. Lower the heat to medium-low and cook, uncovered, stirring a few times, 6 to 7 minutes. While the tomatoes are cooking, remove the rabbit pieces from the marinade and pat dry with paper towels. Reserve the marinade.

SUGGESTED WINES
Medium-bodied red wine, Oltrepò Pavese reds, Sangiovese della Romagna, or even a Valtellina red work. Sonoma's Dry Creek Valley Zinfandels from California are perfect.

Heat the remaining oil in a large skillet over high heat. Add the rabbit and rosemary and cook until the rabbit pieces are lightly golden on all sides, 5 to 6 minutes (You can brown the rabbit in two batches.) Add 1 cup of the wine-vinegar marinade, cook, and stir until it is almost all reduced, 5 to 6 minutes.

Add the tomato sauce to the rabbit and bring to a boil. Reduce the heat to medium-low and season with salt and pepper. Cover the skillet, leaving it slightly askew, and simmer until the rabbit is tender, 40 to 50 minutes. Stir a few times during cooking. If the sauce reduces too much, add a bit more broth.

Add the balsamic vinegar during the last few minutes of cooking and stir to mix thoroughly with the sauce. Taste and adjust the seasoning and serve hot with a generous topping of this delicious sauce.

Makes 4 servings

Coniglio in Agrodolce alla Siciliana

Rabbit in Sweet-and-sour Sauce

Trattoria Primavera is located in the very old section of Palermo. And old it was! After glancing at the run-down trattoria, I almost changed my mind and left, and in doing so, I would have missed a truly delicious dinner. The sweet-and-sour rabbit I had that night was simply wonderful. It was marinated in red wine, onion, and fresh herbs and was cooked in its own marinade with the addition of a syrupy mixture of vinegar, sugar, and raisins. As I finished my dinner and was paying the bill, I smelled something terrific coming from the next table. A steaming bowl of seafood was being ladled over gold, glorious *cuscusu*! I took a deep breath, called the waiter back, and to his amazement, I ordered a whole new dinner of fish stew and couscous (pages 238–40). I was so full, I thought I would burst. But in the line of duty, researching this book, I was willing to sacrifice and add another inch to my waistline!

For the marinade
    1 medium-size onion, thinly sliced
    4 to 5 fresh sage leaves or 2 dried, finely crumbled

1 small sprig fresh rosemary or 1 teaspoon dried

1 tablespoon black peppercorns

3 cups medium-bodied dry red wine, such as Chianti
Classico

To complete the dish

One 4-pound rabbit, cut into serving pieces, washed, and
dried on paper towels

⅓ cup olive oil

1 medium-size onion, finely minced

1 cup unbleached all-purpose flour, evenly spread over a
sheet of aluminum foil

Salt and freshly ground black pepper to taste

½ cup water

¼ cup red wine vinegar

3 tablespoons sugar

½ cup golden raisins soaked in 2 cups lukewarm water
for 20 minutes, then drained and dried on paper towels

In a small bowl combine all the ingredients for the marinade.
Place the rabbit in a deep dish or large bowl and pour the
marinade over it. Cover the bowl and marinate 3 to 4 hours,
basting and turning the rabbit a few times.

Remove the rabbit from the marinade and dry well with paper
towels. Strain the marinade and reserve the wine.

Heat the oil over high heat in a large, heavy skillet. Add the
onion and cook, stirring, until it begins to color, 2 to 3 minutes.
With a slotted spoon transfer the onion to a plate.

Flour the rabbit pieces lightly, shaking off any excess, and
add to the skillet, making sure not to crowd them. (The rabbit
can be browned in two batches.) Cook over high heat until the
pieces are golden on both sides, 6 to 7 minutes. Season with
salt and pepper.

Return the onion to the skillet together with half of the
reserved wine from the marinade and bring to a boil. Reduce
the heat to medium-low and cover the skillet. Cook 30 to 40
minutes, stirring and turning the rabbit a few times during the
cooking.

While the rabbit is cooking, combine the water, vinegar,
raisins, and sugar in a small skillet and bring to a boil over high
heat. Cook and stir 1 to 2 minutes. Transfer the rabbit to a
serving dish. Mix the vinegar-sugar mixture into the sauce,
spoon it over the rabbit, and serve.

Makes 4 servings

SUGGESTED WINES

*The particular taste of this
sweet-and-sour dish needs a
fairly strong-flavored white or
red wine with good, but not too
much, acidity. Try a red such as
Lungarotti's Rubesco or a white
Rhône-style wine from California.*

Coniglio con Pomodori e Olive Verdi

Stewed Rabbit with Tomatoes and Green Olives

This lovely country dish comes from Enoteca Il Gallo della Checca.

2 cups unbleached all-purpose flour, evenly spread over a sheet of aluminum foil

One 4-pound rabbit, cut into serving pieces, washed, and dried on paper towels

⅓ cup olive oil

Salt and freshly ground black pepper to taste

2 cloves garlic, finely minced

10 to 12 fresh sage leaves, finely chopped or ½ teaspoon dried, crumbled

1 tablespoon chopped fresh rosemary or ½ teaspoon dried, crumbled

1 cup good, light red wine, such as a Valpolicella

2 cups canned imported Italian tomatoes with their juice, put through a strainer or food mill to remove the seeds

1 cup meat broth, preferably homemade (see pages 53–54)

1 cup pitted green olives, drained and halved

Flour the rabbit pieces lightly and shake off the excess flour.

Heat the oil in a large skillet over high heat. Add the rabbit pieces, making sure not to crowd them, and cook until they are golden on both sides, 6 to 7 minutes. (The rabbit can be browned in two batches.) Season with salt and pepper. Add the garlic, sage, and rosemary and stir a few times. (At this point the skillet is very hot and the garlic will color in no time at all.) Add the wine and cook, stirring, until it is reduced by half, 3 to 4 minutes.

Add the tomatoes and the broth, stir, and bring to a boil. Reduce the heat to medium-low and cover the skillet, leaving it slightly askew. Cook 30 to 40 minutes, stirring and turning the rabbit a few times during cooking. Add the olives and simmer 5 to 10 minutes longer. At this point the rabbit should be tender and the sauce should have a nice medium-thick consistency. If too thick, add a bit more broth or tomatoes. Taste and adjust the seasoning and serve piping hot.

Makes 4 servings

FISH AND
SEAFOOD

Take a good look at the map of Italy and you will see an odd-shaped country squeezed between two great seas, the Mediterranean and the Adriatic, which seems to be kicking the island of Sicilia into the open sea. The first assumption, therefore, is that this is a country of serious and devoted fish eaters. And yet, not too long ago, before the super-highways and refrigeration made it possible to transport fish quickly and safely from one part of Italy to another, the consumption of fish inland was not what one would expect from a country that is practically surrounded by water. And when fish arrived inland, the quantity and selection were somewhat limited and the freshness of the fish was questionable. Today most of that has changed since fresh fish can reach any destination within a matter of hours.

There is however, an indisputable, special pleasure that comes from eating fish at its place of origin. If you are sitting in a little trattoria in Venezia or Rimini, San Remo, Amalfi, or Taormina overlooking the water, the fish tastes better—or so it seems.

One of the joys of eating fresh fish on the Italian seacoast is the wonderful display of appetizing preparations strategically placed in full view of the patrons. One look at all those tempting fish salads, and marinated fish appetizers, and your resolve of moderation simply fades away.

The best place to see the abundance of Italian seafood in one big sweep is at the fish markets. Every city or small town on the coast has an open fish market and perhaps the best known and most celebrated is the Rialto market in Venezia, which displays an incredible selection of fish caught in the Adriatic, with species of fish hardly seen anywhere else in the world.

The Italian philosophy for cooking fish is quite simple. Choose the freshest fish possible and treat it simply so that the identity of the fish will prevail over the other ingredients used in the preparation.

Fish in Italy is grilled, baked, stewed, fried, poached, cooked on a spit, and eaten raw. (Fresh-caught mussels and oysters on the half shell with lemon juice were very popular in Italy a few years ago, before the water became polluted.)

In this chapter I have included dishes that are representative of the areas I visited, such as the classic *buridda* of Liguria (a mixture of baked fish and shellfish, layered with onions and tomatoes), Swordfish Bundles with Fresh Tomatoes and Capers, which can be found in several slightly different versions all over Sicilia, the delicious, unusual Cod with Tomatoes and Prunes of Trattoria Corsi in Roma, and two appetizing fish stews—Fish Soup Abruzzi Style, which is scented with vinegar and chili pepper, and Sicilian Fish Stew with Couscous.

Almost all the dishes in this chapter can be put together in a very short time and some, like the fish stews, the *buridda*, and the mixed grill of fish, are perfect to prepare for a large group.

In Italy, as in the United States, fish is used much more extensively now than ever before because of its easy availability and freshness and because, as we have finally discovered, it is good for us.

Brodo di Pesce

Basic Fish Broth

2½ to 3 pounds fish frames (see note below)
1 large onion, coarsely chopped
2 medium-size stalks celery, cut into pieces
2 small carrots, cut into pieces
3 sprigs fresh parsley
2 cups dry white wine
3 quarts cold water
Salt to taste

Rinse the fish frames under cold running water, then combine all the ingredients in a large saucepan and bring the water to a boil over medium heat. Reduce the heat to medium-low and, with a slotted spoon or a skimmer, skim the scum that comes to the surface of the water. Simmer, uncovered, about 1 hour.

Line a strainer with a few layers of paper towels, strain the broth into a bowl, and, if you are not planning to use it right away, cool it to room temperature. It can be refrigerated for a few days or frozen for one to two months.

Makes about 8 cups

NOTE OF INTEREST

Fish frames are a mixture of fish heads, bones, scales, etc., available in fish markets, sold for the purpose of making fish broth or any such fish-flavored liquid. You can assemble your own "fish frames" by freezing any odd pieces of fish parts.

A few cups of a flavorful fish broth will enhance the taste of any fish stew, fish soup, or risotto.

Baccalà con il Pomodoro e Prugne

Poached Cod with Tomatoes and Prunes

Corsi is a truly authentic Roman trattoria—a large, unadorned room with an old-fashioned "wine bar" where the local old folks meet to drink and play cards.

This is where I had some of the best trattoria food in all of Roma. Each dish that came out of the kitchen captured your immediate attention with its aroma, color, and taste.

NOTE OF INTEREST
Originally this dish was prepared with salt cod. The cod had to soak for several days in cold water in order to soften.

One of the most interesting dishes I had at Corsi was this stewed cod with prunes. When cooked, the cod was tender and flaky, and the unusual mixture of tomatoes, garlic, wine, and diced prunes was absolutely delicious.

5 tablespoons olive oil
2 cloves garlic, peeled and left whole
1 cup dry white wine
2 cups canned imported Italian tomatoes with their juice, put through a strainer or food mill to remove the seeds
Salt and freshly ground black pepper to taste
Four 1-inch-thick cod fillets (about 2 pounds)
4 ounces pitted prunes, diced
3 tablespoons chopped fresh parsley

Heat the oil in a large skillet over medium heat. Add the garlic and cook, stirring occasionally, until the garlic is golden brown on all sides. Discard the garlic and add the wine. Cook until the wine is reduced by half, 3 to 4 minutes. Add the tomatoes, season with salt and pepper, and bring to a boil. Lower the heat to medium-low and add the cod. Cover the skillet, leaving the lid slightly askew. Cook until the cod is tender and flaky when pierced with a fork, 10 to 12 minutes. Gently place the fish onto 4 serving dishes and keep warm in a low oven while you finish the sauce.

Add the prunes and parsley to the sauce and simmer 2 to 3 minutes longer. Spoon the sauce over the fish and serve hot.

SUGGESTED WINES
Frascati or Est! Est!! Est!!! di Montefiascone would be a traditional pairing.

Makes 4 servings

Baccalà al Forno con Patate

Roasted Cod with Roasted Potatoes

Here is another dish from Corsi in Roma, my favorite little trattoria that seems to be able to cook cod better than anybody. This is a very simple dish to prepare. Thick fillets of cod are seasoned with garlic and rosemary and baked with very thin potato slices until golden. The potato slices *must* be very thin so that they will cook evenly with the fish. To make sure this happens, you may also boil the slices very briefly ahead (about 1 minute), then add them to the baking dish.

    ⅓ cup olive oil, preferably extra virgin
    2 cloves garlic, finely minced
    2 tablespoons chopped fresh rosemary or 1 tablespoon dried, crumbled
    Four 1-inch-thick cod fillets (about 2 pounds)
    3 medium-size potatoes, peeled and cut into very thin rounds
    Salt and freshly ground black pepper to taste
    ⅓ cup plain bread crumbs

Preheat the oven to 375°F.

    Put the oil, garlic, and rosemary in a large baking pan and mix with a wooden spoon. Place the cod fillets in the pan and coat them with the garlic-rosemary mixture on both sides. Put the potatoes all around the cod and toss them with a spoon until they are also coated with the garlic and rosemary. Season with salt and pepper. Bake 4 to 5 minutes, then sprinkle the cod and potatoes with the bread crumbs and bake 4 to 5 minutes longer. At this point the potatoes and cod should be lightly golden and the inside of the fish should be opaque. Serve at once.

Makes 4 servings

TIP

The perfect accompaniment for this dish would be two other baked dishes—Baked Tomatoes with Mint (page 279) and Baked Stuffed Eggplant (pages 269–70)

These are the dishes I love to cook for friends because they are earthy and delicious, and can be prepared several hours ahead and baked at the last moment with no hassle and no fuss!

SUGGESTED WINE
Try a good Orvieto from Barberani or Antinori.

Trancie di Tonno alla Veneziana

Tuna Steaks with Sweet-and-sour Onions

Tuna is a very popular fish with Southern and Northern Italians alike. This delicious fish has a firm, compact texture and a delicate taste and can be prepared in various manners.

    A preparation which is common to both Sicilians and Venetians is to cook the fish in a sweet-and-sour sauce. At Trattoria

Al Million in Venezia, the tuna steaks were cooked quickly in a bit of olive oil, then were topped with onions that had been browned in the same skillet and cooked with a mixture of red wine vinegar and sugar. It was sheer perfection. And here is the bonus: the whole dish can be completed in less than fifteen minutes!

¼ cup olive oil
Four ½- to ¾-inch-thick tuna steaks (about 2 pounds)
2 medium-size onions, thinly sliced
¼ cup red wine vinegar mixed with 3 tablespoons sugar
Salt to taste

Heat the oil in a large skillet over medium heat. Add the tuna steaks and cook until lightly golden, about 2 minutes. Turn the steaks and cook 2 minutes longer on the other side. (Do not overcook the fish or it will be too dry.) Transfer the steaks to a plate and keep warm in a *very low* heated oven.

Add the onions to the skillet. Cook and stir over medium heat until the onions are golden, 5 to 6 minutes. Add the vinegar-sugar mixture and cook, stirring, until the vinegar is almost all reduced and the onions are shiny and glazy, 1 to 2 minutes. Season with salt. Spoon the onions over the tuna steaks and serve at once.

Makes 4 servings

SUGGESTED WINE
Try a light red from the Veneto from Masi or Serègo Alighieri, which will fit this Venetian dish very well.

Stufato di Tonno

Tuna with Olives, Basil, and Tomato Sauce

Tuna is caught off the southern coast of Sicilia and it holds a place of prominence in the Southern Italian diet. This splendid firm-fleshed fish is delicious when it is grilled, but it is absolutely wonderful when it is quickly pan-fried and tossed together with a savory sauce of tomatoes, black olives, onion, celery, and fresh basil.

This preparation is typical of many homes and *trattorie*. Sometimes a different kind of fish is used, or the sauce might have the addition of capers and fresh oregano. But the principal elements of this dish do not change—firm-fleshed fish, tomatoes, garlic, olives, oil. Where did I enjoy this dish? I wish I could remember, but I know it must have been in one of the several hundred *trattorie* I researched for this book!

½ cup plus 1 tablespoon olive oil
1 small onion, diced
2 small white stalks celery, diced
2 cloves garlic, minced
½ cup dry white wine
2 cups canned imported Italian tomatoes with their juice,
    put through a strainer or food mill to remove the seeds
10 large pitted black olives, quartered
Salt and freshly ground black pepper to taste
Four 1-inch-thick tuna steaks (about 2 pounds)
10 fresh basil leaves, shredded or 2 tablespoons chopped
    fresh parsley

Heat ¼ cup of the oil in a medium-size skillet over medium heat. Add the onion and celery and cook, stirring, until it begins to color, 4 to 5 minutes. Add the garlic and cook 1 minute longer. Add the wine and cook, stirring, until the wine is almost all reduced, 2 to 3 minutes. Add the tomatoes and olives and season with salt and several grinds of pepper. Cook and stir for 4 to 5 minutes.

While the sauce is cooking, heat the remaining oil in a large skillet over medium heat. Add the tuna steaks and cook until they are lightly golden on both sides, 3 to 4 minutes.

Add the tomato sauce to the tuna and shake the skillet lightly to distribute the sauce without having to move the steaks. Bring the sauce to a gentle boil, then reduce the heat to medium-low and simmer 1 to 2 minutes. Transfer the steaks to serving dishes, add the basil to the sauce, and stir over the heat once or twice. Taste and adjust the seasonings, then spoon the sauce over the steaks and serve at once.

Makes 4 servings

SUGGESTED WINES
With a Sicilian dish, you should try a Sicilian wine. Try a light red from producers such as Settesoli or Terre di Ginestra, and serve it cool.

Pesce Spada alla Caprese

Marinated Grilled Swordfish Capri Style

In 1986, only a few months after I opened Biba restaurant in Sacramento, I had a delegation of members of the Italian Parliament for lunch who were touring California and had just ended a meeting with the governor. Understandably, I was a little nervous at having such important people at my newly opened restaurant. As it turned out, they were impressed and very pleased with everything, especially the pasta and the freshness of the swordfish. Before leaving, one of the gentlemen approached me and said: "Signora, I want to share with you a dish from my town, Capri. Grill the swordfish *first*, and marinate it *after* it has been grilled." I tried it and loved it and now serve it quite often in summertime.

In June 1991 I had lunch at Il Bocciodromo in Capri, and one of the dishes of the day was marinated grilled swordfish, which was accompanied only by slices of intensely red, ripe tomatoes, basil, and olive oil.

3 cloves garlic, finely minced
½ cup loosely packed fresh oregano leaves or 2 tablespoons chopped fresh parsley, preferably Italian (flatleaf)
¼ cup red wine vinegar
¼ cup water
½ cup extra virgin olive oil
Juice of 1 large lemon
Salt and freshly ground black pepper to taste
Four ½-inch-thick swordfish steaks (about 2 pounds)

In a small bowl combine the garlic, oregano, vinegar, water, oil, and lemon juice and season with salt and several grinds of pepper. Set aside.

Preheat the grill or the barbecue well in advance. Brush the fish lightly with the marinade and put it on the grill. Cook until the fish is lightly golden, 2 minutes on each side.

Place the fish in a large, shallow dish that can accommodate the steaks in one layer and pour the marinade over them. Marinate for about 1 hour at room temperature, basting a few times.

Makes 4 servings

Involtini di Pesce alla Siciliana con Pomodoro Fresco

Swordfish Bundles with Fresh Tomatoes and Capers

In Sicilia, it is almost impossible not to eat fish on a daily basis, since this beautiful island is surrounded by waters that are rich with an incredible variety of fish. Swordfish, just like tuna, is a favorite and used in many preparations.

In this recipe, thin slices of swordfish are stuffed with a mixture of cooked onions, anchovies, raisins, parsley, and parmigiano, and are rolled up into fat little bundles. Then they are browned in oil and finished cooking with strips of peeled fresh tomatoes, garlic, capers, and olive oil. This appetizing preparation comes from Trattoria Pesco Mare in Siracusa, and can be found in one version or another all over Sicilia.

For the bundles

¼ cup olive oil

1 small onion, finely minced

2 cloves garlic, finely minced

4 anchovy fillets, chopped

2 tablespoons plain bread crumbs

3 tablespoons golden raisins, soaked in 1 cup lukewarm water for 20 minutes, squeezed dry, and chopped

3 tablespoons chopped fresh parsley

Salt and freshly ground black pepper

¼ cup freshly grated parmigiano

2 large egg yolks

Eight ¼-inch-thick slices swordfish (about 1½ pounds)

To complete the dish

¼ cup olive oil

2 cloves garlic, finely minced

½ cup dry white wine

2 pounds ripe tomatoes, peeled (see page 16), seeded, and cut into strips

2 tablespoons capers, drained and rinsed

Salt to taste

TIPS

In winter, when fresh tomatoes are less than acceptable, use a good brand of canned imported Italian tomatoes which are ripe red, meaty, and juicy. Seed the tomatoes (they are already peeled) and cut them into strips. Reserve the thin tomato juices in the can for a soup.

These delicious bundles can also be grilled and served without a sauce. In that case, brush the bundles with olive oil mixed with a bit of red wine vinegar and sprinkle the bundles lightly with a bit of bread crumbs, then grill them until they are golden brown on all sides, turning very gently, about 8 minutes. They can be served as an entree or as an appetizer.

Heat the oil in a medium-size skillet over medium heat. Add the onion and cook, stirring, until it begins to color, 4 to 5 minutes. Add the garlic and the anchovies and cook 1 minute longer. Add the bread crumbs, raisins, and parsley and stir once or twice. With a slotted spoon, transfer the mixture to a bowl and cool slightly, then season with salt and pepper and add the parmigiano and the egg yolks. Mix well until the ingredients are well combined. Taste and adjust the seasonings.

Lay the swordfish slices on a work surface and spread some of the onion mixture over each slice, leaving an empty border all around the slice. Roll each slice up into a bundle and secure with 1 or 2 wooden toothpicks. (The bundles can be prepared several hours ahead and kept in the refrigerator tightly covered.)

Heat the oil in a large skillet over medium heat. Add the bundles and cook until they are golden on all sides, 6 to 7 minutes. (Make sure to turn the bundles gently, so they won't open.)

With a slotted spoon, transfer the bundles to a plate. Add the garlic to the skillet and stir once or twice. Add the wine and cook, stirring, until it is almost all reduced, 2 to 3 minutes. Add the tomatoes and capers and season lightly with salt. Cook 1 to 2 minutes, stirring, then return the bundles to the skillet and stir just long enough to coat the bundles with the sauce, less than 1 minute. Serve at once.

Makes 4 servings

SUGGESTED WINES

The most popular Sicilian table wine is Corvo. Try either the white or red served cool. (Swordfish goes well also with light red wines.)

Pesce Spada alla Menta e Balsamico

Grilled Swordfish with Mint and Balsamic Vinegar

NOTE OF INTEREST

If balsamic vinegar is unavailable, substitute a good red wine vinegar. In that case, simmer the sauce for about 1 minute to cut down a bit on the strong taste.

Pierino Jovene is an exuberant Neapolitan who, for twenty years, has owned and operated the well-known Gambero Rosso of Cesenatico. Pierino cooks fish very simply, for he believes that good fish should stand on its own merit.

In this preparation the swordfish is grilled and topped with a few tablespoons of warm uncooked garlic, balsamic vinegar, and mint sauce.

Four ½-inch-thick swordfish steaks (about 2 pounds)
¼ cup olive oil, preferably extra virgin
¼ cup balsamic vinegar (see page 13)
6 to 7 fresh mint leaves, shredded
Salt to taste
1 clove garlic, finely minced

Preheat the grill or the barbecue well ahead of time.

Brush the fish with a bit of oil and place it over the hot grill. Cook 2 to 3 minutes on each side.

While the fish is cooking, heat the remaining oil in a small skillet over medium heat. Add the balsamic vinegar and mint and season with a bit of salt. Cook just long enough to heat up the sauce. Just before removing the sauce from the heat, stir in the garlic. Place the grilled fish on serving plates, spoon the warm sauce over, and serve at once.

Makes 4 servings

SUGGESTED WINES

A full bodied rosé, Ruffino's Rosatello, Antinori's Rosato di Bolgheri, and Mastroberardino Lachrymarosa from Italy. Firestone or Simi Rosé of Cabernet and Phelps Mistral Granache Rosé fit the bill.

La Grigliata Mista

Mixed Grilled Fish

As a teenager, growing up in Bologna, I would spend two weeks every summer at nearby Rimini, a very popular resort on the Adriatic coast, only seventy miles from Bologna. Those were happy, carefree times. I would tan all morning long, sleep in the afternoon, dance all night, and, in between, find the time to eat tons of wonderfully fresh fish. One of my favorite dishes was the *grigliata di pesce misto*, a large plate with small amounts of different types of fish all perfectly grilled and served with only a few slices of lemon and a drizzle of delicious extra virgin olive oil.

The last time I enjoyed this splendid dish was in June of 1991 at Dal Delicato Trattoria in Napoli. It came to the table preceeded by the unmistakable aroma of very fresh fish and was served with a side dish of fried zucchini blossoms (see pages 34–35) and fried zucchini (page 280).

This is a dish that I prepare quite often at my restaurant in Sacramento and it is always a sellout.

In order to make this dish a success, choose not less than four different types of seafood and fish. Some that I use, interchangeably, are halibut, swordfish, tuna, mahi mahi, orange roughy, lobster, large prawns, and calamari. After you choose, ask your vendor to cut them into two-ounce pieces, about one-half-inch thick. Keep in mind that in this dish nothing is hidden under sauces and therefore the quality of your fish must shine.

> 2 pounds assorted fish
> ⅓ cup olive oil
> 1 cup plain bread crumbs mixed with 2 tablespoons chopped fresh parsley
> Salt to taste
> Lemon wedges

Preheat the broiler or the barbecue well ahead of time.

Brush the fish with the oil on both sides and sprinkle with the bread crumb–parsley mixture. Place the fish on the hot grill and cook 2 to 3 minutes on each side. Serve at once with the lemon wedges.

Makes 4 servings

SUGGESTED WINE
Try a Johnson-Turnbull Chardonnay from California.

Zuppa di Pesce alla Siciliana con il Cuscusu

Sicilian Fish Stew with Couscous

At the supermodest Trattoria Primavera in the old quarter of Palermo, I was served a fluffy, golden *cuscusu*, topped by a delicious, spicy fish stew which I promptly tried to reproduce once I was back in my Sacramento kitchen. And, considering the compromises I had to make (no Sicilian fish available in Sacramento, and no old Sicilian women in my kitchen preparing *cuscusu*), I was quite satisfied with the results.

This fish stew is utterly delicious, quite simple to prepare, and, by doubling the recipe, can feed a crowd. Because the fish cooks rather quickly and if left in the sauce too long tends to break into very small, unattractive pieces, I prepare the fish sauce completely several hours ahead then I reheat it gently, add the fish, cook it, and serve at once.

For the soup

⅓ cup olive oil

1 medium-size onion, finely minced

2 small white stalks celery, finely minced

4 anchovy fillets, chopped

3 cloves garlic, finely minced

1 cup dry white wine

2 cups fish broth (see page 229)

4 cups canned imported Italian tomatoes with their juice, put through a strainer or food mill to remove the seeds

Salt to taste

½ teaspoon dried red pepper flakes

2½ pounds mixed fish fillets, such as halibut, sea bass, tuna, swordfish, snapper, or rockfish, cut into 2-inch pieces

3 tablespoons chopped fresh parsley

For the couscous

2 cups medium-grain couscous (see note)

2 tablespoons olive oil

Salt to taste

3 cups fish broth (see page 229)

NOTE OF INTEREST

Cuscusu, *as it is called in Sicilia, is one of the many legacies bestowed on Sicilia by the Arabs, who ruled Sicilia from the ninth to the eleventh centuries. This is a dish that was made by mixing semolina flour with a bit of water and oil and breaking it into very small grains by the expert hands of Sicilian women. Unfortunately, homemade cuscusu is one of those dishes that, with a few exceptions, now belongs to the legacy of the past, since it is quite time-consuming to prepare and requires a skill that takes time and patience to acquire.*

Today, even in Sicilia, chances are that the cuscusu *you eat comes out of a box. There are, however, several commercial brands of instant couscous that are quite good, such as Ferrero, Sipa, Casbah, and Ile de France. Couscous can also be found sold by the pound in health food stores.*

To prepare the fish soup, heat the oil in a large saucepan over medium heat. Add the onion and celery and cook, stirring, until the onion begins to color, 4 to 5 minutes. Add the anchovies and garlic and cook, stirring, about 1 minute.

Raise the heat to high and add the wine. Cook, stirring, until the wine is almost all reduced, 5 to 6 minutes. Add the fish broth and tomatoes and season with salt and the red pepper. Bring to a boil, then lower the heat to medium-low and cook, uncovered, 8 to 10 minutes, stirring a few times.

Add the fish pieces and simmer about 5 minutes. During the last minute of simmering, stir in the parsley and taste and adjust the seasonings.

While the sauce is simmering, prepare the couscous. Mix the

couscous with the oil in a medium-size bowl. Bring the fish broth to a boil in a small saucepan over medium heat. Add 2½ cups of the hot broth to the couscous, mix well, and cover the bowl with aluminum foil. Set aside for about 10 minutes. (Keep the remaining broth warm over very low heat.) Taste the couscous; if it is too crunchy, add the remaining hot broth, cover, and set aside for 5 minutes longer. When done, the couscous should be plumper (because it absorbs the liquid) and should still be firm to the bite. Fluff it up with a fork, breaking any small clusters that may have formed.

Spoon the couscous into bowls and top with the fish stew.

Makes 4 to 6 servings

Buridda

Baked Assorted Fish, Tomatoes, and Onions Genova Style

NOTE OF INTEREST

The frugality of the Ligurian people is proverbial. In this dish, with the addition of the onion and tomatoes, a little fish is made to go a long way and feed more people than it would if the fish were grilled or pan-fried.

Imagine a trattoria that has been in the same location and the same family for over one hundred years, handed down from generation to generation and to the present owner, Bruno Andreani, who has run it for a mere thirty years!

Antica Trattoria dei Cacciatori is located in Sampierdarena, now a suburb of Genova. The food they serve is typical of the area which draws its resources and imagination from the nearby sea. *Buridda* is an interesting, delicious dish that combines the best the sea and the land have to offer—fresh, wonderful fish, ripe tomatoes, sweet onions, fresh herbs, and that important commodity of Liguria, delicious, light Ligurian olive oil.

In this preparation the onions are cooked in olive oil until soft and stirred quickly with a bit of garlic and anchovy. The onions are then spread in the bottom of a baking dish and layered with slices of tomatoes, assorted fish, more onions and tomatoes, and then baked.

This wonderful dish looks good, tastes even better, and can be assembled several hours ahead and baked at the last moment.

⅓ cup olive oil

2 large onions, thinly sliced

3 anchovy fillets, finely chopped

3 cloves garlic, finely minced

2 pounds ripe, juicy, pear-shaped tomatoes, cut into
   ¼-inch rounds

Salt and freshly ground black pepper

1 pound firm-fleshed fish, such as sea bass, halibut, or
   mahi mahi, cut into 4 serving pieces ¾-inch thick

4 ounces sea scallops

4 ounces medium-size shrimp, peeled and deveined

2 tablespoons chopped fresh parsley

Preheat the oven to 350°F.

Heat ¼ cup of the oil in a large skillet over medium heat. Add the onion and cook, stirring, until the onion begins to color, 5 to 6 minutes. Add the achovies and garlic and cook, stirring, about 1 minute.

Spread half of the onions in the bottom of a baking dish, top the onion with half of the tomatoes, and season lightly with salt and pepper.

Arrange the fish and shellfish over the tomatoes and top with the remaining onions, spreading them evenly over the fish. Top the onions with the remaining tomatoes, season again lightly with salt and pepper, and sprinkle with the parsley.

Pour the remaining oil over the tomatoes and bake 25 to 30 minutes. Let the dish settle for a few minutes; then, with a large spoon, remove some of the excess oil and watery juices from the pan and serve.

Makes 4 to 6 servings

SUGGESTED WINES
The fragrant, light, dry white Vermentino of Lupi or the Cinqueterre of the Cantina Sociale would fit nicely.

Brodetto di Pesce

Fish Soup Abruzzi Style

This is one of those dishes embedded in my memory that surfaces every time I see a cornucopia of fresh seafood.

Years ago, while vacationing with my family in Abruzzo, we

dined at Beccaceci, a well-known trattoria in the seacoast town of Giulianova, much renowned for its fish preparations. My pick that night was a *brodetto di pesce* that came to the table loaded with large chunks of fish intensely flavored in a rich tomato-wine-garlic-vinegar-anchovy broth that had the addition of the ever-present *peperoncino* (red pepper flakes).

¼ cup olive oil, preferably extra virgin
1 small onion, finely minced
3 cloves garlic, finely minced
2 anchovy fillets, chopped
½ teaspoon dried red pepper flakes
⅓ cup red wine vinegar
1 cup dry white wine
5 cups canned imported Italian tomatoes with their juice,
    put through a strainer or food mill to remove the seeds
Salt to taste
½ pound halibut fillets, cut into 2-inch-thick pieces
½ pound sea bass fillets, cut into 2-inch-thick pieces
½ pound swordfish steaks, cut into 2-inch-thick pieces
4 ounces shrimp, peeled and deveined
4 ounces sea scallops
6 ounces squid, cleaned as instructed on page 40 and cut
    into 1-inch rings
2 tablespoons chopped fresh parsley
12 small slices Italian bread, toasted or grilled

Heat the oil in a large saucepan over medium heat. Add the onion and cook, stirring, until it begins to color, 5 to 6 minutes. Add the garlic, anchovies, and red pepper and cook, stirring, about 1 minute.

Raise the heat to high and add the vinegar. When the vinegar is almost all reduced, less than 1 minute, add the wine. Cook and stir until it is reduced by half, 3 to 4 minutes. Add the tomatoes and season with salt. Bring to a boil, then lower the heat to medium-low and cook, uncovered, 5 to 6 minutes, stirring a few times.

Add the fish pieces and let simmer 2 to 3 minutes, then add the shrimp and scallops and cook until the fish is cooked through, 2 to 3 minutes. Lastly, add the squid and cook less than 1 minute. Stir in the parsley, taste, adjust the seasonings, and serve at once with slices of grilled bread or polenta.

Makes 4 to 6 servings

SUGGESTED WINES
Here your choice can go from a lightly chilled bottle of young Montepulciano d'Abruzzo from Cornacchia to a full-bodied oaky-style Chardonnay from the California Central Coast. Edna Valley Vineyard, Au Bon Climat, or Firestone would work.

Vongole alla Napoletana

Stew of Clams Neapolitan Style

A friend had told me that Trattoria da Dora in Napoli was excellent, but that the service left a lot to be desired. And she was right on both counts. After I was seated, I had to wait almost 15 minutes before someone offered me a glass of wine, or at least of water. Finally, when I was almost ready to leave, the scruffy owner came to get my order. As I was sipping a glass of ordinary white wine, brooding about the unhappy beginning of this meal, the food arrived. The large bowl of very small clams in a fragrant tomato sauce with specks of garlic floating all over was sinfully delicious. As I was happily dipping the dense slices of bread into the sauce, I forgot all about the unpleasant beginning of the meal.

> ¼ cup olive oil
> 3 cloves garlic, finely minced
> 3 tablespoons chopped fresh parsley
> 1 cup dry white wine
> 3 cups canned imported Italian tomatoes with their juice, put through a strainer or food mill to remove the seeds
> Salt and freshly ground black pepper
> 4 pounds clams, the smallest you can get, thoroughly washed in several changes of water

Heat the oil in a large saucepan over medium heat. Add the garlic and the parsley and cook, stirring, until the garlic begins to color, about 1 minute. Raise the heat to high and add the wine. Cook and stir until the wine is reduced by half, 3 to 4 minutes. Add the tomatoes and bring to a boil, then lower the heat to medium and cook, stirring, 4 to 5 minutes. Season with salt and several grinds of pepper.

Add the clams and cover the saucepan. Cook just until the clams open, 2 to 3 minutes. (Discard any clams that do not open.) Taste and adjust the seasoning and serve hot with good, crusty Italian bread.

Makes 4 servings

TIPS

↬ *Because clams (and mussels) are often very sandy, I soak them in a large bowl of cold salted water for about 1 hour to draw out the sand, then I wash them thoroughly.*

↬ *Mussels can be used instead of the clams, or prepare this appetizing dish with both clams and mussels.*

SUGGESTED WINES

Because of the tomato in this recipe, a nice light red wine such as Mastroberardino's Irpinia Rosé or Lachrymarosa from the Campania region would be perfect.

Insalata di Mare

Trattoria Cannavota Fish and Shellfish Salad

Seafood salads are very popular all over Italy, especially in coastal towns. There, the freshly caught fish is displayed in many different, appealing salad combinations. The important elements in these dishes are two: very fresh fish and shellfish and wonderfully fragrant olive oil. Then the local cook will add his or her touch to the preparation.

At Cannavota in Roma, I lunched on a salad that, besides the oil, lemon, and garlic dressing, also had the addition of the reduced flavorful juices of the clams' cooking liquid. Just a little extra touch that made this salad more memorable.

For the fish

2 pounds small clams, thoroughly washed and scrubbed in several changes of water

2 cups dry white wine

6 cups water

6 ounces bay scallops, thoroughly washed under cold water

6 ounces medium-size shrimp, peeled and deveined

1 pound white fish, such as mahi mahi, orange roughy, or halibut, cut into 1½-inch pieces

6 ounces small squid, cleaned as directed on page 40 and sliced into small rings, without its tentacles

For the dressing

Juice of 2 lemons

Salt to taste

Small pinch of dried red pepper flakes

2 cloves garlic, finely minced

⅓ cup extra virgin olive oil

2 tablespoons chopped fresh parsley

2 small white stalks celery, thinly sliced

Put the clams in a large skillet, add 1 cup of the wine and 1 cup of the water. Cover and bring to a boil. Remove the clams with a slotted spoon as they open. Discard any that do not open.

TIPS

➣ *If your clams are very sandy, soak them in cool, salted water for about 1 hour. Salt will draw out the sand inside the clams.*

➣ *Most of the work for this dish can be done in advance. Wash and cook the fish in the morning and keep it in a tightly sealed bowl in the refrigerator.*

➣ *As you can see from the cooking time in the recipe, all the fish and shellfish cook very fast. Keep in mind that squid cooks very fast and even only a few seconds can make the difference between tender and tough squid.*

Remove the meat from the shells and put it in a large salad bowl. Discard the shells. Cook the clams' juices over high heat until only 3 to 4 tablespoons are left in the skillet. Pour the juice into a small bowl.

In a medium-size saucepan, combine the remaining water with the remaining wine and bring to a boil over high heat. Lower the heat and cook the fish, beginning with the scallops. The scallops will take no longer than 1½ minutes to cook. They're done when opaque all the way through. Remove with a slotted spoon to drain on paper towels. Add the shrimp and cook 1 to 1½ minutes, till opaque. Transfer to paper towels. Add the cut-up white fish and cook 2 to 2½ minutes, till opaque. Transfer to paper towels. Add the squid and cook no longer than 30 to 40 seconds. Drain the squid and immediately put the colander with the squid in a bowl of very cold water to stop the cooking. Place the squid on paper towels to dry. Add all the fish to the clams in the salad bowl.

To prepare the dressing, combine the reserved clam juice, the lemon juice, salt, red pepper, garlic, olive oil, and parsley in a medium-size bowl and mix well to combine. Add the sliced celery to the fish and stir in the salad dressing. Mix well, then taste and adjust the seasonings. Cover the bowl and cool in the refrigerator about 30 minutes. Serve with slices of crusty Italian bread.

Makes 4 servings

SUGGESTED WINES
Try the single-vineyard Frascati Santa Teresa of Fontana Candida, or a Wente Estate Semillon from Livermore in California.

Cozze Impepate

Peppery Mussels on the Half Shell

I first tasted this dish many years ago in a small trattoria on the Amalfi coast, and I soon found out why this delectable dish is one of the most popular of the Campania region. Large, very fresh mussels steamed in a bit of oil and wine (or water) and dressed only with a bit of fresh chopped parsley and *lots* of freshly ground pepper are simply irresistible.

If you happen to be in Amalfi, which is the gem of the

northern coast, go to trattoria Da Gemma and ask for a large serving of *cozze impepate*; then, after your meal, make sure to take a nice leisurely stroll in the small *piazza*, smell the flowers, and take in the breathtaking view of the great blue sea below.

> 5 pounds mussels
> 2 tablespoons olive oil
> 1 cup dry white wine
> 2 tablespoons chopped fresh parsley
> Freshly ground black pepper to taste
> Lemon wedges

Soak the mussels in cold salted water for 20 minutes. Remove the beards of the mussels and scrub them well under cold running water. (Often the mussels are full of grit and need to be scrubbed thoroughly in several changes of water.) Discard any mussels that won't close.

Heat the oil and the wine in a large skillet over medium heat. Add the mussels and cover the skillet. Cook until the mussels open. (This will vary from one mussel to the other; some will open in 30 to 40 seconds, others will take 1 to 2 minutes.) Remove the mussels with a slotted spoon to a large bowl as they open and discard any that won't open during cooking.

Detach and discard the top shell. Return the mussels in their half shells to the skillet. Stir in the parsley and season generously with black pepper (I was told not to use any salt!!!).

Serve the mussels with lemon wedges and eat them on the half shell to fully enjoy the juices that are in the shells.

Makes 4 servings as an entree or 8 as an appetizer

SUGGESTED WINES
Choose a Prosecco from Nino Franco or a crisp Sauvignon Blanc from California, such as Beaulieu or Konocti.

Calamaretti alla Griglia

Grilled Small Squid

Because I love and eat pasta as often as I can, I try judiciously to "lighten up" my diet once in a while with fish. At La Carbonara in Roma, a bustling, busy, well-known trattoria, I was served very small, charred, and tender squid that had been basted with olive oil, lemon, and vinegar. They were heavenly!

When I make this dish at home or at the restaurant, I choose the smallest squid possible, and even though they are not quite as small as the Roman ones, they are still delicious.

While you have the grill or the barbecue hot, before you put on the squid, grill some onions, zucchini, red bell peppers, and eggplant, and serve alongside this delicious squid.

> ¼ cup olive oil
> Juice of 1 lemon
> 1 tablespoon white wine vinegar
> Salt to taste
> 1¼ pounds squid, the smallest you can get, cleaned as directed on page 40
> Lemon wedges

Preheat the grill or the barbecue well in advance. In a small bowl combine the oil, lemon juice, vinegar, and salt. Brush the squid lightly with the oil mixture. Put the squid on the very hot grill. When one side is lightly charred, about 45 seconds, turn them to grill on the other side. Serve with the lemon wedges.

Makes 4 servings

TIP

ᔍ *With squid, there is one simple rule. Do not overcook it, or it will become tough and rubbery.*

SUGGESTED WINES
Try a good Soave from Masi or Boscaini, or Ivan Támás Trebbiano from Livermore in California.

Fritto Misto di Frutti di Mari

Deep-fried Shellfish

Most restaurants and *trattorie* of the seacoast serve the popular *fritto misto di pesce*. At Antico Pizzo in Venezia, a bustling, colorful trattoria a few minutes away from the well-known Rialto fish market, I was served a delicious crisp concoction of mixed fried shellfish. Octopus, squid, shrimp, and small scallops had been tossed in flour and fried to perfection. They were sprinkled with salt and served with lemon wedges.

This deceivingly simple dish can, at times, be quite disappointing, because of poor frying techniques.

To prepare this dish successfully at home this is what you should do:

NOTE OF INTEREST
In Italy a fritto misto is generally never served with sauces, because Italians feel that the goodness and crispness of quickly fried fish should stand on its own merit.

1. Prepare all your ingredients on a tray, ready to go.
2. Have the oil very hot, but not smoking. The ideal temperature of the oil should be 375°F.
3. When you add the fish to the hot oil, do not crowd the pan, or you will lower the temperature of the oil and you'll get soggy results.
4. The moment the fish is golden, transfer it to paper towels and add more fish to the pan. (Do not attempt to do this dish for a crowd unless you are skilled with frying and can juggle a couple of pans at the same time.)
5. Have your family or friends at the table because fried food, just like pasta, *does not wait for anyone*, and must be served immediately.

Oil for frying
½ pound medium-size shrimp, peeled and deveined
1 cup unbleached all-purpose flour
½ pound fresh scallops, preferably bay scallops or the smallest you can get
½ pound small squid, cleaned as instructed on page 40 and cut into ½-inch rings
Salt to taste
8 lemon wedges

Wash all the shellfish under cold running water and pat dry thoroughly with paper towels.

Heat 2 inches of oil in a medium-size saucepan over high heat. Place the shrimp in a large colander and put the colander over a large bowl. Sprinkle the shrimp heavily with the flour and shake off the excess flour. With a slotted spoon, lower a limited number of shrimp into the hot oil and fry until they are golden on both sides, 1 to 2 minutes.

Remove with a slotted spoon and transfer to paper towels to drain.

Flour and fry the scallops in the same manner, and remove when they are golden on all sides, 1 to 2 minutes.

Flour the squid and fry in the same manner. Remove when they are golden, about 1 minute. (Squid will cook faster—do not overcook or they will become quite tough.)

Place the *fritto misto* on individual serving dishes, sprinkle with salt, and serve piping hot with lemon wedges.

Makes 4 servings

SUGGESTED WINES
Try the Napa Valley Trefethen Riesling, or Château Ste. Michelle's Dry Riesling from Washington state.

Gamberi alla Cannavota

The Shrimp of Trattoria Cannavota

When Romans are tired of their appetizing spicy pastas, of their goats and lambs cooked on a spit, and of their savory oxtail stews, they turn to fish. And whether the fish is stewed, grilled, fried, poached, or sautéed, it still retains that essential Roman quality. Character!

This tasty, flavorful shrimp dish comes from Trattoria Cannavota. At the first bite, I knew there was something more in the sauce than the "mere touch" of wine, oil, butter, and chile pepper. The secret, I was told, after I soaked up every bit of sauce left in my plate, was the addition of some "broth" made with the shells from the shrimp.

For the shrimp broth
    Shells of 1½ pounds medium-size shrimp
    6 cups water
    1 cup dry white wine
    1 medium-size carrot, cut into pieces
    1 small onion, peeled and quartered
    1 stalk celery, cut into pieces
    Several bay leaves
    Several sprigs fresh parsley

For the shrimp
    ¼ cup olive oil
    1½ pounds medium-size shrimp, peeled and deveined
    2 cloves garlic, finely minced
    1 cup dry white wine
    1 cup shrimp broth
    Salt to taste
    Pinch of dried red pepper flakes
    1 tablespoon unsalted butter
    2 tablespoons chopped fresh parsley

Prepare the shrimp broth by putting all its ingredients in a medium-size saucepan. Bring to a boil over medium heat, then reduce the heat to medium-low and cook, uncovered, until the

TIPS

↬ *At the end of the cooking the sauce should have a nice, medium-thick consistency. If too thin, after you have removed the shrimp to serving dishes, reduce it over high heat, then spoon over the shrimp.*

↬ *Peel and devein the shrimp and make the broth ahead of time. At dinnertime, it will take you less than 10 minutes to put this dish together.*

↬ *If you have any leftovers, use them over pasta. Cook some spaghetti, linguine, or penne, add them to a skillet with some oil and the leftover shrimp, and toss quickly together. Buon appetito!*

broth is reduced to about 1 cup, 1 to 1½ hours. Strain the broth through a fine sieve and discard the shells. Put the broth in a bowl and cool, then cover the bowl and refrigerate until ready to use.

To prepare the shrimp, heat the oil in a large skillet over medium heat. Add the shrimp and cook until the shrimp are lightly golden on all sides, 1 to 2 minutes. Transfer the shrimp to a plate while you finish the sauce.

Add the garlic to the skillet and cook, stirring, until the garlic begins to color, less than 1 minute. Add the wine and shrimp broth and season with salt and the pepper. Cook, stirring, until the liquid is reduced by half, 6 to 7 minutes. Return the shrimp to the skillet and add the butter and parsley. Cook, stirring, about 1 minute longer. Place the shrimp in individual serving dishes and top with a bit of the sauce. Serve at once.

Makes 4 servings

SUGGESTED WINES
The snap of Sauvignon Blanc fits this dish well. Try Felluga Sauvignon Blanc from Friuli or Sterling Sauvignon Blanc from the Napa Valley.

VEGETABLES
AND SALADS

It has been said that Italians prepare vegetables better than anybody else in the world. I don't know if that is true but I do know that vegetables are an essential part of a family meal and that Italians passionately wait for the changing of the seasons to enjoy the *primizie*, the first produce to reach the market. Those special first crops of asparagus, peas, tender string beans, lettuce, and ripe, red tomatoes are eagerly sought and sometimes dearly paid for by the housewife who knows that good cooking begins at the market with the freshest possible ingredients.

One of the extraordinary sights in an Italian open market is its vegetable stalls filled to capacity with mounds of colorful, fresh vegetables and fruit. As a child I sometimes followed my mother to the glorious medieval open market in Bologna. She would inspect the vegetables and fruit with a critical eye, then would pick a few tomatoes or peppers with the greatest of care and would prepare them the same day with a minimum amount of fuss.

There is so much that can be done with vegetables. They can be tempting appetizers or side dishes, they can be turned into cooked or raw salads, and quite often they can become the whole meal. I, and scores of other Italians, could exist on pasta and vegetables alone.

The vegetables I found in the *trattorie* I researched were the kinds that could have been prepared by mothers or grandmothers in country kitchens. They were quite simple, always straightforward, mostly uncomplicated, generously seasoned, and often had the mark and the inventiveness of the cook who prepared it.

In this chapter you will find vegetables that are stuffed, baked, fried, sautéed, and grilled. There is a mashed potato that will melt your thoughts of moderation away, a warm potato salad that is sinful, a stewed lentil dish that will fill your stomach and your heart with warmth, and an unusual deep-fried whole artichoke. There is also the creamy spinach of Masuelli in Milano, the fried spicy eggplant of Trattoria Paola in Roma, and the Potato and Onion in a Skillet of Gabriella in Trieste, all of which will win you over.

Salad in Italy is never served before the first course, unless it is a composed salad such as calamari salad (pages 40–41), meant to be served as an appetizer. An *insalata verde*, green salad, or an *insalata mista*, mixed green salad, is likely to follow an entree, especially at a formal meal. There are, of course, other salads that play different roles. For example, in a family meal a composed or simple salad might become the whole meal. A composed salad might be made with assorted greens and cheese, or with rice and shellfish, or with cooked meats and cooked vegetables, or simply with a variety of boiled or grilled vegetables, such as the *Verdure Cotte in Insalata* (pages 260–61) and the *Insalata di Melanzane e Pomodori alla Griglia* (pages 257–58).

It is also not unusual in a trattoria to see customers ordering a plate of pasta followed by an *insalatona* (pages 256–57), a large salad with mixed greens, vegetables, and cheese. If all this is confusing to you, keep in mind a few basic rules.

If you are planning an Italian meal for company, serve the green or mixed green salad after the entree. Keep it simple, and remember that this salad is served not because your guests are still hungry, but because it is meant to cleanse and refresh the palate at the end of a meal, or to prepare it for what follows (cheese, desserts, etc.). If you are preparing a salad for your family and you are serving several courses in the Italian manner, follow the same rule.

If you are planning a salad for a relaxed meal at home, there are no rules, and as stated above, the salad might become the whole meal with the addition of several different ingredients.

All this leads us to the Italian salad dressing. Don't believe the commercials you see on television where the advertised bottle of Italian dressing contains all the herbs in the world, with the addition of a hefty dose of garlic. Italian salad dressing doesn't know diversity or regionality. It consists simply of the best possible olive oil, good red wine vinegar, and salt. (Lemon juice is often used with boiled vegetables instead of vinegar.) Pepper is optional.

Even though I have given proportions for the salads in this chapter, I believe that proportions for salad dressing in cookbooks should be abolished, since much of it depends on the intensity of the oil and the vinegar used. As a general rule, be generous with the oil but stingy with the vinegar. Taste the salad and adjust it to your liking.

The following are some basic guidelines for a perfect salad.

∞ Make sure that your greens are washed and, most important, dried well.

∞ Season the salad lightly with salt.

∞ Add just enough oil to coat the salad.

∞ Add the vinegar very judiciously, perhaps starting with only a few tablespoons. You can always add more.

∞ Toss the salad well, then taste and adjust it to your liking.

∞ Serve the salad at once or the dressing will make the salad soggy.

Insalata Capricciosa

Capricious Salad

Insalata capricciosa is prepared with a variety of mixed greens and vegetables, depending on the capriciousness of the cook. This popular salad is a standard item in *trattorie*, where it is generally served in large, individual bowls, undressed. The oil and vinegar are brought to the table in pretty glass containers so the customers can dress their own salads.

Don't limit yourself to the choice of ingredients in this recipe; add as many kinds of lettuce as you like. You should always include, however, some radicchio, arugula, or Belgian endive for that touch of tartness that Italians like so much in their salads.

> 1 small head radicchio
> ½ head curly chicory
> ½ head butter lettuce
> 1 medium-size red bell pepper, seeded and cut into thin strips
> 2 white stalks celery, thinly sliced
> 3 medium-size, ripe tomatoes, cut into wedges
> 20 pitted black olives, halved
> ½ small red onion, thinly sliced
> Salt to taste
> ⅓ cup extra virgin olive oil
> 3 to 4 tablespoons red wine vinegar

Wash all your greens and vegetables and dry them well. Tear the greens into medium-size pieces and toss all the salad ingredients together in a large bowl. Season with salt and dress with the oil and vinegar. Taste and adjust the seasonings and serve.

Makes 4 to 6 servings

Rape Rosse in Insalata

Red Beet Salad

This, just like fennel, is another vegetable that many people tend to shun. Perhaps it is the fear of cooking something new that intimidates. But once you have prepared it a few times, you will be completely hooked on the delicate taste of fresh cooked beets. Red beets are very popular in Italy and are often part of a family meal. They are also standard items in restaurants and *trattorie*, where they are displayed on large platters alongside other vegetables.

Beets can be boiled or baked. A red beet salad mixed with very thin slices of sweet onion and dressed simply with extra virgin olive oil and wine vinegar is unbeatable.

2 pounds red beets, trimmed and peeled
½ medium-size sweet onion, thinly sliced
Salt to taste
¼ cup extra virgin olive oil
2 tablespoons red wine vinegar

Preheat the oven to 375°F.

Wrap the beets all together or separately in aluminum foil and place in the oven. Bake until tender, 50 minutes to 1 hour, depending on the size of the beets. When they are cool enough to handle, remove the foil and cut the beets into thin rounds. Place them in a salad bowl and let cool to room temperature. When you are ready to serve, add the sliced onion, season with salt, and dress with the oil and vinegar. Mix gently and serve.

Makes 4 servings

TIPS

∾ *Bake or boil the beets several hours or a day ahead, then slice them and keep covered in a salad bowl in the refrigerator. Serve beets at room temperature, however, to fully savor their delicate taste.*

∾ *To boil beets, bring a medium-size saucepan of water to a boil over medium-high heat. Add the beets and 1 teaspoon of salt. Cook, uncovered, until tender, 45 minutes to 1 hour.*

Patate Calde in Insalata

Warm Potato Salad

At Re di Coppe in Trieste, a very pleasant wine bar–trattoria, I lunched on a cheese platter and a delicious warm potato salad. The potatoes were meltingly soft and were dressed with a lovely green extra virgin olive oil and strong red wine vinegar. This is another one of those basic, homey dishes.

2 pounds old boiling potatoes
Salt and freshly ground black pepper to taste
⅓ to ½ cup extra virgin olive oil (see note on page 256)
¼ cup red wine vinegar
2 tablespoons chopped fresh parsley

Place the potatoes in a large saucepan and cover them generously with cold water. Bring the water to a boil over medium heat and cook until tender, 45 minutes to 1 hour.

TIPS

∾ *Sometimes, to avoid the mess of a dirty pot, I wrap the potatoes in aluminum foil and bake them at 350°F for 40 to 50 minutes. This way I can keep them warm in the oven until I need them. Then, at the last moment, I peel and slice the potatoes and toss them quickly with the oil and vinegar.*

∽ *Old potatoes absorb a
great deal of oil because they are
drier and flourier. This dish was
served to me with a lot of delicious green extra virgin olive oil
which I scooped up with the potatoes and lots of bread. Increase
or decrease the amount of oil to
suit your taste.*

Drain the potatoes, then peel them as soon as they are cool enough to handle and cut into ¼-inch-thick rounds. Place the potatoes in a large salad bowl and season with salt and pepper. Add the oil, vinegar, and parsley and mix well. (Do not worry if the potatoes break up while you mix them.) Taste and adjust the seasoning and serve warm.

Makes 4 to 6 servings

L'Insalatona del Ghiottone

The Glutton Salad

NOTE OF INTEREST

*At Boni, the mozzarella used
was ovoline, small balls of delicious buffalo mozzarella. Ovoline can sometimes be found in
specialty Italian stores. If you
cannot find them, look for the
best possible mozzarella, preferably imported from Italy. However, very good domestic
mozzarella is now available in
specialty food stores.*

The name of trattoria Boni in Bologna has appeared a few times throughout the book. This is because I simply love it. Boni is a modest-looking trattoria that serves the food my mother used to cook—great homemade pastas, mixed boiled meats, mashed potatoes, all those real, heartwarming dishes of my childhood. One night when I dined there with my family, my sister-in-law, Emma, who is almost a vegetarian, ordered the *insalatona del ghiottone*, a very large salad which was served in a bowl and contained a variety of mouthwatering ingredients. This is the exact dish that came to the table.

1 small head radicchio, torn into bite-size pieces
½ small bunch arugula, torn into bite-size pieces
2 Belgian endive, pulled apart into separate leaves
½ head Boston lettuce, shredded
2 white stalks celery, thinly sliced
4 medium-size ripe tomatoes, cut into wedges
¼ pound white cultivated mushrooms, thinly sliced
6 ounces mozzarella, cut into 2-inch pieces (see note above)
4 ounces parmigiano-reggiano, cut into small chunks
6 ounces sliced speck (see page 11), cut into strips
Salt to taste
⅓ cup extra virgin olive oil
3 to 4 tablespoons balsamic vinegar (see page 13) or
   ¼ cup red wine vinegar
4 large hard-boiled eggs, shelled and cut into wedges

Assemble all the greens and vegetables, the cheeses, and speck in a large bowl and season with salt. Dress with the oil and balsamic vinegar and mix well. Taste and adjust the seasonings. Serve in individual bowls or plates and arrange the hard-boiled eggs over each serving.

Makes 4 servings

Insalata di Melanzane e Pomodori alla Griglia

Grilled Eggplant and Tomato Salad

The Sicilians' love of eggplant is evident in the many ways they use it. It is fried as an appetizer, sautéed and served over pasta, baked as an entree, and grilled for a salad. One of the loveliest salad preparations comes from Taverna Aretusa in Siracusa. There, eggplant is sliced, grilled, and tossed together with aromatic green extra virgin olive oil, vinegar, garlic, and fresh basil, and left to marinate in the dressing for a few hours. I have added a personal touch to this popular preparation. Alongside the eggplant I also grill a few tomatoes, then dice them and add to the salad for additional color and taste.

For a light supper and a change of pace, serve this salad with two or three different types of cheese, a nice loaf of bread, and a good bottle of Chardonnay. I bet nobody will miss the meat!

TIPS

Choose the smallest eggplants with shining, unpocked skin and a firm texture.

Onions, zucchini, and red bell peppers can also be grilled and added to the salad.

2 small, firm eggplant (about 1½ pounds), cut into
   ¼-inch-thick rounds
Salt to taste
⅓ cup extra virgin olive oil
3 medium-size, ripe but firm tomatoes (about 1 pound),
   halved and squeezed to remove the seeds and watery
   juices
3 to 4 tablespoons red wine vinegar
1 clove garlic, minced
10 to 11 fresh basil leaves or 2 tablespoons chopped fresh
   parsley

Preheat the grill, barbecue, or broiler. Place the eggplant slices in a large dish and sprinkle generously with salt. Let stand for 30 minutes to allow the salt to draw out the eggplant's bitter juices. Pat the slices dry with paper towels.

Brush the eggplant slices on both sides with olive oil and place on the hot grill or under the broiler. Cook until golden and a bit charred, 1 to 2 minutes, then turn them over to cook on the other side. Grill the tomatoes the same way, and remove when they are colored on both sides and a bit wilted, 1 to 2 minutes.

Cut the eggplant and tomatoes into medium-size strips and place in a salad bowl. Season with salt and dress with the oil, vinegar, garlic, and basil. Toss well, then leave at room temperature for a few hours before serving.

Makes 4 to 6 servings

Panzanella

Bread, Tomato, and Tuna Salad

TIP

The salad can be prepared ahead of time and refrigerated. In this case both the tuna and the dressing should be added just before serving.

Panzanella is an unusual bread salad, a classic dish of Firenze. Its most important ingredient is the coarse-textured Tuscan bread, used when it is several days old. Since Tuscan bread isn't available here, we need to compromise, and will make the salad with four- to five-day-old coarse Italian bread.

This version of *panzanella* comes from a little *caffè* just outside Montecatini, where my husband and I had stopped for a quick bite before continuing our trip to Liguria. We sat at an outside table, under a large umbrella covered with the Cinzano sign, and ordered some local *salame*, prosciutto, and the *panzanella* salad. The salad was delicious and had, besides the bread, tomatoes, fresh basil, and red onion, in addition to tuna and black olives. We piled the *salame* and the prosciutto on the wonderful Tuscan bread, drank a few glasses of local Chianti wine, and almost forgot about our trip to Liguria.

8 ounces coarse-textured Italian bread without the crust,
   4 to 5 days old
3 medium-size, ripe tomatoes, roughly diced
1 medium-size red onion, minced
12 large fresh basil leaves, shredded
10 to 12 pitted black olives, quartered
3 tablespoons red wine vinegar
3 cloves garlic, finely chopped
⅓ cup extra virgin olive oil
Salt and freshly ground black pepper to taste
One 7-ounce can oil-packed tuna, drained
Fresh tomato slices for garnish

Break the bread into pieces and soak in a bowl of cold water for 2 to 3 minutes. Drain and squeeze the bread dry, making sure to remove all the water completely. Place the bread in a large bowl and break it up into small pieces with a fork. Add the tomatoes, onion, basil, and olives.

In a small bowl combine the vinegar, garlic, and olive oil and mix well. Season the salad with salt and several grinds of pepper. Add the dressing and mix well to combine. Add the tuna and mix gently into the salad. Place the salad on serving dishes, decorate with tomato slices, and serve.

Makes 4 to 6 servings

La Caprese

Mozzarella and Tomato Salad

I didn't want to write this recipe. I reasoned that this salad had been written about too much already. I changed my mind because mozzarella and tomato salad was the single most sought-out item of the *trattorie* I visited, and because my husband, Vincent, pointed out to me that before I opened Biba in Sacramento in 1986, we had never found this salad anywhere locally, in spite of the fact that mozzarella was already available in specialty food stores and that tomatoes are harvested all around Sacramento!

TIP

⌒◞ *I love sweet onions, so occa-*
sionally I top the tomatoes with
very thinly sliced onion. I also
love extra virgin olive oil, which
I add liberally so that I can
scoop it up with good crusty Ital-
ian bread.

Mozzarella and tomatoes is, undoubtably the national Italian salad. Everyone loves it. Perhaps the origin of this salad was in Capri, thus the Italian name of *La Caprese*. This great salad can be served as an appetizer, a light entree, or at the end of a meal. In order to prepare it successfully you need the best possible mozzarella (sometimes imported buffalo mozzarella can be found in Italian specialty food stores), ripe, juicy, fresh tomatoes, extra virgin olive oil, and fresh fragrant basil. Four basic Italian ingredients that can be identified with the sunny nature of Italian cooking.

1 pound ripe, juicy tomatoes, cut into ¼-inch-thick slices
¾ pound imported Italian mozzarella (see page 9), cut into ¼-inch-thick slices
Salt to taste
¼ cup extra virgin olive oil
10 to 12 fresh basil leaves, shredded

Arrange the tomato and mozzarella slices alternatingly on individual serving dishes and season lightly with salt. Sprinkle with the olive oil and basil. Serve at room temperature.

Makes 4 servings

Verdure Cotte in Insalata

Mixed Cooked Vegetable Salad

Often in the restaurants and *trattorie* of Northern Italy, cooked vegetables are individually displayed in separate bowls and presented attractively on a counter, table, or serving cart, so that the customer can pick and choose the ones he wants for his mixed vegetable salad.

A nice, colorful mixed cooked vegetable salad is a great way to end a meal. I love cooked vegetables, dressed simply with good extra virgin olive oil and a strong red wine vinegar. Often, at the end of a long day at the restaurant when I am ready to sit down for dinner, which can be anytime between 9 and 11 P.M., I choose a mixed cooked vegetable salad because it is light but thoroughly satisfying. Use this salad as a guideline, then add other vegetables as you like. Boil all your vegetables ahead and use them during the week, since they can be kept quite well in the refrigerator, covered in a bowl, for several days. Just remember to let them come to room temperature before serving.

> 1 small bunch broccoli (about 1 to 1½ pounds)
> 2 medium-size carrots, peeled
> 1 medium-size onion, peeled
> 2 medium-size boiling potatoes, unpeeled
> Salt to taste
> ⅓ cup olive oil, preferably extra virgin
> 3 to 4 tablespoons red wine vinegar

Bring a medium-size saucepan of water to a boil over medium heat. Wash the broccoli and remove and discard ⅓ of the tough stalks. Separate the florets from the stalks and cut the stalks into rounds. Add them to the boiling water together with 1 teaspoon of salt. (The salt will keep the broccoli nice and green.) Cook, uncovered, until they are tender to the touch, 5 to 6 minutes. Drain and dry on paper towels.

Bring another medium-size saucepan of water to a boil and add the carrots and the onion. When the carrots are tender to the touch, 6 to 8 minutes, transfer them to paper towels to drain. Keep cooking the onion until tender, another 30 to 40 minutes. (Test its doneness by pricking it with a long, thin knife.) Drain and place on paper towels.

Place the potatoes in another saucepan with water to cover, bring to a boil, and let boil until tender, 30 to 40 minutes. Drain and cool on paper towels.

Cut the carrots into small rounds and the onion into thin slices. Peel the potatoes and cut them into small chunks. Place in a large salad bowl with the broccoli. Season with salt, add the oil and vinegar, and mix gently. Serve at room temperature.

Makes 4 to 6 servings

TIP
The vegetables should be boiled separately because their cooking times are considerably different. By cooking them separately, they will also retain their bright colors and unique identity.

Asparagi con la Fontina

Asparagus with Fontina and Cream Sauce

Young, tender asparagus topped with parmigiano and melted butter and baked for the briefest amount of time is a classic dish of Parma, the lovely city that gives us the incomparable parmigiano-reggiano, and is a favorite of Northern Italians.

This new interpretation comes from A Ca' Mia Trattoria in Moncalieri, just outside Torino, which uses asparagus in many interesting preparations.

2 pounds asparagus
Salt
4 tablespoons (½ stick) unsalted butter
⅓ cup heavy cream
2 ounces Italian fontina cheese, diced
¼ cup freshly grated parmigiano

NOTE OF INTEREST

In Italy the asparagus are cooked according to the method given here. The boiling water cooks the larger stalks, while the tender tips are cooked with the steam.

❉ ❉ ❉

VARIATION

For Asparagi alla Parmigiana, boil the asparagus as instructed above, drain them, and place in a buttered baking dish. Sprinkle them generously with parmigiano, dot with butter, and bake in a preheated 350°F oven until the cheese is melted, 5 to 10 minutes.

Cut off the tough asparagus ends. With a potato peeler or a small, sharp knife, trim away the outer skin. Wash the asparagus gently under cold water and tie them together into one or two bunches with string or rubber bands. (Do not tie them too firmly or, as they cook, they will break.)

Bring three inches of water to a boil in a tall stockpot over medium heat (I use an old coffeepot so that the asparagus stay snugly upright in the water). Add 1 teaspoon of salt and asparagus. Cover the pot with a lid or with aluminum foil and cook until tender, 6 to 10 minutes, depending on the size of the asparagus.

As the asparagus are cooking, prepare the sauce. Melt the butter in a medium-size skillet over medium heat. Add the cream and fontina cheese. Cook, stirring, until the cheese melts and the cream has thickened and reduced by half, 1 to 2 minutes. Season lightly with salt.

Drain the asparagus and pat dry with paper towels. Place them in individual dishes with their tips facing the center. Spoon some sauce over, sprinkle with a bit of parmigiano, and serve at once.

Makes 4 servings

Fagioli in Umido

Beans Stewed with Pancetta and Tomatoes

Beans, just like pasta and bread, have a wholesome, basic appeal that speaks the unaffected language of country food. I grew up with bean soups and bean stews, especially after the war when it was almost impossible to find meat at any price.

However, my family was lucky, because we had an aunt who had a farm, and somehow she managed to give us an occasional chicken or a few pounds of sausage. Then my mother would prepare these great bean stews with the addition of the chicken or the sausage, and she could stretch those preparations into several dinners.

These robust, humble dishes can still be found in countryside *trattorie* and are still enjoyed and appreciated even today. At Trattoria della Rubbiara outside the city of Modena the stewed beans are served with several slices of boiled cotechino (page 189), a large pork sausage. This is a filling dish, perfect for a cold winter day.

NOTE OF INTEREST

Borlotti beans are an Italian bean variety that has a pinkish color with red speckles. They can be found in Italian markets. Substitute cranberry beans if you can't locate them.

1 pound dried borlotti beans (see note above), picked over and soaked overnight in cold water to cover
¼ cup olive oil
2 tablespoons unsalted butter
1 small onion, minced
4 ounces sliced pancetta, cut into small strips
2 cloves garlic, minced
2 tablespoons chopped fresh rosemary or 1 tablespoon dried, crumbled
3 cups canned imported Italian tomatoes with their juice, put through a strainer or food mill to remove the seeds
Salt and freshly ground black pepper to taste

Discard any beans that come to the surface of the water. Drain and rinse the beans under cold running water and put them in a large pot. Cover the beans generously with cold water and bring to a boil over medium heat. Reduce the heat to medium-low and cook until the beans are tender, about 1 hour. Stir a few times during cooking. Drain the beans and set them aside. (The beans can be cooked a day ahead and kept in the refrigerator, tightly covered in a bowl.)

Heat the oil and butter together in a large skillet over medium heat. When the butter has melted, add the onion and pancetta and cook, stirring, until they begin to color, 5 to 6 minutes. Add the garlic and rosemary and cook, stirring, 1 to 2 minutes longer. Add the beans and mix once or twice, then stir in the tomatoes and season with salt and pepper. Cover the skillet and reduce the heat to medium-low. Cook 10 to 15 minutes, stirring a few times during cooking. Serve hot with boiled cotechino (page 189) or pan-fried sausage.

Makes 6 to 8 servings

Fagioli all'Uccelletto

White Beans with Fresh Tomatoes and Sage

Bologna is known for its superlative pasta dishes, Roma for its artichoke preparations, and Firenze for its famous bean dishes. *Fagioli all'uccelletto* is perhaps the most popular bean dish of Firenze and Toscana. It is a straightforward winter preparation that combines white cannellini beans with fresh tomatoes, sage, and olive oil.

At the very popular Il Cibreo in Firenze, this dish had the addition of a bit of pancetta, which made it extremely appetizing.

½ pound dried white cannellini beans or white kidney beans, picked over
⅓ cup olive oil
2 ounces pancetta, cubed
2 cloves garlic, minced
8 to 10 fresh sage leaves or 1 teaspoon dried, crumbled
1 pound ripe tomatoes, roughly diced
Salt and freshly ground black pepper to taste

Soak the beans overnight in cold water to cover and cook them as instructed on page 69.

Heat the oil in a medium-size skillet over medium heat. Add the pancetta and cook 2 to 3 minutes, stirring. Add the garlic and sage, stir, and cook 1 minute longer. Add the tomatoes. Cook 2 to 3 minutes, then stir in the beans. Season with salt and pepper and cover the skillet. Reduce the heat to medium-low and cook until the sauce has a medium-thick consistency, 15 to 20 minutes. Stir a few times during cooking. If the sauce seems a bit dry, add a bit of chicken broth or water. Serve next to roasted or grilled meats or sausage.

Makes 4 servings

Lenticchie in Umido

Stewed Lentils with Pancetta

Lentils, just like mashed potatoes, roasted potatoes, and beans, are perfect trattoria food—inexpensive, nutritious, hearty, filling, and, when properly prepared, absolutely delicious. Lentils are great in thick, heartwarming soups or stewed and served alongside fried sausages, boiled meats, or lamb.

Trattoria Da Ornella in Bergamo cooks lentils with pancetta, onion, and tomatoes and serves them with cotechino (page 189), a Bolognese pork sausage, and with *gallina bollita* (pages 215–16), boiled chicken.

> 1 pound dried lentils, picked over and soaked overnight in cold water to cover
> ⅓ cup olive oil
> 1 small onion, minced
> 1 medium-size carrot, minced
> 2 ounces sliced pancetta, diced
> 1 cup canned Italian tomatoes with their juice, put through a strainer or food mill to remove the seeds
> 1 cup chicken broth, preferably homemade (see pages 54–55)
> Pinch of dried red pepper flakes
> Salt to taste

Discard any beans that come to the surface of the water. Drain and rinse the lentils under cold running water. Place them in a large pot, cover generously with cold water, and bring to a boil over medium heat. Reduce the heat to medium-low and simmer, stirring a few times, until the lentils are tender but not completely cooked, 25 to 30 minutes. Drain the lentils and set aside.

Heat the oil in a large skillet over medium heat. Add the onion, carrot, and pancetta and cook, stirring, until they begin to color, 5 to 6 minutes. Add the lentils, tomatoes, and broth, and season with the red pepper and salt. Cover the skillet, reduce the heat to medium-low, and cook 10 to 15 minutes, stirring a few times. Serve hot.

Makes 6 servings as a side dish or 4 servings as an entree

Carote e Cipolline al Marsala

Carrots and Small Onions with Marsala Wine and Raisins

NOTE OF INTEREST
I generally serve this at Thanksgiving and Christmas, next to a large golden turkey. It is perfect, however, next to any kind of roasted meat.

Just say Peck in Milano, and people will smile knowingly and direct you to this shrine of food. Peck is not a trattoria or a restaurant (even though a restaurant is the newest addition to the Peck's empire). Peck is simply a gourmet food store that will take your breath away! This store has everything that is relevant and necessary to Italian cooking. Innumerable kinds of hams, sausages, cheeses, olive oils, balsamic vinegars, sun-dried tomatoes, fresh and dried porcini mushrooms, and large trays of varied homemade pastas are dazzlingly displayed. But what gets my immediate, undivided attention is the incredible display of exquisitely prepared food. Roasts of all kinds, colorful, mouthwatering seafood, and vegetable salads that dazzle you with their color and aroma.

This is one of Peck's prepared vegetables. It was displayed on a large white platter. The carrots and the small onions were lightly browned and glazed with the thickened Marsala wine and laced with golden raisins and fresh green Italian parsley. I simply had to add this lovely dish to this book and, next time you are in Milano, go to Peck, buy whatever appeals to you, then go to a park or back to your hotel room and have a feast!

1 pound small white boiling onions
4 tablespoons (½ stick) unsalted butter
1 pound small young carrots, peeled and cut into ¼-inch-
    thick rounds
1 cup dry Marsala, preferably imported Florio
¼ cup golden raisins, soaked in 2 cups water for
    20 minutes, drained, and dried on paper towels
2 tablespoons chopped fresh Italian (flatleaf) parsley
Salt to taste

Bring a medium-size saucepan of water to a boil over medium heat. Cut a cross at the root end of each onion and add to the boiling water. Cook 3 to 4 minutes, then drain the onions and rinse under cold running water. Peel the onions and remove their dangling tails. (This step can be prepared up to a day ahead of time.)

Melt the butter in a large skillet over medium heat. Add the carrots and onions and cook, stirring, until they begin to color, 4 to 5 minutes. Add the Marsala and cover the skillet. Cook until the carrots and onions are tender but a bit firm to the bite, 4 to 5 minutes. Stir a few times during cooking, and add a bit more Marsala if needed.

Remove the lid (at this point there should still be a few tablespoons of Marsala in the skillet) and raise the heat to high. Add the raisins and parsley and season with salt. Cook and stir until the Marsala is almost all evaporated and the vegetables are golden and glazed. Serve hot.

Makes 4 to 6 servings

Le Verze Piccanti del Corsi

Signor Corsi's Spicy Braised Cabbage

One thing that can be said about trattoria cooking is that it always delivers dishes that are hearty and thoroughly satisfying. Flavors are often intense and a reminder of the cooking of the peasants. Signor Corsi of Trattoria Corsi in Roma loves such dishes. During my last visit to his bustling establishment, he kept bringing me samples of dishes to taste. I particularly liked this cabbage dish because of its spiciness. It was served as an accompaniment to Stuffed Beef Bundles, pages 183–84.

1 medium-size head Savoy cabbage (about 1½ to 2 pounds)
1 cup water
⅓ cup olive oil
1 cup dry white wine
Salt
A generous pinch of dried red pepper flakes

Remove and discard the bruised outer leaves from the cabbage. Slice the cabbage in half and remove the inner core. Cut the cabbage into thin strips and place it in a large skillet.

Add the water, oil, and wine and season with salt and red pepper. Cover the skillet and cook over medium heat until the cabbage is soft, 20 to 30 minutes. Stir a few times during cooking. Remove the lid and raise the heat to high and cook, stirring, until no more liquid is left in the pan and the cabbage is lightly golden. Taste and adjust the seasonings.

Makes 4 to 6 servings

Melanzane Fritte Piccanti

Fried Spicy Eggplant

Cooks everywhere have their own versions of popular dishes. I have had fried eggplant in Italy many times, up and down the peninsula, but the first time I had fried spicy eggplant was in Roma at Trattoria Paola. Signora Ida's love for eggplant was evident in the many ways she prepared them. This was simply terrific because of the addition of a little bit of hot peperoncino to the eggs. Throw away the dips and the crackers and use this dish as a down-home, tasty appetizer.

1 large eggplant, peeled and sliced into ¼-inch-thick
  rounds
Salt
A generous pinch of dried red pepper flakes
2 large eggs, lightly beaten in a small bowl
Olive oil for frying
1½ cups plain bread crumbs, evenly spread over a sheet
  of aluminum foil

TIPS

༈ Use two- to three-day-old
bread to make the bread
crumbs. Place the old bread, cut
into chunks, in a food processor
and process until finely chopped.
Refrigerate or freeze it until
needed; they'll keep a few weeks
in the refrigerator and a few
months in the freezer.

༈ In a trattoria, the temperature of the oil is not measured
with a thermometer, but with a
bit of the food that is going to be
fried. Drop a bit of what you
are frying into the hot oil and,
if it turns golden almost immediately and the oil sizzles and
bubbles all around the morsel,
the oil is ready. In case you need
more assurance, use a thermometer which should read 375°F.

Place the eggplant slices on a large platter, sprinkle generously
with salt, and let stand for about 30 minutes to allow the salt
to draw out the eggplant's bitter juices. Pat the slices dry with
paper towels.

Add a bit of salt and as much red pepper as you can stand
to the beaten eggs and mix well.

Heat one inch of oil in a medium-size skillet over medium-
high heat. When the oil is hot, dip the eggplant slices into the
eggs and coat them with the bread crumbs, pressing the crumbs
into the slices witth your hands. Fry the slices a few at a time
until they are golden and crisp on both sides, 2 to 3 minutes.
Remove with a slotted spoon and transfer to paper towels to
drain. Serve piping hot.

Makes 4 servings

Melanzane Ripiene

Baked Stuffed Eggplant

The beautiful thing about vegetables is that they can interchangeably be served as appetizers, side dishes, or as a light
lunch or supper. Both Trattoria Paola and Settimio all'Arancio
in Roma serve these delicious baked stuffed eggplants as an
appetizer. Italian eggplant is considerably smaller than its American counterpart and in fact is closer in look to the Japanese
eggplant. For this dish, select the smallest eggplants possible,
with a glossy, smooth skin and compact, firm texture.

2 eggplants, the smallest you can get (about 1½ pounds), cut in half lengthwise
2 small, ripe tomatoes (about 10 to 12 ounces), halved, seeded, and diced
¼ pound whole milk mozzarella, diced
5 to 6 fresh basil leaves, shredded
2 tablespoons chopped fresh parsley
2 cloves garlic, finely minced
¼ cup extra virgin olive oil
Small pinch of dried red pepper flakes

Preheat the oven to 350°F.

With a tablespoon, scoop out some of the pulp from the eggplant halves, making sure not to break the skin. Place the eggplant halves on a large platter and sprinkle generously with salt. Let stand about 20 minutes to allow the salt to draw out the eggplant's bitter juices. Pat the eggplant dry with paper towels.

Dice the pulp of the eggplant and put it in a bowl with the tomatoes, mozzarella, basil, parsley, garlic, and olive oil. Season with salt and pepper flakes. Fill the eggplants' cavities with this mixture.

Oil a baking dish lightly, and put the eggplant halves into the dish. Bake until they are lightly golden, soft to the touch, and easily pierced with the tip of a thin knife, 15 to 25 minutes, depending on the size of the eggplants. Serve hot or at room temperature.

Makes 4 servings

Finocchi al Forno con Besciamella

Baked Fennel with Béchamel and Parmigiano

In Italy one looks forward to the changing of the seasons not only to break the monotony of a long hot spell or a cold winter, but also for the delight of seasonal ingredients. Fall is my favorite time of the year, because besides fresh porcini mushrooms it also brings another vegetable I love. Fennel.

Fennel, or anise as it is also called, comes to the market in late fall and is available throughout the winter. This white, crunchy vegetable, with its subtle anise taste, is delicious eaten raw in a salad, and it is absolutely wonderful when it is sautéed, fried, or baked.

At Caminetto d'Oro in Bologna, a trattoria that specializes in grilled meats, fowl, game, and vegetables, it was baked with a layer of white, creamy béchamel and topped with parmigiano. I simply loved it.

2 large fennel (about 3 pounds)
3 tablespoons unsalted butter
1 cup béchamel (see pages 127–28)
⅓ cup freshly grated parmigiano-reggiano

Trim off the long stalks from the fennel. If the thick outer leaves of the fennel are bruised or discolored, remove them. Cut the fennel lengthwise through its bulbous base into ¼-inch-thick slices. Place the slices in a large skillet and cover completely with water. Bring the water to a boil over medium heat and cook, uncovered, until the slices are tender but still a bit firm to the touch, 10 to 12 minutes. With a slotted spoon transfer the slices to paper towels to drain.

Preheat the oven to 375°F.

Spread 2 tablespoons of the butter over the bottom of a baking pan. Place the fennel slices in the baking pan, slightly overlapping each other. Spoon the béchamel over each slice, sprinkle with the parmigiano, and dot with the remaining butter. Bake until the top of the fennel begins to color, 15 to 20 minutes. Serve hot.

Makes 4 servings

NOTE OF INTEREST

Until a few years ago, fennel was seldom available in supermarkets, and when it finally began to appear regularly, many people didn't know exactly what to do with it.

Restaurants in this country, especially Italian restaurants, might serve fennel raw, cut into wedges to be dipped in a bowl of olive oil and salt (in pinzimonio), *or as a component of a mixed salad, and very seldom have I seen it prepared any other way.*

Fennel comes in two different shapes. One is short, fat, and round, the other is thin and elongated. Choose the fat one as it is less stringy.

Keep in mind that fennel is sold attached to its long, leafy stalks which add considerably to the weight of the fennel and which are discarded. A large, fat fennel should feed two. So when you buy fennel, don't buy it by the pound, buy by the piece.

Piselli alla Pancetta Fritta

Peas with Fried Pancetta

Fresh young peas are at their best when cooked quickly and simply. In Italy there are many preparations for peas that are quite similar to each other. The peas are shelled and boiled briefly with a bit of salt, then they are tossed together in a skillet with some oil, pancetta, prosciutto, or lard. Sometimes onions or diced tomatoes are added, but quite often the peas stand on their own merit so their sweetness can be fully savored. Fresh peas are available in summer, and I urge you to seek them out to make this simple, appetizing dish. Sometimes I use this preparation as a topping for some penne or shells.

At the charming trattoria Quintilio in Altare, a small hamlet at the border of Liguria and Piemonte, these peas were served next to a roasted rabbit.

> 2 pounds unshelled fresh peas or two 10-ounce packages
>   frozen peas, thawed
> ¼ cup olive oil, preferably extra virgin
> ¼ pound sliced pancetta, cut into thin strips
> Salt and freshly ground black pepper to taste

If you are using fresh peas, bring a medium-size saucepan of water to a boil. Shell the peas and add them to the boiling water. Cook, uncovered, until tender, 5 to 10 minutes, depending on their size. Drain the peas and set aside.

Heat the oil in a medium-size skillet over medium heat. Add the pancetta and cook, stirring, until it is lightly golden and a bit crisp, about 1 minute. Add the peas and season with salt and several grinds of pepper. Cook and stir about 1 minute, then serve.

Makes 4 servings

Peperonata

Peppers, Onions, and Tomatoes in a Skillet

Peperonata is a medley of peppers, onions, and fresh tomatoes cooked in a skillet. This is a straightforward, comforting dish that satisfies the eye as well as the palate. In Emilia-Romagna, *peperonata* is finished cooking with a touch of good red wine vinegar, which seems to highlight the flavors of the vegetables, and is served next to a *bollito misto* (boiled meats) or a *gallina bollita* (boiled chicken, pages 215–16). It is a perfect trattoria food and calls for good, firm bread to soak up all the delicious juices.

⅓ cup olive oil, preferably extra virgin
5 large red, yellow, and green bell peppers, seeded and cut into 1- to 2-inch strips
1 large onion, thinly sliced
2 large, ripe tomatoes, cut into small chunks
Salt and freshly ground black pepper to taste
¼ cup red wine vinegar

Heat the oil in a large skillet over medium heat until fragrant. Add the peppers and cook, stirring, until the skin begins to color, 2 to 3 minutes.

Add the onion and cook, stirring, until it is lightly colored, 5 to 6 minutes. Add the tomatoes, season with salt and pepper, and cook 5 to 6 minutes, stirring several times. Raise the heat to high and add the vinegar. Cook and stir until the vinegar is reduced. Taste and adjust the seasonings and serve hot.

Makes 4 to 6 servings

Le Patate in Tecia di Gabriella

Gabriella's Potatoes and Onions in a Skillet

Many rustic dishes with a somewhat rough apperance are wholesomely delicious, and perfectly in tune with the *cucina casereccia*—home cooking—of the area. This dish comes from Trattoria Gabriella Gregori, a very pleasant establishment in Padriciano, a small suburb of Trieste, that serves the delicious hearty food of the area. The potatoes are first boiled, then sliced and finished cooking with onions, pancetta, fresh sage, and broth, which will impart its distinctive taste to the potatoes. At the end of cooking, the onions are soft and creamy and the potatoes, laced with the strips of pancetta, are tender to the breaking point. I find this a most appetizing dish.

2 pounds old boiling potatoes
⅓ cup olive oil
2 large onions, thinly sliced
2 ounces sliced pancetta, cut into small strips
10 fresh sage leaves, shredded, optional
1 cup chicken broth, homemade or made with bouillon
    (pages 54–55)
Salt and freshly ground black pepper to taste

Put the potatoes in a large saucepan and cover them generously with cold water. Bring the water to a boil over medium heat and cook until tender, 45 minutes to 1 hour. Drain the potatoes and peel them as soon as they are cool enough to handle, then cut them into thick wedges.

Heat the oil in a large skillet over medium heat. Add the onions, pancetta, and sage and cook, stirring, until the onion and pancetta begin to color, 7 to 8 minutes. Add the potatoes and broth and season with salt and pepper. Cook, stirring, until the broth is completely reduced, 5 to 6 minutes. (It's okay if, as you cook and stir, the potatoes break into smaller pieces.) Serve piping hot.

Makes 4 to 6 servings

Le Patate Arrosto del Signor Vernizzi

Signor Vernizzi's Roasted Potatoes

At Trattoria Vernizzi, located in the flat, fertile, gastronomically rich Emilia countryside, the roasted potatoes are in a class by themselves. The day I ate at this cozy country trattoria, the potatoes were the mere accompaniment to a wonderful roast, and yet, after the first bite, they became the stars of the meal. They came out of the oven golden and crisp, shining with oil and laced with the aroma of roasted garlic cloves and fresh rosemary. Suddenly, I was a child again, knowing no restraint, wanting to scoop up those golden potatoes and pile them onto my plate.

2 pounds old boiling potatoes, peeled and cut into thick
    wedges
4 cloves garlic, peeled and left whole
3 tablespoons roughly chopped fresh rosemary or 1 to 2
    tablespoons dried, chopped
Salt and freshly ground black pepper to taste
½ cup olive oil
1 cup water

Preheat the oven to 400°F.

Place the potatoes in a baking pan together with the garlic and rosemary, and season with salt and several grinds of pepper. Add the olive oil and mix well to coat the potatoes. Stir in the water and bake 45 minutes to 1 hour, *without touching or stirring the potatoes.* When they have a deep golden color, they are ready to be served.

Makes 4 to 6 servings

TIPS

൦ഄ At the end of the cooking, all the water will be evaporated and the potatoes might stick a bit to the bottom of the pan. Just get a spatula and scrape them off gently.

൦ഄ When I make these potatoes, I sometimes add a few ounces of sliced pancetta cut into small strips during the last 10 or 15 minutes of cooking for added taste.

Puré di Patate

Mashed Potatoes with Parmigiano

Some dishes are so basic to the cooking of many nations that we tend to dismiss them because they are too common. Take the humble mashed potato, for example. I prepare it regularly, and perhaps you do too. So what is so special about it? I will let you decide after you try this version, which comes from Trattoria Lo Sterlino in Bologna, and has the addition of sweet butter, cream, and parmigiano-reggiano.

This luscious, velvety preparation has become, by popular demand, a standard item on the menu at my Sacramento restaurant.

1½ pounds old boiling potatoes
4 tablespoons (½ stick) unsalted butter
⅓ cup heavy cream
Salt to taste
⅓ cup freshly grated parmigiano

TIP

൦ഄ Mashed potatoes can be prepared several hours ahead. To reheat, place the potatoes in the top part of a double boiler or in a small saucepan, and heat over simmering water, stirring, until the mixture is nice and hot.

Put the potatoes in a large saucepan and cover them generously with cold water. Bring the water to a boil over medium heat and cook until tender, 45 minutes to 1 hour. Drain the potatoes and peel them as soon as they are cool enough to handle, then mash them through a food mill or with a potato masher; do not use a food processor.

Heat the butter and the cream in a medium-size saucepan over medium-low heat. When the butter melts, add the mashed potatoes, season with salt, and add the parmigiano. Mix the potatoes energetically with a wire whisk or a wooden spoon until everything is well combined and the potatoes are hot, soft, and creamy. Taste and adjust the seasonings and serve at once.

Makes 4 servings

Tortino di Patate

Potato Cake with Garlic and Parmigiano

The first thing that is noticeable when you enter a trattoria is the aroma that comes from the kitchen. Something smells good! And you feel instantly at home.

When this potato cake came out of the oven, golden and crisp, bubbling with melted butter, smelling of cooked sweet garlic and melted parmigiano, I instantly realized that the best things in life are the simplest!

TIP

∾ *Trattoria cooking, just like home cooking, is very "relaxed." Don't worry about the exact thickness of the potatoes, or how fine the garlic should be chopped. Add a bit more garlic or parmigiano if you like it. When you cook with a relaxed attitude, your food will taste better and you will enjoy it more.*

1½ pounds old boiling potatoes, peeled and cut into ¼-inch-thick rounds
Salt and freshly ground black pepper to taste
2 cloves garlic, roughly minced
2 tablespoons chopped fresh parsley
¼ cup freshly grated parmigiano
¼ cup plain bread crumbs
3 tablespoons unsalted butter, cut into small pieces

Preheat the oven to 350°F.

Butter a baking pan generously.

Place the potatoes in the baking pan in one layer, overlapping each other. Season with salt and pepper and sprinkle with the garlic, parsley, parmigiano, and bread crumbs. Dot the potatoes with the butter. Bake until the tops of the potatoes are golden brown, 25 to 30 minutes. Serve hot or at room temperature.

Makes 4 to 6 servings

Fagiolini con le Alici e Aglio

String Beans with Anchovies and Garlic

This tasty string bean dish proves, once again, that the less you fuss with vegetables, the better they are. Italians don't cover vegetables with heavy sauces, they simply complement them with other savory ingredients.

For this dish, choose the smallest string beans with a smooth skin and a deep green color. All you then have to do is toss them with a bit of good oil, some garlic, and a few anchovies and—*pronto*—you'll have one of those delicious dishes that are sought out in the *trattorie* of Italy.

> 1 pound small string beans
> 1 teaspoon salt
> ¼ cup olive oil, preferably extra virgin
> 2 cloves garlic, minced
> 4 anchovy fillets, chopped
> Freshly ground black pepper to taste

Snap off both ends of the beans and wash them under cold running water.

Heat a medium-size saucepan of water over medium heat until boiling. Add the salt and beans. Cook, uncovered, until tender, 5 to 7 minutes, depending on the size of the beans. Drain the beans well of all water.

Heat the oil in a large skillet over medium heat. Add the garlic and anchovies and cook, stirring, until the garlic begins to color, about 1 minute. Add the string beans and season with salt and several grinds of pepper. Cook and stir about 1 minute, then serve.

Makes 4 servings

Spinaci con Panna e Parmigiano

Spinach with Cream and Parmigiano

The king of the Italian cheeses, parmigiano-reggiano, is used extensively in the cooking of many regions. I grew up with this great cheese, and my mother would use it liberally not only over pasta but on meat and vegetables. She used to cook a spinach dish that had the addition of a bit of cream and parmigiano that was great. At Masuelli in Milano, a real old-fashioned trattoria with the mother in the kitchen and the father and the son serving the food, I recaptured the delights of this delicious vegetable dish.

2 pounds fresh spinach, stems and bruised leaves discarded, or two 10-ounce packages frozen spinach, thawed and squeezed of any water
2 tablespoons unsalted butter
⅓ cup heavy cream
⅓ cup freshly grated parmigiano
Salt to taste

If using fresh, wash the spinach thoroughly under cold running water. Bring a large saucepan halfway full of water to a boil over medium heat, then add the spinach and cook until tender, 5 to 6 minutes. Stir a few times during cooking. Drain the spinach and squeeze out any excess water.

Heat the butter in a medium-size skillet over medium heat. When it begins to foam, add the cream and bring it to a gentle boil. Add the spinach and parmigiano and season lightly with salt. Cook, stirring, until the cheese is melted and the cream is almost all reduced, 2 to 3 minutes. Serve hot, next to grilled or roasted meat.

Makes 4 to 6 servings

Pomodori al Forno con la Mentuccia

Baked Tomatoes with Mint

In Italy, baked stuffed vegetables are very often served as an appetizer, as well as an accompaniment to meats. At Trattoria Paola in Roma, I enjoyed these tomatoes alongside baked stuffed eggplant (pages 269–70). It was a hot Roman evening and these vegetables were served at room temperature. I could have made a whole meal out of them.

> 4 medium-size, firm, ripe tomatoes (about 1¼ pounds), halved and seeded
> ½ cup olive oil
> Salt and freshly ground black pepper to taste
> 2 cloves garlic, minced
> 5 to 6 fresh mint leaves, finely shredded or 2 tablespoons roughly chopped fresh Italian (flatleaf) parsley
> ½ cup loosely packed, finely shredded fresh basil

Preheat the oven to 350°F.

Place the tomatoes, cut side down, on paper towels to drain their excess juices.

Cover the bottom of a baking pan lightly with some of the olive oil. Season the tomatoes with salt and pepper.

In a small bowl combine the garlic, mint, and basil with a few drops of olive oil. Place some of this mixture in the tomato cavities, dribble the tops of the tomatoes lightly with olive oil, place them in the baking dish, and bake until they are soft and the tops are lightly browned, 20 to 25 minutes. Serve hot alongside meat or fish, or at room temperature with other vegetables as an appetizer.

Makes 4 servings

Zucchine Fritte con la Mentuccia

Pan-fried Zucchini with Mint and Vinegar

These zucchini are pan fried (not deep fried), meaning that they are cooked over medium-high heat in a minimum amount of oil.

When the first zucchini come to the Italian markets in spring, with their shiny, smooth, bright glossy skin, they are a sight to behold. And when they are small and firm, and are quickly pan fried and tossed together with warm oil, vinegar, garlic, and fresh mint, they are absolutely irresistible. This recipe comes from Trattoria La Botte in Taormina, Sicilia, which serves these zucchini at room temperature as an appetizer or warm as a side dish.

⅓ cup olive oil
1½ pounds small, firm zucchini, cut into ¼-inch-thick
    rounds
1 cup unbleached all-purpose flour
2 cloves garlic, minced
2 tablespoons red wine vinegar
6 to 7 medium-size fresh mint leaves, finely shredded or
    2 tablespoons chopped fresh parsley
Salt to taste

Heat the oil over medium-high heat in a large skillet.

Place the zucchini in a large colander and put the colander over a large bowl. Sprinkle the zucchini generously with the flour so it's coated on all sides and shake off the excess. Test the heat of the oil by slipping in a slice of zucchini. If the oil sizzles and splatters, it's ready. With a slotted spoon, lower some zucchini into the hot oil, making sure not to crowd the skillet. As they turn golden on one side, turn them to color on the other side, 1 to 2 minutes. Remove with a slotted spoon and transfer to paper towels to drain. When all the zucchini are done, place them in a deep dish or a salad bowl.

Add the garlic to the skillet and stir once or twice. Stir in the vinegar and mint. Cook and stir quickly, then pour the hot dressing over the zucchini. Season with salt, mix well, and serve warm as a side dish or at room temperature as an appetizer.

Makes 4 servings

Zucchini in Agrodolce

Sweet-and-sour Fried Zucchini

Raisins, pine nuts, sugar, and red wine vinegar are ingredients with contrasting flavors that are often joined harmoniously in Sicilian cooking. This delicious dish is another version of the fried zucchini with mint on the preceeding page, made a bit more interesting by the addition of raisins and pine nuts.

⅓ cup olive oil
1½ pounds small, firm zucchini, cut into ¼-inch-thick rounds
1 cup unbleached all-purpose flour
2 tablespoons red wine vinegar
2 anchovy fillets, finely chopped
2 cloves garlic, minced
2 tablespoons sugar
2 tablespoons golden raisins, soaked in 1 cup lukewarm water for 20 minutes, drained, and patted dry
2 tablespoons pine nuts
Salt to taste

Heat the oil in a large skillet over medium-high heat.

Place the zucchini in a large colander and put the colander over a large bowl. Sprinkle the zucchini generously with the flour so it's coated on all sides and shake off the excess. Test the heat of the oil by slipping in a slice of zucchini. If the oil sizzles and splatters a bit, it's ready. With a slotted spoon, lower some of the zucchini into the hot oil, making sure not to crowd the skillet. As they turn golden on one side, turn them to color on the other side, 1 to 2 minutes. Remove with a slotted spoon and transfer to paper towels to drain. When all the zucchini are fried, place them in a deep dish.

In a small bowl combine the vinegar, anchovies, garlic, and sugar and add it to the skillet. Stir briefly over medium heat. Add the raisins and the pine nuts, cook and stir 10 to 20 seconds, then pour the hot mixture over the zucchini. Season with salt, mix well, and serve warm as a side dish or at room temperature as an appetizer.

Makes 4 servings

Padellata di Verdure in Agrodolce

Sweet-and-sour Mixed Sautéed Vegetables

⅓ cup olive oil

3 large red bell peppers, seeded and cut into medium-size strips

1 small eggplant, peeled and cut into small pieces (about the size of an olive)

2 small, firm zucchini, cut into ¼-inch-thick rounds

1 medium-size onion, thinly sliced

2 clove garlic, finely minced

2 large, ripe tomatoes, cut into medium-size pieces

Salt and freshly ground black pepper to taste

Olive oil for frying

2 medium-size old potatoes, peeled and cut into ¼-inch-thick rounds

2 tablespoons sugar mixed with ¼ cup red wine vinegar

Heat the oil in a large skillet over medium heat. Add the peppers and cook, stirring, until the skin of the peppers begins to color, 2 to 3 minutes.

Add the eggplant, zucchini, and onion and cook, stirring, until they are lightly colored, 5 to 6 minutes. Add the garlic and cook less than 1 minute. Add the tomatoes, season with salt and pepper, and cook 8 to 10 minutes. Stir several times during cooking.

While the vegetables are cooking, heat one inch of oil in a large skillet over medium-high heat. Add the potatoes (be careful not to crowd them or the oil temperature will go down) and fry until they are lightly golden, 2 to 3 minutes. Remove the potatoes with a slotted spoon to paper towels to drain.

Add the fried potatoes to the vegetables. Raise the heat to high and add the sugar-vinegar mixture. Cook and stir until the vinegar is reduced, less than 1 minute. Taste and adjust the seasonings and serve hot as a side dish, or at room temperature as an appetizer.

Makes 4 servings as an appetizer or 8 servings as a side dish

TIPS

꙰ *For a lighter preparation, the potatoes can be boiled until tender instead of fried.*

꙰ *If you have any left over, turn it into a filling for calzone.*

PIZZA, CALZONI, AND OTHER GOOD THINGS

PIZZA

It is hard to explain why pizza, a specialty of Napoli, that for so long was the food of poor people, has become today one of the most popular foods in the world. Pizza is simple food, made just like bread, with flour, yeast, and water. The dough is then flattened and seasoned with a variety of flavorful ingredients. The first pizzas were probably topped only by oil and garlic, cheese and fish, since the tomato didn't arrive in Italy until the sixteenth century from America. In 1830 Napoli opened the first true pizzeria, Pizzeria Port'Alba, which baked its pizzas in a wood-burning brick oven, and the pizza began to be what it is today The rest is history!

Several *pizze* in this chapter come from this venerable old pizzeria which still stands and is run by direct descendants of the original owners.

Pizza is still somewhat traditionally prepared, especially in Napoli, but even in Italy there is more experimentation today and therefore many more variations of the classic pizzas.

A good pizza should have a crisp crust, fresh-tasting ingredients, and, to my mind, a light hand in using them. In this chapter you will find mostly traditional pizzas, but once you have tried them and have succeeded in producing the most important thing in pizza making, a crisp crust, then you can go on to create your own pizza.

Basic Pizza Dough

1½ cups unbleached all-purpose flour
1 package active dry yeast, dissolved in ½ cup plus
    2 tablespoons lukewarm water
1 tablespoon olive oil
1 tablespoon salt

TIPS

✤ *For a crisp crust, place a large baking stone or unglazed terra-cotta tile in the middle of the oven before preheating. The pizza can be cooked directly on the baking stone or in its own pizza pan placed over the stone. If you don't have a baking stone, make sure to have a very hot oven.*

Made by hand. Put all the ingredients in a medium-size bowl and mix well with your hands until they are incorporated. Put the dough on a working surface and knead 5 to 6 minutes. At this point the dough should be smooth and pliable. If the dough seems a bit sticky, knead in a little more flour. Dust the dough lightly with flour and place in a large bowl. Cover the bowl with a moist kitchen towel or plastic wrap and put it in a warm, draft-free place to rise, about 3 hours. At this point the dough should have doubled in volume, be springy, and have small gas bubbles all over its surface.

Made in an electric mixer. Put the flour in the bowl of an electric mixer. Add the dissolved yeast, oil, and salt and, with the dough hook, mix well at medium-low speed until all ingredients are incorporated. Increase the speed to high and knead the dough 4 to 5 minutes. Dust the dough lightly with flour and place it in a large bowl. Cover the bowl with a moist kitchen towel or plastic wrap and let it rise in a warm, draft-free place for about 3 hours.

Made with a food processor. Put the flour and salt in a food processor fitted with the metal blade. Add the dissolved yeast and oil and pulse the machine on and off until the dough is loosely gathered around the blade.

Remove the dough and knead it by hand 2 to 3 minutes. Dust the dough lightly with flour and place it in a large bowl. Cover the bowl with a moist kitchen towel or plastic wrap and let it rise in a warm, draft-free place for 3 hours.

Finishing the pizza. Preheat the oven to 450°F 30 minutes before baking. Flatten the dough down with your hands. Roll out the dough into a 12-inch circle, making sure to leave the edges a bit thicker than the center so that the filling won't spill over.

Brush a flat 12-inch pizza pan with a bit of olive oil and spread the dough onto the pan with your fingertips. Top with your favorite filling and bake until golden.

Even though active dry yeast is quite reliable, it is a good idea to proof the yeast. Add a pinch of sugar to the dissolved yeast and, if the yeast is okay, tiny bubbles will appear on the surface of the water. Make sure always to check the expiration date on the yeast package before using it.

The dough for the pizza can be prepared in the morning and, after it has risen, can be punched down, shaped into a ball, and kept in the refrigerator covered with plastic wrap until ready to use. The dough can also be made to rise, at a slower rate, in the refrigerator.

Pizza dough can also be made with a combination of all-purpose flour and finely ground semolina (hard wheat durum flour) or only with semolina.

Pizza con Cipolle, Pomodori e Olive

Pizza with Onions, Tomatoes, and Olives

We had been told that there was an excellent trattoria hidden in the Ligurian mountains which specialized in hearty game dishes typical of the Ligurian tradition. We understood that the trattoria was about a one-hour drive from Alassio, the lovely seacoast resort town in which we were staying. We left Alassio at seven, confident that we would meet our 8:30 reservation. I should have known better! In spite of the map in our hands we got lost several times because of the lack of signs. Finally we began climbing the mountain road that was to lead us "straight into the Trattoria dei Cacciatori." Naturally, nobody had mentioned to us that the road was one of the narrowest and steepest in all the Ligurian region. As we were climbing and I was taking in with awe and apprehension the awesome view of the valley way, way below, the sun was setting and the idea of coming back down that twisted road in the dark after having consumed a rich meal and perhaps a few bottles of wine really frightened me. So I convinced my husband to turn around and forget about the "hearty game" dishes of the trattoria. Finally, back in the valley again, a little unsettled by the experience and also quite hungry, we spotted a sign that read "Enoteca Il Gallo della Checca." We decided to stop at this wine shop for a glass of wine and what we found was not only wine, but also some delicious savory treats such as this thick-crusted Ligurian pizza. Perhaps because I was now safely back in the valley, no pizza had ever tasted so good.

> Pizza Dough for one 12-inch pizza (see pages 284–85)
> 1 pound fresh, ripe plum tomatoes, cut into small pieces, or 2 cups loosely packed, drained, diced canned imported Italian plum tomatoes
> 2 cloves garlic, minced
> 4 to 5 flat anchovy fillets, cut into small pieces
> 10 pitted black olives, halved or quartered
> 3 tablespoons olive oil
> Salt to taste
> ½ medium-size onion, thinly sliced

Prepare the pizza dough and let it rise.

Preheat the oven to 450°F 30 minutes before baking.

In a medium-size bowl combine the tomatoes, garlic, anchovies, olives, and 2 tablespoons of the olive oil and season lightly with salt.

In a small bowl mix the sliced onion with the remaining tablespoon of oil.

Roll out the dough into a 10-inch-thick circle and place it on the pizza pan. Spread the onions over the dough and top with the tomato mixture, making sure to cover the onions completely.

Bake until the dough is golden brown, 15 to 20 minutes. Serve hot.

Makes 2 servings

TIPS

✑ In summer, when plum tomatoes are very red and very ripe, they have an unsurpassed sweet flavor and a tender skin. I generally dice or slice them into rounds and use them over pizza. In winter, when tomatoes are not at their best, I use canned imported Italian plum tomatoes.

✑ Make sure to cover the onions completely with the tomatoes or they will burn while baking.

✑ Ligurian pizza has a thicker crust than most other Italian pizza.

SUGGESTED WINES
Simple, easy drinking whites like Vermentino or Cinqueterre from The Cantina Sociale delle Cinqueterre, or a Chenin Blanc from Gran Cru or Hacienda in California work deliciously

Pizza Bianca

White Pizza

Apparently the original Neapolitan pizza was a *pizza bianca* and it was made without tomatoes. At Antica Pizzeria Port'Alba in Napoli, I came across a "white pizza" that was utterly delicious. It had a crisp, medium-thick crust and was topped by four different cheeses: mozzarella, smoked mozzarella, gorgonzola, and pecorino. Because the pecorino cheese available here is the strong, assertive pecorino romano, of which I am not terribly fond, I have substituted the soft, mild Italian fontina.

> Pizza dough for one 12-inch pizza (see pages 284–85)
> 2 tablespoons olive oil, mixed with 1 clove garlic, minced
> 2 ounces mozzarella, grated or diced
> 2 ounces smoked mozzarella, grated or diced
> 2 ounces gorgonzola cheese, diced
> 2 ounces fontina cheese, diced
> 8 flat anchovy fillets

Prepare the pizza dough and let it rise.

Preheat the oven to 450°F 30 minutes before baking.

Roll out the dough into a 12-inch circle and place it on the pizza pan. Brush the dough lightly with the oil and garlic. Spread the cheese on the dough, forming 4 large triangular wedges. Mark each wedge of cheese with 2 anchovy fillets and bake until the dough is golden brown, 15 to 20 minutes. Serve hot.

Makes 2 servings

SUGGESTED WINES
Choose a light, fragrant red wine such as Masi Valpolicella from Italy, or Saintsbury Garnet from California.

Pizza con le Vongole

Pizza with Clams

The day I was at the Antica Pizzeria Port'Alba in Napoli, I ordered several pizzas because I wanted to taste as many as I could. The waiter asked me twice if I understood that one pizza was more than enough for one person and, when I nodded, he left shaking his head. When the four pizzas I had ordered arrived and were put on the table, I could feel the stares of everyone in the room. I suppose that the sight of a five-foot, two-inch-tall lady methodically skipping from one pizza to another with great enthusiasm was quite amusing.

Pizza dough for one 12-inch pizza (see pages 284–85)
2 pounds fresh clams, the smallest you can get
1 cup water
3 tablespoons extra virgin olive oil
1 to 2 cloves garlic, finely minced
Salt to taste
1 pound fresh ripe plum tomatoes, cut into small pieces, or 2 cups loosely packed, drained, diced canned imported Italian plum tomatoes
2 tablespoons chopped fresh parsley

Prepare the pizza dough and let it rise.

Preheat the oven to 450°F 30 minutes before baking.

Put the clams in a medium-size skillet with the water and bring to a boil over high heat. Cover the skillet and cook until the clams open, about 2 minutes. With a slotted spoon transfer the clams to a bowl and detach the meat from the shell, discarding the shells.

Heat 1 tablespoon of the oil in a small skillet over medium heat. Add half the garlic and stir once or twice. Add the clam meat and season lightly with salt. Stir a few times and remove from the heat.

In a medium-size bowl combine the tomatoes, parsley, and the remaining oil and garlic. Season lightly with salt. Add ¼ cup of the tomato mixture to the clams and mix well.

Roll out the dough into a 12-inch circle and place it on the pizza pan. Spread the tomato mixture over the dough. Bake until the dough is golden brown, about 15 minutes. Spread the clams over the pizza and put it back in the oven *very briefly*, less than 1 minute. Serve hot.

Makes 2 servings

Pizza alla Siciliana

Sicilian Pizza

The components of this lovely pizza, which I enjoyed at Trattoria La Botte in Taormina, were ripe, juicy tomatoes, plump black olives, anchovy fillets, buffalo mozzarella, and tiny broccoli florets, everything laced with a delicious, aromatic green olive oil. When fresh, ripe tomatoes are not available, I use canned pear-shaped tomatoes imported from Italy, without their juices. I cut the tomatoes into pieces and toss them with a bit of olive oil and garlic, then spread them on the pizza.

> Pizza Dough for one 12-inch pizza (see pages 284–85)
> 1 pound fresh, ripe plum tomatoes, cut into small pieces or 2 cups loosely packed, drained, diced canned imported Italian plum tomatoes
> 10 large pitted black olives, quartered
> 2 tablespoons extra virgin olive oil
> 2 cloves garlic, finely minced
> 2 to 3 anchovy fillets, cut into pieces
> Salt to taste
> 4 ounces mozzarella, grated or diced
> 3 ounces broccoli florets, steamed until tender but still firm

Prepare the pizza dough and let it rise.

Preheat the oven to 450°F 30 minutes before baking.

In a medium-size bowl, combine the tomatoes, olives, oil, garlic, and anchovies. Season lightly with salt and mix well.

Roll out the dough into a 12-inch circle and place it on the pizza pan. Brush the dough lightly with oil. Spread the mozzarella over the dough and top with the tomato mixture.

Bake for 10 minutes, add the broccoli, and then bake until the dough is golden brown, about 5 minutes longer. Serve hot.

Makes 2 servings

SUGGESTED WINES

Choose a light, fragrant red wine such as Masi Valpolicella from Italy, or Saintsbury Garnet from California. Or try a fragrant, fairly acid, full-bodied white wine. Good choices would be Concannon Sauvignon Blanc from California and Falchini Vernaccia di San Gimignano from Italy.

Pizza con Funghi, Prosciutto Cotto e Mozzarella

Pizza with Mushrooms, Ham, and Mozzarella

This is another delicious pizza from the venerable Antica Pizzeria Port'Alba in Napoli.

Pizza dough for one 12-inch pizza (see pages 284–85)
3 to 4 tablespoons olive oil
10 ounces white cultivated mushrooms, thinly sliced
1 clove garlic, minced
Salt to taste
2 ounces sliced boiled or baked ham, cut into small strips
4 ounces mozzarella, grated or diced

Prepare the pizza dough and let it rise.

Preheat the oven to 450°F 30 minutes before baking.

Heat the oil in a large skillet over high heat. Add the mushrooms and cook, stirring, until they begin to color, about 1 minute. Stir in the garlic and season lightly with salt. Mix once or twice and remove from the heat.

Roll out the dough into a 12-inch circle and place on the pizza pan. Spread the mushrooms over the dough and top with the ham and mozzarella. Bake until the dough is golden brown, about 15 minutes. Serve hot.

Makes 2 servings

SUGGESTED WINE
With this classic pizza have a good beer.

CALZONE

Calzone is made with pizza dough. The dough is rolled out into a large circle, filling is put in the center of the dough, and then the dough is folded over the filling and sealed Then, just like pizza, it is baked in a very hot oven until it looks like a large, golden puffed-up turnover.

Calzone, just like pizza, is simple, rustic, ancient food that was once stuffed with very humble but tasty ingredients. Even though calzone has evolved and has become somewhat more sophisticated, in the South of Italy it still retains its traditional, rustic qualitiy.

The *calzoni* in this chapter are, just like pizza, somewhat traditional because they come from traditional establishments. After you have experimented with them, you should feel free to create your own *calzoni*.

The tips for pizza, can also be applied to calzone. But unlike pizza, the contents of the calzone should not be too moist or they will make the dough a bit soggy.

Calzone con Melanzane e Radicchio

Calzone with Eggplant and Radicchio

One of the most delicious *calzoni* I enjoyed in Napoli was filled with an appetizing mixture of sautéed eggplant, garlic, capers, and black olives. It also had the addition of a slightly bitter cooked chicory which I could not identify. Yearning to recapture that flavor, I tried to reproduce it with another bitter chicory from the North of Italy, radicchio, and the unusual pairing of eggplant and radicchio turned out to be a winner.

NOTE OF INTEREST
The filling for this calzone has a slightly bitter taste which comes from the radicchio.

1 recipe Basic Pizza Dough (see pages 284–85)

For the filling
    1 medium-size eggplant (about ¾ pound), peeled and
      cut into ¼-inch-thick slices
    Salt
    5 tablespoons olive oil
    1 clove garlic, minced
    2 tablespoons capers, drained and rinsed
    10 pitted black olives, quartered
    2 tablespoons chopped fresh parsley
    1 small head radicchio (about ½ pound)
    ½ cup freshly grated parmigiano
    6 ounces whole milk mozzarella, grated or diced
    1 large egg, lightly beaten

Prepare the pizza dough and let it rise.

Preheat the oven to 450°F 30 minutes before baking.

Put the eggplant slices on a large dish and sprinkle them with salt. Let stand for about 30 minutes. (The salt will draw out the eggplant's bitter juices.) Wipe the slices with paper towels and cut them into small cubes.

Heat 3 tablespoons of the oil in a medium-size skillet over medium heat. Add the eggplant and cook, stirring, 4 to 5 minutes. Add the garlic, capers, olives, and parsley and season with salt. Cook 1 to 2 minutes longer, stirring. With a slotted spoon transfer the mixture to a bowl.

Discard any bruised radicchio leaves. Wash the radicchio leaves well and pat dry with paper towels. Cut the radicchio into small strips.

Heat the remaining oil in the same skillet over medium heat and add the radicchio. Cover the skillet and cook until the radicchio begins to wilt, 4 to 5 minutes. Stir a few times during cooking. Season lightly with salt. Add the radicchio to the bowl with the eggplant mixture. Add the parmigiano and mix everything well.

Divide the dough into two equal parts and roll out two circles approximately 8 inches in diameter. In the center of each circle of dough place the mozzarella and the radicchio and eggplant mixture. Fold the dough over the filling, combining the edges. Fold the edges slightly to form a border, then pinch them with your fingertips or with a fork to seal. Place the *calzoni* on a baking sheet and brush with the beaten egg. Bake until they are golden brown, 15 to 20 minutes. Cool slightly and serve.

Makes 2 *calzoni*

SUGGESTED WINES

For this calzone choose a full-bodied red wine, either Italian or Californian, such as a Barbera, a Merlot, or a nice dry Lambrusco.

Calzone Rustico

Calzone with Ricotta, Salame, Smoked Mozzarella, and Tomatoes

The stuffing for calzone is limited only by one's imagination. In Napoli, however, where traditional food still prevails, the most popular *calzoni* are the ones that use the much-loved ingredients of the area, namely, mozzarella, ricotta, and fresh, ripe tomatoes. This calzone comes from Lombardi a Santa Chiara, a very popular Neapolitan pizzeria that serves some of the best *pizze* and *calzoni* of Napoli.

1 recipe Basic Pizza Dough (see pages 284–85)

For the filling

    4 ounces whole milk ricotta

    4 ounces thinly sliced salame, cut into thin strips

    4 ounces smoked mozzarella (see page 9), grated
       or diced

    8 ounces mozzarella, grated or diced

    2 medium-size, ripe tomatoes, diced

    2 tablespoons chopped fresh parsley

    Salt to taste

    1 large egg, lightly beaten

Prepare the pizza dough and let it rise.

Preheat the oven to 450°F 30 minutes before baking.

In a medium-size bowl combine all the ingredients for the filling, except the egg. Taste and adjust the seasoning.

Divide the dough into two equal parts and roll out two circles approximately 8 inches in diameter. Place half of the filling in the center of each circle of dough. Fold the dough over, combining the edges. Fold the edges slightly to form a border, then pinch with your fingertips or a fork to seal. Place the *calzoni* on a baking sheet, then brush them with the beaten egg. Bake until they are golden brown, 15 to 20 minutes. Cool slightly and serve.

Makes 2 *calzoni*

SUGGESTED WINE
Choose a full-flavored, oaky Chardonnay from Simi or Far Niente in California.

Calzone con Bietole

Calzone with Swiss Chard

In this calzone, uncooked Swiss chard, tossed together with garlic, anchovies, salt, chile pepper, and oil, becomes the filling. The Swiss chard cooks while the calzone is baking, just as if it were cooked "in parchment." Another delicious dish from Lombardi a Santa Chiara in Napoli.

1 recipe Basic Pizza Dough (see pages 284–85)

For the filling

    12 ounces Swiss chard
    2 cloves, garlic, finely minced
    4 anchovy fillets, chopped
    ¼ cup olive oil
    Pinch of red pepper flakes
    Salt to taste
    6 ounces mozzarella, grated or diced
    1 large egg, lightly beaten

Prepare the pizza dough dough and let it rise.

Preheat the oven to 450°F 30 minutes before baking.

Remove the Swiss chard leaves from the stems. Wash the leaves well, dry them thoroughly, and place in a salad bowl. Add the garlic, anchovies, oil, red pepper, and salt and mix well.

Divide the dough into two equal parts and roll them out into two circles approximately 8 inches in diameter. Divide the mozzarella and place in the center of each circle of dough. Divide the Swiss chard filling and place over the mozzarella. Fold the dough over the filling, combining the edges. Fold the edges slightly to form a border, then pinch them with your fingertips or with a fork to seal.

Place the *calzoni* on a baking sheet and brush with the beaten egg. Bake until golden brown, 15 to 20 minutes. Cool slightly and serve.

Makes 2 *calzoni*

SUGGESTED WINES

Try the new Italianate-style reds from Monteviña, Brioso and Montanard. For whites, try the new California white Rhône types such as Viognier.

Calzone con Funghi, Peperoni e Salame

Calzone with Mushrooms, Red Bell Peppers, and Salame

The delicious pizza and *calzoni* of the South are in a class by themselves. These preparations can be found in *trattorie, pizzerie,* and, often, in snack bars and *caffè*. One morning, after having walked the streets of Napoli for over two hours, I was suddenly hungry, so I did what most Italians do, I stopped at a *caffè* for a little "pick-me-up" and at 11:30, two hours before my lunch,

I had a warm, delicious calzone that was stuffed with mush-rooms, red bell peppers, *salame*, and mozzarella.

1 recipe Basic Pizza Dough (see pages 284–85)

For the filling
> 2 to 3 tablespoons olive oil
> ½ pound small white cultivated mushrooms, thinly sliced
> 1 clove garlic, finely minced
> 1 tablespoon chopped fresh parsley
> Salt to taste
> 4 ounces whole milk mozzarella, diced
> 2 large red bell peppers, roasted (see page 32), peeled, seeded, and cut into thin strips
> 4 ounces thinly sliced Italian salame, cut into thin strips
> 1 large egg, lightly beaten

Prepare the pizza dough and let it rise.

Preheat the oven to 450°F 30 minutes before baking.

Heat the oil in a large skillet over high heat. Add the mush-rooms and cook, stirring, until they begin to color, about 1 minute. Stir in the garlic and parsley, season lightly with salt, mix once or twice, and remove from the heat.

Divide the dough into two equal parts and roll out into two circles approximately 8 inches in diameter. Divide the mozzarella and place in the center of each circle of dough. Divide the mushrooms, peppers, and *salame* and place over the mozzarella. Fold the dough over the filling, combining the edges. Fold the edges slightly to form a border, then pinch the edges with your fingertips or with a fork to seal. Place the *calzoni* on a baking sheet and brush them with the beaten egg. Bake until they are golden brown, 15 to 20 minutes. Cool slightly and serve.

Makes 2 *calzoni*

SUGGESTED WINES
Try a lighter, uncomplicated red such as Sutter Home Soléo or Pecota Gamay Beaujolais from California.

"OTHER GOOD THINGS"

"Other good things" are a mixture of dishes that belong everywhere and nowhere in particular. The *focaccia Ligure*, for example, is a savory bread, often eaten between meals as a snack or instead of other bread during meals. The *crescentine fritte* are made with a bread dough that is rolled out quite thin and fried. In Bologna *crescentine* are often part of a rustic meal, served next to prosciutto and *salame*. They can also be served as a delicious snack. The *erbazzone all'Emiliana*, a savory ricotta and spinach pie, studded with delicious crisp pancetta, is one of those dishes that will fit anywhere, lunch, dinner, snack, or appetizer, and will surely please everyone. Then there are the *frittate*, delicious open-faced Italian omelets, which can be used as homey appetizers or simply as a spur-of-the-moment light lunch or dinner.

Mastering some of the dishes in this chapter will allow you not only to enjoy some truly delicious food but also to have fun while preparing them.

Focaccia Ligure

Savory Ligurian Bread with Sage

Italy is studded with a cornucopia of savory flat breads. The names change according to the regions and so do the flavorings that go into them. The principal ingredients, flour, yeast, and water, are kneaded together into a ball and left to rise; then the bread is spread flat on a baking sheet or over a baking stone and cooked until golden. The Ligurian *focaccia* is a bit thicker than most savory breads and is generally kneaded together with wonderful fragrant fresh sage or rosemary and oil.

❋ ❋ ❋
VARIATIONS

To make focaccia *with rosemary, substitute the sage with ½ cup roughly chopped fresh rosemary or 2 to 3 tablespoons dried.*

To make the Bolognese savory bread called crescenta, *substitute the sage with the same proportions of rosemary given above, plus ½ pound chopped pancetta which should be kneaded into the dough together with the rosemary during the preparation of the second rising.*

For the sponge
1 cup unbleached all-purpose flour
1 package active dry yeast dissolved in ½ cup lukewarm water

For the second rising
2½ cups unbleached all-purpose flour
2 packages active dry yeast dissolved in 1 cup lukewarm water
½ cup loosely packed, shredded fresh sage leaves or 2 tablespoons crumbled dried
3 tablespoons olive oil
1 tablespoon coarse salt

Prepare the sponge by putting the flour in a medium-size bowl or in the bowl of an electric mixer Add the dissolved yeast and mix with the flour. Knead the dough approximately 10 minutes by hand or 3 to 4 minutes by machine. If the dough is a bit sticky, dust it lightly with flour. After the kneading, the dough should be smooth and pliable. Put the dough in a lightly floured medium-size bowl, cover it tightly with plastic wrap, and let it rise in a warm draft-free place until doubled in bulk, 2 to 3 hours.

Combine all the ingredients of the "second rising," except the salt, in a large bowl or in the bowl of an electric mixer. Add the "sponge" and knead energetically 10 minutes by hand or 3 to 4 minutes by machine. After the kneading, this dough should be smooth and pliable. Dust the dough lightly with flour, place in a large bowl, and cover with plastic wrap. Let it rise in a warm, draft-free place for 2 hours. The dough should double in size and have small gas bubbles over its surface.

Preheat the oven to 450°F 30 minutes before baking.

Lightly oil a 10- or 12-inch-long baking sheet.

Roll the dough out to about ½-inch thickness and place on the baking sheet. With your fingers spread it evenly into the baking sheet, and in doing so make hollow fingertip indentations all over the dough. Spread the coarse salt over the *focaccia* and bake until the *focaccia* has a nice golden brown color, 20 to 25 minutes. Serve warm or at room temperature.

Makes 10 to 12 servings

SUGGESTED WINES

Light, dry, not fragrant wines, either white or red, are traditional with these focaccie. *Try with a glass of French champagne.*

Crescentine Fritte

Bolognese Fried Flat Dough

There is a whole category of food that conjures up homey images. When I think of *crescentine fritte*, I see my mother and grandmother in the kitchen rolling out a large sheet of dough, the dough cut into large triangles and deep fried. My brother, sister, and I watch in fascination as the *crescentine* puff up as they fry, and become golden almost instantly. The aroma of fried food is all over the kitchen. My mother sprinkles a bit of sugar on the *crescentine* and hands the plate to us. Sheer paradise!

Homey food, street food, country food, deliciously appetizing, this is what *crescentine* are. In country *trattorie*, *crescentine* come to the table sprinkled with salt You drink a glass of wine, munch on those delicious, crisp *crescentine*, and wait for the food to come, and then you realize that you are not hungry anymore because you have devoured a whole plate of them.

1½ cups unbleached all-purpose flour
2 tablespoons olive oil
2 tablespoons unsalted butter, melted
1 teaspoon salt
½ package active dry yeast, dissolved in ½ cup lukewarm
  water
Vegetable oil for frying

Put the flour, oil, butter, and salt in a medium-size bowl. Add the dissolved yeast and mix the ingredients well with a wooden spoon or your hands until they are incorporated. Place the dough on a work surface and knead 2 to 3 minutes. Add a bit of flour if the dough is a little sticky. Wrap the dough with plastic wrap and let it rest in a warm draft-free place for about 30 minutes.

Lightly flour a wooden board or work surface and roll out the dough into a large, thin rectangle. With a scalloped pastry wheel, cut the sheet of dough into 5-inch-wide strips, and zigzag each strip into large triangles. Lay the triangle on a tray lined with a clean kitchen towel.

Heat one inch of oil in a medium-size skillet over medium-high heat. When the oil is very hot, slide a few pieces of dough into the skillet and fry a few at a time. When they are golden on one side, 20 to 30 seconds, turn them to fry on the other side. Transfer to paper towels to drain. Sprinkle the *crescentine* lightly with salt and serve piping hot.

Makes 14 to 16 *crescentine*

TIPS

ᴄᴡ⹀ *The dough can be prepared several hours ahead and kept refrigerated. Bring it back to room temperature before rolling it out.*

ᴄᴡ⹀ *Just like most fried food, these* crescentine *should be eaten immediately after they are fried, or they will become somewhat soggy.*

ᴄᴡ⹀ Crescentine *can be served as an appetizer as part of a rustic dinner, or as a snack. They are delicious when paired with a few slices of prosciutto or* salame.

SUGGESTED WINES

If using these crescentine *as an appetizer, try a good Fino Sherry from Spain such as Tio Pepe from Gonzalez, Byass or Manzanilla from Hidalgo, or a dry, fragrant, crisp Italian sparkling wine such as Nino Franco Prosecco.*

Pizzelle Fritte alla Napoletana

Neapolitan Fried Little Pizzas

I discovered these little fried *pizzelle* at Dal Delicato in Napoli. They were brought to the table piping hot, golden and crisp, topped with juicy red tomatoes, milky white mozzarella, and fresh basil. They were so appetizing I could not stop eating them. The crisp fried dough reminded me of the *crescentine fritte* (Bolognese Fried Flat Dough—pages 297–98) that my mother used to make. Serve them as an appetizer or as a snack.

1 recipe Basic Pizza Dough (see pages 284–85)
Vegetable oil for frying
1 pound fresh, ripe plum tomatoes, diced and mixed with
    2 tablespoons olive oil and salt to taste
6 ounces whole milk mozzarella, grated or diced

Prepare the pizza dough and let it rise.

Roll out the dough into a large circle, approximately ¹⁄₁₆ of an inch thick.

With a 4-inch glass or cookie cutter, cut the dough into circles. Fold the edges of the dough over slightly, then press them with a fork to make a small border. Poke the circles of dough with a fork in several places.

Heat one inch of oil to 370°F in a large skillet over medium-high heat. The oil is ready when a piece of the dough turns brown in 20 to 30 seconds. Add only 2 to 3 circles of dough at a time. When one side of the little pizza is golden, 20 to 30 seconds, turn it over to cook the other side. Drain on paper towels.

Preheat the oven to 375°F.

Top each small pizza with some of the diced tomatoes and mozzarella and place on a baking sheet. Bake just long enough for the cheese to melt, 6 to 7 minutes. Serve hot.

Makes 10 to 14 small pizzas

TIPS

↬ *During the frying, the dough will puff up. Poke it with a fork and press it down lightly with a long wooden spoon, then turn to fry the other side.*

↬ *After the frying, the shape of each small pizza will be somewhat different. That is okay; this will add to the rusticity of the dish.*

↬ *After the dough is cut into circles, gather up the scraps and roll them out again so that nothing will go to waste.*

↬ *The* pizzelle *can be fried ahead and kept at room temperature on a tray covered with a kitchen towel for a few days. (Do not use plastic wrap; that will make the fried dough soft.)*

SUGGESTED WINES
You can serve these little pizzas as appetizers either with a cocktail of your choice or with an Italian Campari and soda. I also enjoy them with a nice glass of light white wine, such as a Breganze Bianco from Maculan.

Erbazzone all'Emiliana

Spinach and Ricotta Pie

Erbazzone is a delicious, savory spinach and ricotta pie, a specialty of Reggio-Emilia, a small, lovely city north of Bologna. There are many variations of this time-honored dish. At Taverna Sette Torri in Reggio-Emilia, the pie had the addition of crunchy bits of pancetta and garlic that made it extremely appetizing.

Erbazzone can be served as an appetizer, a light lunch or supper, or, as in Italy, a midday "pick-me-up."

For the pie crust
2 cups unbleached all-purpose flour
¼ pound (1 stick) unsalted butter (at room temperature for hand mixing, cold and in small pieces for the food processor)
1 teaspoon salt
1 large egg
¼ to ⅓ cup chilled dry white wine

For the filling
2 pounds fresh spinach or one 10-ounce package frozen spinach
3 tablespoons olive oil
4 ounces sliced pancetta, diced
1 clove garlic, minced
3 large eggs, separated
¾ cup freshly grated parmigiano
Salt to taste
1 pound whole milk ricotta
1 egg, lightly beaten

In a medium-size bowl or in a food processor fitted with the metal blade, mix the flour and butter until crumbly. Add the salt, egg, and wine and mix into a soft dough. Divide the dough into two balls, one a little larger than the other. Wrap them in plastic wrap and refrigerate for one hour.

Prepare the filling. If you are using fresh spinach, discard the stems and any bruised leaves. Wash the spinach thoroughly under cold water. Put the spinach in a large saucepan with 1 cup cold water and a pinch of salt. Cook until the spinach is tender, 7 to 8 minutes. If you are using frozen spinach, cook it according to the package directions. In either case, drain well and squeeze out any water with your hands. Chop the spinach quite fine.

Heat the oil in a medium-size skillet over medium heat. Add the pancetta and cook, stirring, until it begins to color, about 2 minutes. Add the garlic and stir once or twice. Set aside.

Beat the egg yolks in a large bowl with the parmigiano and salt. Add the ricotta and spinach mixture and mix everything until thoroughly combined.

Beat the egg whites in a medium-size bowl with a pinch of salt until stiff peaks form, then fold into the spinach-ricotta mixture.

Preheat the oven to 375°F.

Butter a 10-inch springform cake pan.

On a lightly floured surface roll out the larger ball of dough into a 12-inch circle and place it in the buttered cake pan, fitting the dough against the sides of the pan. Pour the ricotta-spinach mixture into the pastry and level the filling with a spatula.

Roll out the remaining dough and place over the filling. Pinch the edges of the top and bottom dough together to seal the pie. Brush the top crust with the beaten egg and prick it in several places with a fork. Bake until the crust is golden brown, 40 to 50 minutes. Cool the pie completely to room temperature, remove from the pan, and cut into slices or a serving dish.

Makes 8 servings

SUGGESTED WINES
A Trebbiano di Romagna or Albana from Cesari would be a good first-course accompaniment. A Sauvignon Blanc from Meridian or Fetzer would also work well.

Frittata alle Erbe

Frittata with Herbs

A frittata is perfect trattoria food—simple, unassuming, inexpensive, and delicious. At Ai Provinciali, a popular tavern-trattoria in the center of Udine, one can choose from the several frittatas of the day, quite popular with lunch patrons who opt for a light meal.

> ½ cup finely shredded assorted fresh herbs, such as basil, sage, and mint
> 2 tablespoons chopped fresh parsley
> ½ cup freshly grated parmigiano
> Salt to taste
> 6 large eggs, lightly beaten in a medium-size bowl
> 2 tablespoons olive oil

Stir all the ingredients, except the oil, into the beaten eggs and mix well. Heat the oil over medium heat in a nonstick 10-inch skillet.

Add the egg mixture and cook until the bottom of the frittata is lightly browned and the top begins to solidify, 5 to 6 minutes.

Place a large plate over the skillet and turn the frittata onto the plate. Slide the frittata back into the skillet to cook the other side. Cook until the bottom is lightly browned, 3 to 4 minutes longer. Slide the frittata onto a serving dish and serve warm or at room temperature.

Makes 2 servings as an entree or 4 servings as an appetizer

SUGGESTED WINES

Choose a nice aromatic wine such as an Alsatian, Californian, or Italian Gewürztraminer. A dry, pungent Sauvignon Blanc such as Dry Creek from Sonoma would also be wonderful.

Frittata di Patate e Erbe

Potato-herb Frittata

A frittata is an open-faced omelet. In Italy, frittatas are generally served as an appetizer or for a light lunch or supper; it is almost never served at breakfast. Frittatas can be prepared with a variety of fillings, such as vegetables, cheeses, meats, fish, and even pasta and rice. At Trattoria La Botte in Taormina, this potato-herb frittata was served as an appetizer. At my house, however, I serve it as a light Sunday supper, next to a nice mixed green salad. After all, Sunday is a day of rest and a frittata takes only minutes to prepare.

1 medium-size boiling potato (about 6 to 7 ounces)

½ cup freshly grated parmigiano

2 tablespoons chopped fresh parsley

6 large eggs, lightly beaten in a medium-size bowl

Salt to taste

2 tablespoons olive oil

5 to 6 fresh sage leaves, finely shredded, or 1 teaspoon
   dried, crumbled

1 clove garlic, minced

Bring a small saucepan of water to a boil over medium heat, add the potato, and cook until it is tender, 25 to 30 minutes. Drain and cool the potato, then peel and cut into small cubes.

Stir the parmigiano and parsley into the beaten eggs and season lightly with salt.

Heat the oil over medium heat in a nonstick 10-inch skillet. Add the potatoes, sage, and garlic and stir for about 1 minute.

With a slotted spoon, scoop up the potatoes and stir into the eggs. Put the skillet back over medium heat and add the egg mixture. Cook until the bottom of the frittata is lightly browned and the top begins to solidify, 5 to 6 minutes.

Place a large plate over the skillet and turn the frittata onto the plate. Slide the frittata back into the skillet to cook the other side. Cook until the bottom is lightly browned, 3 to 4 minutes longer. Slide the frittata onto a serving dish and serve warm or at room temperature.

Makes 2 servings as an entree or 4 servings as an appetizer

TIP

∽ *If you have problems turning the frittata onto a plate, turn on the broiler and place the skillet briefly under the broiler to cook the top part.*

SUGGESTED WINES

As an appetizer, dry vermouth or Fino Sherry; as a snack or light meal, a light red wine such as a Valpolicella.

Frittata di Cipolle all'Aceto Balsamico

Onion Frittata with Balsamic Vinegar

Aceto balsamico is synonymous with Modena, a small, prosperous city north of Bologna. There, balsamic vinegar is treated with respect and used with restraint in many dishes. At Trattoria La

Francescana, I had an onion frittata that had been cooked with a few drops of very old balsamic vinegar. It was incredibly good.

½ cup freshly grated parmigiano
1 tablespoon chopped fresh parsley
6 to 8 fresh basil leaves, shredded
6 large eggs, lightly beaten in a medium-size bowl
Salt to taste
3 tablespoons olive oil
2 large onions, thinly sliced
1 to 2 tablespoons balsamic vinegar (see page 13)

Stir the parmigiano, parsley, and basil into the eggs and season with salt.

Heat the oil in a nonstick 10-inch skillet over medium heat. Add the onions and cook, stirring, until they are lightly golden and soft, 8 to 10 minutes. Stir in the balsamic vinegar and mix once or twice.

With a slotted spoon, scoop up the onion and stir into the eggs. Put the skillet back over medium heat and add the egg mixture. Cook until the bottom of the frittata is lightly browned and the top begins to solidify, 5 to 6 minutes.

Put a large flat plate over the skillet and turn the frittata onto the plate. Slide the frittata back into the skillet and cook until the bottom is lightly browned, 3 to 4 minutes longer. Slide the frittata onto a serving dish, and serve hot or at room temperature.

Makes 2 servings as an entree or 4 servings as an appetizer.

TIPS

ↄ҂ *The amount of balsamic vinegar you use really depends on the strength of the vinegar. The older the vinegar, the less you need. In Modena I was given a thirty-year-old vinegar to sprinkle a few additional drops over the frittata, and it was simply wonderful.*

ↄ҂ *My favorite way to eat a frittata, the day after it is made, is between two slices of bread, accompanied by a nice glass of dry white wine!*

SUGGESTED WINES

Sweetness of onions, sweetness of balsamic—go with any dry red or full-bodied white of your choice.

DESSERTS

Desserts are pure gratification. They are the icing on the cake at the end of a meal, and yet they are not vital to a well-balanced meal. They are there simply to be indulged in.

Italian desserts can be divided into two categories—the rich, elaborate, luscious desserts displayed in pastry shops and caffès, and the uncomplicated, simple desserts of the home.

Because trattoria food is basically home food, the desserts served in *trattorie* are not the rich concoctions of pastry shops, which are treats for special occasions, but rather the *dolci casalinghi*. These are simple, unprepossessing preparations that require no particular skill or elaborate equipment, yet capture your attention because of their sense of place and tradition.

In a home, as well as in a trattoria, fruit plays a very important role. After an Italian meal, with its orchestrated sequences of appetizer, pasta, entree, and vegetable, with the rich flavors of each course still lingering in the mouth, a poached pear, a baked apple, or a colorful fruit salad will refresh the palate and end the meal on a light, pleasant note.

While eating in *trattorie* all over Italy, I got excited by baked apples, still hot from the oven, oozing with melted sugar, butter, and thick, rich Marsala wine, by the slice of rice-hazelnut cake and the sweet ravioli, so similar to the ones my mother used to make, and by the almond cookies which, I could dip with abandon into a glass of Vin Santo.

Some desserts in this book, however, even though simple to prepare, look and taste as if they were made by pastry chefs, such as the popular *tiramisù*, which today seems to be everybody's favorite, the *zuccotto*, with its impressive dome shape, the Sicilian cannoli, with their delicious crunchy homemade shells, and the *bonet*, a luscious baked chocolate custard.

The desserts in this book are simple, homespun creations. They are the treats of one's childhood, as delicious as American apple pie, and just as much loved.

Torta di Nocciole e Cioccolata

Hazelnut Chocolate Cake

This delicious cake was given to me by Ugo Faligna, a master baker from Parma. It is the sort of cake that is often found in the *trattorie* and homes of the area, since it is quite simple to prepare and keeps well for several days. At my restaurant in Sacramento I serve it over a layer of warm zabaglione (page 331) or with a glass of very old Marsala or Vin Santo wine.

6 ounces whole hazelnuts

½ pound (2 sticks) unsalted butter, at room temperature

6 large egg yolks

1 large whole egg

1 cup granulated sugar

5 ounces semisweet chocolate, finely chopped

¼ cup dark rum

2 cups unbleached all-purpose flour

6 large egg whites, beaten in a large bowl until stiff peaks form

Confectioners' sugar for garnish

Preheat the oven to 350°F. Butter and flour a 10-inch spring-form cake, shaking off any excess.

Place the hazelnuts in a single layer on an ungreased baking sheet and bake until lightly golden, 3 to 4 minutes. Wrap the hazelnuts in a large kitchen towel and rub off as much skin as possible. Put the hazelnuts in a food processor and chop them into fine pieces. (Be careful not to process them into powder.)

In a large bowl or in the bowl of an electric mixer, beat the butter with the egg yolks, whole egg, and sugar at high speed until pale yellow and fluffy. Add the hazelnuts, chocolate, and rum and mix into the eggs. Add the flour slowly, beating gently to incorporate. (The batter should have a soft, somewhat loose consistency.) Fold in the egg whites thoroughly. Pour the mixture into the buttered cake pan, level the top with a spatula, and bake until the cake is golden brown and a thin knife inserted in the center of the cake comes out just slightly moist, 30 to 40 minutes. Cool to room temperature, remove from the pan, sprinkle with confectioners' sugar, and serve.

Makes one 10-inch cake; 10 to 12 servings

Torta di Riso e Nocciole

Rice-hazelnut Cake

I feel positively exhilarated when I come across food of my youth that looks and smells much like the one my mother used to make. Rice-hazelnut cake, a specialty of Bologna, was a favorite in our household. My mother prepared it ritually, as my grand-mother did before her. This version comes from Trattoria Giannina in the small town of Campotto, near the beautiful city of Ferrara.

4 cups milk
½ cup granulated sugar
½ cup short-grain rice, preferably imported Italian
    Arborio
½ cup granulated sugar
4 ounces whole hazelnuts
2 large eggs, lightly beaten
2 tablespoons almond liqueur
3 large egg whites, beaten with ¼ cup granulated sugar
    until stiff peaks form
Confectioners' sugar for garnish

Preheat the oven to 350°F.

Butter and flour a 9-inch springform cake pan, shaking off any excess. In a medium-size saucepan, combine the milk and sugar and bring to a gentle boil over medium heat. Add the rice, reduce the heat to medium-low, and cook, stirring, until the rice is quite tender and the milk is all reduced, 35 to 40 minutes. (During the last few minutes of cooking, as the milk evaporates, make sure to keep stirring or the rice will burn. At this point the rice should have a moist consistency.) Transfer the rice to a large bowl and cool to room temperature.

Put the hazelnuts in a single layer on an ungreased baking sheet and bake until they are lightly golden, 3 to 4 minutes. Wrap the hazelnuts in a large kitchen towel and rub off as much skin as possible. Put the hazelnuts in a food processor and chop them into very fine pieces. (Be careful not to process them into powder.)

Add the hazelnuts, eggs, and almond liqueur to the rice, and mix thoroughly. (The rice mixure should have a soft, loose consistency. If too stiff and compact, beat in another egg.) Fold in the egg whites thoroughly. Place the rice mixture in the buttered baking pan and level the top evenly with a spatula. Bake until the top of the cake is golden brown and a thin knife inserted in the center of the cake comes out clean, 30 to 40 minutes.

Cool to room temperature, remove from the pan, sprinkle the cake with confectioners' sugar, and serve.

Makes one 9-inch cake; 6 to 8 servings

TIPS

෴ *The traditional rice cake is prepared with toasted blanched almonds, not hazelnuts. I have substituted hazelnuts out of personal preference.*

෴ *This cake can be kept for several days tightly wrapped in the refrigerator. Serve it at room temperature.*

෴ *If you don't have a springform cake pan, you can use a regular baking pan. However, you must first butter the bottom and sides of the pan and line the bottom with a round of parchment paper. When the cake is cool, place a large plate over the pan and invert the cake onto the plate.*

Torta di Mele della Trattoria Montagliari

Trattoria Montagliari Apple Cake

Signor Capelli, owner of Trattoria Montagliari in the Chianti region, is an exuberant man whose love for food and wine is immediately evident from your first encounter. The food we had that night was delicious, earthy, and satisfying in the true Tuscan way. The highlight of the meal was an almost flourless apple cake with an intense caramelized apple flavor.

> 6 pairs Amaretti di Saronno cookies (see page 17), finely chopped, or ½ cup dry, plain bread crumbs mixed with 1 tablespoon sugar
> 3 large eggs
> 1½ cups granulated sugar
> 1 tablespoon yeast
> ⅓ cup unbleached all-purpose flour
> ½ cup milk
> 2 tablespoons unsalted butter, melted
> 6 large Golden Delicious apples, cored, peeled, and very thinly sliced
> Confectioners' sugar for garnish

Butter a 10-inch springform cake pan and sprinkle the chopped *amaretti* over it, coating the bottom and sides of the pan evenly. Place in the refrigerator until needed. Preheat the oven to 375°F.

Combine the eggs and sugar in a large bowl or in the bowl of an electric mixer. Beat at high speed until the eggs are thick and pale yellow, then add the yeast, flour, milk, and melted butter, mixing well at low speed. Add the apples and mix thoroughly by hand.

Cover the outside of the cake pan with a large sheet of aluminum foil. This will prevent the juices in the soft apple mixture from leaking out of the bottom of the pan. Pour the apple mixture into the pan and level with a spatula. Place the cake pan on a cookie sheet and put in the oven. Bake until the top of the cake is golden brown and a thin knife inserted in the center of the cake comes out just barely moist, about 1 hour.

TIPS

~ *This is a deliciously light cake that contains very little flour and butter. For this reason it is a bit tricky to produce, since the only ingredient that keeps it together are the three eggs. For the best results,*

~ *The pan must be buttered and generously coated with the chopped cookies to prevent the cake from sticking to the bottom and sides of the pan.*

~ *The consistency of the apple mixture when you put it in the pan will be somewhat loose. That is okay because the milk will evaporate during baking.*

~ *The cake needs to cook between 1 and 1½ hours, depending on the oven, or it will fall apart.*

~ *When the cake is done and is still hot, it might stick a bit to the sides of the pan. Take a knife and gently separate it from the sides.*

~ *Don't worry if the cake is a bit burned—it tastes even better because the sugar is caramelized.*

Cool the cake 10 minutes before removing from the pan. (Don't remove the bottom of the pan as the cake is quite soft.) Refrigerate a few hours before serving, then sprinkle the top with some confectioners' sugar.

Makes one 10-inch cake; 8 to 10 servings

Torta di Mele e Mandorle

Apple-almond Cake

Masuelli is an old-fashioned trattoria situated about 10 minutes from the bustling center of Milano. Eating at Masuelli is just like eating in a private home. Signora Masuelli in the kitchen prepares the daily menu according to what she finds in the market in the morning. The day I was there, my eye caught sight of an apple cake dusted with powdered sugar that was displayed next to a large bowl of *macedonia di frutta* (page 325). Since I simply adore apples, I had to order it. It had a compact, not too sweet texture, with a faint taste of espresso and a chunkiness given to it by the chopped almonds and the almond macaroons. The reason I liked it so much was that it reminded me of some of the homey desserts of my youth, which, while lacking the sophistication of pastry-shop desserts, had an abundance of taste.

1½ cups blanched whole almonds
6 large Golden Delicious apples, cored, peeled, and diced
Grated zest of 1 lemon
¾ cup sugar
¼ pound (1 stick) unsalted butter, at room temperature and cut into small pieces
3 large eggs
4 pairs Amaretti di Saronno (see page 17) or almond macaroons, finely chopped
1½ cups unbleached all-purpose flour
¼ cup almond liqueur
⅓ cup cold strong espresso or very strong coffee
2 tablespoons honey
Confectioners' sugar for garnish

Preheat the oven to 400°F. Put the almonds in a single layer on an ungreased baking sheet and bake until lightly golden, 3 to 4 minutes. Put the almonds in a food processor and chop them into very fine pieces. (Do not process them into powder.) Set aside.

Butter and flour a 10-inch springform cake pan, shaking off any excess.

In a large bowl combine the apples and lemon zest. Place the sugar, butter, and eggs in a medium-size bowl or food processor and mix to combine. Add the *amaretti* and flour and pulse the machine on and off to mix. Add the almond liqueur, espresso, and honey and mix well.

Fold this batter into the apple mixture. Pour the mixture into the cake pan, shake the pan a few times to spread the mixture evenly, and smooth the top with a spatula. Bake about 1 hour. The cake is done when a thin knife inserted in the center comes out clean. Cool it completely to room temperature, remove from the pan, and serve sprinkled with confectioners' sugar.

Makes one 10-inch cake; 8 to 10 servings

TIPS

ᐁ *When done, this cake will have a dark brown color, given to it by the espresso. It is best served at room temperature.*

ᐁ *For a more elegant presentation, cover the bottom of a dessert dish with a few tablespoons of zabaglione (page 331) and place a nice slice of the apple cake over it.*

Bensone

Modena's Coffee Cake

Bensone is a dessert that falls into the category of sweet breads and coffee cakes. It is a simple, unassuming dessert that has been around for centuries. *Bensone* is prepared by combining flour with melted butter, eggs, sugar, yeast, and milk. These ingredients are kneaded together just like bread, then the dough is shaped into a ring, or a loaf, or some other shape, and baked. *Bensone* has a dense texture typical of country breads, but it is delicious topped by a bit of good jam, or dunked in a *caffè latte* or cappuccino or a glass of sweet Marsala.

When my daughters were little, I used to bake *ciambella*, Bologna's counterpart of *bensone*, because I could put a few slices in their lunch pails and I could keep it for four or five days.

This recipe comes from Osteria della Rubbiara in the small town of Nonantola, near Modena, where they serve delicious, old-fashioned food.

NOTE OF INTEREST
There is no need to refrigerate this cake. Keep it at room temperature, covered with plastic wrap.

6 cups unbleached all-purpose flour

¼ pound (1 stick) unsalted butter, melted

6 large eggs, 5 lightly beaten together, 1 beaten by itself

1¼ cups sugar

Pinch of salt

Grated zest of 2 lemons

1 tablespoon yeast dissolved in 1 cup warm milk (if it is good, it will foam slightly)

In a large bowl or the bowl of an electric mixer, combine the flour with the butter, 5 eggs, sugar, salt, lemon zest, yeast, and milk into a dough. Knead the dough 10 minutes by hand or 5 minutes by machine. At this point the dough should be soft, pliable, and just a bit sticky. (Resist the temptation to add more flour during the kneading if the dough is a bit sticky.) Flour the dough lightly, place it in a large bowl, cover with plastic wrap, and let rest about 1 hour in a warm place.

Preheat the oven to 350°F.

Butter and flour a 15- by 12-inch baking dish, shaking off any excess.

Shape the dough into a ring or wide loaf and brush it with the remaining beaten egg. With a long, thin knife, make an incision in the top of the dough and sprinkle the top generously with the remaining ¼ cup of sugar. Bake until golden brown, about 1 hour. The cake is done when a thin knife inserted in the center of the cake comes out clean.

Makes 10 to 12 servings

Torta Sbrisolona

Crumbly Cake

NOTE OF INTEREST

Try this torta *served next to some zabaglione—it is simply delicious.*

One of Mantova's typical and classic desserts is *torta sbrisolona*. This cake is assembled by combining all the ingredients into a soft, moist dough which is spread in a baking pan and baked. The name *sbrisolona* comes by the fact that the cake is quite crumbly. This homey, yet delicious dessert, popular with the many *trattorie* of the city, is generally served with a glass of sweet dessert wine.

This recipe comes from Trattoria Due Cavallini in Mantova. The only liberty I have taken with it was to add a few tablespoons of honey to the dough mixture, which made the cake a little less crumbly.

- 1 cup unbleached all-purpose flour
- ½ cup fine cornmeal
- ¾ cup sugar
- Grated zest of 2 lemons
- 6 ounces hazelnuts, toasted, skinned (see page 307), and finely chopped
- 2 large eggs, lightly beaten
- ¼ pound (1 stick) unsalted butter, melted
- 3 to 4 tablespoons honey

Preheat the oven to 350°F.

Butter the bottom and sides of a 9-inch springform pan and line the bottom with a piece of parchment paper.

In a large bowl combine all the ingredients until thoroughly combined. (At this point the mixture should be fairly moist.) Pour it into the baking pan and smooth the top with a spatula. Bake until the top of the cake is golden and a thin knife inserted in the center of the cake comes out clean, 30 to 35 minutes. Cool to room temperature and serve.

Makes one 9-inch cake; 8 servings

La Torta di Ricotta di Settimio

The Ricotta Cake of Signor Settimio

Fresh Roman ricotta is simply outstanding, and, for me, it is in a class by itself. At Settimio all'Arancio in Roma I had a *torta di ricotta* that was smooth, velvety, and quite light.

Back in Sacramento, I have had no problem reproducing the

cake. What I could not reproduce entirely was the taste that the Roman ricotta gave the cake, since it is unavailable here. Nevertheless, I urge you to try it, because it is still delicious.

> 2 pounds whole milk ricotta
> ¾ cup granulated sugar
> 6 ounces candied citron, finely diced
> Grated zest of 2 lemons
> 1 cup golden raisins, soaked in Marsala or rum for 20 minutes, drained, patted dry, and diced
> 6 large egg yolks, lightly beaten
> ¾ cup unbleached all-purpose flour
> 4 large egg whites beaten with ¼ cup granulated sugar until stiff peaks form
> Confectioners' sugar for garnish

Preheat the oven to 350°F.

Butter and flour a 10-inch springform cake pan, shaking off any excess.

Put the ricotta and sugar in a large bowl or in the bowl of an electric mixer or food processor and mix energetically until the sugar is all incorporated and the ricotta is smooth. Combine the candied citron, lemon zest, and raisins with the egg yolks and mix well with a large wooden spoon. Add the ricotta and mix thoroughly. Fold in the flour and mix until smooth. Fold in the egg whites thoroughly and pour the mixture in the buttered pan. Bake until the top is golden brown and a thin knife inserted in the center of the cake comes out clean, 40 to 45 minutes. Cool to room temperature, remove from the pan, sprinkle with confectioners' sugar, and serve.

Makes one 10-inch cake; 10 to 12 servings

La Zuppa Inglese del Pantheon

Rum Cake

Zuppa inglese is to an Italian what apple pie is to an American. My mother would prepare it only on special occasions, and on those occasions the kitchen had the aroma of freshly baked pound cake and hot custard cream.

Zuppa inglese falls into the category of *dolci al cucchiaio*, moist, puddinglike desserts that are eaten with a spoon. The pound cake is soaked in rum or brandy and Alchermes (see note) and is completely smothered with custard cream.

At The Pantheon trattoria in Roma, I found a variation on the classic theme. There they top the last layer of custard cream with a thick layer of chocolate topping.

For the custard cream
    8 cups milk
    Few drops of pure vanilla extract
    10 large egg yolks
    1 cup sugar
    ¾ cup unbleached all-purpose flour

To complete the dish
    1½ pounds pound cake, cut into ¼-inch-thick slices
    1 cup dark rum, combined with ½ cup cherry brandy
    2 cups milk
    ¼ cup sugar
    ¼ cup unsweetened cocoa powder
    2 tablespoons unbleached all-purpose flour

To prepare the custard cream, put the milk and vanilla in a medium-size saucepan and bring it short of a boil over medium heat.

In a large bowl or in the bowl of an electric mixer, beat the egg yolks with the sugar at high speed until pale yellow and thick. Beat in the flour slowly, until it is well blended with the eggs.

Slowly pour the hot milk into the eggs, mixing constantly.

Return the custard to the saucepan and cook over medium-low heat 8 to 10 minutes, stirring constantly. At this point the custard should have a nice dense consistency.

Choose a deep 8-cup dish or a large glass bowl and cover its bottom with a layer of pound cake. Sprinkle the cake generously with some of the rum and brandy mixture. Cover the pound cake with a thick layer of the custard cream. Repeat with two more layers of pound cake and cream, ending it with a layer of cream and sprinkling each cake layer with the rum mixture. (Do not fill the bowl all the way to the top. Leave about 1 inch of space for the chocolate topping.)

In a medium-size saucepan combine the milk, sugar, cocoa,

NOTE OF INTEREST

Alchermes is always used in the traditional zuppa inglese. *This liqueur has a bright red color and a distinctive flavor. To my knowledge, Alchermes is not available in this country, so I substitute it with a nice cherry brandy.*

TIP
ᴧᴥ *Because the chocolate covering settles in no time at all, you need to pour the hot chocolate over the cake in one uninterrupted, quick motion.*

and flour. Stirring quickly with a wire whisk, cook over medium heat until the milk begins to boil. Lower the heat and cook 1 to 2 minutes, stirring constantly. Pour the hot chocolate over the last layer of custard cream. Let cool for 10 to 20 minutes, then cover the bowl and refrigerate several hours or overnight before serving from the bowl.

Makes 10 to 12 servings

Zuccotto

Stuffed, Rum-Soaked Pound Cake

NOTE OF INTEREST
Don't let the several steps needed to make this cake scare you away. The hardest thing here is to line the bowl properly with the cake, and after you have done it a few times, you will have mastered that technique.

The beautiful thing about zuccotto *is that it can be prepared 2 to 3 days ahead of time and, when unmolded and sprinkled with the powdered sugar, will look quite impressive.*

Zuccotto is a delicious dome-shaped dessert that is associated with the city of Firenze. This is one of those beautiful desserts that is invitingly displayed in the caffè and pastry shops of Italy. *Zuccotto* does not need baking and is literally stuffed to capacity with ingredients—chocolate, nuts, and whipped cream—which are enclosed in slices of rum-soaked pound cake.

If you are in Firenze, you must sit at a nice outdoor caffè and, while you take in the glory of this enchanting city, sip a frothy cappuccino and indulge in a nice slice of *zuccotto*.

7 ounces whole hazelnuts or blanched almonds
7 ounces semisweet chocolate
3 cups heavy cream
1 cup confectioners' sugar
1 pound store-bought pound cake, cut lengthwise into ¼-inch-thick slices
½ cup dark rum
Confectioners' sugar for garnish

Preheat the oven to 400°F.

Place the hazelnuts in a single layer on an ungreased baking sheet and bake until they are lightly golden, 3 to 4 minutes. Wrap the hazelnuts in a large kitchen towel and rub off as much skin as possible. Put the hazelnuts in a food processor and chop them into very fine pieces. (Be careful not to process them into powder.) Place them in a large bowl.

Chop half of the chocolate into very fine pieces and add to the bowl with the hazelnuts. Melt the remaining chocolate in the top of a double boiler over medium-low heat, or in a metal bowl or saucepan in a 200°F oven, and let cool.

Beat the cream with the confectioners' sugar at high speed until stiff peaks form. Fold the cream into the hazelnuts and chocolate.

Line a round bowl with plastic wrap. Cut each pound cake slice lengthwise into two long triangles. Line the bowl by putting one slice with its *widest* side up, reaching the top of the bowl, then place the next slice with its *narrow* side pointing to the top of the bowl. Continue lining the bowl this way, alternating the placement of the slices. With a glass or a round cookie cutter, cut a round piece of cake to cover the bottom of the bowl. Fill any opening between the slices with small pieces of cake. Brush the cake with the rum.

Spoon only half of the whipped cream mixture into the cake and, with a spatula, press it gently against the bottom and sides of the cake, leaving an empty cavity in the center.

Fold the melted chocolate into the remaining half of the whipped cream mixture, then press it lightly into the empty cavity of the cake. Cover the top of the cake with slices of pound cake (do not cut these slices into triangles), and brush them with rum. Cover the bowl with plastic wrap and refrigerate overnight.

When you are ready to serve, unwrap the cake, place a flat dish over the cake, and turn it upside down. Lift off the bowl carefully, peeling the plastic wrap away. Dust the cake generously with confectioners' sugar, cut it into slices, and serve.

Makes 10 to 12 servings

Cassata di Ricotta alla Siciliana

Sicilian Ricotta Cake

The traditional *cassata alla Siciliana*, made with ricotta, chocolate, and mixed candied fruit, is a delicious but filling dessert and, as the name implies, is a specialty of Sicilia. Today this

TIP

🞥 *Do not use the candied fruit sold in supermarkets because it too dry and tough. Good candied fruit should be moist and a bit sticky. Check your local specialty food store or Italian market for a better product.*

dessert has a somewhat loose connotation, since it is made commercially with ice cream and has very little to do with the real thing.

At Trattoria Stella in Palermo, I was served an enormous slice of *cassata*, loaded with moist pieces of candied fruit and small chunks of chocolate. The waiter kept watching me, somewhat saddened by the fact that I still had more than half a slice of *cassata* on my plate. So, in order to please him, I slowly finished it. I was so full I thought I would burst.

I hope you will make this dessert because it is truly delicious, but *please*, serve only a *small* slice if you ever want your friends to talk to you again!

2 pounds whole milk ricotta
½ cup granulated sugar
6 ounces semisweet chocolate, finely chopped
8 ounces mixed candied fruit, finely chopped (see tip)
One 10- to 12-ounce store-bought pound cake, cut lengthwise into ½-inch-thick slices
¼ cup cherry liqueur
Confectioners' sugar for garnish

Place the ricotta and sugar in a large bowl or the bowl of a food processor and pulse briefly until smooth. Fold in the chocolate and candied fruit. Cover the bowl and refrigerate until ready to use.

Line a 10-inch cake pan 2½ inches deep with plastic wrap, then line the bottom and sides of the pan with slices of the pound cake, filling any opening between the slices with small pieces of cake. Brush the cake with the cherry liqueur.

Spoon the ricotta mixture into the pan, spreading it evenly. Top with slices of pound cake and brush with the cherry liqueur. Cover the cake with plastic wrap and refrigerate for several hours or overnight.

When you are ready to serve, unwrap the cake, place a flat dish over it, and turn it upside down. Lift off the cake pan carefully and peel the plastic wrap away. Dust the cake with confectioners' sugar and serve.

Makes one 10-inch cake; 10 to 12 servings

Tiramisù

Ladyfingers and Mascarpone Cake

Tiramisù, literally translated "pick me up," doesn't need any introduction. It is *always* made with mascarpone, a delicious, sweet, soft Italian cheese, not unlike a very thick, slightly acidic whipped cream, and *never* with any other cheese or with whipped cream.

At the fancy Osteria Trattoria Laguna in Cavallino, near Venezia, this dessert had a particularly extra light texture.

> 8 large egg yolks
> ½ cup sugar
> 1½ pounds imported mascarpone cheese (see page 10)
> 4 large egg whites, beaten in a medium-size bowl until stiff peaks form
> 2 cups cold strong Italian espresso coffee
> ¼ cup brandy
> 42 ladyfingers, preferably imported from Italy
> ½ cup unsweetened cocoa powder
> Semisweet chocolate for garnish, optional

In a large bowl or in the bowl of an electric mixer, beat the eggs with the sugar until thick and pale yellow. Fold the mascarpone into the eggs until thoroughly incorporated and smooth. Fold the egg whites into the mascarpone mixture thoroughly.

In a medium-size bowl combine the espresso and brandy. Dip the ladyfingers quickly into this mixture, one at a time, and place a layer of them very close together in a 14- by 10-inch dish. Spread half of the mascarpone mixture evenly over the ladyfingers. Sprinkle the cocoa powder evenly over the mascarpone through a small fine-mesh strainer. Dip more ladyfingers in the espresso-brandy mixture and place over the mascarpone, making another layer. Top with the remaining mascarpone and sprinkle with the cocoa powder through a fine-mesh strainer. Cover the dish with plastic wrap and refrigerate several hours.

Just before serving, shave some chocolate with a carrot peeler or a knife and sprinkle over the cake.

Makes 10 to 12 servings

Bonet

Piemontese Baked Chocolate Custard

Bonet is the lovely baked chocolate custard of Piemonte often found in restaurants and *trattorie* that carry on the cooking traditions of the region.

Custard molds are coated with a thick chocolate caramel syrup, then they are filled with a delicious chocolate custard to which *amaretti* have been added. If you like custards, you will love this version which comes from Trattoria del Bricco.

For the chocolate caramel syrup
2 ounces semisweet chocolate, cut into small pieces
1 cup sugar
1 cup water
1 tablespoon fresh lemon juice

For the chocolate custard
7 ounces semisweet chocolate, cut into small pieces
3 cups warm milk
8 pairs Amaretti di Saronno cookies (see page 17), finely chopped
4 large egg yolks
2 large whole eggs
¼ cup sugar

To prepare the caramel, put the chocolate in a small bowl or in the top part of a double boiler and set it over simmering water. Melt the chocolate over low heat, mixing a few times, then turn off the heat.

Combine the sugar, water, and lemon juice in a medium-size skillet. Cook over high heat until the mixture is thick and bubbling and has a rich golden color, 5 to 6 minutes. Pour the chocolate into the caramel and mix quickly to combine. Pour the chocolate caramel into 6 small custard molds, tilting and rotating the molds to coat evenly. Set aside.

To prepare the custard, combine the chocolate and milk in a medium-size bowl or in the top part of a double boiler and set it over simmering water. Cook over low heat, stirring a few times, until the chocolate is completely melted, 8 to 10 minutes.

TIP
↶ *Caramel is achieved by cooking sugar and water together until all the water is evaporated and the sugar bubbles and begins to burn and turns golden brown in color. Keep your eyes on the skillet as the sugar begins to thicken and change color. Do not let it become too dark or the syrup will be too firm and the sugar will taste bitter. When the syrup is thick and bubbly and has a nice rich golden color, pour it into the molds* quickly and carefully. *The syrup will firm up in no time at all.*

Cool slightly, then add the *amaretti* and let soak for 10 minutes.

Preheat the oven to 350°F.

In a small bowl beat the yolks, whole eggs, and sugar with a wire whisk until well combined. Add the eggs *slowly* to the milk, mixing lightly. Pour into the prepared molds and place them in a large baking pan. Pour enough water in the pan to come halfway up the sides of the molds. Cover with aluminum foil and bake 15 minutes. Remove the foil and bake 15 to 20 minutes longer. The custard is done when a thin knife inserted into the center comes out clean.

Cool the custards in the refrigerator. When you are ready to serve, run a knife all around the custard to detach it from the mold. Place a serving dish over each mold and carefully invert the dish to hold the custard and its chocolate caramel sauce. Serve cold.

Makes 6 servings

Budino agli Amaretti

Baked Custard with Almond Cookies

Quintilio is an upscale, yet homey trattoria in Altare, a Ligurian town that borders on Piemonte. Therefore the food served at Quintilio draws from the best of both regions. This baked custard, prepared with Amaretti di Saronno, is an interpretation of the chef, Paolo Bazzano, of the famous Piemontese *bonet* (see preceding recipe).

For the caramel syrup
    1 cup sugar
    1 cup water

For the custard
    2½ cups milk
    8 pairs Amaretti di Saronno cookies (see page 17), finely
        chopped
    6 large eggs
    6 tablespoons sugar

TIPS

∾ *Custards can be prepared several hours or a day ahead. When you are ready to serve, if the caramel is too firm and makes it hard to unmold the custard, place the mold halfway into a bowl of hot water briefly to soften the caramel, then turn it into the plate.*

∾ *Custards can be topped with whipped cream or fresh pureed berries mixed with a bit of brandy or rum.*

To prepare the caramel, combine the sugar and water in a small saucepan. Cook over high heat until the mixture is thick and bubbling and has a rich golden color, 5 to 6 minutes. Pour the caramel quickly into 6 small custard molds, tilting and rotating the molds to coat evenly. Set aside.

To prepare the custard, in a medium-size saucepan heat the milk short of a boil over medium heat. Add the amaretti and let soak for about 10 minutes.

Preheat the oven to 350°F.

In a medium-size bowl beat the eggs and sugar until well combined. Add the eggs to the milk *slowly*, mixing constantly. Pour the mixture into the prepared molds and place the molds in a large baking pan. Put enough water in the pan to come halfway up the sides of the molds. Cover with aluminum foil and bake 15 minutes. Remove the foil and bake 15 to 20 minutes longer. The custard is done when a thin knife inserted into the custard comes out clean.

Cool the custards in the refrigerator. When you are ready to serve, run a knife all around each custard to detach it from the mold. Place a serving dish over each mold and carefully invert the dish to hold the custard and its caramel sauce. Serve cold.

Makes 6 servings

Mele e Pere al Forno

Baked Stuffed Apples and Pears

Because Italians eat desserts only sporadically, they often satisfy their need for something sweet with baked fruit. Baked apples and pears are common fare in Italian homes, especially in the wintertime. Often, they are stuffed with a variety of ingredients, turning this humble baked fruit into a delicious treat. In Bologna, the wonderful food store Tamburini, a shrine for food lovers, bakes the apples and pears with a filling of butter, sugar, *amaretti*, and Marsala wine. When you bake this at home, you will have an added bonus: the wonderful aroma that will spread throughout the house.

4 large Golden Delicious apples, washed and cored
4 large bosc pears, washed and cored, if desired
4 tablespoons (½ stick) unsalted butter
½ cup sugar
1½ cups sweet Marsala wine
4 pairs Amaretti di Saronno cookies (see page 17) or 8
    almond cookies, finely crushed

Preheat the oven to 375°F. Butter a large baking dish generously.

Fill each apple and pear cavity with a small cube of the butter,
1 tablespoon of the sugar, 1 tablespoon of the Marsala, and 1
crushed amaretto cookie. Place the fruit in the buttered dish
with the remaining Marsala wine and bake until the apples and
pears are golden in color and tender, and the skins begin to
split, 35 to 45 minutes.

Serve hot or at room temperature, topping each fruit with a
bit of the pan juices.

Makes 8 servings

Prugne Cotte al Marsala

Dried Prunes Poached in Marsala

If you have traveled to Italy, you might have noticed the Italian
preoccupation with dried prunes. They are served in hotels and
pensioni for breakfast, poached in water, sugar, and lemon juice.
They appear again at the end of a meal in restaurants and *trattorie*, poached in wine and displayed in glass bowls—they seem
to be everybody's favorite. Perhaps it is the Italian belief that
prunes aid the digestion which makes them so popular. I had
to include them here, since when I am in Italy, I too become a
pruneaholic!

¾ pound pitted prunes
Juice of 1 lemon
⅓ cup sugar
1 cup dry Marsala

Wash the prunes well under cold running water and place them in a medium-size nonreactive saucepan. Add the lemon juice, sugar, and Marsala, and marinate them for 2 to 3 hours at room temperature.

Put the saucepan over medium heat and cook until the prunes are tender, 10 to 15 minutes. Pour the prunes and their wine sauce into a medium-size serving bowl, cool to room temperature, and serve. The prunes actually taste better if they are left to soak in their cooking wine overnight. Serve them at room temperature.

Makes 4 servings

Pesche con il Lambrusco

Peaches Marinated in Red Wine

NOTE OF INTEREST
Lambrusco is a dry, frothy wine, typical of Emilia-Romagna. In this country, Lambrusco is not dry, but slightly sweet.

Most of the time, Italians like to end their meal with fruit. A very popular preparation is to marinate berries, oranges, peaches, or cherries in wine or in lemon juice and sugar.

Fruit prepared this way refreshes the palate and satisfies the desire for something sweet.

At Trattoria Da Nello in Bologna the peaches were served in large stemmed glasses, completely covered with a local dry, bubbling, and fruity Lambrusco.

4 cups Lambrusco or any good, medium-dry red wine
½ cup sugar
4 medium-size ripe peaches, peeled, pitted, and sliced

In a wide bowl, combine the wine and sugar and stir to dissolve the sugar. Add the peaches, cover the bowl with plastic wrap, and refrigerate 1 hour.

Put the peaches and enough wine to almost cover the peaches in stemmed glasses or in fruit bowls and serve.

Makes 4 servings

La Macedonia di Frutta Fresca

Fresh Fruit Salad

I could not have ended this chapter without including *la macedonia di frutta fresca*, because fresh fruit salad seems to be the natural way to end a meal in a trattoria.

Since it seems to me that anyone can assemble a fruit salad, instead of a recipe, I will give you ideas on how to compose an Italian-tasting fruit salad.

꙳ A nice *macedonia* should have a considerable variety of fruit.

꙳ All the fruit should be peeled and cut approximately the same size, 1-inch cubes or smaller.

꙳ The cut-up fruit should be assembled in a large bowl and dressed with enough sugar to suit your taste. Then it should be stirred with either fresh lemon juice, sweet Marsala wine (my favorite), sweet white wine, port, or brandy, depending on the preference of the cook.

꙳ It should be kept refrigerated for a few hours, and served chilled.

Biscottini di Prato

The Almond Cookies of Prato

Even though these little almond cookies are a specialty of Prato, a small industrial town outside Firenze, they are very popular all over Toscana. They are so deliciously wholesome that the *trattorie* and restaurants of the region invariably have them on their dessert list. At Il Cinghiale Bianco in Firenze, we enjoyed

NOTE OF INTEREST

These biscotti *have a hard, crunchy consistency perfectly suited for dipping into sweet wine. If you prefer softer cookies, bake them only 15 to 20 minutes and do not put them back into the oven to dry.*

them dipped in the traditional Vin Santo, a sweet wine of the region.

½ pound almonds
4 cups unbleached all-purpose flour
1 cup sugar
1 tablespoon yeast
Small pinch of powdered saffron
½ teaspoon salt
6 large eggs, lightly beaten
1 large egg lightly beaten with 1 teaspoon water in a small bowl

Preheat the oven to 375°F.

Place the almonds in a single layer on an ungreased cookie sheet and bake until they are lightly golden, 6 to 7 minutes. Put the almonds in a food processor and pulse on and off until the almonds are broken into very small pieces. (Do not process the almonds into powder.)

In a large bowl combine the almonds, flour, sugar, yeast, saffron, and salt and mix well. Add the eggs and mix well with a wooden spoon or your hands, until a soft paste forms. Place the mixture on a work surface and knead lightly for 2 to 3 minutes, sprinkling the dough with a bit of flour if it sticks heavily to the board and to your hands. (After kneading, the dough should still be just a bit sticky.)

Butter and flour a cookie sheet, shaking off any excess. Divide the dough into several pieces about the size of an orange. Flour your hands lightly and shape each piece of dough into a roll about the thickness of a sausage. Place the rolls on the cookie sheet and brush them lightly with the beaten egg. Bake until the rolls have a nice golden color, 20 to 30 minutes.

Remove from the oven and turn the heat off. As soon as the rolls are cool enough to handle, cut them diagonally into 2½- to 3-inch-long cookies.

To dry out the cookies completely, put them back in the unlit, warm oven for about 1 hour.

Makes approximately 40 to 45 cookies

Cannoli alla Siciliana

Sicilian Cannoli

Cannoli are probably one of the best-known Italian pastries in the world. The very best place to eat cannoli, however, is in Sicily. *Nobody* makes cannoli like a Sicilian. During my last trip to Sicilia, I ate cannoli in bars, coffee houses, pastry shops, and *trattorie*, comparing one with the other. And while the filling for cannoli changed slightly from place to place, the shells were rather similar, fresh and crisp.

To make cannoli shells at home is not that difficult, and I urge you to do so, because you cannot have good cannoli without good crisp shells. The cannoli dough is assembled and kneaded much like pasta dough, but it is rolled out just like pie dough, which is much simpler to do.

To make cannoli at home, you need to buy metal cannoli tubes which are available in specialty appliance and houseware stores as well as in the housewares section of some department stores.

This version of the Sicilian cannoli is pretty much the standard one. The only variation is the fat used for the cannoli dough, for which I have substituted butter for the traditional lard.

For the cannoli dough

1 cup unbleached all-purpose flour
Pinch of salt
2 tablespoons granulated sugar
2 tablespoons unsalted butter, soft for hand mixing, cold and in medium-size pieces for the food processor
1 large egg, lightly beaten
¼ cup dry Marsala wine, preferably an imported one such as Florio
Peanut or corn oil for frying

For the filling

1 pound whole milk ricotta
½ cup granulated sugar
⅓ cup finely chopped semisweet chocolate
¼ cup candied orange peel, finely minced
¼ cup almonds, finely chopped

TIPS

∾ Test the temperature of the oil before frying with a bit of scrap dough. If the oil sizzles and the pastry turns golden brown almost immediately, the oil is ready. If it turns too dark, the oil is too hot and you should lower the heat. If you have a thermometer, heat the oil to 370°F.

∾ Do not drop the cannoli into the hot oil; gently lower them in, by holding the metal tube with your hand or with long tongs or a slotted spoon.

∾ Keep in mind that the cannoli will fry very quickly and they will be golden brown within 30 to 40 seconds. You need to be literally on top of it. Fry one at a time; then when you are ready to remove it from the oil, add another one. Be careful because it is a bit tricky to remove the cannoli, since the metal tube is quite slippery and you don't really want to pick up the pastry with the tongs because it could break. Start taking out the cannolo when it is just golden, and by the time you position and secure the tongs on the metal tube, the cannolo will be already golden brown.

∾ Cool the fried shells completely; then they can be stuffed or placed in an airtight container and kept in the refrigerator for a few weeks. Cannoli shells can also be frozen for several months. In that case, bring them back to room temperature, then stuff and serve them.

To decorate the cannoli

Chopped semisweet chocolate or chopped candied red cherries
Confectioners' sugar

To prepare the cannoli dough by hand. Place the flour, salt, sugar, and butter in a medium-size bowl and mix thoroughly, rubbing the flour and butter between the palms of your hands until crumbly. Pile the flour mixture on a wooden board or other clean surface. With your fingers, make a hollow, round well in the center of the flour. Pour the egg and Marsala into the well. Mix the egg and wine together with a fork until well combined, then begin to draw some of the flour mixture from inside the well over the eggs. Add the flour a little at a time, always mixing with the fork. When you get to the point that a soft paste begins to form, start adding more flour with your hands and knead the mixture lightly into a ball.

With a pastry scraper clean the board and your hands. Sprinkle just a bit of flour on the board and dust your hands lightly, then knead the dough until it is soft and pliable, 7 to 8 minutes. (At this point the dough should be pockmarked by a few small bubbles, produced by the wine in the dough.) Work the dough into a ball, wrap in plastic wrap, and refrigerate about 1 hour.

To prepare the cannoli dough in a food processor. Place the flour, salt, sugar, and butter in a food processor fitted with the metal blade and pulse on and off until the mixture is crumbly. Add the egg and wine and pulse until the dough is gathered loosely around the blade. Put the dough on a lightly floured wooden board. Dust your hands lightly with flour and knead the dough 3 to 4 minutes. Wrap the dough in plastic wrap and refrigerate about one hour.

Lightly flour a wooden board or other work surface and roll out the dough (just as if you were rolling out pie dough) as thinly as you can. (If the dough is too thick, the shells will be chewy.) The dough can also be rolled out with a pasta machine.

Using a 4-inch round cookie cutter or glass, cut the sheet of dough into circles. (Gather up all the dough scraps into a ball, wrap them in plastic wrap, and refrigerate for later use.)

Place a metal cannoli tube horizontally over each circle. Wrap one part of the dough lightly over the tube and roll gently forward toward the far end of the dough. Before rolling the dough all the way to the end, lightly brush the far end of the dough with a bit of beaten egg to seal. Place the prepared cannoli on a lightly floured platter or cookie sheet.

Heat 2 inches of oil in a medium-size saucepan over high heat (see the frying tips which precede the recipe). Carefully, lower one *cannolo* at a time into the hot oil. When golden brown, 30 to 40 seconds, remove the *cannolo* with a slotted spoon and drain on paper towels. When all the cannoli are fried and slightly cool, slide the pastry off the metal tubes, making sure not to break them. Cool the cannoli completely before filling them.

To prepare the ricotta filling, mix the ricotta and sugar energetically together in a medium-size bowl with a wooden spoon to give the mixture a creamy consistency. (This step can be done quite well in a food processor.) Fold in the chocolate, orange peel, and almonds, making sure everything is well combined. Cover the bowl and refrigerate for about one hour.

When you are ready to serve, put the filling in a small pastry bag and fill the cannoli generously, all the way to the ends of the shells.

Decorate the ends with the chopped chocolate, or cherries. Sprinkle generously with confectioners' sugar and serve.

The filling for cannoli can also be prepared several hours or a day ahead. However, do not fill the cannoli more than one hour or so ahead of time or the shells will become soggy.

Eat the cannoli with your hands as they do in Italy, because the pastry is crumbly and hard to cut with a knife.

Use the leftover cannoli scraps to make more cannoli shells.

Because the ricotta available in this country is quite different from the luscious Italian ricotta, sometimes I add just a bit of whipped cream to the ricotta mixture for a softer, more voluptuous texture.

Ravioli Dolci

Sweet Ravioli

Emilia-Romagna is known throughout Italy for its delicious stuffed pasta. This is a region that stuffs not only pasta, but desserts. Zia Rina, the oldest aunt I have left in Bologna, is a sprightly, ninety-three-year-old, seemingly feeble woman who still makes an occasional batch of tortellini by hand and, at Christmastime, she still rolls out the dough for *ravioli dolci*, which she stuffs with good, thick plum jam.

These delicious ravioli (or *raviole* as they are called in Bologna) can also be stuffed with a variety of other ingredients, such as the ones I had at Trattoria Lo Sterlino in Bologna, which were filled with ricotta mixed with chopped *amarene*, imported cherries in heavy syrup.

For the pastry dough

2 cups unbleached all-purpose flour
¼ pound (1 stick) unsalted butter
1 large egg
¼ cup granulated sugar
3 to 4 tablespoons chilled sweet Marsala wine or sweet white wine

For the filling

10 ounces whole milk ricotta
¼ cup granulated sugar
Grated zest of 1 lemon
6 ounces imported Amarene Fabbri, diced (see note on page 333)

To complete the dish

Confectioners' sugar for garnish

TIPS

↩ Make sure to completely seal the ravioli or some of the filling might leak out during baking.

↩ Filling the ravioli will be much faster if you use a pastry bag.

To prepare the pastry dough, in a medium-size bowl or food processor fitted with the metal blade, mix the flour with the butter until crumbly. Add the egg, sugar, and wine and mix, pulsing the machine on and off, until the dough is loosely gathered around the blade or until it sticks together and can be assembled easily into a ball. Place the dough on a work surface and assemble into a ball. Wrap it in plastic wrap and refrigerate for a few hours.

In a medium-size bowl combine the ricotta with the sugar and lemon zest. Fold in the *amarene*. Refrigerate until ready to use.

Preheat the oven to 350°F.

Line a cookie sheet with aluminum foil or parchment paper.

On a lightly floured wooden board or other surface, roll out the dough to pie-dough thickness. With a large glass or round cookie cutter, cut the dough into 3- to 4-inch circles. Put about 1 teaspoon of filling in the center of each circle of dough. Fold each circle in half over the filling, and press the edges of the dough firmly to seal. Line the ravioli on the cookie sheet and bake until golden, 15 to 20 minutes.

Serve the ravioli warm or at room temperature, sprinkled with confectioners' sugar.

Makes approximately 25 to 30 ravioli; 10 to 12 servings

Zabaglione Caldo

Hot Zabaglione

Zabaglione is a classic Italian dessert that needs no introduction. It be found in restaurants and *trattorie* in Italy and abroad. It is a favorite homey dessert because with a batch of eggs, sugar, and some aromatic wine, one can whip up a soft, cloud-like, sinful concoction in no time at all. Classic zabaglione is generally prepared in a large, round copper pot or in a double boiler. The egg yolks are beaten with a large wire whisk over low heat, then wine, liqueur, or some other flavorful liquid is added to it, and everything is beaten together and cooked very gently, until the eggs have swollen into a soft mass. Zabaglione can be served hot by itself or chilled over fresh berries. Either way it is simply delicious.

> 8 large egg yolks, at room temperature
> ½ cup sugar
> 1 cup dry Marsala wine

In a large bowl or the top part of a double boiler set over simmering water, beat the eggs with the sugar until thick and pale yellow. Do not let the water boil or you will cook the eggs. Add the Marsala wine slowly, beating energetically with a large wire whisk to incorporate it. The zabaglione is ready when the mixture has doubled in volume, is soft and fluffy, and is hot to the touch, 4 to 6 minutes. Pour into individual glasses and serve hot.

Makes 4 to 6 servings

Gelato di Zabaglione

Zabaglione Ice Cream

NOTE OF INTEREST

Italian gelato has a soft, smooth consistency, and it should be eaten that way. When I prepare the gelato, I freeze it for only a few hours, just enough to firm it up a little so that when I serve it, it is still light and soft.

There are certain things that are so basically entrenched in the habits and culture of a country that they need no explanations—they simply *are*. A perfect example is the *passeggiata* on a warm, sunny day. Friends, families, and couples just strolling along, window shopping, or relaxing in an outdoor caffè with a large glass of gelato. That is Italian!

Italians love *gelato* and rightly so, because Italy makes the best ice cream in the world. In *caffè* and *gelaterie* (ice cream shops), the *gelati* are displayed in a kaleidoscope of colors and flavors, tempting, inviting, and utterly irresistible.

> 8 large egg yolks
> ½ cup sugar
> ¾ cup sweet Marsala wine, preferably Florio
> 2 cups heavy cream, whipped with ¼ cup sugar to a medium-thick consistency

In a large bowl or in the top of a double boiler, beat the eggs and sugar together with an electric mixer at high speed until thick and pale yellow. Set over simmering water (do not let the water boil too fast or it will cook the eggs). Add the Marsala slowly, beating energetically with a large wire whisk to incorporate it. Cook and beat constantly until the zabaglione has doubled in size and is hot to the touch, 4 to 5 minutes. Place the bowl with the zabaglione in a larger bowl half-filled with ice and whisk a few minutes to cool. Fold the whipped cream into the zabaglione.

Put the zabaglione mixture in the bowl of an ice cream machine and run for 15 to 20 minutes, or until the ice cream is ready. Place the ice cream in a plastic container and freeze it until you are ready to serve.

Makes 4 cups (1 quart) gelato

Gelato di Vaniglia con le Amarene

Vanilla Ice Cream with Italian Cherries

If *gelato* is served in *trattorie*, chances are that it is not made on the premises. It might be bought at the caffè across the street, or from a nearby *gelateria*.

In spite of the fact that *gelato* is not the quintessential trattoria food, I wanted to put in the book some of my favorite *gelatos*, since *gelato* is universally loved and passionately consumed by Italians.

For the custard cream
  2½ cups milk
  1 cup heavy cream
  7 large egg yolks
  ¾ cup sugar

To complete the dish
  4 cups heavy cream
  1 tablespoon pure vanilla extract
  1½ cups minced amarene (see note above)

To prepare the custard cream, in a medium-size saucepan bring the milk and cream short of a boil over medium heat.

In a large bowl or in the top of a double boiler off the heat, beat the egg yolks and sugar together with an electric mixer at high speed until pale yellow and thick.

Pour the milk *very slowly* into the eggs, beating constantly with a wire whisk until all the milk has been added. Set the bowl or top of the double boiler over simmering water and cook, whisking constantly, until the cream coats the back of a spoon evenly, 6 to 8 minutes. (Do not let the cream boil as it cooks or it will curdle the eggs.) Cool the custard completely to room temperature. (The custard cream can be prepared a day or so ahead and kept in the refrigerator in a tightly sealed bowl.)

Stir the heavy cream and vanilla extract into the cooled custard cream and place it in the bowl of the ice cream machine. Run the machine for 15 to 20 minutes.

NOTE OF INTEREST
Amarene, *or* amarena, *are wild Italian cherries in heavy syrup that are imported from Italy. These delicious, large, black cherries are quite popular in Northern Italy and are often served over ice cream or incorporated into desserts. They are available in specialty Italian markets and gourmet stores.*

Put the ice cream into a bowl and fold in the cherries. Transfer the ice cream to a plastic container and freeze it for several hours or until you are ready to use it.

The custard cream makes 4 cups (1 quart); the completed *gelato* **makes 8 cups (2 quarts)**

Gelato di Panna e Limone

Creamy Lemon Ice Cream

This is a luscious, creamy, and refreshing *gelato* which I simply adore. It is not exactly the lightest of all *gelato*, since it is made with a substantial amount of heavy cream. However, if you exercise some moderation in the amount you eat, you should be able to enjoy it without guilt.

2 cups custard cream (see page 333)
6 cups heavy cream
⅔ cup fresh lemon juice
⅔ cup sugar
Grated zest of 1 lemon

TIP

᧒ *It is a good idea to chill the bowl of the ice cream machine in the freezer for 10 minutes before using it. It will shorten the time needed to make the ice cream.*

Prepare the custard cream and let cool completely.

In a large bowl, combine the custard cream with the heavy cream and set aside.

In a small skillet, combine the lemon juice with the sugar and zest. Cook over medium heat, stirring, until reduced by about half. Cool to room temperature.

Stir the sugar mixture into the custard cream and place in the bowl of the ice cream machine. Run the machine for 15 to 20 minutes. Transfer the ice cream to a plastic container and freeze for several hours or until you are ready to use it.

Makes 8 cups (2 quarts) *gelato*

Eating Out In Italy
A personal guide to some Italian trattorie

The following is a list of suggested *trattorie* and *osterie* (see page 4) scattered throughout Italy. I have taken into consideration that some cities attract a larger group of tourists than others, such as Milano, Venezia, Firenze, and Roma, and therefore those cities have a higher number of *trattorie* listed. This selection is purely personal and certainly does not represent a complete national coverage. I've tried to provide telephone numbers when I was able to.

The North

Trattoria della Posta
Strada Mongreno, 17
Torino
890-193

Osteria Valenza
Via Borgo Dora
Torino

Osteria dell'Amicizia
Corso Casale, 221
Torino
890-188

Trattoria del Bricco
Frazione Quarto Superiore, 50
Asti
293-118

Trattoria della Pace
Boves (Cuneo)
9880-298

Trattoria Pertinace
Località Pertinace
Alba
30-000

Trattoria da Katti
Via Giovo, 11
San Candido (Cortina d'Ampezzo)
76-736

Trattoria Gabriella Gregori
Località Padriciano, 36
Trieste
226-112

Re di Coppe
Via Geppa, 11
Trieste
370-330

Trattoria "Max"
Via Nazionale, 43
Trieste-Opicina
211-160

All'Antica Ghiacceretta
Via dei Fornelli, 2
Trieste
305-641

Trattoria Pod Tabrom
Località Zolla, 8
Trieste
327-120

All'Allegria
Via Grazzano, 18
Udine
505-921

Trattoria Da Mario
Corso Terme, 4
Montegrotto Terme
Padova

Trattoria Antico Pizzo
San Polo, 814 (Rialto)
Venezia
523-1575

Aeciughetta
Campo San Filippo e Giacomo
Venezia
522-4292

Osteria Da Franz
Castello, 754
Venezia
522-7505

Osteria Trattoria Laguna
Via Pordello, 444
30013 Cavallino (Venezia)
968-058

Vini da Gigio
Cannaregggio, 3628/A
Venezia
528-5141

Cantina Do Mori
San Polo, 429
Calle do Mori
Venezia
522-5401

Al Million
Cannaregggio, 5841
Corte del Million
Venezia
522-9302

Le Carampane
San Polo, 1911
Venezia
524-0165

Alla Pigna
Via Pigna, 4
Verona
800-4080

Alla Cucina delle Langhe
Corso Como, 6
Milano
655-4279

Trattoria al Matarel
Via L.S. Mantegazza, 2
Milano
654-204

Trattoria Masuelli San Marco
Viale Umbria, 80
Milano
5518-4138

Il Verdi
Piazza Mirabello, 5
Milano
651-412

Antica Trattoria della Pesa
Viale Pasubio, 10
Milano
655-5741

Casa Fontana
Piazza Carbonari, 5
Milano
689-2684

Trattoria dei Cacciatori
Viale Trieste, 2
Peschiera B.
Milano
753-1154

Da Ornella
Via Gambito, 3
Bergamo
232-736

Vecchio Mulinetto
Viale Milazzo, 39
Parma
526-721

Dei Corrieri
Via Conservatorio, 1
Parma
234-426

Trattoria Vernizzi
Frascarolo di Busseto
Parma
92-423

La Francescana
Via Stella, 22
Modena
210-118

Trattoria Cervetta
Via Cervetta, 7
Modena
241-107

Osteria di Rubbiara
Via Risaia, 2
41015 Rubbiara (Nonantola,
Modena)
549-019

Osteria Novecento
Via Emilia-Romagna, 299
Savignano sul Panaro (MO)
730-434

Alla Grada
Via della Grada, 6
Bologna
523-323

Birreria Lamma
Via de' Giudei, 4
Bologna
358-519

Caminetto d'Oro
Via dei Falegnami, 4
Bologna
263-494

Trattoria Leonida
Vicolo Alemagna, 2
Bologna
239-742

Trattoria Boni
Via Saragozza, 88/A
Bologna
585-060

Trattoria Gianni
Via Clavature, 18
Bologna
229-434

Da Nello
Via Montegrappa, 2
Bologna
236-3311

Trattoria Lo Sterlino
Via Murri, 71
Bologna
342-751

Gambero Rosso
Molo di Levante
Cesenatico (FO)
81-260

Trattoria "E' Parlaminte"
Via Mameli, 33
Imola
30-144

Antica Trattoria Il Cucco
Via Voltacasotto, 3
Ferrara
760-026

Antica Trattoria dei Cacciatori
Corso Martinotti, 317
Sampierdarena (Genova)
467-382

Antica Trattoria Piccolo
Mondo
Via Piave, 7
San Remo
509-012

Enoteca Il Gallo della Checca
Località Ponte Rotto, 31
Ranzo (Imperia)
318-197

Quintilio
Via Gramsci, 23
17100 Altare
58-000

Osvaldo a Boccadasse
Via della Casa, 2R
Genova
377-1881

Trattoria Bruxiaboschi
Via F. Mignone, 8
Genova
345-0302

Central Italy

Osteria del Cinghiale Bianco
Borgo San Jacopo, 43
Firenze
215-706

Latini
Via Palchetti, 6
Firenze
210-916

Sostanza
Via del Porcellino, 25
Firenze
212-691

Il Francescano
Largo Bargellini, 16
Firenze
241-605

Antico Fattore
Via Lambertesca, 1R
Firenze
261-215

Il Fagioli
Corso dei Tintori 47R
Firenze
244-285

Coco Lezzone
Via del Parioncino, 26
Firenze
287-178

Cibreo
Piazza Ghiberti, 35
Firenze
234-1100

Trattoria Da Burde
Via Pistoiese, 6R
Firenze
317-206

Trattoria Cammillo
Borgo San Jacopo, 57R
Firenze
212-427

Trattoria Montagliari
Via di Montagliari, 29
Panzano in Chianti (Firenze)
852-184

La Biscondola
Via Grevigiana
Mercantale (Firenze)
821-381

Antica Trattoria Sanesi
Via Arione, 33
Lastra a Signa (Firenze)
872-0234

Trattoria Le Vigne
Podere Le Vigne
Radda in Chianti (Siena)
738-640

Locanda Marchetti
Via Fulvio Testi, 10
Castelnuovo di Garfagnana
(Lucca)
63-157

Trattoria Toscana
Via Vittorio Emanuele, 2
Capalbio (Grosseto)
896-028

The South

Trattoria da Settimio
all'Arancio
Via dell'Arancio, 50
Roma
687-6119

Hostaria da Pippo lo Sgobbone
Via de Podesti, 8-10
Roma
390-798

La Taverna (or Trattoria, as
the owners call it) Paola
Via Paola, 46-47
Roma
686-1805

Arancio d'Oro
Via Monte d'Oro, 17
Roma
686-5026

La Carbonara
Piazza Campo dei Fiori, 23
Roma
686-4783

Il Piedone
Via del Piè di Marmo, 28
Roma
679-8628

Hosteria Cannavota
Piazza San Giovanni in Later-
ano, 20
Roma
775-007

Al Pantheon
Via del Pantheon, 55
Roma
679-2788

Lucia
Vicolo del Mattonato, 2
Trastevere
Roma
580-3601

Evangelista
Via delle Zoccolette, 11
Roma
687-5810

Antica Trattoria al Moro
Vicolo delle Bollette, 13
Roma
679-3513

Da Gigetto
Portico d'Ottavia
Roma
686-1105

Trattoria Corsi
Via del Gesù
Roma

Angelino ai Fori
Largo Corrado Ricci, 40/30
Roma

Da Augustarello a Testaccio
Via G. Branca, 98-100
Roma
574-6585

Osteria dell'Angelo
Via G. Bettola, 24
Roma
389-218

Vecchia Roma
Via di Monserrato, 96
Roma
656-9389

Beccaceci
Via Zola, 30
Giulianova Lido (Teramo)
800-3550

Salvatore alla Riviera
Via Riviera di Chiaia, 91
Napoli
680-4940

Dal Delicato
Largo Sermoneta, 34-37
Margellina, Napoli
667-047

Da Dora
Vicolo F. Palasciano, 52
Napoli
684-149

Antica Pizzeria Port'Alba
Via Port'Alba, 18
Napoli
459-713

Vini e Cucina
Corso Vittorio Emanuele, 762
Napoli
660-302

Trattoria Da Sica
Via Bernini, 17
Napoli
556-7520

Il Bocciodromo
Traversa Lo Palazzo, 2
Capri
837-7414

La Fattoria
Dragonea di Vietri sul Mare
Salerno
210-518

Santa Lucia
Via Roma, 182
Salerno
225-696

Da Gemma
Via Fra Gerardo Sasso, 9
Amalfi (Salerno)
871-345

Trattoria Casalinga
Via Biondi, 19
Catania
311-319

Trattoria A Cuccagna
Via Principe Granatelli 21/A
Palermo
587-267

Trattoria Stella (La Patria)
Via Aragona, 6
Palermo
616-1136

Trattoria La Botte
Piazza San Domenico, 4
Taormina
24-198

La Bussola
Via Nazionale
Taormina–Isola Bella
21-176

A Zammara
Via Fratelli Bandiera, 15
Taormina
24-408

Trattoria Pesco Mare
Via S. Landolina, 6
Siracusa
21-075

Taverna Aretusa
Via Santa Teresa, 32
Siracusa
68-720

Index